G000268949

Doctor of Souls

DOCTOR OF SOULS

A biography of
Dr. Leslie Dixon Weatherhead

John Travell

Lutterworth Press
Cambridge

The Lutterworth Press
P.O. Box 60
Cambridge
CB1 2NT

e-mail: publishing@lutterworth.com
website: www.lutterworth.com

British Library Cataloguing in Publication Data
A catalogue record is available from the British Library

ISBN Hardback: 0 7188 2991 3
ISBN Paperback: 0 7188 3004 0

Copyright © John C. Travell, 1999

First hardback edition 1999, Reprinted 2000
First paperback edition 2000

All rights reserved. No part of this publication may be reproduced, saved in a
retrieval system or transmitted in any form or by any means, electronic,
mechanical, photocopying, recording or otherwise, without the prior permission in writing of the Publisher.

Printed by
Redwood Books

For Annette

The preacher has admiration for his peculiar reward, but the pastor has affection: if the preacher be ill there are paragraphs in the newspapers; if the pastor, there is concern in humble homes. No man in human society gathers such a harvest of kind feeling as the shepherd of souls, none is held in such grateful memory.

John Watson: *The Minister's Prayer Book*

And in the early morning the people flocked to listen to him in the temple.

St. Luke 21. v.38

Foreword

This is not just the story of a remarkable man, it charts the end of an era in church life, that of the preacher as star performer who drew the crowds and enjoyed the kind of fame now reserved for television celebrities and sports personalities. To the very end of his long life, Leslie Weatherhead could fill the largest hall in town, though he never made the mistake of drawing optimistic general conclusions from his individual success. Yet a poignant paradox runs through this book. The fact that succeeding generations of preachers have been unable to do a 'Weatherhead' will strengthen the conviction of those who insist that preaching as a rhetorical art died with him, ours is the age of pulpit conversations, dialogues and over-the-garden-wall type chats. And yet, it is not easy to see by what other means than the sermon as a formal act of proclamation could congregations have been confronted with the mercy and judgement of God in war-time London. Nor in what other manner many thousands throughout the world could have been invited to wrestle with the Gospel not as a discussion topic but as part of a liturgical act through which God was made real to them and their lives transformed by the friendship of Jesus – to use one of Weatherhead's favourite phrases.

Temperamentally, Weatherhead was a preacher to his finger-tips. I recall the last time I went to visit him at his last home in Bexhill on Sea. He seemed at a loose end, the old charm was still there but not the spark. He was a public performer robbed of his audience; had he been a West End star, one would have said he was missing the roar of the crowd and the smell of grease paint. He complained about his rotten health and catalogued the miseries of being old. Eventually, he looked at the clock and excused himself, he was taking a mid-week service at the old people's home just down the road. He collected his bible and book of prayers, he squared his shoulders and suddenly the lassitude had gone, he seemed to have a new access of energy, he was about to do what he did best. And the great preacher strode off to address the smallest congregation he had had in over sixty years.

In an easy, lucid style of which Weatherhead would have approved, John Travell conveys something of the glory of great preaching and its cost. Phillips Brooks' famous definition of preaching as truth conveyed through personality implies the limitations as well as the strengths of the art. Some of the most revealing and moving passages in this book are those in which Weatherhead shares his deepest feelings by letter with another popular religious personality, the Bible translator J B Phillips, about the spiritual and psychological cost of being a pulpit star. He was painfully aware of the absurd irony of being highly successful at commending one who was in earthly terms a failure, who came to his own people and unlike the popular preacher was not feted but despised and rejected.

I read this book expecting to be choked with nostalgia about a man I revered and an era whose passing I deeply regret. So I was, but I also found John Travell's analysis of Weatherhead's ministry in its general context deeply disturbing. Leslie's great friend, Donald Soper, died as I was reading this manuscript., the last of the great Methodist triumvirate with Edwin Sangster, had gone. Despite the passing of the, last of the Titans, I cannot accept either the option of writing off formal preaching as a lost art nor that of prophesying its renaissance as part of a religious revival just around the corner. So what are we preachers to do? Well, if this story underlines our dilemma, it must also offer some clues to the way forward, for Leslie Weatherhead, like all great men and women of God, had discovered how to make God real to whoever was within range of his voice. Perhaps his secret was so simple that we could easily overlook it in our quest for complex answers. In the end, preaching is not the art of making a sermon and delivering it; it is the art of making a preacher and delivering that. Leslie Weatherhead made the Christian doctrine of redemption credible because he looked and talked and behaved like some-one redeemed.

Leslie had the courage to run the gauntlet of public ridicule by exploring ideas and experiences which are regarded by many in the Church as cranky, such as spiritualism, reincarnation, out-of-the-body experiences, psychic heal-ing and the like. In particular, he was passionately interested in communica-tion from beyond the veil. Though I have never had the nerve nor the convic-tion to follow him into such esoteric realms, I will go so far as to suggest he is speaking to us through this book.

Colin Morris
1999

Preface and Acknowledgements

In 1975, a year before his father's death, Professor Kingsley Weatherhead produced a biography, *Leslie Weatherhead: A Personal Portrait*. This has been the main – almost the only – source of information about Dr Weatherhead available for subsequent writers and commentators.

This present work is not intended to replace Professor Weatherhead's excellent book, which contains intimate knowledge and insights that only a son could give; but to supplement it by giving a fuller account of his father's public ministry and career.

Growing up in the Methodist National Children's Home (now NCH Action for Children), I became aware of Leslie Weatherhead's name and fame while I was still at school. I began attending his church, the City Temple, in 1956. There I met my wife, joined the choir, and there both our children were baptised by him, my daughter Diana on the occasion in 1961 described by Dr. Leonard Griffith in his autobiography.

It was due to Dr. Weatherhead's influence on me that I applied to enter the Congregational ministry soon after he retired in 1960. I was effectively the last person to enter the ministry directly from his ministry, and he took a considerable interest in my progress, freely giving me his encouragement, guidance and help. When I was ordained he presented me with my preaching robes, and only illness prevented him from giving the charge at my ordination and induction.

From the time of my son's baptism in 1958 we entered into a personal correspondence which lasted almost twenty years, until his death in 1976. In his will he left me, as well as his gowns, his interleaved pulpit Bible, books, files, note-books, and press cuttings. My retirement in 1989 provided me with the time and opportunity to study this material and use it as the basis of research on his ministry. I successfully submitted the resulting thesis as a doctoral dissertation in the University of Sheffield under the title: 'Psychology and Ministry: with special reference to the life, work and influence of Leslie Dixon Weatherhead'. This biography is a further outcome of that research.

In addition to Dr. Weatherhead's private papers, files, letters and books in my possession, the main sources used for this study were personal correspondence and interviews. The material in the Weatherhead Archive at the University of Birmingham, including Dr. Weatherhead's own notes for his biographer (which formed the basis of the biography written by his son) was particularly valuable. The City Temple Archives, and the *City Temple Tidings,* provided a remarkably full record of the life of the City Temple for the whole of the period under review. Other sources used included the Methodist Missionary Society Archives, the Dr. Williams Library, the Leeds Record Office and the Leeds Local History Library, the records of the Wesley Historical Society, the British Council of Churches Archives and the British Newspaper Library.

In compiling this record I am particularly grateful to Dr. Weatherhead's family for all their support and encouragement; Professor Kingsley Weatherhead's own biography of his father has been invaluable. I am grateful to the authorities at the City Temple for allowing me to examine their records, and to many former members of the church for their memories, most of all Mr. Cyril Dewey, whose knowledge of the City Temple is unrivalled. The Birmingham University Archivist, Miss Christine Penney, has been most generous in her assistance, and my friend Dr. Lynne Price readily made the material of her researches available to me. Dr. Rodney Maliphant gave me the benefit of his expert knowledge of psychology, the Rev. Ian Randall shared with me his studies on the Fellowship of the Kingdom, and the Rev. John Munsey Turner his memories of Brunswick, Leeds. Mrs. Vera Phillips kindly made available to me the correspondence between Dr. Weatherhead and her husband, Dr. J. B. Phillips. Dr. Edwin Robertson not only let me have a copy of his book on J.B. Phillips but was very informative and helpful on Dr. Weatherhead's broadcasting, as also was Dr. Kenneth Wolfe, and the Rev. Eric Lord also generously made his own researches available to me. Mrs. Benita Kyle very kindly provided me with valuable information about her husband's work, and the Rev. Edmund Heddle freely shared with me his correspondence and his intimate knowledge of Dr. Weatherhead's last years. I am indebted to the Rev. Barry Gent, Dr. William Davies, the late Rev. T. Alan Beetham, Mrs. Margaret Kingston for the letter to her father and the photograph on p. 15, Mr. John Vickers, Mr. Colin Dews, Miss Rosalie Temple, Miss Rosemary Bishop, Miss Vera Harris, Sister Kathleen Lee, and the Rev. Ronald Ward for their information and assistance. My son Richard proved an invaluable research assistant, and I am very appreciative of all his time and help in searching the newspaper records. Dr. Gordon Powell shared with me his memories of Dr. Weatherhead's visit to Australia, and I have received a considerable amount of correspondence from many people who knew or remembered Dr. Weatherhead and readily shared their memories and knowledge of him with me. Not all of this material could be included, but I am very grateful for it as it added considerably to my own knowledge and appreciation of Dr. Weatherhead's life and ministry. I am particularly appreciative of the personal interest, encouragement and help I have received from Dr. Gordon Barritt. My friend Jo Draper patiently read the typescript and I am more than grateful to her for her expert advice and encouragement. I am especially grateful to Dr. Colin Morris, undoubtably one of the foremost, most challenging and inspiring preachers of today, for his kindness in providing a Foreword, which, as one great preacher's tribute to another, adds much to the merits of this book. My thanks are due most of all to my friend and Supervisor, Dr. Clyde Binfield, without whose willingness to undertake this task, his patience with me and his constant demand for more thorough research and higher standards of presentation this study would be considerably poorer than it is; and to my wife Annette, without whose insistence this project would never have been undertaken. She was more keen than I was that I should start it, and no less eager to have it completed. Our own shared memories have also contributed to this, so that it has been a special joy to recall a ministry and friendship to which we owe more than we can say.

Contents

Foreword   7
Preface and Acknowledgements   9
1. Background and Early Influences   13
2. India and War   23
3. Return to India 1919   34
4. Manchester 1922-1925   41
5. Leeds   52
6. The Mastery of Sex   63
7. Weatherhead's Christology: The Oxford Groups   72
8. Speaking, Writing, Broadcasting   78
9. From Leeds to London   89
10. The City Temple   97
11. The Approach of War   115
12. The Impact of War   123
13. St. Sepulchre's   133
14. On Being a Minister   142
15. The Final Years of War   148
16. The Immediate Post-War Years   166
17. Plans for Rebuilding: Debate, Delays and Frustrations   175
18. Travels Abroad   178
19. Psychology, Religion and Healing   185
20. Rebuilding; Thanks to Rockefeller   196
21. President of the Methodist Conference   209
22. The City Temple Re-Opens   224
23. Into Retirement   237
24. Bexhill   245
25. The Christian Agnostic   257
26. The Last Years   273
27. Envoi   297
28. Conclusion   300
Bibliography   309

Illustrations

Wesley Guild Outing, Saxe Coburg Church, 1900   15
College Student, Richmond, 1913   20
Ordination Certificate   24
Army Report   27
'The Weatherhead Way'   85
Albert Schweitzer, 1935   92
The Last Interruption, interior of the old City Temple   95
"Youth looks at Europe", Weatherhead's article about Hitler   116
Leslie Weatherhead, 1940   124
Neville Chamberlain addressing the Assembly   126
City Temple after its destruction by bombs   130
Service of Anglo American Unity, 1942   149
Leaving for a preaching and lecturing tour of the U.S.A.   203
Telegram from Billy Graham   205
Wichita Falls, 1954   206
Induction as President of the Methodist Conference   210
The Queen Mother at the rededication of the City Temple   229
Exterior of the rebuilt City Temple   230
Interior of the rebuilt City Temple   231
Evelyn and Leslie with Gertie Hutchinson   247
Leslie Weatherhead with the Archbishop of York   283
Opening of the Leslie Weatherhead Room   288

I. Background and Early Influences

'our relation to God was a matter of the first importance'

On Monday morning, August 18, 1958, the *Daily Mirror* printed a picture of a packed queue of people, which stretched from a building on Holborn Viaduct, London, past the ancient parish church of St. Andrews, then rounded the corner and continued for several hundred yards along Shoe Lane. The picture was captioned with a question: 'Can you guess what these people are queuing for?'

The answer, which the *Mirror* obviously regarded as extraordinary, was that they were waiting to attend the opening service of a newly re-built church, the City Temple, and especially to hear the church's distinguished minister, Dr. Leslie Dixon Weatherhead. Unusual though this scene was in the late 1950s, such queues had been normal on Sundays on the Viaduct in the years before the church was destroyed by bombs in 1941. They became a regular sight once again when the church returned to its original home, and they continued to appear whenever Weatherhead preached, even well after he had retired, and long after the days of people flocking to listen to famous preachers were held to be over.

The exceptional interest in this event (which attracted the attention not only of the national press in Britain but of newspapers in several other countries as well) is an indication of the remarkable international reputation that Leslie Weatherhead had acquired, and the influence of his ministry. From the mid-1920s to well into the 1960s, he became established as the best known and most widely popular English preacher. A prolific author of best-selling religious books, he was well known as one of the first and most successful religious broadcasters, as a pioneer and populariser of the use of psychology in the pastoral work of the Church, and as a major influence in the revival of the Church's ministry of healing. His liberal theology, outspoken criticisms of Christian orthodoxy, and his questioning of the Church's traditional doctrines and creeds, as well as his interest in unorthodox medicine, spiritualism and psychic research, made him a highly controversial figure. The exceptional appeal of his personality, his rare gifts of communication, and his remarkable ability to enter into the minds of his hearers; to perceive and articulate their anxieties as well as their religious doubts and difficulties, won him a vast following throughout the world, as people listened to him preach, read his books, and found that he knew how to put their thoughts and feelings into words, providing them with answers to their questions in language which they could understand, and answers they found persuasive and satisfying.

Leslie Weatherhead's life spanned the period of enormous changes that took place during the first two-thirds of this century. When he was born, in Harlesden, in north west London, on 14 October, 1893, into a modest but comfortably off nonconformist family, Queen Victoria was still on the throne, and Britain was at the height of its influence and power. The British Empire spread around the globe, and the nation as a whole shared a confident belief in its continual progress, through the development of industry, the beneficial findings of science, improvements in medicine and health, in education and domestic comfort, the development of the means of transport and communication, and the generally increasing prosperity which all this had brought about.

This general sense of well-being and progress was particularly strong among the members of the Free Churches, who, at the turn of the century, were more numerous and more influential in the affairs of the nation than at any time in their history, before or since. The great nonconformist pulpit personalities, such as R.W. Dale of Birmingham, the Baptist C.H. Spurgeon, and Joseph Parker at the City Temple, were national figures. In business the nonconformist presence was considerable, including great industrialists such as W.H. Lever, Samuel Morley, Titus Salt, W.H. and H.O. Wills, H.V. Mackintosh and Henry Tate. The Quaker confectioners, Cadbury, Rowntree and Fry, were becoming household names through their products. Within nonconformist circles, and particularly in Wesleyan Methodist families like the Weatherhead's, there was considerable confidence in the strength of their faith and in the future of their churches.

It was into this national atmosphere of confidence and rising expectations that Leslie Weatherhead was born and in which he grew up. Although through-out most of his active life he was regarded as a moderniser, his most basic attitudes and beliefs were shaped by his Victorian background, though they were modified later by his experiences in war and his contact with Indian religions. The various changes in theological and philosophical fashion during the twentieth century left him largely unaffected. He was more excited by the latest discoveries of science, in which he included research into psychic phenomena and the paranormal, and in medicine, particularly psychology and all non-physical methods of healing. His general outlook and underlying religious beliefs remained mainly those current in liberal evangelical nonconformist churches during the late nineteenth century in which he was born, although he was constantly challenging and questioning received religious ideas and encouraging others to do so in the pursuit of truth and the greater knowledge of God.

Leslie's family attended Wesley's Chapel in City Road, London, where his parents had met and were married and taught in the Sunday School. His father, Andrew, who was the manager of a hosiery warehouse, was the son of a baker in Moffat, in the Scottish border country. His family were Presbyterians, members of the United Free Church of Scotland. Andrew's brother James later became its Moderator. Leslie's mother, Elizabeth Dixon, was a schoolteacher, and her brother, W.G. Dixon, was a Wesleyan Methodist minister. Leslie had two older sisters; Muriel, born in 1888, and Alice, born in 1890. When Leslie was two-and-a-half the family moved to Leicester, where they attended the Saxe Coburg (later Saxby) Street Methodist Church.

Leslie Weatherhead's home was typical of that of many Nonconformist families at that time. He greatly admired his father although he seems to have been in some awe of him, particularly as Andrew Weatherhead found it difficult to show warmth and affection. He was a man of strong principles, and actively supported the Passive Resistance Movement against paying rates to finance denominational schools, (particularly strong in Leicester). In January, 1904, some 150 passive resisters were summoned at Leicester Police Court for non-payment of

Wesley Guild outing, Saxe Coburg Church, around 1900. Leslie Weatherhead, front row, far left.

the Education Rate. Andrew Weatherhead avoided both the tax and a police record by coming to an arrangement with the police that when the tax became due he allowed them to enter the house and remove some small article of furniture which he later bought back for the same money. This enabled him to preserve both his principles and his respectability.

Elizabeth Weatherhead is described by her grandson as

a Christian of terrible and serious aspect. . . . She seems to have been a great forbidder; no one in the family could enjoy what she disapproved of, and what she disapproved of covered a wide spectrum of recreations – dancing, smoking, drinking, gambling, theatre, cinema, and a number of other pastimes for weekdays – the list of Sunday prohibitions being of course, longer.[1]

Donald Soper, born just ten years later, grew up in a home remarkably like Weatherhead's, with the same strong piety, strict discipline and prohibitions on worldly pleasures and amusements. Not only was Soper's father also 'a man of impregnable convictions,'[2] he was similarly austere and reserved with his children. Soper's mother was also a schoolteacher, although Elizabeth Weatherhead seems to have been far more dauntingly severe. Leslie's feelings about his mother were very mixed. His daughter says that he was both afraid and fond of her at the same time.[3] Her influence on him was very strong. He came to realise later in life that his mother had not wanted him. 'As a boy he feared his mother and yet earnestly desired her love.'[4]

Much of Weatherhead's later psychological understanding was based on his own childhood memories. Describing in *Psychology and Life* the exceptional sensitivity of a child he says,

Probably before birth occurs, the child's mind is sensitive to the mental preoccupations of its mother . . . even now we do not exactly know to what extent the condition of a mother's mind influences that of her unborn child.[5]

Even before he was born, his mother had set her heart on his being a minister, and her schoolmarmish severity towards him, which seems to have been displayed more often than maternal affection, was no doubt the expression of her desire to make him as worthy a candidate for his vocation as it was within her power to do. She not only beat him savagely on occasion for boyish misdemeanours, but intensified his punishment by withholding forgiveness. In Weatherhead's later writings, his sermons and his psychology, the need to forgive and to know oneself forgiven is central to his thinking, and a major reason why psychotherapy and analysis need to be allied with religion.

Religious observances dominated the Weatherhead household. Family prayers were held every day, and church attended three times each Sunday, with family prayers beforehand in the morning and a prayer meeting in the chapel after the evening service. Between tea and evening chapel Andrew Weatherhead taught his children the shorter catechism. In a sermon on 'Why People Don't Go To Church', Weatherhead sympathises with those who were forced to attend as children and for whom 'Religion was a dreary duty which had to be carried out in obedience to adult command', yet he does not seem to have resented it himself. In another sermon on 'Religion in the Modern Home' he regrets the loss of the habit of family prayers and gives an affectionate picture of the practice in his own home. He attributes his knowledge of the Bible to his mother's daily readings and says that

> into the minds of her children my mother drove a most important considera-
> tion, namely the thought that religion mattered, and that our relation to God
> was a matter of the first importance.[6]

For a lonely and imaginative boy, growing up at that time in a home like his, it was as natural for him to see glamour, adventure and fame in the lives of the great preachers and missionaries as it is now for children to dream of becoming space-explorers or pop-stars. As a child of seven he would play a favourite game of pretending to be a preacher, using a kitchen chair as a pulpit and an old table cloth as a gown and hood. This was one Sunday game that his mother did allow, and no doubt it gave her much satisfaction. In spite of the austerity of his childhood, he remembered his home with real affection:

> In my childhood I was brought up in a Presbyterian home which compared
> with modern standards, would be called very strict. . . . Yet I must add that
> the Sundays of my childhood remain in my memory as days of great
> happiness. Frankly, it never occurred to any of us to do anything else on
> Sunday but attend church and Sunday school. What would have happened
> if we had suddenly decided to go for a day's picnic, I don't know. Yet,
> Sunday was not irksome and unpleasant, and I do not think there were
> many homes in which there was more laughter and fun than mine.[7]

When he was five, Weatherhead entered the Board School in Medway Street, Leicester. His memories of this school were harsh, and he never forgot the effect the place had on him.[8] Recalling his schooldays over fifty years later, in *That Immortal Sea* (1953) he says

> I hated school with all my heart. I can even remember hearing that if you got
> your feet wet you developed a cold that could keep you from school. I
> clearly remember taking a jug of water up to my bedroom and pouring water
> over my feet and getting into bed with them sopping wet, in the hope that in
> the morning I should have a cold and need not go to school [p.109].

He was never physically robust, and whether from this practice or not he suffered from colds and bronchitis, which frequently kept him away from school. His absence on one occasion led to an incident that left him all his life with burning sense of injustice and indignation:

> When I was seven I was away from school when my classmates learnt subtraction sums. On my return I was humiliated to find that I could not understand how they were done. . . . The teacher was one . . . who caned every pupil who got a sum wrong. I was a very sensitive and nervous child and in continual ill-health, and I was in terror of her violence and her loud, hysterical voice. Finding myself behind the others. . . . I got a large sheet of paper and persuaded my elder sister to set me twelve subtraction sums. How I slaved that evening! I can recall even now how hot my head grew, how shaky and inky my hands! . . . I took it up to the teacher in the morning. I wanted to show her that at least I had tried to understand. I shall never forget that moment. She never looked at the sums. She tore the paper across and dropped it into the waste-paper basket. "Oh, anyone can copy them when someone else has done them," she said. I can remember how I flushed at the injustice. It occurred to me afterwards that she had glimpsed another handwriting because my sister had set them out for me, and deduced that I had copied them. But that happened nearly forty years ago. Yet I can still hear the tearing of that paper. I can remember her name, her dress, her face, her large, white, flabby hands, as clearly as if it happened yesterday. . . . The incident so affected me that I always feel a sympathy for little children sometimes amounting to anguish, and injustice to them makes me more angry than anything else.[9]

At the age of thirteen he moved to the Alderman Newton Secondary School in Leicester. His memories of this school were not particularly happy either. It was strict, and he still received beatings from time to time, but its justice was reasonably fair. He still missed lessons through periods of ill-health, which meant that he often found himself behind the rest of the class and having to strive to catch up. He did, however, have some successes, which must have given him some pride of achievement and strengthened his confidence. In 1909 he was recommended for a distinction in passing a Cambridge University examination in 'The History of Scientific Progress from the Beginning of the 19th. Century'. He took his matriculation with the University of London in 1912. In his last year he was awarded the popularity prize which was voted on by all the boys. The extraordinary appeal of his personality was evidently felt even then. He was absent from school at the time of the vote owing to another of his frequent bouts of illness, and the news took him greatly by surprise.

These years were significant in the development of his religious awareness and his deepening sense of personal vocation. On January 3, 1903, when he was nine, he entered into his diary his determination to serve Christ for the rest of his life. The intensity of his religious feelings was strengthened through an exceptional and mystical sensitivity to nature. During his teens the family regularly holidayed at a farm near Leicester known as Onebarrow Lodge, and he always remembered these times with a special delight. Other holidays were spent at the family's old home in Moffat, and he came to know and love the streams and mountains of the Scottish border country. His son says, 'Never have I known anyone in whom the sights and sounds of nature, especially the peaceful ones, could induce such unalloyed pleasure.'[10] In a sermon, 'This Haunted World', Weatherhead reveals how powerfully the beauty of nature impressed him with a sense of wonder and worship.

> Nature just breathes the beauty of God. Who has not known high mystic moments on some lovely morning amidst the Scottish hills, or heard the birds calling on a Yorkshire moor . . . sometimes through the glory of the night sky, or the majesty of the mighty mountains, you have known that this is a haunted world, that behind it or should one say interwoven with it, there are realities of another and you know that essentially it is to that other world that you belong.[11]

Andrew and Elizabeth Weatherhead both taught in the Sunday School at Saxe Coburg Street, and Andrew became Senior Steward there in 1910. The Superintendent Minister of the circuit from 1910-1913 was the Rev. James Cooke, who had previously spent five years in the West Indies. This missionary connection undoubtedly appealed to the young Leslie, and Cooke's ministry made a great impression on him. Following a service in which Cooke had preached power-fully on the theme of the Cross, Weatherhead went to see him and made his first serious step towards entering the ministry.

He was further influenced in this decision by the ministry in Leicester of the Rev. Charles Ridge, and by his Sunday School Superintendent, Thomas Ellis. In a letter to Ellis, dated 10 June 1912, telling him of his intention to become a missionary, Weatherhead wrote:

> This is the result I think first of the influence of the Rev. Chas. Ridge on my life, secondly of the direct appeal of the Rev. Wm. Goudie but all along I have been impressed and enthused with your tremendous enthusiasm for the cause of Foreign Missions and I feel that much of my enthusiasm is due to you, and for this, in this jolly lame way I thank you. [12]

Saxe Coburg Street had a strong missionary emphasis. Charles Ridge had also spent some thirteen years in the West Indies before serving in home circuits, including Leicester. With his father, Leslie had gone to hear the Rev. William Goudie speak at a missionary meeting. Goudie had served in India and was the Wesleyan Missionary Society's Secretary for West Africa. Goudie had excited Leslie's sense of adventure, and he told his father that he wanted to be a medical missionary in India. Andrew Weatherhead said that he could not afford to pay for both medical and theological training and Leslie had to choose which to follow. He chose theology, and determined to go to India as a missionary, but he remained interested in medicine all his life.

He preached his first ever sermon on 3 September 1911, just six weeks before his eighteenth birthday, at the village chapel in Houghton-on-the-Hill, six miles from Leicester, on the text from St. Matthew's Gospel chapter 11. 'Come unto me all ye that labour and are heavy-laden, and I will give you rest'. He was so nervous that he succeeded in unpicking the cord from around the cushion on the pulpit desk without realising what he was doing. Returning from the chapel he had what he described as 'the crowning experience' of the presence of Christ which deeply affected him and profoundly influenced his understanding of the nature of the Christian faith. In order for lay-preachers to get to their destinations the circuit provided a pony and trap. Those who were going in the same direction set out together, but as Leslie was going furthest he was left driving the trap on his own, and had to drive it all the way back by himself. He had never driven a horse before and the weather was bitter, with hard frost and snow. Going home in the dark after the service it was snowing, and he was terrified as the horse slithered on the icy ground. He says,

> Then a most liberating thought came to me. How small was all this compared to the sufferings of Him whom I had set out to serve! How cowardly to be afraid! I began to pray aloud, and then it happened – I don't know how – but as I prayed and longed for Him, He came. He seemed more real than the snow. My heart just sang with that kind of joy which is full of awe and wonder and wild delight.[13]

Throughout his life he always placed the greatest value on such mystical experiences, and belonged to an important tradition in Methodism, going back to John Wesley, which emphasised 'experiential religion', which to Weatherhead meant the 'personal experience of Jesus'. He acknowledged that such experiences were rare, but this made them particularly important and precious. In later life he had a number of other such experiences: during a service in a Y.M.C.A. hut in Mesopotamia in the First World War; in a railway carriage at Vauxhall station; watching a sunset in Charnwood Forest; among the foothills of the Himalayas. He wrote:

> These for me have been times when the sun has shone out in all His splendour. The presence of Christ then has been so real that to lift the head and see a form would not occasion surprise.[14]

His preaching at Houghton was well received. The Leicester Wesleyan Methodist Messenger, reporting the Local Preachers' Meeting on 8 September 1911 said, 'A good report was given of the preaching and general conduct of the Service taken by Bro. Leslie Weatherhead at Houghton and he was unanimously recommended to be put on trial.' When his trial sermon was preached at Saxe Coburg Street some months later, The Messenger again reported,

> Those who heard Bro. Leslie Weatherhead preach his trial sermon at Saxe Coburg Street on August 29th. had a treat. And his examination confirmed the impression that he is "called" of God to preach. The Brethren had a very great joy in supporting his nomination to the position of a fully accredited Local Preacher.[15]

It appears from this that Weatherhead was only 'on trial' for a year – an unusually short time then, and impossible now.

After taking preliminary examinations in theology and the Bible and preaching more trial sermons, Weatherhead entered Cliff College to begin training for the ministry in October 1912. Cliff was intended to provide laymen with theological and evangelical skills and there was no requirement for ministerial students to spend time first at Cliff, but many chose to do so before their candidacy was accepted for the ordained ministry. As Weatherhead's period on trial had been so short, it may have been considered wise for him to have an initial period at Cliff before going on to a ministerial training college. He entered Cliff the same year that its first Principal, Thomas Cook, died and was succeeded by Samuel Chadwick, who was noted for the brilliance of his biblical exposition. Chadwick possessed great gifts of spiritual insight, and encouraged the use of imagination in a detailed study of the texts. He had the power – which Weatherhead also possessed, and may have first discovered here – to bring

College Student, Richmond, 1913.

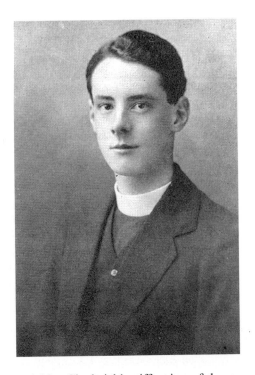

them vividly to life. But Cliff did not suit him. Chadwick's stiff regime of classes in the morning and agricultural work in the kitchen gardens every afternoon he found heavy going. At the end of the Easter term he left and, in September 1913, entered Richmond College, London.

Richmond had a long missionary tradition. It was founded originally through the Centenary Fund of 1838, commemorating the conversion of John Wesley a century before. In 1863 it was taken over by the Missionary Society, and until 1885 only those preparing for work overseas were trained there. This segregation of training from those preparing for the home ministry was then recognised as being unhelpful, but Richmond retained its strong missionary associations and continued to attract many of those wishing to go overseas. Weatherhead enjoyed his time there and got on well with his fellow students who, during his first year, elected him secretary of the year, during his second, chairman of the year, and in his third year, chairman of the college. Among the members of the staff who made a lasting impression on him were the Principal, W.T. Davison, from whom he acquired his theological foundation, T.H. Barratt, 'a great soul and a great saint', and Harry Bisseker. When he was leaving he asked Davison for a signed photograph. Davison said, 'I wonder if any of the other men would care to have a copy?' Leslie found half-a-dozen who said they would. Davison 'seemed so pleased to be assured of the affection in which he was held.'[16]

The member of the staff who impressed him most and had the most lasting influence on him was Bisseker, who taught Biblical Literature and Classics. It was Bisseker who was responsible for awakening Weatherhead's interest in psychology. Weatherhead later dedicated *A Plain Man Looks at the Cross* to him, describing him as 'My first tutor in Greek Testament and Psychology, and still my teacher and my friend.'

That Bisseker was teaching psychology in a theological college as early as 1913 is remarkable. The explanation must lie in the fact that psychology was traditionally a branch of philosophy. The ancient Greek philosophers were interested in the human soul – the psyche – and their works of philosophy and ethics were also about psychology. It was not until the late nineteenth century that psychology came to be treated as a separate experimental science. Freud's *The Interpretation of Dreams* appeared in 1899, and the International Psycho-Analytical Society, which grew out of Freud's circle in Vienna, was established in 1910. Freud's *Totem and Taboo* was published in 1913, the year Weatherhead entered college, and *The Ego and the Id* was not produced until 1923. There were other Methodists interested in psychology as well as Bisseker: George Jackson had used psychological insights in his Vanderbilt lectures, *The Fact of Conversion* in 1908. The 'New Psychology' was, nevertheless, still very new, and it was only much later that it came to be accepted in the training of ministers. Weatherhead was among the first to press for it to be introduced.

The outbreak of war in 1914 disrupted the life of the college. Many of the men enlisted at once and although enlistment was left to each individual to decide for himself, by March 1915 twenty-two men had left the college. Weatherhead hesitated, feeling it was not right to fight, but not right to remain in safety when others were sacrificing their lives. The choice was made for him when he was rejected as medically unfit. Then, in 1915, his college career was suddenly cut short when Richmond was taken over by the Westminster Training College, whose premises had been commandeered by the Australian forces. The first and second year students were moved to Manchester, and the third year men were given appointments. Weatherhead became minister of the Methodist Church in Farnham, Surrey, close to the army base at Aldershot, and he was also given charge of three churches in the neighbouring villages.

Weatherhead began his ministry with a missionary zeal for the conversion of individuals, and a clear message to preach of the real presence of Christ, which he later defined as the 'transforming friendship'. There was also a disciplined, if naive and puritanical, piety. He had acquired an imaginative rather than an academic approach to biblical exposition, a good knowledge of New Testament Greek which he carefully maintained (often later referring to the original Greek in his exposition of a text), an enthusiasm for psychology and a frustrated interest in medicine. But the fact that his theological education was ended before he could take his degree undoubtedly affected him. He never regarded himself as a scholar, and treated those whom he did consider to be such with considerable respect.

1. Kingsley Weatherhead: *Leslie Weatherhead, A Personal Portrait* (H. & S. 1975) p.17.
2. William Purcell: *Portrait of Soper* (Mowbrays 1972) p.39.
3. Private conversation with Mrs Caunt.
4. K. Weatherhead, *op. cit.*, p.18.
5. Leslie Weatherhead: *Psychology and Life* (H. & S. 1934) p.168. In his notes for his biographer, he says that it was his period of analysis with J.A. Hadfield that enabled him to recognise the effect of his childhood, and particularly of his mother's attitude on him.
6. Leslie Weatherhead: *The Eternal Voice* (S.C.M. 1939) p.154.

7. Leslie Weatherhead: *When the Lamp Flickers* (H. & S. 1948) p.128.

8. *Leicester Evening Mail* 19 October 1960. 'Those were terrible days. I was very unhappy there.'

9. *The Eternal Voice op. cit.*, p.144f.

10. K. Weatherhead, *op. cit.* p.28.

11. *That Immortal Sea, op. cit.*, p.57. Weatherhead's delight in nature made a strong impression on his Australian host, Gordon Powell, in 1951. 'He told us how he drew strength from beauty. He was particularly fascinated with the beauty of gum trees. He pointed out the wonder of a flock of birds in flight.' [Powell to Travell, Letter and article, 7 July 1991].

12. Letter, 10 July 1912. Weatherhead to Ellis. Copy in my possession.

13. Leslie Weatherhead: *Jesus and Ourselves* (Epworth 1930) p.19f.

14. Leslie Weatherhead: *His Life and Ours* (H. & S. 1932) p.363.

15. *The Wesleyan Methodist Messenger* October 1912.

16. Richmond College 1843-1943 (Ed. Frank Cumbers) (Epworth 1944) p.63f.

2. India and War

'I am not doing my maximum for my country in her hour of need'

In the few months he was at Farnham Weatherhead began to build a reputation for the power and effectiveness of his preaching. His enthusiasm and evangelical zeal attracted attention and gained a response. The local press soon reported crowded congregations. It was a common practice in Wesleyan churches at the time for the minister to ask those who had been converted during the service to stand up at the end to indicate their decision. Weatherhead started doing this at Farnham and recorded in his diary the numbers and names of those who had responded, filling four pages with the names of those who had been converted through his ministry from the time he began preaching until he joined the army in 1917. 'With what enthusiasm' he wrote, 'does a man go to his first church! . . . I remember that I went at short notice because a senior man had gone to the war. . . . The services were a great joy, and many open conversions were witnessed in those days.'[1]

The closeness of Farnham to the military establishment at Aldershot brought him into contact with the many soldiers and young recruits, and he valued the opportunity this gave him to minister to them. He felt some sense of guilt that he was not involved in the war as they and most of his contemporaries were. He applied for a chaplaincy, but was again turned down and told he was already doing a chaplain's work there. His heart was still set on becoming a missionary, when to his delight he heard that there was a vacancy in Madras and he had been appointed to fill it.

Before sailing to India he was ordained, on 13 September 1916, almost exactly three years after he had entered Richmond and only five years since he had preached his first sermon. This was an unusually short time for entry into the Methodist ministry. Candidates were normally required, when they began as local preachers, to spend one year on trial before being accepted onto the full plan. The process of taking examinations, preaching trial sermons and being approved by the relevant committees could take another year or two before the candidate started his training at theological college. After three years in college – or four if taking a degree – there was then a three- or four-year period of probation, making at least seven years in all, before he could be recommended for full connexion and finally ordained, along with the other candidates of the year, at the annual Conference. Leslie Weatherhead's ordination therefore took place some four years earlier than was normally allowed. This was largely due to the exigencies of the war which cut short his theological education, and also to the fact that those going to missionary service overseas were usually ordained at a separate service before leaving to take up their appointments in order that they should be properly authorised to administer the sacraments, which they would be required to do once abroad. The normal probationary period was therefore not always insisted upon. But the Methodist authorities must have been sufficiently impressed with him to proceed with his ordination after so

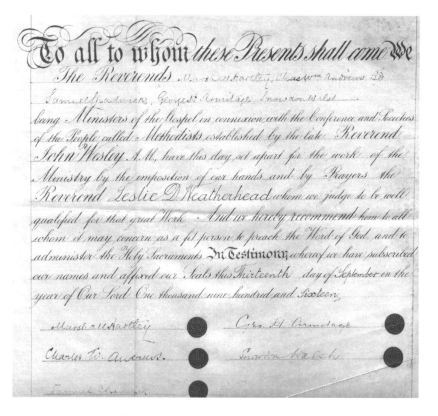

To all to whom these Presents shall come We
The Reverends Marshall Hartley, Chas Wm Andrews, & D.
Samuel Chadwick, George H Armitage, Snowdon Welsh —
being Ministers of the Gospel in connexion with the Conference and Societies
of the People called Methodists, established by the late Reverend
John Wesley A.M., have this day set apart for the work of the
Ministry by the imposition of our hands and by Prayers the
Reverend Leslie D Weatherhead whom we judge to be well
qualified for that great Work And we hereby recommend him to all
whom it may concern as a fit person to preach the Word of God, and to
administer the Holy Sacraments In Testimony whereof we have subscribed
our names and affixed our Seals this Thirteenth day of September in the
year of Our Lord One thousand nine hundred and Sixteen,

Marshall Hartley   Geo. H Armitage

Charles W. Andrews.   Snowdon Welch

Samuel Chadwick

Ordination Certificate

short a time.

Among those who officiated at the ceremony and signed his ordination document were his former principal at Cliff College, Samuel Chadwick; the General Secretary of the Wesleyan Methodist Missionary Society, Marshall Hartley; and the W.M.M.S China Secretary, Charles Andrews. Weatherhead set out for Madras a month later, arriving in India to take up his appointment in mid-November, 1916.

His first few months were spent as assistant to W.A. Kirkham, at St. Thomas Mount, a small village ten miles outside Madras. He moved to the city at the beginning of 1917 to become minister of the Georgetown Church, the oldest Wesleyan church in India.

Methodist missionary work in India had its origins in the vision of Dr. Thomas Coke, who in 1783 had produced a *Plan of the Society for the Establishment of Missions among the Heathens* with India particularly in mind. It was not until 1813 that the Methodist Conference gave him permission to set out with a small team to go to Ceylon. Coke himself died on the way, but the rest of the party arrived and began working there in June 1814. Around 1816 a number of English Methodists living in Madras began to meet for prayer and fellowship. Hearing of the arrival of Coke's team in Ceylon they asked for one of the missionaries to be spared for the mainland, and James Lynch was sent to them. Lynch established the Georgetown Church in 1817, which meant that the church was celebrating its centenary during the year in which Weatherhead arrived.

Being so new on the scene he did not take any prominent part in the centenary services which took place in March, but he quickly established himself in the pulpit, recording in his diary for 25 February that twenty-two people stood up to be counted at the end of the service. Two weeks later he recorded thirteen more. The church was in the university district of Madras, so that beside the English expatriates and Anglo-Indians, the congregation was made up largely of Indian students. The university lectures were in English, so there was no language problem to be overcome in conducting the services. Even so, the Methodist Church required all missionaries in foreign postings to be fluent in the native tongue within two years of their being appointed, so Weatherhead was given three months away from the circuit in order to take Tamil lessons from an Indian teacher named Venkatachari. He found the Tamil boring but enjoyed the opportunity to learn about Indian culture and religions with his teacher.

At the same time, although now so far away from it, he was unable to forget the war in Europe. The news of the battles in France and the slaughter of so many of his contemporaries continued to trouble his mind. On the first of January 1917 he wrote in his diary, 'I am not doing my maximum for my country in her hour of need.' Once again he applied for a chaplaincy but was once more turned down. Weatherhead was young, idealistically patriotic and eager still to share in the excitement of war before it was too late. He recorded his frustration and disappointment in his diary:

Ever since leaving the Aldershot District I have felt restless and dissatisfied concerning the claims of the nation.

Now I feel it my duty to go. This war may go on for years, and the need for men is urgent, especially in the East. My chaplaincy offer has not been accepted, possibly through a bad health record, but if I don't go now I shall despise myself and never be able to preach sacrifice again. . . . This is no temporary emotion. It is the fruit of long thought and prayer. I have reached the stage where it becomes a clear matter of conscience and duty, and whatever happens I must go. I love my work and I hate war, but this call seems to me pre-eminent.[2]

On 17 April he wrote to his District Chairman, C.H. Monahan, describing his dissatisfaction with his position ever since leaving Aldershot. He had spoken to his senior colleague, Kirkham, who was also feeling the urge to enlist, 'and told him how eager I was to enter the Army.' He asked permission to make a statement to the Local Committee 'in order if possible to obtain the approval of the brethren.' In his statement he said,

I now feel it my duty to go. I am young, single and have no ties, and I feel that if I go on any longer like this I shall despise myself. . . . I do not bring before you such a suggestion without a great deal of prayer. Now however,

I have got to the stage when I feel that whatever happens I MUST go.[3]

Understandably, the members of the Local Committee were not pleased to have this request from someone so recently appointed, and their displeasure was further increased by having to consider a similar application from Kirkham at the same time. Monahan wrote to Marshall Hartley, informing him of the situation and saying that the Local Committee 'was unanimous in feeling that it was quite outside our province to give permission to any brother to enlist'. They had not expressed either approval or disapproval, but their chief criticism was that 'in a corporate body such as our ministry, they should have been guided by the conscience of the Church as a whole and not solely by the individual conscience.' They added the information that Weatherhead had already proceeded to apply for a commission since their meeting. Hartley immediately cabled back: 'Kirkham Weatherhead Committee declines sanction', and followed this with a strongly worded letter insisting that 'they are doing their best service to the Empire by remaining at their posts.'[4]

In spite of the strength of this official disapproval, Weatherhead's mind was made up. He felt he could not submit to his superiors even though his father cabled him to accept the Society's ruling, and he knew that he might be dismissed from the ministry for such disobedience. This was for him an overriding issue of conscience, and for him, conscience had to take precedence over all other authority. He wrote in his diary, 'To say conscience bids me go, and then let conscience be overruled by another, is no conscience at all.'

This incident gives an indication of the independence of Weatherhead's character, and his attitude to external authority. It contrasts with that of his close friend, W.E. Sangster, who accepted the decisions of the Methodist Conference as the will of God, even if sometimes reluctantly.[5] Weatherhead was anxious to have the approval of Conference for his appointment to the Congregational City Temple in 1936, but it is very probable that he would have gone ahead and accepted the call even if this approval had been withheld, and he appreciated the freedom from authority that this famous Independent Church enabled him to have.

Weatherhead was commissioned in the Indian army in May 1917, and sent to an Officers' Training Camp at Sabbathu, in the Himalayas. He found the training hard, and not being physically robust, would collapse on the floor after returning from a route march and lie there until he had recovered enough to remove his kit. His sheltered Methodist upbringing meant that until he left for India, he had rarely met anyone who was not a practising Christian and involved in the Church. He was now for the first time having to adjust to living with men, who it seemed to him, broke all the rules of respectable behaviour which he had been brought up to accept; who habitually used strong language, drank alcohol (a particularly serious sin among Methodists!) and gambled over cards. Yet he enjoyed their company, finding them friendly, companionable and courageous.

Although his pleasant and cheerful personality made him popular, he found himself the butt of teasing and jokes for his piety and puritanism. On one occasion, he was accused of being snobbish and stand-offish because he refused to take part in a bet the men of his platoon were having on who would do best at a session on the rifle range. He silenced his critics by proving himself to be a better shot than any of them; getting a full score of bulls-eyes, first with a rifle and then a machine-gun. This impressive demonstration of an unsuspected skill led to him being appointed as officer in charge of musketry training.

The posting at Sabbathu gave him the opportunity to spend his free time, especially his Sundays, alone in the mountains, revelling in the Himalayan scenery, taking with him his Bible and Methodist hymn book as devotional aids. In the quiet of the lonely spaces he felt that the mountains were 'alive with divine companionship and friendliness' and the impressions and insights gained then remained with him throughout all his life.

Army report, February 1918

Then, in October 1917, he was attached to the 88th Carnatic Infantry Regiment and stationed near Madras, and so found himself back among his friends there and able to continue preaching and conducting services. His senior officer's report on him at this time describes him as 'an hardworking and promising young officer with an high sense of duty. Is returning to the Church after the war. Good at games and gets on well with all ranks'. The Brigadier General who counter-signed the report remarks, 'a particularly nice mannered young officer. Keen and capable.' According to the document, he is fit for active service, likely to be fit for promotion in the ordinary course, but it does not recommend that his promotion be accelerated.[6] In February 1918 he was ordered to join the 83rd. Wallajabad Light Infantry in Mesopotamia.

Trevor Wilson in *The Myriad Faces of War* (1986) refers to the campaign against the Turks in Mesopotamia as a 'sideshow' to the main conflict going on in Europe [p.378]. Turkey had joined the war on the side of Germany in 1914 in order to attack her main enemy, Russia. When Turkey attacked Egypt, the British brought in detachments of Australian and New Zealand troops to safeguard the Suez Canal, and then a division of Indian troops to protect their vital oil supplies, provided by the Anglo-Persian oil wells through a pipeline 140 miles long which stretched from southern Persia to Abadan, at the head of the Persian Gulf. The terrain was uninviting and not encouraging to an invading army. The climate ranged from extreme heat to extreme cold, and the country was rife with disease.

Weatherhead's regiment was stationed at Tanooma on the banks of the Tigris, near Basra. The forces in Basra were not involved in any attack during his time there, though they suffered from the constant harassment of Arab snipers.

After five months he was transferred to the army political department as Arab Liaison Officer with the rank of Staff Captain. One of the main aims of the British campaign in Mesopotamia was to impress the Arabs and to reassure those sheiks who were sympathetic to the British. Although he always insisted 'I was no Lawrence!' Weatherhead's chief duties were similar to those of T.E. Lawrence, 'Lawrence of Arabia': to discover whether the sheiks with whom he stayed were friendly or hostile to the British forces. In addition (unlike Lawrence) he had to negotiate with the local sheiks for provisions of grass and hay for the army's horses.

Weatherhead's assignment was difficult and dangerous. It required considerable diplomatic skills of tact and shrewd judgment, and an ability to establish very quickly a relationship of trust and friendship with his Arab hosts. In order to show the Arabs how grass could be grown with proper irrigation in that desert area, he was given six skilled farm workers from the 1st/4th Devonshire Regiment, with an interpreter and a group of armed Indian soldiers to protect them. They journeyed round the Arab villages, seeking to persuade the Arabs to co-operate with them. The Arabs were not always as friendly as they seemed, and on one occasion in particular they had to leave in a hurry having been warned that their hosts planned to murder them while they slept. Weatherhead's time with the Arabs was brought to an end when a sore knee became infected and he developed sandfly fever, which resulted in his being admitted to the British Hospital in Amara.

In March 1918 he was invited to become an army chaplain. He was officially appointed on 22 June and ordered to report to Baghdad. He spent some months at Nasiria and then in November he was posted to Bakubah where he became chaplain to the 1st/4th and 1st/6th Devons, and also of a military hospital. The two Devon battalions were territorials of the Wessex Division who had been first sent to India in 1914 to free the regulars there to join the war in France. The 6th Devons were transferred to Basra in January 1915 and the 4th. had followed them in February 1916. In addition to the casualties lost in fighting the Turks, the heat and conditions in Mesopotamia (together with poor rations) caused a great deal of sickness amongst the troops. At one time the 4th battalion was reduced to ten officers and 266 other ranks. When they were required to move their position five officers and 170 men had to be left behind as unfit to march ten miles. The situation improved during 1917, but the great influenza epidemic of 1918-1919 laid low many more of them. There were also in the area 35,000 Armenian refugees depending on the army for living facilities and medical care.[7]

Weatherhead found his change of role tougher than he had expected. There was a great deal of apathy and even hostility to chaplains among his fellow officers, which disconcerted and depressed him. He wrote in his field notebook: 'Not unbelief but indifference we have to fight. They have all heard but not seen.' Such indifference was new to him, and he found it not only difficult to deal with but hard to understand. He recorded the criticisms of the Church he heard among his fellow officers, even that 'People blame the Churches for the war.' He worried about how the men returning from the war would regard the Churches, and what the Churches would need to do to attract them back. Weatherhead's criticisms of the Church's traditional practices, the outdated language of its creeds and doctrines and its unhelpful divisions, which he believed were the main obstacles to people accepting the claims of Christ, date from this wartime experience.

He filled several pages in his notebook with ideas for improvements in services and organisations which he intended to implement when he returned to the regular ministry after the war. As well as making plans for visiting, the use of music in worship, and other aspects of church work, he includes giving his Sunday School teachers lectures on Child Psychology, and lecturing on Temperance, Foreign Missions, and other religions such as Hinduism. He sets out a personal programme which includes '2 hours before breakfast at General Reading, Macaulay &c.' 'Membership' he says, 'should not depend on Class meeting but attendance at the Lord's Supper.' This had been a particular problem for Methodists with considerable debate as to how membership should be recognised. (Methodism had begun as a 'Society' and it was only in 1893, the year Weatherhead was born, that the description, 'Wesleyan Methodist Church' first appeared on class-tickets.[8]) He outlines his 'Ideal Service: 1hr. 15mins' which includes time for 'Silent Prayer to realise God's Presence' and lays out the pattern he followed throughout his ministry.

More pages are devoted to 'Questions for Discussion'. He is interested in the questions that science and the theory of Evolution raised for religion, speculating on the evolution of the soul after death, and asking whether evolution denies immortality, and whether we evolve as a race or as individuals.

Giving lectures to Sunday School teachers on child psychology was an idea that did not get put into regular practice, but the reference indicates that he was already thinking of the science of psychology as a practical aid to ministry. His belief that the universe was a rational unity meant that he did not consider the latest findings of science as a threat to religion but as revealing more of the mind of God.

Challenged by contact with those – including practising Christians – who enjoyed the things which his upbringing had taught him were sinful, he writes down for and against arguments on the benefits of teetotalism, the evils of gambling, the 'disgusting' habit of swearing, the moral dangers involved in the theatre. He concludes that 'Religion does not consist of doing a no. of things Christ never commanded, nor in not doing a lot of things He never disapproved.' There is a pious, and even priggish earnestness about much of this, and his direct experience of the evils of these sinful pleasures must have been very limited. Coming from his innocent and church dominated background, his first contact with his new companions in the army was something of a shock. On one occasion the Church of England chaplain, who had been drinking heavily, sang a bawdy song, waving his glass to the music. Weatherhead liked to be popular, and he did not find it easy to be condemnatory. He liked people, and was by nature tolerant and easy-going. His cheerful good humour meant that his fellow officers, who may not have shared his principles or his prudishness, usually came to like and respect him. He preached to them about the Christ who 'never condemned by words but by His life and death.' 'Thou shalt not', he told them, 'is not found in the New Testament. It was superseded by Thou Shalt.'

His first services attracted only a handful of worshippers – at one camp only four men turned up out of a battalion of eight hundred – but within a few weeks he records that the church is packed on Sunday nights. William Whitehead, one of the Devonshires who knew him then, remembered that Weatherhead's stay with his regiment was brief, since, having made a promise to speak at the Y.M.C.A. tent one evening, he refused to break it even when the colonel, 'a hard Canadian', ordered him to attend the Officer's Mess instead.

> Leslie took the service at the Y.M.C.A. and next day he was expelled for disobeying the Colonel's command. Later . . . I was sent to Basra and it was Armistice Day and at a gathering of troops in the Y.M.C.A. I met Leslie again. Hearing that day of the Armistice Leslie said, 'In half-an-hour's time we will have a service', and I still at 95 remember his text, 'Blessed is that nation whose God is the Lord'.[10]

During his rounds in the military hospital Weatherhead met an R.A.M.C. captain who was using psychological techniques, including hypnotism, in treating patients in his care. Weatherhead recorded in his field notebook:

> Captain Tombleson curing by Hypnotism. . . . Paralysed soldier put to sleep and then walking down the ward. . . . Cured cases given up by other doctors. Then curing by praying for a man on a hillside. . . . Said to Hindle [the senior Methodist chaplain] 'You padres ought to be doing this.

Tombleson made a deep impression on Weatherhead who took every opportunity to discuss his methods and theories with him. He was a Quaker, and as well as practising medicine and psychology, he believed strongly in the power and value of prayer in healing

In his Preface to *Psychology, Religion and Healing* (1951), the published version of his London University doctoral thesis, Weatherhead sets out more fully the effect that this young doctor had on him:

> That doctor was a remarkable man. He practised psychological treatment of an impressive kind when what was then called 'The New Psychology' was very new indeed. He practised hypnotism, both as a means of investigating the deep mind of the patient and also of giving him suggestions of courage, confidence and recovery. Further, he had as great a spiritual faith and power as I have ever seen. He would go out into the desert, and for hours he would concentrate his mind on one patient with a kind of spiritual intention. On returning he would sometimes find remarkable results. The patient, previously sleepless, would be asleep; or, discontented, would have found peace of mind; or, in despair, had begun to believe in his own recovery. In one case, a man apparently unable to walk was walking about the ward. The doctor claimed that when he had done all he could for a patient by all the arts of medicine, the turning point in the illness was sometimes determined by adding this form of prayerful concentration. . . . The combination of healing and religion had always fascinated me. When this doctor turned to us two chaplains and said, 'You padres ought to be doing most of this,' I felt he was right. I remembered that Jesus said, "Heal the sick," and I had always had an uneasy feeling that to relegate all healing to the material methods of the doctors, splendid though that work is, did not really answer the challenge of our Lord's words. Nor could I believe that His challenge was met by the psychologists, especially those who had no place for religion in their thought or practice. I therefore determined to learn all I could about non-physical ways of healing. When the doctor and my fellow-chaplain were both killed, I felt an even greater urgency to try to understand the ways in which

psychology, religion and healing were related.

Turkey signed an armistice with the allied powers on 30 October, 1918. Following the end of hostilities Weatherhead was sent to Baquba, north of Baghdad, for demobilisation. He took the opportunity to go with Major Hindle to visit units of the Indian and British troops along the north-west borders of Persia. Hindle wanted to find out how many chaplains were needed for these scattered troops. During the journey both men conducted services and preached wherever they could. After this Weatherhead was sent to Bombay where he was released from the army in April 1919 and returned from there to resume his ministry in Madras.

Joining the war when and where he did, Weatherhead did not have to experience the awful conditions in the trenches in France nor to take part in any major battle, though there were dangerous situations in his field of operations. On one occasion he was lucky to escape with his life when an Arab sniper shot at his tent while he was sleeping. Fortunately the tent was pitched over a foxhole, so that he was lying below ground level, and the bullet passed over his head. But the war inevitably affected him deeply, as it did most of his generation. It shattered people's assumptions about living in a civilised and increasingly Christian world and had a devastating effect on religious faith. Christian theologians, professional clergy, as well as lay people, found it difficult to fit their experience of total war into their religious beliefs, and very often their faith was destroyed by what they had endured.

The war also changed people's ideas about heaven and hell. Speaking in the City Temple on 10 November 1914, Lloyd George declared,

> We are in the war from motives of purest chivalry to defend the weak . . .
> The brave men who have died need not fear Judgment, because it is our faith that 'sacrifice is ever the surest road to redemption.'[11]

Such theological tailoring to suit the purposes of war did not satisfy many people for very long, but the hell on earth that the Flanders' mud became did make the threat of hell in an after life lose much of its potency and force, since it could not imaginably be worse than what was being suffered already, and by so many who could not conceivably be held to have deserved it.

Weatherhead was young enough when the war started, to feel something of the excitement of war. In his book, *Thinking Aloud in Wartime*, written during the first two months of the next war, in 1939, he admits that he only started thinking seriously about war after it was over.

> When it broke out I was twenty, and more irresponsible than most. I remember being examined by a doctor and told I should be rejected on medical grounds, and being at that time rather relieved. I was at college in London and wanted to get on with my work. Then, when in India I tried to join the Indian Army as a subaltern, and I remember half-hoping that the war wouldn't be over before my commission came through! . . . I got back to England in 1922 and began to think furiously about the whole problem of war. I found myself moving towards pacifism because I had seen the beastliness and waste and evil of war [p.11f.].

The war confronted him directly with the problems of evil, pain, suffering and death, and these remained constant themes in his sermons and books to the end of his ministry. In spite of all he had seen and experienced of the waste, tragedy and suffering of war, it does not seem to have caused him to doubt the existence, the goodness, nor the love of God, though he understands, sympathises with, and seeks to give reasoned answers to those who do.

His first book as sole author, *After Death*, published in 1923, was a direct result of his wartime experiences and the questions provoked by them. In Mesopotamia he and a small group of fellow officers, 'a chaplain, a doctor, a Y.M.C.A. secretary and the writer', had met whenever they could to discuss the issues of life and death prompted by the war, and his book was the outcome of the conclusions that they had reached then. One particular tragedy stuck in his mind and made him determined to write the book:

> A young captain in the Air Force, known to us, with a mechanic behind him, had set out in an aeroplane loaded with bombs for the front. For some unknown reason he had crashed while still in sight of the aerodrome. The chaplain had buried all that remained of both. The machine was a mess of twisted and half-molten metal. . . . Gradually a full moon lifted itself across the swirling waters of the Tigris. The whole landscape was lit up with an unearthly radiance. . . . 'Where is he now?' someone asked. 'What is he doing?' Thousands have asked these and similar questions since August 1914. . . . Never before were such questions so insistent. What has Christianity to say? [p.8]

Weatherhead felt that the traditional Christian answers were no longer acceptable.

> How would you comfort a father who had been brought up in the old school of theology, and who had been taught the doctrine of a physical resurrection, if the news were brought to him that his son had been blown to atoms by a H.E. shell so that no trace of the body could be found? [*ibid.* p.182]

After Death is, and was intended to be, a comforting book. Weatherhead's aim was to give hope and comfort to those who had lost loved ones and who lacked the faith that the Christian gospel provided, that death could not destroy the life that God had given: that there was life beyond the grave. He grounds his proof of immortality in the character of God, arguing that

> if ultimately the purposes of God can be defeated by a bullet or a germ or a brick then he He is not a God fit to be on the throne of the universe. His universe has run away with Him. [*ibid.* p.22]

Since human personality created by God contains faculties, instincts, hopes and desires that are unattainable in this life, then, unless the universe is irrational, it must be God's purpose for these to be fulfilled in another life than this. Heaven and hell are not different states or places, 'but one spiritual world, which is hell or heaven, according to the spiritual condition of the soul which passes through the veil.' Hell is not a place of eternal torment, 'God is not to be thought of as delighting in a useless revenge over souls no longer able to avoid Him.' Hell 'means a sense of deprivation' in which souls which have neglected spiritual values in their life on earth find themselves unprepared and unable to enter into the delights of living in a wholly spiritual realm. Heaven by contrast is the ability to enter more fully than was possible in this life into the delights of a spiritual world, and into closer communion with God. Heaven, like hell, is also 'self-revelation', in which a humble person who made no pretence to religious faith or goodness but 'who lived the straight life and served God in the service of his fellows' would find themselves receiving an unexpected reward.

One thinks of men who would say to one, 'I'm not a religious bloke, Padre', and yet lived a life (not only in the trenches where definite calls for heroism and unselfishness were continually being made, but the ordinary life of the camp) full of unselfish deeds, very dear to the heart and spirit of Christ, showing that fellowship of the kingdom which is the very first necessity of the Christian. [*ibid.* p.82f]

Weatherhead was a convinced universalist, believing in the 'ultimate triumph of Love', since nothing can finally defeat the purpose of God for every human life. He allows the possibility that there may be some who 'so hate goodness' that they still hold out against him, yet, 'When one increasingly realizes the "good in the worst of us" one feels that the great refusal will not in one single instance be made'. This belief in 'the good in the worst of us' was a constant note in his preaching, and one of the reasons why so many people 'heard him gladly.'

In a chapter on 'Our Present Relation to Those who have Passed to the Life After Death', he speaks tenderly to the recently bereaved about the possibility of continued communication or communion with those who have died. This leads him to consider the claims of Spiritualism, recognising that it had become more popular because of the widespread bereavement caused by the war. Examining the evidence for it he accepts that it contains an element of truth, but warns against it, stating that Spiritualism had not made any valuable or original contribution to Christian thought concerning the life beyond the grave. He allows that 'Truth of great and permanent value may yet come through these channels' yet insists that the Christian 'has in his own faith a heritage which if more fully explored, will give to him more than all that is supplied for his comfort and encouragement by modern Spiritualism.'

Weatherhead's own mother had died while he was in India, and the book is dedicated to her. In spite of her harsh treatment of him as a child, he loved and admired her, and it was a great grief to him that he was not able to be with her before she died.

1. Albert Clare: *The City Temple 1640-1940* (Independent Press) p.250.
2. Clare, *op. cit.*, p.252f.
3. Methodist Missionary Society Archives. School of Oriental and African Studies, London. Madras Correspondence 1817-1945. KH-2713/1.
4. *ibid.*
5. Paul Sangster: *Doctor Sangster* (Epworth 1962) p.18.
6. Document dated 6 February 1918, in my possession.
7. C.T. Atkinson: *The Devonshire Regiment, 1914-1918* (Simpkin, Marshall, Hamilton and Kent 1926) p.196f.
8. *Methodist History* Vol.3. *op. cit.* p.156f.
10. Letter, 25 March 1991. W. Whitehead to Travell.
11. Alan Wilkinson: *Dissent or Conform? War, Peace and the English Churches 1900 – 1945* (SCM. 1986) p.27

3. Return to India

'Everything good in Hinduism may be found in Christianity'

Returning to India in April 1919, Weatherhead was appointed Superintendent Minister of the Egmore Church, with the oversight of three churches in the Madras circuit. He also became one of the Free Church Chaplains to the Governor of the Province, Lord Willingdon, who later became Viceroy.

He joined a small study group of doctors and ministers, including the Anglican bishop, who each week took turns in introducing a new book and presenting papers for study and discussion on medical and psychological topics. He describes this as having been 'strenuous training', but found it an invaluable opportunity to develop his interest and increase his knowledge in this field.

On 24 August 1920, he married Evelyn Triggs, the Vice-Principal of the Royapettah Girls' High School in Madras, whom he had met during his first period in India. She was the daughter of a Methodist minister and former missionary, the Rev. Arthur Triggs, and had been born in Ceylon. They spent their honeymoon in Darjeeling, in northern India, within sight of the Himalayas. The sight of the peak of Everest in the early morning, catching the sun while the rest of the world was still dark, remained vividly in his memory and imagination all his life. He eagerly seized an opportunity to go over the mountains into Tibet, where he was fascinated by its Buddhist culture; the chanting of the monks and the prayer wheels everywhere turning in the wind.

Mrs. Weatherhead started a Sunday School at the Egmore Church, and Leslie introduced a Fellowship Group, which included periods of discussion and study, along the lines he had set out in his Field Notebook during his time in Mesopotamia.

The congregations were made up largely of university students. Since the university lectures were in English, they were drawn to the church because its services were in English, and this provided them with a way to improve their command of the language. Weatherhead was excited by the opportunity of preaching the Christian message to those who had never heard it before, and his resumed ministry gained the same effective response as it had received before he had left for the war. Congregations were larger than before, and increasing numbers of both men and women stood up after the service to declare their conversion.

He was sensitive to the fact that for those Indians who were persuaded to change from their native religion to the Christian faith there was often a considerable price to be paid. One law student came to him and asked to be baptised secretly. Weatherhead explained that this was not possible, since baptism was an open confession of faith in Christ. He asked the young man the reason for the request, and was told that if he was baptised during a public service, his father would cut off his allowance and he would not be able to complete his degree, which meant that his whole future career would be finished. Weatherhead was deeply sympathetic, conscious that his own faith had never cost him that much, but felt that he had to insist that baptism must be an open confession of faith or it was nothing. The student accepted the condition, and was duly baptised during a public service, crowded with his fellow students. Then everything happened as he had expected. His father cut off his allowance and he had to leave the university. Instead of becoming a barrister he became a clerk to a fishery concern. Giving an account of this incident in a sermon preached many years later, in 1945, on 'Has a Country at War the Right to Export the Gospel of Peace?', Weatherhead described how, when he came to leave India, the young man was at the station in Madras to see him off. Weatherhead told him how sorry he was that his conversion had meant such a sacrifice for him. 'I cannot describe to you folk here today the thrill in his voice and the light in his eyes, when he gripped my hand and said, "But it is worth it."'

The Weatherheads' first child, Arthur Dixon, was born the following year in the Vellore Hospital, some seventy miles from Madras. Weatherhead had come to know well the American founder of Vellore, Dr. Ida Scudder, and he supported her pioneering work throughout his life. When she died, in 1960, he preached and paid tribute to her at her Memorial Service, which was held in the City Temple, and every year during his ministry there, the church contributed funds towards the work at Vellore.

The culture, customs and conditions in which people lived in India affected him deeply. He learnt as much as he could about their ways and traditions, but he was appalled by much of what he saw and disturbed by many of the practices associated with religion in India. His visits to his church members often took him through the slums of Madras, and he could not forget or shrug off the scenes of poverty and wretchedness he met there. In his book, *Discipleship* (1934), he describes visiting a leper colony, spending the day with the lepers, and then going home to his bungalow. He contrasts this visiting and then leaving with the Christian belief in the Christ who remains always among the poorest and most needy.

> Sometimes, on some errand of love I go to the slums or some foul den of thieves or some haunt of evil. I pity, I sympathize. I try to help. God forgive me, I can hardly keep from patronage. Then I come home. I bathe. I eat. I sleep. But He stays there. He is still in that foul den, that slum, that brothel [p.145f.].

During his time in the army, in 1918, he had prepared and given lectures on Hinduism and Islam. In his comments on Hinduism he concludes that 'Everything good in Hinduism may be found in Christianity.' In the concept of Brahman he recognises many of the attributes that Christians ascribe to God, but finds that 'Nowhere is Brahman said to be holy, or righteous or good, no, nor even moral. . . . The dwelling place of the gods is in many Hindu minds a hell of immorality and lust. By that one fact Hinduism remains for ever condemned.' He deplores the caste system, which 'hinders any social reformation [and] keeps 50 million people in servile tyranny', and the 'immorality and obscenity'; condemning as 'the greatest evil of all 'The cruel and immoral treatment of women and girls'.

Possessing an Edwardian gallantry towards women, he was shocked by a system that forced girls into marriage with a stranger, and made them mothers as young as eleven, and which exposed girl babies, regarding them as having been born female because of some sin in an earlier life, and in which young girls were made to become temple prostitutes. His lecture is illustrated with incidents he knew at first hand. On one occasion, during a cholera epidemic, when scores of people had died, offerings of sheep and goats had been made to placate the Hindu goddess so that 'the place of sacrifice was steaming, stinking with blood', but to no avail.

Suddenly there is a more terrible development; a devil priestess is wanted. A little well favoured Christian girl is seized. She is told that on the following day she must help the priest, she must kill some of the sacrifices. What this involves few people in this country realise. It means that for ever afterwards she must be one of the public prostitutes of the town. She is thirteen years old. In the case of which I am thinking the evangelist pleaded all night with the priests, and that, together with bribes, procured the girl's release.

In a later sermon he describes an incident in which he intervened to save a little girl in Madras 'whom we were just able to purchase in time before she was thrown away by an indignant father, who refused to admit the shame in his own family circle which was involved in a little girl being born'. His abhorrence of so much that he finds in Hinduism is because 'it is being done in the name of religion, associated with the holiest name we know, the name of God.'

His censure of Hindu practices derives not from an exclusive Christian attitude which dismisses other religions as false, but from an acceptance of all religions as ways of acknowledging and serving the Divine. Jesus, he says, came to fulfil all that is best in all religions, but 'Christ's Gospel is not a thing that can be merely added to Hinduism without the purging away of a great deal of evil first.'

In a similar lecture he praises Islam for the way it has 'bound the Arab. It has done more to tame that untameable race and to bind it into some sort of nation than anything else.' He approves the Muslim belief that God is one, but questions whether He is holy, since a Muslim worshipper may be a liar or a thief without insulting God. Islam is a religion without a Saviour. 'God is not Love. God does not save.' The Muslim God is an 'unknown, unlovable despot.' He considers the Muslim concept of heaven immoral, stating that a religion can be judged by its ideas about God and the after life, and that the treatment of women 'as dictated by their religious life and custom . . . is ever the test of the finer senses of a nation.' He deplores the Muslim treatment of women as 'the blackest of all the blots which besmirch the name and teaching of Muhammad'; recounting an incident in which a man cut off his wife's nose, and then repented, and wanted a missionary doctor to provide a new one. Told by the doctor that it would cost 30 rupees, the man replied, 'Oh, I can buy another wife for that.' He praises much of the teaching of Muhammad, but finds that when compared to the life and teaching of Jesus 'Muhammed and the Muhammedan faith fade away as the light of a faint and far off star before the glory of the sun.'

Weatherhead's experience of the unpleasant aspects of the religions of India, and his compassion for her people, strengthened his evangelical and missionary commitment, since he believed that only the religion of Jesus had a Saviour with power to save and rescue the people from 'the shadows of idolatry and superstition, of sin and of shame'. 'Never think again that Hinduism is best for Hindus. Its ideals are one thing, its practices are another. Christ will fulfil the best in Hinduism. He will destroy the worst.' Even so, his attitude towards religions other than his own, in spite of everything in their practices that he finds not only unacceptable, but even abhorrent, remains one of respect for truth, and he examines them as a searcher after insights that will lead to a greater knowledge of God.

Many years later, in 1945, in a sermon, 'Is Christianity the Final Religion?' which even then was well ahead of its time, he insists that

the Christianity we know is not the final religion, because you and I are seeing an Eastern religion through Western eyes. . . . In olden days missionaries used to go to the ancient countries of the East with their Western Christianity . . . wrapped up in a parcel and tied up with string, bearing British manufacture. . . .The real missionary goes to learn from the East what Christianity is because he recognises this: that when the Easterner looks at the Master, he sees something different from what we see. . . . You don't go to Africa, you don't go to India, you don't go to China, you don't go to the South Sea Islands and say 'All that you have thought is all wrong. You must listen to us. We have got the truth.' You sit down and say, 'Will you talk to me about your religion, and will you let me talk to you about mine?' And you show them Christ as you see Him, and, as the other man understands and sees and prays, your own conception of Christ is incredibly enriched. He is the truth of all religions. He is the way of God for all men.

And in a second sermon, preached the same day, he continued,

I have a hope myself that . . . the sunrise for religion will come from the East; that having preached to other peoples and having refrained from taking our religion seriously, there may well come back to us from those lands such an interpretation of our own Christianity as shall lift us out of our materialism.

Weatherhead believed that the British had a civilising effect on India, particularly in outlawing such practices as suttee (the burning of widows) but he was no imperialist. The beginning of his second period in India coincided with the India Act (1919), which established the all-Indian Parliament of two houses (though with strictly limited powers), and the beginning of Mahatma Gandhi's movement for civil disobedience and non-co-operation with the British authorities; and it ended in 1922, just before Gandhi was arrested, tried and imprisoned. It was a time of great political unrest and Weatherhead could not remain aloof and indifferent to what was taking place.

The War had a profound impact on India and Indian attitudes, especially towards the British Imperial power. It changed Indian perceptions of Britain and its place in the world. When the war began there was much loyalty and support for the British,

In the early stages all opposition to the government ceased and there was general support for war measures. 1,200,000 men, of whom 800,000 were combatants, were recruited, a hundred million pounds were given outright to Britain and between twenty and thirty million pounds contributed annually towards war expenses. India undertook her own defence so that for a time there were only 15,000 British troops in the country.[1]

In spite of this, the British government failed to respond with any positive recognition of India's contribution to the war effort by making worthwhile concessions to her aspirations. The experiences of the Indian troops in the trenches further disillusioned 'village India' with the supposed superiority of the west. The war against Turkey strained the loyalty of Indian Muslims, who revered the Sultan of Turkey as the leader of their faith.

The same month in which Weatherhead arrived back in India, April, 1919, General Dyer ordered his troops to fire on a crowd of between ten and twenty thousand unarmed demonstrators at Amritsar, killing nearly four hundred and wounding over twelve hundred. This action, the punitive measures which followed it, and the reception given to Dyer's actions by the government, press and public in England, caused further resentment in India. Only Gandhi's influence prevented large-scale outbreaks of violence. Dyer was retired, but people in India were greatly offended by a vote in his favour in the House of Lords, and by some of the British press, in particular the *Morning Post* which not only treated him as a national hero but raised a heavily subscribed fund in appreciation of his services. Gandhi, who had previously argued for co-operation with the British, now became an opponent. He denounced the British rule as evil and proclaimed that 'co-operation in any shape or form with this satanic government is sinful.' In August he carried the Congress with him in launching a non-co-operation movement with the government. Weatherhead returned to a much-changed atmosphere in a highly rebellious India, and he could not remain impervious to it.

Soon after he returned to England in 1922, Weatherhead was asked to give a lecture on Mahatma Gandhi to the Didsbury Literary Society and Reading Club. He strongly defended Gandhi, whom he described as 'the greatest personality in India today', at a time when he was being ridiculed by much of the British press. Weatherhead was appalled by the way the Indian situation was being misrepresented by the English newspapers, and he described the action of General Dyer as 'that worst of all the dark blots on the British name.' He praised the way Gandhi reacted to the tragedy, and criticised the British Government, which, he said, could have avoided a great deal of harm if only it had co-operated with Gandhi, and especially if it had seriously apologised for the actions of Dyer.

In January, 1922, the Prince of Wales made a visit to India, including Madras. Gandhi's response was to call for the Indians to boycott the proceedings and ceremonies. Weatherhead sympathised with Gandhi's reaction to the visit, which he regarded as 'untimely' and 'unhappy'. The Prince's stay in Madras lasted five days and was taken up with official receptions. Weatherhead was not impressed. He made a critical note: 'What an Indian Prince would do – Races – Polo – Dancing – Medals. No kingly thing spoken. Doesn't represent anyone. No meeting with Indians or understanding of problems. Pointless visit. 25,000 rupees.' [Presumably the cost of the visit to the city.] 'A young man out for a good time.' No doubt Weatherhead failed to appreciate the constitutional constraints which bound the Prince from anything which looked like interference in political matters, but his disappointment with and disapproval of the way the Prince carried out his responsibilities as heir to the throne clearly remained with him. Years later, in a sermon preached towards the end of the Second World War, he recalled the Indian reaction to the Prince's visit:

You may criticise the Indian religions . . . but the Indian is religious. . . . I was chaplain to the Governor of Madras, Lord Willingdon, when Edward Windsor, who was then Prince of Wales, came out to Madras, and the

Indian University students, amongst whom I was working, could not understand it. They said, "We in our Hindu temples, we in our Mohammedan mosques pray every day, and we pray for your Prince of Wales, but he never goes anywhere to pray." Indeed it was with the greatest difficulty that he could be persuaded to spend twenty minutes inside the Madras Cathedral, and when the seriousness of this attitude was pressed upon him, he sent, to my knowledge, an aide-de-camp from Government House round to the Bishop's residence, to say, "If the service is not over in twenty minutes I shall walk out."

Weatherhead was always careful not to be identified with any political party, but he was often outspoken in his views. Discussing the caste system in his lecture on Hinduism, he condemned also the 'English Caste System' as 'pernicious and utterly at variance with the spirit of Christ'.

Gandhi was arrested on 10 March, 1922, just after Weatherhead had left for England. He took a close interest in Gandhi's trial and gained an eyewitness account of it from an Indian friend. Gandhi's statement at the trial he considered 'a most terrible indictment of the British system.' In his lecture on Gandhi he refers to a letter that he says Gandhi sent to every Englishman, 'and the reply some of us in Madras sent to that letter.' Gandhi had written about the exploitation of Indian resources for the benefit of Britain, and accused the British authorities of encouraging the traffic in drink and drugs, of 'degrading treatment of Indians in the Dominions' and 'Total disregard for Indian sentiment by glorifying the Punjab administration and flouting the Muslim sentiment.' Weatherhead said that not one of the charges made by Gandhi could be denied, and attacked the 'irreligious spirit' of the British in India, accusing them of building a pagan civilisation which 'imperils the future of India more than any other influence.'

He recalled sharing a first-class carriage in a train in India with an English Government official. Late at night, when the train stopped, a Brahmin lawyer approached the compartment and asked if there was room for him. It was a sleeping compartment, and two berths were unoccupied, but Weatherhead's travelling companion angrily said, 'No, there isn't, we don't want any bloody niggers in here.' And a group of people on the station laughed. Weatherhead commented that the 'fatal assumption of racial supremacy . . . and total lack of brotherliness and sympathy' was what lay beneath all the problems in India then.

Early in 1922 Weatherhead received an invitation to return to England and become minister of the Methodist Church in the London suburb of Kensal Rise. In 1920, the Weatherheads had been visited by Newton Flew, a distinguished Methodist scholar, who had also been an army chaplain in Mesopotamia, where Weatherhead had first met him. It was on Flew's recommendation that the invitation had come to be issued. Weatherhead's health was causing concern. He had never been physically robust, and the harsh climate and conditions during his service in Mesopotamia had taken their toll. He had returned to Madras immediately on his discharge from the army without taking any leave, in order to release an older colleague, the Rev. William J. Tunbridge, who had been in India six years and urgently needed to return home. The heat and dust of India had undermined his health still further. He decided to accept the invitation, and in February, 1922, returned to England with his family.

The six years Weatherhead had spent in India and at war were the most formative in his life, taking him from his narrow Nonconformist home, bringing him into contact for the first time with those he later described as 'lovable agnostics', and with those whose life style and attitude to religion were very different from his own. In India and Mesopotamia he experienced other religions and cultures. As a missionary, serving officer and army chaplain, he had come up against disagreeable authority which he had refused, on the grounds of conscience, to obey. His meeting with the Quaker doctor Tombleson was the single most important influence on his life and gave his vocation its direction and purpose, and his meeting with Newton Flew introduced him to the Fellowship of the Kingdom where he was to find his closest friends and the chief influences on his theology and message. He returned from India aged twenty-nine, married, with a family, matured, but with his youthful enthusiasm for the gospel undimmed.

1. Percival Spear: *A History of India* (Vol 2, Penguin 1965) p.181f.

4. Manchester 1922-1925

'The Philistines have invaded the Epworth Press with the hypothesis of
"science falsely so-called" and the puerilities of half-daft criticism'

Weatherhead returned to England in February, 1922, having arranged with the church at Kensal Rise to take up his ministry there in September of that year, but the Methodist Conference intervened. The Chairman of the Manchester District, J. Oliver Hornabrook, had put in a strong request to Conference for a younger man to take on the challenge of the Oxford Road church in a particularly difficult part of Manchester. Hornabrook had spent a year there himself, in 1913, just before joining the forces as a chaplain for five years. Conference considered that Weatherhead was too young for a comfortable suburban church and decided to appoint him to Manchester instead.

The Oxford Road church was in a down-town area of industrial Manchester. The church manse, at 61 Cecil Street, was an old terraced house in the middle of a row, with a pub on one side and a brothel immediately opposite. The state of the manse and the condition of its furnishings was so poor that Weatherhead, understandably unhappy about his wife and family having to live in such a place, wrote a letter, supposedly coming from a minister's mother-in-law, to the *Methodist Times and Leader*, describing it and saying 'Any girl who marries a Wesleyan minister is either a heroine or a fool.' He signed it, 'Amelia Ray Tatwunce.' His second son, Andrew Kingsley, was born there in 1923.

The Church situation in England in the 1920s was very different from when he had left in 1916. The war had considerably affected people's attitudes and beliefs, leaving them largely disillusioned with religion. The greater freedom from pre-war social constraints that wartime conditions had allowed, especially for women, led to behaviour and manners considerably different from what the pre-war generation, and church-goers in particular, had considered acceptable. The Nonconformist Churches suffered most of all, and felt it the more sharply by contrast with their previous prosperity and expectations. The Liberal Party had gone into sharp decline, and the political influence of Nonconformity declined with it. Churches lost confidence as their attendances fell, and became increasingly uncertain about the future. There was an accelerating movement of populations from the city centres to the suburbs, and although suburban churches might be well attended this made it more difficult for Free Church opinion to be heard. Where the Church of England retained the advantage of its great cathedrals, the vast preaching houses of Nonconformity were becoming costly liabilities, and were steadily abandoned. The great days of the Nonconformist pulpit were effectively over.

There was a steady drift of people from the north to the south, where life was growing more prosperous, providing new opportunities and entertainments. The cinema, and especially radio, were having a considerable influence on people's habits and widening their knowledge of the world.

The Oxford Road church was a vast Victorian building with a seating capacity of twelve hundred. It had been a fashionable church in the past, but by the time Weatherhead became its minister it had declined along with the surrounding district. Its regular congregations then numbered about thirty in the morning and sixty at the evening service. It was, however, almost opposite the Manchester University, so that once again Weatherhead had the opportunity to work with young students as he had in Madras.

He and his wife opened the manse to young people for whom he always had a special liking. With the help of groups of students from the university he visited three thousand homes in Manchester, each three times. Weatherhead had some cards printed, with a personal message and a photograph of himself in military uniform, to be handed to the people visited. With the students he formed a Fellowship Group, similar to the one he had started in Madras, which met for discussion on Friday evenings in the manse, and after each Sunday evening service he organised a social hour. These efforts, combined with the appeal of his preaching, began to attract increasing congregations to the church.

He also began to use his knowledge of psychology in his pastoral work, and to apply the principles and methods he had been taught by Captain Tombleson. He was encouraged to continue by the evident success of his first cases, which included some remarkable results. A Manchester man who had been told he would never walk again made a full recovery when treated by Weatherhead. He expressed his gratitude by presenting him with a large roll-top desk, which took pride of place in Weatherhead's study, and which he continued to use for the rest of his life.

The poverty of the unemployed, the prevalent materialism and lack of interest in spiritual things, caused him to ask what the role of the Church should be, and what it had to offer, to the mass of the underprivileged and socially disadvantaged. Tawney's *Christianity and the Rise of Capitalism*, based on his Holland Memorial Lectures of 1922, impressed him with a concern for social justice, and stories of personal hardship among miners' families and those working in factories moved him to indignation in Manchester, just as the plight of the poor in India had affected him there. Aware of the difficulties in the way of social change, he wrote in his notebook, 'Hosts of employers wish to do the Christian thing, but are bound by Society as it is today same as miners are.'

He was delighted to find already active in the Oxford Road church an organisation that exactly fitted in with his understanding of Christian service. This was The League of Good Samaritans, which had been founded by Herbert Buckley, a member of the church, in 1910. Buckley was the leader of a Young Men's Class, one of whose members was unable to earn a living. Buckley and the other members of the class would frequently discuss what they could do for him. From this came the idea of starting a men's group to provide help for others in need, and the League was formed, based on the story of the Good Samaritan. Weatherhead was impressed by this organisation and, after he left Manchester, founded further Lodges in Leeds and London and encouraged the setting up of Lodges in other churches as well. He greatly valued the League, because it proved a practical and efficient way of helping people in need and because it provided a means of useful service for the men of the church, so meeting the criticism that churches gave little opportunity for men to employ their time and talents. It also helped the minister, who had no time to investigate everyone who appealed to him for help, and was able to protect him from those who fraudulently preyed on his sympathy and goodwill. The Samaritan League held regular meetings to discuss the most practical ways of helping individuals whose names had been passed on to them, usually by the minister. This went further than simply giving a small sum of money that might salve a conscience but not make any real difference. The League members drew on their own wide knowledge and experience to give practical advice and assistance, sometimes even setting a man up in business, providing support until he was able to become completely independent.

While he was in India, Weatherhead had learned from Newton Flew about a new organisation known as the Fellowship of the Kingdom, and he joined it immediately he returned to England. This was a movement which had grown rapidly from groups of younger Methodist ministers, especially those who had, like Weatherhead, returned from serving in the forces as chaplains and who shared a strong feeling that the Church needed to re-think both its organisation and its traditional theology if it was to meet the serious questions and challenges to faith provoked by the war. They also shared a dissatisfaction with the spiritual state of Methodism and an impatience with older methods of evangelism.

The heart of the Fellowship was the annual conference it held at Swanwick from 1920. The F.K. sought to get away from the influence of dominant individuals and to put the emphasis on small groups sharing with each other, but inevitably the personalities of the speakers and leaders made themselves felt. Weatherhead attended in 1922, and from then on became an enthusiastic member. Throughout his ministry, even after he became minister of the Congregational City Temple, he held regular meetings of the Fellowship in his home.

At Swanwick he rapidly became established as a leading personality, often acting as either the Conference's chairman or secretary. The F.K. gave him the opportunity he had lacked in India, to meet and get to know many of his fellow ministers. Friendship was of great importance to him, and he coveted the fellowship of other ministers. His attachment to Methodism, which he was so anxious not to break when he went to the City Temple, owed a great deal to the F.K. and the companionship he found there. In his notes to his biographer he describes it as 'the source of nearly all my dearest friends, and which has meant more to me than I can say.' Among those whom he came to know at this time were W.E. Sangster and Donald Soper. His love of people and interest in them, and his lively and attractive personality made a considerable impression on those who met him there for the first time. One of these was C. Ryder Smith, then Theological Tutor at Richmond College and later its Principal. After meeting him at the Conference Smith wrote to him,

The Hayes
Swanwick,
Friday.

Dear Mr. Weatherhead,

. . . Please, I am going to ask a question I hope you aren't tired of them – what does 'D' stand for in your name? There are great controversies about it, don't you feel honoured? Don't forget to see us when you come to Richmond – I shall tell the Students what a great man you are etc. etc. – So I expect you will come. – I can't realise I've only known you for 4 days – its more like 4 ages.

Yours,
Ginger.

One of the themes of the 1922 conference was 'The Christian Preacher and Social Righteousness', and the chief speakers were H.G. Tunnicliffe, and S.E.Keeble – who had studied Karl Marx and was a leading advocate of Christian Socialism within Methodism. Weatherhead, although never a Socialist, was much impressed with their arguments, which he recorded fully in his notebook. According to these notes, the arguments about inequalities of wealth and poverty were presented as breaching the fellowship which was meant to exist between 'All men . . . God and their fellows.' He writes, 'We must learn the social implications of Christianity', and suggests the setting up of a Christian political party. This idea remained with him; he advocated it later during the political crises of the 1930s and attempted to establish such a party himself during the Second World War.

Although Weatherhead was not among the founders of the Fellowship, he quickly established himself as one of its most important figures.

The spiritual leader of this movement was William Russell Maltby (1866-1951), Warden of the Wesley Deaconess Order, aided by J.A. Findlay (1880-1961) T.S. Gregory . . . who became a Roman Catholic, R.N. Flew, and the young Leslie Weatherhead . . . who were able to combine a rich catholic spirituality with an intense concern to follow the 'historical Jesus' as he had been revealed to them by the Protestant biblical scholarship which they had studied. The influence of this style of liberal evangelicalism . . . was very great upon ministry and intelligent laity alike.[1]

It is not easy to determine which was the greater, Weatherhead's influence on the Fellowship or the Fellowship's influence on him. Weatherhead wrote regular papers for it, and if these expressed the theology of the Fellowship, then this also appeared in his sermons and books. The Fellowship emphasised the importance and possibility of an encounter with the living Jesus, who was the same person as the historical figure of the Gospels, and this, interpreted as a 'transforming friendship' between the believer and his Lord, was central to Weatherhead's teaching. An appreciation of the value of silence in worship was a feature of the Swanwick conferences and a significant part of services conducted by Weatherhead. The belief that the Christian life could be understood as an adventure and a quest found expression notably in Weatherhead's book, *In Quest of a Kingdom*, which clearly owes its title and its theme to the Fellowship of the Kingdom.

Maltby and Findlay were both considerable influences on Weatherhead, and he collected and filed their frequent articles in the Methodist and other religious papers. Findlay was Tutor in New Testament Language and Literature at Didsbury College, during Weatherhead's time in Manchester, and an outstanding New Testament scholar who 'persuasively expounded a "Come to Jesus" religion.' William Strawson[2] attributes Weatherhead's emphasis on the reality of the friendship of Jesus to Findlay, but this is to overlook the significance of Weatherhead's own 'Damascus Road' experience of the presence of Christ when he was seventeen. According to one of his former students, Findlay was apparently irritated by the frequency with which his ideas appeared in Weatherhead's books. Weatherhead owed much to Findlay, who provided him with the scholarship to support and interpret his experience, and his influence may also be seen in Weatherhead's belief in an innate human goodness, deriving from a perception of the perfect goodness of God, who, as the Supreme Artist, could never have deliberately created anything evil. Even the horrors of the Second World War, which revealed the terrible deeds of which human beings were capable, did not succeed in completely shaking this belief.

Maltby, more than any other, was the one to whose thinking he responded. Maltby had been one of the speakers at the Swanwick Conference in August, 1922, and Weatherhead recorded in his notebook the substance of Maltby's address on fellowship and loving one's neighbour. Maltby had become Warden of the Wesleyan Deaconess Order in 1920 after 25 years as a circuit minister. In 1925 he toured India, Burma and Ceylon, lecturing on behalf of the Student Christian Movement. Maltby's theology was 'liberal' but his chief emphasis was on the personal relationship of the Christian believer to Jesus Christ. Strawson notes the way this teaching of Maltby's was powerfully expressed through the preaching of Weatherhead.

> The Gospel is the incredible story of God coming near to us in Jesus. Jesus is the one who inevitably draws to himself, and so to God, those who look at him. This is a wonderful message . . . a message which filled to overflowing such great chapels as Brunswick, Leeds, and the City Temple, London, when Leslie Weatherhead preached it. . . . Along with Findlay and Weatherhead, he had an extraordinary grasp of the reality of Jesus; known in personal experience as the Saviour. As Weatherhead said to Findlay when they visited Maltby on his deathbed, "I've come to see the master of us all".[3]

Weatherhead developed a close attachment to Maltby, who baptised the Weatherheads' daughter, Margaret, on Christmas Day, 1929, at the Brunswick Church in Leeds. Weatherhead dedicated his book, *Jesus and Ourselves* to Maltby, 'In glad acknowledgement of a debt that can never be repaid.'

Manchester gave Weatherhead the opportunity to meet and hear others who were admired by him and influential in his life. The Bishop of Manchester then was the great William Temple, and they became good friends. Temple's book, *Christus Veritas*, published in 1924, dealt with the sufferings of God in a way that harmonised with Weatherhead's own thinking and response to the sufferings caused by the war. He carefully kept the reports of the visits of distinguished preachers to Manchester Central Hall. Among these were A.E. Whitham, whom he was to succeed as minister of Brunswick in Leeds; W.E. Orchard, and the famous American, Harry Emerson Fosdick, who preached at a mid-day service on Tuesday, 3 June 1924, which Weatherhead was able to attend. Orchard and Fosdick were particularly important to the development of his style and approach to public prayer. Weatherhead acquired Orchard's famous book of prayers, *The Temple,* published in 1913, during his time at Richmond, and he cherished it all his life. He frequently adapted and used Orchard's prayers in his services, and much of the style of his own prayers was modelled on Orchard. Fosdick's books, *The Manhood of the Master, The Meaning of Prayer* and *The Meaning of Faith* he kept with him during his time in the army, and Fosdick was much moved when they met to learn from Weatherhead that even when he was having to travel on horseback in Mesopotamia and could take very little with him, these books, together with his Bible and hymn book, remained with him as his constant companions. The title of one of Weatherhead's best-loved books, *The*

Transforming Friendship, comes from Fosdick's *The Meaning of Prayer*.

Weatherhead's notebooks show others who influenced him in the early years of his ministry. Prominent among these were the distinguished Congregationalist, J.H. Jowett, whose weekly sermons, published in the *British Weekly*, he regularly filed, and the articles featured as 'The Correspondence of the Rev. Prof. David Smith, D.D.' The cuttings of Smith's column appear more often than those of any other writer in the early notebooks, and provided Weatherhead with a constant source of illustrations and ideas. Smith, who was a Professor of Theology at Queen's College, Belfast, dealt with the individual's doubts and difficulties in a direct and honest way which appealed to Weatherhead, and which was similar to that of Weatherhead himself.

Weatherhead's university education having been cut short by the war, he took the opportunity to enrol at the university for a three year M.A. course in the Department of English. This enabled him to identify more closely with the students as one of themselves, so that they were even more ready to help him build up his congregation and attract people to his church.

In 1923, he collaborated with a fellow minister, J. Arundel Chapman, in producing *The Old Testament and Today*. This had its beginnings in a pamphlet Weatherhead had written and which was published by the Christian Literature Society for India during his ministry there. Chapman was a founder member of the Fellowship of the Kingdom and one of its strongest influences; as its literary editor and Propaganda Secretary, he was responsible for all its publications. From 1924 to 1930, he was Theological Tutor at Didsbury College, Manchester, but it is most likely that he first met Weatherhead at the 1922 Swanwick conference. Like Weatherhead, he was a modern liberal in his beliefs. Like Weatherhead also, Chapman had had a mystical experience of the presence of Jesus which had transformed not only his faith, but both his theology and political outlook, and completely changed his life. Sharing this common outlook and experience they discovered each other as kindred spirits and Weatherhead counted Chapman as 'one of my dearest friends.' Chapman suffered from severe bouts of depression, and during one of these, in June 1934, apparently committed suicide by walking over a cliff. Weatherhead was devastated, especially since at the time he was away on holiday in Venice. Just before he went he had advised Chapman to see a psychologist, but Chapman had said that he would wait until Weatherhead returned.

In their book the authors set out to help young people especially to read and appreciate the Old Testament in the light of modern biblical scholarship. For all the criticisms Weatherhead made of much of the Old Testament throughout his career he retained a love and respect for the Bible as a whole. He preached mainly from biblical – and often Old Testament – texts, and in his very last book, *The Busy Man's Old Testament,* he again returned to encouraging people to read it with understanding and discrimination.

The book was generally well received, being favourably reviewed by – among others – the *Expository Times* and the *Times Literary Supplement*. Professor Willert F. Howard, in the *Methodist Recorder*, commended its scholarship as 'sound and adequate' and recommended that it be read by every local preacher and candidate for the ministry. The *Methodist Times and Leader* thought the book was 'noteworthy as indicating the viewpoint of the younger Methodist ministry on Biblical criticism.' Dr. George Jackson, of Didsbury College, in a personal letter to Weatherhead, congratulated them both 'on an eminently useful bit of work' and promised to say a word about it in the *Manchester Guardian*, though he chided them for the over use of the phrase 'as to' and suggested they run through the book again to see how many times it occurred. He closed the letter with a kindly piece of advice: 'And remember, neither University classes or anything else must interfere with your short afternoon rest. As you love me lay that duty on your soul.'

There were other, less appreciative comments. One writer in the *Irish Christian Advocate* (28 March 1923) considered the book directly opposed to Methodist doctrine. It was dangerous, as it contradicted 'many of the plain statements of the Old Testament' and ignored 'the place and value of sacrifice.'

All sceptics and unbelievers should be comforted by the wholesale way in which all positions attacked by them have been surrendered from the fact of the Fall to the "omniscience" or divinity of our Lord. . . . It is time a stop was put to all the nonsense that is being poured out of and into the modern mind of professed Methodists, and that they began seriously to believe what God has seriously caused to be written. The Philistines have invaded the Epworth Press with the hypothesis of "science falsely so-called" and the puerilities of half-daft criticism.

In the same year, 1923, Weatherhead published his first book as sole author, *After Death*. The manuscript of this book had also been prepared during his time in India, and was the outcome of his experiences during the war. In order to get the book produced, his publishers, James Clarke & Co., required him to put up thirty pounds towards the cost of publication in case the book was not a success. This was a large amount of money for a young minister, whose stipend then was £280 per year. He felt he could not afford to do this, but his wife insisted that he should go ahead.

Her faith was justified. The book sold well, dealing as it did with a subject then very much in people's minds. It gained considerable additional publicity, notoriety, and subsequently increased sales, following an attack on it and its author by another Wesleyan minister, who accused Weatherhead of propounding heretical theories which were contrary to Methodist doctrine as set out by John Wesley. This led to him being arraigned before the Methodist Conference discipline committee on fourteen charges of heresy. He was given a list of the charges, and prepared his defence, but when he appeared before the committee he discovered that the charges had been altered. His objection was accepted, and the hearing was postponed to the following Conference. When this met a year later, he was completely exonerated. The committee, and then the full Conference, voting some four hundred in favour and twenty against, decided that the book did not exceed the freedom of interpretation that the Methodist church allowed its ministers. The adverse critical reactions to the book not only surprised him but made him less respectful of orthodox theology. Thereafter he was less inclined to take notice of ideas from that source unless they coincided with his own.

The book continued to sell, and by 1956 had gone into its twelfth impression and had been published in Canada, America, South Africa and Australia. In 1926, an anonymous churchgoer gave its author £200 to have eight hundred copies distributed to members of his church.

Weatherhead's success at Oxford Road, and his rapidly growing wider reputation were quickly recognised. After only six months in Manchester he was invited to follow A.E. Whitham at Brunswick Church, Leeds, when Whitham ended his outstanding ministry there in 1925. Before he left Manchester, he heard that the Manchester Mission, which had previously refused to take over Oxford Road, regarding it as a hopeless cause, had agreed to adopt the church, to convert the building and continue with it as the 'Oxford Hall.'

In 1925 he was awarded an M.A. Honours degree in English Literature for a thesis which was later published (in 1929) as *The Afterworld of the Poets*. This book was in part Weatherhead's answer to the critics who had attacked him for his views in *After Death*, one of whom had mentioned his frequent references to nineteenth-century poets in that book, arguing that he would have done better to have consulted more theologians, and such early Christian thinkers as Origen and Ambrose instead. In reply to his critics, Weatherhead stated that 'the most modern theological conceptions concerning the life beyond the grave . . . were almost all contained in the poetry of the Victorians', indicating that the poets were fifty years ahead of the theologians.

The book contains a Foreword by A.S. Peake, who was then Rylands Professor of Biblical Exegesis in the University of Manchester. Weatherhead had gone to him for advice concerning this choice of subject for study. Peake predicts for him

> a distinguished career in the ministry. . . . I am the more confident because he has not yielded to the temptation to stake his future on his talent for popular speech . . . he has recognised the duty of strenuous study and hard thinking.

The book presents a number of ideas that remained fundamental to Weatherhead's thinking. He refuses to distinguish between the poet and the religious mystic and visionary, placing poets in the 'same category' as Bunyan, the author of Revelations, St. Francis of Assisi, 'and a thousand more' who have 'a different way of arriving at truth.' He compares the theologian, inhibited by his training which makes him dogmatic and afraid of being unorthodox, with the poet who is free and 'soars to a pinnacle of truth' and whose way of arriving at truth is the same as that of the biblical writers who ascribed their ideas to God.

> Isaiah says, "The word of the Lord came unto me saying. . . ." Browning says: "God has a few of us whom he whispers in the ear" . . . the "inspiration" is the same in quality in both cases. [*ibid*. p.22]

Weatherhead insists that truth, like beauty, is perceived through feeling as much as by reasoned thought, argument and the presentation of evidence: 'we are not to say, "We feel a thing deeply and therefore it is true," but rather "It is true, therefore we feel it deeply."' This conviction is at the root of his understanding of what constitutes authority in religion, and it is at the heart of his approach to preaching and writing. His aim is less to persuade by argument and logical presentation (though he always sought to do this) than to share his insights with his hearers and readers, so that they might 'see' what he 'sees' (a much used word in his preaching) and in another favourite phrase, 'feel it in their ductless glands.' For Weatherhead, the 'authority' of the preacher is not derived from his being an official representative of his Church, or from his declaration of the Church's doctrines, dogmas and traditional teaching, but from the sincerity of his insights and the sharing of his own deeply held convictions, which have come to him through his study, prayer, imagination and reason, and which have authenticated themselves in his understanding. His 'authority' therefore is not his, but only the authority of whatever genuine truth is contained in his preaching, as it is received, recognised and authenticates itself in the mind and heart of his hearers.

> Christ's authority was the inward authority of truth, and its weight lay in the people's own intuitive appreciation of truth. He did not argue, but, when he spoke, something in the hearer leaped up in recognition of the truth. [ibid. p.26]

In *The Christian Agnostic* (1965) he explains how this conviction came to him, in an experience which he likens to the conversion of John Wesley, when in Wesley's own words, 'I felt my heart strangely warmed . . . and an assurance was given me that He had taken away my sins, even mine, and saved me from the law of sin and death.' Weatherhead uses this story to explain that,

> The experience of Aldersgate Street meant that the inner authority based on experience and the outer authority of the church met, and the doctrine of Forgiveness for Wesley ever afterwards had the highest authority man ever knows in religion. For Wesley, there occurred that intuitive leap which possesses truth or is possessed by it. In Oman's phrase, "Reality spoke to him." [p.29]

In an account of his own experience he says,

> In a Y.M.C.A. tent pitched on the banks of the Tigris in Mesopotamia, one night early in 1918 . . . there came to me, who had long assented to the idea of forgiveness and offered it to others, a sudden overwhelming sense of being possessed by this truth for the first time. No outward authority or teaching of the church had brought me the authority which that experience brought. It was utterly convincing and final and no one could take it from me. [*ibid.* p.21]

Weatherhead was convinced that unless an individual had made this intuitive response to the truths of religion, their so-called 'beliefs', which may have been accepted only on the basis of some external authority, would lack the power to make any real or vital difference to them. It was not enough just to assent to an idea, it had to be felt in the emotions. 'Truth may certainly be true whatever my opinion may be, but it has no authority with me until I perceive it to be true. When I do, reality has spoken to me.' [*ibid.* p.26]

In *The Afterworld of the Poets* he considers the poems of Wordsworth, Shelley, Tennyson, Arnold, Clough, Swinburne and Browning. In Tennyson he finds 'A New Projection of Christian Thought Born of the Fear of Death', and in Robert Browning 'The Climax of Development'. Tennyson, he says, harmonized Christianity with the latest theories and findings of science, and that 'all the main positions taken up in modern theology with regard to the subject of eschatology may be found in *In Memoriam* written three quarters of a century ago.' But it is Browning who 'takes us farthest and shows us most . . . no poet of the century, we think, saw so clearly or so far.' Weatherhead finds in Browning support for much of his own thinking on life after death. His conviction that 'nothing good can ever be lost', leads Browning 'to accept the theory of universalism, since there is indestructible good in all men.' Nor could Browning accept that 'a soul created by God ever passes out into the darkness, whether we regard that darkness as the extinction or annihilation of the soul or whether we regard it as endless punishment for the wicked.' Browning believes that the ultimate destiny of the human race is that 'man should become divine.' By this he does not mean become God, 'but that manhood should be so raised to its highest power that it could only be called godhead. . . . Men shall be as gods.' Weatherhead argues that this position is in harmony with much in religious and philosophical thought and that even 'In Christianity the idea is not absent'. Citing Paul's Letter to the Romans and the Second Epistle of Peter, which 'speaks of men as partakers of the Divine Nature''', as well as St. John's Gospel and the Revelation of St. John, he says 'We may ask whether the whole purpose of the Incarnation was not to show the possibility of the godhood as yet potential of man.'

Browning was undoubtedly Weatherhead's favourite poet, the one whose thoughts, themes and feelings he found most compatible with his own, but Alan Wilkinson's claim that 'Weatherhead disliked modern music, poetry and art'[4] is too sweeping. *The Christian Agnostic*, for example, contains quotations from a wide range of poets, including C. Day Lewis, Robert Bridges, John Masefield and such modern poets as Stevie Smith and Christopher Fry. During the Second World War, his sermons and pastoral letters in the *City Temple Tidings* contain quotations and references to poems by Yeats, Lord Wavell and Siegfried Sassoon, as well as a poem by a Canadian pilot killed in action, and even, just after the war, a poem written by a German woman, Wanda Hageman. Steve Odum, in his analysis of Weatherhead's published writing, as well as his pastoral letters in the *City Temple Tidings*, lists 140 different poets to whom and whose works Weatherhead refers – a total of 515 references in his books alone. Odum fairly remarks,

His interest in literature was motivated by more than a need for sermon illustrations. The world of literature had been a part of his world since childhood. He learned to see his world through the eyes of the poet, the novelist and the dramatist.[5]

Weatherhead possessed a great love of language and an exceptional feeling for words, acquired through his boyhood reading – in spite of his parents' disapproval – of the popular adventure stories of George Henty, R.M. Ballantyne, Conan Doyle and Rider Haggard, and especially through the family practice of daily Bible reading, so that he learnt to know and love the cadences of the Authorised Version.

Weatherhead's time for general reading in addition to his study of psychology and his religious reading – which was considerable – was bound to be limited. Clarity of meaning and fresh insights into new truths were what he looked for most, and he had no time for anything that did not have something to say which he could share with his congregations or his readers. Macbeth's plea to the doctor, 'Canst thou not minister to a mind diseas'd, Pluck from the memory a rooted sorrow?' was the sort of challenge from literature that he could relate to, as it expressed precisely the limitations of orthodox medicine and the kind of need that he believed only psychology and religion together could meet.

1. J.M.W. Turner: *A History of the Methodist Church in Great Britain Vol.3* (Epworth 1988) p.319f.
2. William Strawson: 'The Significance of the Rev. Leslie Dixon Weatherhead as a Preacher.' Unpublished lecture to the Lincolnshire Branch of the Wesley Historical Society, 17 May 1977.
3. *History of Methodism* Vol.3 *op. cit.*, p.218.
4. Alan Wilkinson: *Dissent or Conform? War, Peace and the English Churches 1900-1945* (S.C.M. 1986) p.241.
5. S.A. Odum: 'Identification as a key to effectiveness in the preaching of Leslie Dixon Weatherhead.' Unpublished Ph.D. thesis, Southern Baptist Theological Seminary. 1985. p.165.

5. Leeds

'The aim of practical psychology is that of the New Testament . . . namely
the facing up to life bravely, and the making of it that vigorous,
radiant, confident, healthful thing God meant it to be.'

In September 1925, Weatherhead moved to the Brunswick Church, Leeds, and
to what he always regarded as the happiest and most rewarding period of his
ministry.

Brunswick was a large and thriving church, with a prosperous congregation.
When it was built, in 1825, exactly 100 years before Weatherhead became its
minister, it was described as the largest Chapel in the kingdom, holding 3,000
people. It was a square, grey, stone building, 'sparsely Classical' in style, built
on a prominent hill site just north of the city centre, and it represented the
strength of Methodism in Leeds at that time. Methodist preaching had begun in
Leeds in 1742, the first chapel being built in 1751. In 1837, the newly arrived Vicar
of Leeds wrote that 'the de facto established religion is Methodism.'

The Methodist Magazine of October 1825 reported of the building of Brunswick
Chapel,

> Our friends in Leeds at length erected a place of worship in that town, in
> some degree commensurate with the wants of the growing population, and
> the demands of one of the largest societies in Methodism. This very neat
> and elegant structure is 96 feet in length by 72 feet broad, within; and the
> gallery, to which there is access by four flights of stairs, passes entirely
> round it.[1]

It also had a large central two-decker pulpit and a perfect acoustic.

Within a few months of the opening of Brunswick a huge and acrimonious
dispute followed a decision of the trustees to install a large pipe organ. This was
attacked as introducing popery and ritualism, and as a serious departure from
Methodist practice and belief. As a result, 2,400 members left Leeds Methodism
and formed the Leeds Protestant Methodists. This movement spread to other
neighbouring towns and then, in 1836, it united with another such group to form
the Wesleyan Association. From this eventually developed the United Methodist
Free Churches. The organ was inaugurated in September 1828, when Samuel
Wesley gave the first recital.

The Brunswick Church was in the Jewish quarter of the city, and as the Jewish
population around the church grew, the congregation came increasingly from
further afield, until, with the growth of the suburbs and public transport, most of
those attending came from outside the city centre. It had enjoyed a long and
famous preaching ministry from Weatherhead's predecessor, A. E. Whitham, a
man of great spirituality, whose approach to preaching and worship emphasised
the mystical and sacramental. In 1935, he helped to found the Methodist
Sacramental Fellowship. Whitham had built up the church and extended the
range of its organisations and activities, particularly in response to the acute
social needs of the city, and under his leadership the church had raised

considerable sums of money in support of a large number of charities. He was a supporter of the peace movement, and had established an active branch of the League of Nations at the church. Weatherhead shared these concerns and quickly introduced the League of Good Samaritans to Leeds where it became active in working with the poor in the area surrounding the building.

The harsh economic conditions that followed the First World War affected the people of Leeds as they did all the major industrial towns. Mass unemployment fluctuated from a high point just after the end of the war, declining until 1927, and then rapidly rising again, more than doubling in the two years 1929 to 1931. The city had an acute housing problem with large areas of Victorian slums. In 1932 the Improvements Committee of the Leeds City Council invited the Leeds Free Church Council to submit a statement to them on the housing conditions in the city. This reported that there were 72,000 back-to-back houses, of which 33,000 consisted of houses built before 1872

in long unbroken rows, with narrow streets, consisting of 2 rooms with a cellar, usually unlighted, with practically no provision for the storage of food, that personal and domestic washing has to be done in the living room, that there is no internal W.C., no accommodation for the storage of household refuge, that outdoor ashpits and W.C.'s are used for groups of houses, and that the houses themselves are crowded together at the rate of 70 to 80 to the acre.

There were another 28,000 houses built in blocks of eight, 'with sanitary conveniences situated between the blocks' and 13,000 with somewhat better accommodation and facilities. The overcrowding and extreme poverty of these slum areas resulted in health statistics which, according to the report, 'are simply appalling.' In some streets the death rate between the years 1920 to 1930 was nearly 70% above the average for the city as a whole, and the infant death rate as high as 85% with rates of tuberculosis and respiratory diseases reaching as much as 133% above the rest of the city.

The concern for the social conditions, bad housing and poverty in the city expressed by the Free Church Council was shared by all the churches in Leeds. An Anglican, the Rev. Charles Jenkinson, who came from the East End of London, was elected as a Labour member to the Leeds City Council in 1930. In February 1931, within three months of his election, he called for a survey of the slums, and his drive and determination were a major factor in bringing about the slum clearance and new housing schemes the Council undertook. In July, 1929, Brunswick's near neighbour, Rev. James Sutherland, of the Belgrave Central Church, started a 'Never-Seen-the-Sea Fund', to enable slum families to have a holiday by the sea. He also started a 'Boots for Bairns' appeal, which the members of Brunswick actively supported.

Weatherhead became minister of Brunswick just a few months before the 1926 General Strike, which caused some disruption to the city's public services. He had a strong sympathy for those suffering from the hardships and inequalities of society, and in his preaching he frequently made reference to the topics and concerns of the day. A former member of Brunswick recalled: 'He always stood up for the workers, and used to say that if people were paid according to their usefulness to society, dustmen would be among the more highly paid.'

In a broadcast on 22 May 1932, he expressed his concern for the slums and the appalling conditions in which so many of his fellow citizens were forced to live:

> let any man go into the slums of one of our great cities . . . in which men and
> women are herded together so that even one room is sometimes shared by
> more than one family . . . slums in which gambling and immorality are rife. . . .
> How can anyone who knows our slums – some of them owned by so-called
> religious people and some by landlords who live in luxury – say that Jesus
> reigns? Or take our modern competitive business and industrial life with its
> antagonism that rarely stays to see another's point of view, its restless,
> feverish quest to make money . . . with its unscrupulous over-riding of the
> rights of personality . . . all through our national and international life there
> are elements of bitter and unforgiving hostility.

Between 1918 and 1939 the city had extended its boundaries by 50 per cent. The movement of the population from the city centre meant that Brunswick's congregation was becoming more scattered and coming from a wider area, since Brunswick drew most of its congregation, not from the nearby slums, but from the skilled working-class, trade and business people who lived further out. At his first Leaders' Meeting in September, 1925, Weatherhead requested that an accurate list of the members of each class be supplied to him before the beginning of December, and at a further meeting suggested introducing a public recognition service for new members.

To strengthen the spirit of fellowship within the church, always difficult with a widely scattered congregation, he introduced the Friday Fellowship which had been so successful in Manchester. This was organised along the lines of group discussions with a set topic, each group having its own leader and 'scribe' to report back to the whole fellowship at the end of the evening, with the minister himself in the chair. Brunswick's Sunday school teachers and church officials found it helpful to attend, along with increasing numbers of students and young people, and many came from other churches to enjoy the stimulation of the discussions, as well as some who did not belong to any church organisation. Weatherhead later introduced the Friday Fellowship to the City Temple, stating, 'In my ministries both in Leeds and London such fellowship has been spiritually the strongest thing in our Church life.' His successor at Brunswick, W.E. Sangster, when he inherited it, 'found it a wonderful meeting' and introduced it to the Central Hall Westminster when he moved there in 1939, with considerable success.

Weatherhead suggested a weekend Conference of Church members at regular intervals, and the first of these was held in June 1929 with W.R. Maltby as its leader. As his reputation grew, more and more people began to attend Brunswick regularly from an increasingly wide area. To further meet the problem of uniting a growing but scattered congregation he introduced area groups of twenty or so church members and adherents living close to one another, with a group leader responsible for arranging for them to meet and offering some pastoral care of the members. Early in his ministry a question was raised in the Leaders' Meeting about an organisation for boys of intermediate age. Weatherhead was asked to look into this, with the result that a Boys' Brigade Company was successfully formed.

His evangelical zeal was as vigorous as ever, and with two colleagues, W.M. Cherry and Wilfred Gower, he arranged and took part in a series of open-air meetings in June, 1930. A large number of cards were printed and distributed inviting people to come and hear the three of them speaking about Jesus. The meetings were held by the Post Office, opposite the Mexborough Arms, near the Old Manor House, and ended with a Rally in the Thorner Methodist Church. Although open-air preaching has always been a traditional Methodist practice, it is much more associated now with Donald Soper than Leslie Weatherhead, who always preferred to preach in the atmosphere of worship. His light voice, and personal and intimate style of preaching, were not really suited to speaking in the open-air, and though there is no reason to suppose he was not good at it, and he must have preached many times in the open during his army chaplaincy, he does not seem to have repeated the experiment.

In 1928 he produced one of his best-loved and most influential books, *The Transforming Friendship*. The title comes from a passage in one of Weatherhead's favourite books; H.E. Fosdick's, *The Meaning of Prayer* (1915):

> The most transforming influences in life are personal friendships. . . . Friendship opens the heart to the ideas, ideals and spiritual quality of another life, until we are susceptible to everything that the friend is and sensitive to everything that he thinks. . . . Consider then what persistent fellowship with God will mean in changing life's quality and tone. Henry Drummond said, 'Ten minutes spent in Christ's society every day; aye, two minutes, if it be face to face and heart to heart, will make the whole life different. . . .' Some things cannot be bought or earned or achieved; they must be caught, they are transmitted by contact as fragrance is. . . . True prayer is habitually putting oneself under God's influence.[p.74]

The Transforming Friendship originated in a series of sermons begun in Madras and Manchester and continued in Leeds, and which had appeared as a series of articles in the *Methodist Recorder*. It demonstrates the central importance of the person of Jesus in Weatherhead's religious thinking and personal faith. In the Prologue to a subsequent book, *Jesus and Ourselves* he states this in the form of a letter to a young man who has just become a church member. 'You ask me in your letter to try to tell you something of what religion means to me. My religion is so centred in Jesus that your question becomes, "What does Jesus mean to me?" He had discovered through his experience of counselling and in private interviews that the personality and character of Jesus had a powerful appeal which evoked a direct response from individuals, where discussions of doctrine and abstract theology had much less effect. He believed that these had unnecessarily complicated the essentially simple Christian message, which he defined as 'the acceptance of the gift of the friendship of Jesus'.

The book begins with a Prologue in the form of a dream in which Weatherhead sees Jesus in various modern situations; with a business man at his place of work, with a family, with a university student, with a poor and lonely girl. He imagines Jesus asking searching questions and changing each of the individuals through the influence of his own presence and personality. The further chapters go on to explore the possibility and nature of this 'transforming friendship' as a real and vital experience for his contemporaries, recognising at the same time the doubts and difficulties that must surround such a claim.

In a chapter on 'The Reality of the Friendship' he builds on W.R. Maltby's book, *The Meaning of the Resurrection,* in which Maltby explains the purpose of the appearances of Jesus between the resurrection and the ascension as being to teach the disciples to realise that he is always present with them, even though they cannot see him, and that it was this belief that made all the difference to them and the kind of people they became. Weatherhead states:

> Christianity is meaningless unless this friendship can do as much for us. What Jesus once was, He is eternally. . . . We can, as Brother Lawrence said, "practise the Presence of God" but the only way I know of practising the presence of God is by practising the presence of Jesus, who makes God credible and real, and entering into the transforming friendship which He offers. . . . The reality of this transforming friendship is reached, not through argument but through experience. [p.47]

The style of the book may seem dated and even sentimental, but it was well reviewed and on the whole favourably received at the time, and added to his growing popularity and reputation. In its review, *The Methodist Leader* referred to Weatherhead as 'one of the few great preachers in the Methodist Church', indicating how considerable his standing had already become, at least within his own denomination. Mark Guy Pearse, writing in the *Methodist Recorder*, praised the book, finding in it a 'tender human sympathy' and a 'compulsion of conviction that is convincing'. He described it as 'a good book, beautiful and blessed, full of grace and truth . . . the style . . . glows with celestial fire.' There was further warm praise in the *Methodist Times* which found the book 'stamped with a remarkable personality' and 'very courageous.' It chose it as its 'Book of the Week' and recommended that 'It should be put into the hands of every young man and young woman in Methodism.'

Several other reviewers commended the book in similar terms, but there were some who were less enthusiastic. In the *Journal of the Wesley Bible Union*, the Rev. Dr. H.C. Morton, in an article headed, 'Methodism in May and the Modernist Minister', deplored the book as indicating that the Wesleyan Church had 'long since surrendered to Modernism.' Although he found the book often moved him to tears – 'It has pathos and a touching human appeal' – he attacked Weatherhead for denying 'the sin-bearing of the Son of God' on the Cross and for sweeping 'out of his path whatever in Bible teaching and Methodist and Christian Creed he thinks in his way.' For Morton the book was not only deeply offensive, it provided a 'tragic ministerial self-portraiture' which 'openly denies a part of the Gospel, and flouts the Foundations upon which the whole Gospel rests.'

In spite of Morton, the book rapidly became a best-seller and continued in print for thirty years, selling over 100,000 copies in ten different languages.

Popular as the book was, it continued to attract criticism from the more academic and orthodox. As late as 1945, the Dean of Chapel of Corpus Christi College Cambridge, Canon Charles Smyth, in a Lent book on *The Friendship of Christ*, took Weatherhead to task for his definition of Christianity as 'the acceptance of the gift of the friendship of Jesus', saying that this was true 'only with very formidable qualifications.' He argued with some justification that it could not possibly be 'the essence of the Christian message' since it was no part of the *kerygma* of the early church. Smyth makes a distinction between the friendship of Jesus of which he disapproves, because in his view it is based sentimentally on a non-biblical view of the historical Jesus, and the friendship of Christ, offered corporately to the Church, and not, on the analogy of human friendship, by one individual to another. This he feels, preserves the lordship of Christ, and the *Mysterium Christi*. He acknowledges that 'for many people the historical Jesus of the Gospels is a more real person than the living Christ of the Acts. But this is a paralysing limitation. . . . The Jesus of history belongs to history.' In spite of such criticisms, even seventy years after it was first published, the book continues to have a remarkable power to move and inspire, and in America it is still in print.

The Transforming Friendship was sub-titled, 'A book about Jesus and ourselves', and this became the title of Weatherhead's next book on this theme, which was once again based on a series of sermons and articles in the *Methodist Recorder* and the *British Weekly*. This book expresses Weatherhead's deepest conviction,

> that Christianity is Christ. Christianity's greatest appeal is Christ. The man who finds that Christianity gives him all he needs – gives him that satisfaction for which his heart is, and has always been, hungry – knows that satisfaction is derived, not from any way in which organized Christianity is presented to him, not in the logic of the creeds, not in ritual or ceremony, but in the offer of a personal relationship between the soul and Jesus Christ Himself.[2]

This conviction was expressed in much of Weatherhead's writing, including the sequel to *Jesus and Ourselves,* titled *His Life and Ours* (1932), and especially in a much later book, *Over His Own Signature* (1955).

By focusing on the person of Jesus, Weatherhead was able to present Christianity as something separate and distinct from the Church, its institutions, rituals, dogmas and creeds. This enabled him to appeal to those whom the events of the recent war, and the inadequacies of the institutional Church which it so clearly revealed, together with the materialism and hedonism of the post-war world, had made disillusioned and cynical. It also provided a fresh approach to young people, who had doubts and criticisms of so much of organized religion and were, he felt, so often put off by it. He thus avoided having to defend the Church or justify and explain its creeds and doctrines in order to persuade people to faith. Instead, he was able to sympathize with the Church's critics and those who found its teachings hard to accept, and yet still to offer Christianity as an attractive, satisfying, intellectually acceptable and desirable way of life. That he was highly successful in this is shown by the fact that this book also immediately went into several editions, and like the previous volume, continued in print for the next thirty years.

The Transforming Friendship and *Jesus and Ourselves* represent one major aspect of Weatherhead's appeal and popularity (his gifts as a preacher and communicator of an intensely personal, devotional and evangelical religion). Between these two books he published, in 1929, *Psychology in Service of the Soul*, which demonstrated another aspect, for which he became equally well-known. He was acquiring a growing reputation as a psychologist, pioneering the use of psychological knowledge and techniques in the pastoral work of the ministry.

The 'New Psychology' was still being regarded by many in the Church – among them some who were highly placed and influential – with considerable suspicion, as the enemy of religion. In 1927, for example, a fellow Methodist, the

Rev. William H. Lax, well-known then for his work in the East End of London, wrote,

> Psychology now claims to displace the saving grace of Christ, and puts in the counter-claim of ability to do all that the Christian religion has been doing for ages. This is a new aspect in the controversy, and creates greater difficulties than it professes to cure. Dr. Garvie has truly said "at the present hour it is psychology which is the most dangerous menace to the Christian view of life, as biology was in a former generation and geology in an earlier time."[3]

That same year Weatherhead addressed the F.K. Swanwick Conference, where he argued that it was God's will that everyone should be in perfect health of body, mind and soul. This started a considerable debate within the F.K. and the Methodist press, and led to a new and continuing interest in healing and psychological counselling among Methodist ministers. Even so, Weatherhead attracted a great deal of hostility and criticism because of his interest in psychology. It was his special insight to recognise in the New Psychology a real aid to the minister as pastor. By focusing on what psychology had to say about the importance and effects of guilt in personality, Weatherhead recognised that here was a possible way of building a bridge between the two disciplines of theology and psychology. He saw that combining the distinctive insights of both would provide a dynamic new pastoral approach which brought together the psychologist's recognition of the destructive effects of guilt with the healing power of forgiveness offered by the Christian faith.

Weatherhead's psychological insights informed his writing on 'Jesus and Ourselves' and influenced his devotional works. The first chapter of *Jesus and Ourselves*, for example, headed, 'Jesus' Respect for Our Personality' begins with a discussion on the different ways in which one person can impose his will on another. Weatherhead's understanding of the way Jesus responded to the people who came to him, and the way he dealt with them, owes a great deal to his own knowledge of human psychology. At the same time, his writings on psychology were strongly devotional and expressed his Christian convictions. Psychology was for him a means of ministry – a healing tool which could not be completely successful unless it pointed people to God and led them to a fuller relationship with him. In his Preface to *Psychology in Service of the Soul* he says:

> The aim of practical psychology is that of the New Testament – which contains in other language so much of what is valuable in the new psychology – namely the facing up to life bravely, and the making of it that vigorous, radiant, confident, healthful thing God meant it to be.

Psychology in Service of the Soul ends with a chapter on 'The Soul's Urge to Completeness', in which Weatherhead argues that this is a drive 'to self-realization' which human nature shares with all nature, and in human beings this 'urge to completeness, means 'universally a craving for God.' The final pages of this book are as devotional and direct in presenting a Christian message as anything in his other, apparently more specifically religious books:

> If a man's body is out of harmony with its environment we call him ill; if a man's mind is out of harmony with its environment we call him neurotic, or insane, but if a man's soul is out of harmony with its environment – or in

other words, God – we do not think of him as abnormal. He flies to the doctor, and in these days to the psycho-analyst. But thousands of people who do not know what is the matter with them yet find the poise and harmony they need in a return to God, for whom every soul is hungry, and without whom they can never have self-realization and the fullness of life. The words of Jesus still echo down the ages and call to those whose soul is sick, with a more serious illness than body or mind can ever contract, "Ye will not come to Me that ye might have life". [p.209]

From the time when he had first begun to use his psychological skills in Manchester Weatherhead had developed his knowledge of psychology and his competence. This was officially acknowledged when in 1926 he was granted a Certificate of Recognition as a Teacher by the West Riding Education Department, and began to conduct classes in psychology in technical and evening schools throughout the county. In Leeds, he acquired a set of rooms near the church, and spent each afternoon interviewing people who came seeking his help. He developed a relationship with doctors who began to send him patients. One of the doctors was Maxwell Telling, then Professor of Medicine in the University of Leeds. Telling asked him to see a patient of his, a young woman, whom Weatherhead subsequently saw more than seventy times. His treatment was successful, and she was able to go back to work. Telling wrote an appreciative preface to *Psychology in Service of the Soul.*

Preaching at the City Temple in London, on 7 October 1928, Weatherhead mentioned using psychology and hypnotism in his ministry. This attracted the attention of the national press and he was besieged by reporters the following day at St. Pancras Station as he was about to catch his train back to Leeds. He gave them an explanation and an account of his psychological work that was fully printed not only in the London daily papers but in all the major provincial newspapers throughout the country as well. Those which had not had a correspondent at St. Pancras interviewed his wife in Leeds instead.

The extent of this press interest indicates how very unusual and even sensational it was at the time for a Christian minister to be a practising psychologist, and even more remarkably, to be using hypnotism to heal people. The newspapers reported his claim to have cured more than fifty cases of people suffering from such ailments as insomnia, neurasthenia, depression, and other nervous disorders during the previous five years. Weatherhead explained that he worked in co-operation with a doctor who sent him patients he was unable to diagnose. He revealed that to hasten matters, he sometimes used hypnotism, which he had been studying for over five years, although he only treated cases where a doctor could find no physical cause. He found that hypnotism acted upon about 70 per cent of people. In Manchester he had treated a man suffering from paralysis. Under hypnotism, Weatherhead discovered this was due to the shock the man had experienced in losing his wife, his son and all his money within one week. Once Weatherhead had uncovered the repression, the man was freed from the paralysis and able to walk again.

This publicity made Weatherhead the centre of controversy in the national as well as the religious press during the next few weeks. This was fuelled by a further account of his work, which he gave to the City Temple Literary Society on 25 October, in a lecture on 'The Meaning and Interpretation of Dreams.' The

Manchester Guardian headline, 'Minister and Doctor Work Together' made less impression than such headlines in other papers as 'When Doctors Fail', or 'Minister Claims Success Where Medical Men Fail', which provoked sharp criticism and comment in the correspondence columns. A letter signed simply 'A Doctor' in the *Yorkshire Evening Post*, (11 October 1928) waxed indignant on behalf of the medical profession. Quoting Weatherhead as saying 'There are many illnesses today which no doctor can possibly cure', the writer replied,

Surely Mr. Weatherhead does not seriously mean that it requires a minister of religion for these cases. He must know that many doctors have devoted their lives to this work. Men like Professor Hadfield, Dr. Brown, Dr. Crichton Millar, who are all the better fitted for it in that the patient does not need to see another doctor first, to make sure there is no physical cause for the illness as Mr. Weatherhead admits has to be done in his case. The minister who combines psychological treatment with his other activities is apt to be biased in his treatment of patients . . . neither the layman nor the doctor desire to be the patient's conscience in the way the clergy appear to. . . . Mr. Weatherhead may certainly succeed where other doctors have failed, but not because they were doctors, but just as one doctor may succeed in one case where another fails. But an average of 10 cures a year is indeed small for a man who professes to have been practising for five years.

Other writers were opposed to the use of hypnotism, especially by a minister of religion. One insisted, 'This is a power which may be used for good by qualified specialists, but if freely permitted to anybody who chooses to practise it, might lead to very serious consequences, and sometimes vicious ones.' Another writer declared that 'to heal through psycho-analysis and hypnotism' was 'a system which received such scathing condemnation from the Founder of Christianity. . . . To use hypnotism in the name of religion is a travesty of Jesus' teaching.'

Weatherhead was so taken aback by the amount of publicity and criticism that he had attracted, that he returned to the subject when he stood up to preach in the City Temple again the following week. The *Christian Herald* (18 October, 1928) reported that he began by making

an emphatic statement concerning the "unwanted and entirely distasteful publicity into which he was hurled. . . . . The publicity" he said, "was concerned with some psychological work which I regard as part of any normal ministry. You see . . . there are certain disharmonies of mind (or even of body) which really arise not from any physical cause, nor even from a psychological cause, but from disharmony of soul. For instance, if a man refuses to forgive any injury done to him by another and broods upon it for a number of years, that repression may cause a disharmony even in the body. If that be so it is no use him taking drugs; it is no use him taking physical measures. It would be very little use his going to the ordinary psychotherapist, who is not likely to tell him that what he needs is the forgiving love of God. That is a case in which the person who ought to be able to help is a minister who has specialized in psychology. That is all I have been trying to do. And the great pity to me is to see that my position – which has been confirmed as sound by the most eminent medical authorities of my own city – has been turned by certain newspapers into a stunt. That is the last thing I wanted, because I regard that particular work

. . . as part of a normal ministry.

Psychology in Service of the Soul had appeared first as a series of articles Weatherhead had written for *The Methodist Magazine* and *The Methodist Recorder* between 1927 and 1929. The book is dedicated 'In Admiration and Gratitude' to J. Arthur Hadfield, who was a major influence on Weatherhead. Hadfield was the son of a Congregational missionary, the Rev. James Hadfield. After attending Eltham College he went first to Queen's College, Oxford, and then entered Mansfield College to train for the Congregational ministry. From 1906 to 1914 he was minister of the Kirk Memorial Church in Edinburgh. There he came under the influence of the psychologist, William McDougall, and became his research assistant. This led him to study medicine at Edinburgh University, specialising in the treatment of nervous disorders. During the war he served first as a Surgeon-Lieutenant in the Royal Navy and then transferred to the army, where he worked again with McDougall as neurologist at the War Hospital in Oxford. After the war he practised in Harley Street and became Lecturer in Psychopathology and Mental Hygiene at Kings College, London. He was one of the founders of the Tavistock Clinic and became its first Director of Studies for the training of doctors in psychological medicine. It was to Hadfield that Weatherhead turned after a serious breakdown of health in 1942. Hadfield took him through an intensive period of psycho-analysis which had a profound effect upon him.[4]

Shortly before Weatherhead's book, one by the Rev. J.G. McKenzie, *Souls in the Making*, was published in 1928. MacKenzie, who was eleven years older than Weatherhead, was a Professor of Sociology and Psychology at Paton College, Nottingham. Like Weatherhead, his interest in psychology had begun during his time at theological college, but unlike Weatherhead, his motivation was theological and evangelical rather than pastoral. McKenzie was interested in analysing the traits in human personality that encouraged or inhibited religious belief. He felt that theology by itself was inadequate for the pastor since 'it may tell him what his people ought to believe, but cannot help him when he comes to ask how they come to believe or disbelieve.' Weatherhead quoted appreciatively from McKenzie in his own book, and valued McKenzie's distinction between pastoral psychology and psychotherapy: 'The former deals with those who have become mal-adapted to the realities of life; the pastor deals with the building up of a spiritual personality from the beginning.' Like Weatherhead, McKenzie recognised the psychological importance of confession and forgiveness, but he put less stress on this than Weatherhead, and was more theological in his approach, believing in the value of specific Christian doctrines in helping people with their troubles. Weatherhead's interest was always pastoral: he wanted to be a healer, if not in medicine, since this was denied him, then in ways that were open to him. Psychology fitted in with his deep interest in people and his desire to help them. His approach to it was always practical. He was eclectic, belonging to no school, but taking from each those ideas which seemed to him of most use in his pastoral and counselling work.

Two Forewords were contributed to *Psychology in Service of the Soul*, the first by Eric Waterhouse, who at the time was Tutor in Philosophy at Richmond College. Weatherhead in his Preface pays tribute to him as 'the greatest psychologist in my denomination.' He was an early guide and supporter of

Weatherhead, later acting as supervisor for his doctoral thesis. Waterhouse commends the book, and praises Weatherhead's gifts, but warns,

The only danger attending Mr. Weatherhead's bold handling of the matter is that those without his knowledge or his gifts should copy his example, and seek to do, not only what he can do, but what he would never try to do.

Maxwell Telling, who provided the other Foreword, was even more concerned about the effect the book might have in producing unqualified imitators. These warnings were necessary. The book was immediately popular, going into four editions in less than a year. The clarity of its style, together with the insights it contained, gave it an obvious appeal to many ministers seeking to improve their pastoral skills. W.J. Smart, in his book, *Miracles of Achievement* (1961), describes the effect it had.

Many men, with no other guidance than *Psychology in Service of the Soul* set out on well-meaning efforts to imitate Leslie Weatherhead. Lots of little Weatherheads sprang up all over the country talking psychology, sniffing around other people's complexes, interpreting dreams, and telling everyone how not to be tired tomorrow. [p.150]

In its review of the book, the *Leeds Mercury* (23 August 1929) described the impact Weatherhead was already making:

He is still young, or at any rate, youngish, but already he has become an inspiring force. He has this great pulpit gift: he can bring home to a congregation – bring home, not merely say – how noble every life might be and how we so often by self-seeking make it a paltry thing. This seems a platitude when set forth in cold type. You should hear it from this man's lips. . . . Those of us who are not scientists and have been bewildered by the more fanciful pages of Freud and Jung will judge Mr. Weatherhead's claims chiefly by the results he reports. I think they will be convinced with him that the suitably trained minister may be a true healer where the origin of the trouble is a disharmony of soul (or shall we say, conscience.)

1. *Brunswick Chapel Centenary Booklet* 1925. p.22.
2. *Jesus and Ourselves* (Epworth 1930) p.10.
3. William H. Lax: *Lax of Poplar* (Epworth 1927) p.253. A.E. Garvie was Principal of Hackney and New College, London, from 1907 to 1933.
4. Leslie Weatherhead: *On Being a Minister*. Joseph Smith Memorial Lecture, Selly Oak, Birmingham, 8 October 1966. p.4. 'I had two hundred separate hours of psychoanalysis with Dr. J. A. Hadfield and am quite prepared to believe that the pulpit was the only stage open to me to "strut my ego" as he quite kindly put it.'

6. The Mastery of Sex

'It is no characteristic of religion to be afraid to face facts, and I would
go so far as to call it a crime that young people should be sent out
into a world which shrieks sex at them without a knowledge of
those facts which are relevant'.

In 1931, Weatherhead produced one of the most controversial of all his books,
which added considerably to his reputation and greatly increased his notoriety,
making him more widely known and bringing him to the attention even of those
outside religious circles and the borders of his own country as well. This was
The Mastery of Sex Through Psychology and Religion, and though it was a
serious and sensitive work, its explicitness scandalised many, especially within
the churches. His usual publishers, the Epworth Press, after much nervous
deliberation, declined to accept the book. Frank Cumbers, later its Book Steward
and Director recorded,

> The records of the publishing house from which I write, contain details of
> the long and agonizing discussions which followed upon his offer of *The
> Mastery of Sex* before the MS was declined. Things are different today; but
> those were "early days" for that study. All the greater honour to the young
> man who was thus giving a lead.[1]

The book was published instead by the Student Christian Movement, which
seems to have had no such qualms.

In his Foreword to *Psychology in Service of the Soul* Maxwell Telling had said
that 'Many of the cases today which need a soul doctor do so because of the
disturbance in the realm of sex.' He asked what the professional clergyman was
going to do about the difficulties people had with sex matters with which ministers
were bound to be confronted. Telling was concerned that many of the clergy
had a narrow and conventional religious bias in their attitude to sex which was
not only unhelpful but even dangerous. Weatherhead shared this concern. His
psychological training, as well as his ministry among young people, had
convinced him that ignorance of sex and prudish social attitudes were the cause
of a great deal of misery and individual guilt, as well as much unhappiness and
spoilt relationships between young men and women within marriage itself. When
he was in Manchester a group of men came to ask him why the Church had
nothing to say about sex, although this was the subject of so many films, novels
and plays, and the source of their greatest temptation and moral problems. This
was a challenge he felt he could not ignore, especially when it was reinforced by
a report in August, 1926, of a Y.M.C.A. World Conference in Helsingfors, on the
theme 'Youth Faces Life' which stated

> the outstanding feature of the discussions was the importance given by the
> delegates to the sex problem and their determination to deal satisfactorily
> with it. . . . There was evidence . . . of a more insistent demand for scientific
> research and instruction in this matter of sex than in any other problem with
> which youth is concerned today.

This was not a new and post-war anxiety. There was an internationally shared concern over sexual behaviour, and what were regarded as the dangers to society and the nation's well-being of unfettered sexual appetites. The widespread ignorance of sex, which was the cause of considerable distress, individually, socially and morally, had been exercising the minds of psychologists as well as religious moralists and thinkers for several decades before the upheaval in social attitudes brought about by the war. During the last decades of the nineteenth-century there had developed a new science of 'sexology' with works by a number of writers. The most influential of these were, together with Freud; the Professor of Psychiatry at the University of Vienna, Kraft-Ebing; Magnus Hirschfeld, who founded the Institute of Sexual Science in Berlin, and Havelock Ellis, who in 1894 had published *Man and Woman*, a detailed study of the psychology of sex, and later sponsored the British Society for the Study of Sexual Psychology. At the same time, moralists such as the Rev. J.M. Wilson were calling for social purity 'for the good of your nation and your country', warning that 'Rome fell, and other nations are falling.'[2]

The teaching of Freud on the psychological dangers of the repression of instincts was seen as providing a justification for less inhibited and more active sexual behaviour, although in 1905, in his *Three Essays on the Theory of Sexuality,* he insisted that it was socially and economically necessary for the survival of civilisation that sexual development and behaviour in the young should be retarded and controlled by parents, schools and religious institutions. The success of movements for religious revival, such as the missions sponsored by the Free Church Council in 1901 and 1902, together with an internationally held belief that sexual promiscuity led to racial degeneration, brought about a growth in purity movements and increasing campaigns for legislation against vice and for the young to be educated to avoid 'unhealthy' sexual practices. New youth movements such as the Boy Scouts and the Boys' Brigade sought to teach adolescents ideals of purity and clean living, and a number of Christian ministers, most notably the Baptists Henry Varley and F.B. Meyer, gave outspoken lectures on purity to meetings of men only.

From the 1880s to well after the end of the First World War, the various societies concerned with public morals produced a host of tracts, lectures, books, lantern shows and films aimed at the 'education for chastity' of adolescents. Information on birth-control was becoming more available for married couples, although not without opposition. In 1886 the Leeds Vigilance Association had Dr. H.A. Allbutt struck off the medical register for publishing his *Wife's Handbook,* but the book went into 450,000 copies before the war. The first volume of Havelock Ellis' *Studies in the Psychology of Sex* was declared 'lewd and obscene' by a court of law in 1897, and Iwan Bloch's study of sexual behaviour, *Sexual Life of Our Times*, was prosecuted in the 1900s.

Education on birth control was greatly affected by the war, particularly because of the spread of venereal disease amongst the troops. In 1917 nearly 55,000 British soldiers were hospitalised with V.D. This had a considerable influence in changing official attitudes and prejudices. In 1918, Marie Stopes, the most famous of the advocates of sex education and birth-control, had published *Married Love,* which sold over 2,000 copies in its first fortnight, and by the end of 1923 had sold over 400,000 copies. Her *Wise Parenthood*, also published in 1918, sold over 300,000 by 1924. The famous preacher, Maude Royden, who was a predecessor of Weatherhead's at the City Temple, was also active in speaking and writing on sexual matters. Her book, *Sex and Common Sense,* came out in 1921. This was concerned with helping women to come to terms with their sexuality, particularly the many thousands whose chances of marriage had been destroyed by the war. Two years later, the Presbyterian, Dr. Herbert Gray, produced another highly successful book, *Men, Women and God* which dealt with sex questions from a Christian point of view.

Weatherhead's book was therefore one of a succession by medical, psychological and Christian writers attempting to educate and change people's attitudes to sex. As so often in his career, he sensed and responded to the climate of the time. Yet he was not merely an opportunist, leaping on to a popular band-wagon. His book was a serious and courageous attempt to break down the obstacles, to personal well-being and happiness and to harmonious relationships within marriage, caused by ignorance. He set out to make plain what earlier writers had in the main continued to hedge around with obscure language. Herbert Gray, for example, had, in the first chapter of his own book, headed 'Knowing the Facts', insisted that the facts ought to be known, but avoided attempting to explain them, saying, 'I do not think they can be fully conveyed through any printed page. They are too delicate for such handling.' Weatherhead had no such inhibitions, and Gray contributed an admiring foreword to *The Mastery of Sex* praising it as 'the best comprehensive book on sex that I have ever read. . . . Mr. Weatherhead writes with a frankness which is new in English books.'

Weatherhead's achievement in writing and getting published at this date a book about sex so detailed and uninhibited in its descriptions was remarkable. Even the most responsible medical writers were criticised if they attempted to be too specific and popular. Havelock Ellis was censured by the medical profession in England because his books were too popular in tone. Subsequent volumes of his *Studies in the Psychology of Sex* were published in America, where their sales were strictly confined to the medical profession. They were not generally available until 1936. Even as late as 1953 Alfred Kinsey in America was advised to have his research on *Sexual Behaviour in the Human Male* and *Sexual Behaviour in the Human Female* published only by a medical publisher. Weatherhead's daring in writing his book added to his dangerous reputation in conservative religious circles and aroused opposition to him even within his own denomination which directly affected his future career.

Unlike Henry Varley and F.B. Meyer, who set out deliberately to produce in their audiences embarrassment, shame and guilt, Weatherhead sought to combine his knowledge of the psychology of sex as a major instinct with his religious belief that it was God given, and therefore good, even beautiful and pleasurable, though he continued to hold that sex should be kept within marriage. He had the co-operation of a medical friend, Dr. Marion Greaves, who provided the notes for the chapters dealing with 'the more physical aspects of sex problems.' The book included an Epilogue written by the distinguished Methodist biblical scholar, Principal W. F. Lofthouse, who was Chairman of the Copec (the Conference on Christian Politics, Economics and Citizenship) Commission on the Relation of the Sexes. Weatherhead gratefully quoted the Archbishop of

Canterbury, Cosmo Gordon Lang, who, in a speech in the Mansion House on 4 April 1930, had said,

> I would rather have all the risks that come from free discussion of sex than the great risks we run by a conspiracy of silence. . . . We want to liberate the sex impulse from the impression that it is always to be surrounded by negative warnings and restraints, and to place it in its rightful place among the great creative and formative things.

The book was reviewed by over sixty newspapers and publications in several different countries. Some, such as *The Manchester Guardian* and *The News Chronicle,* while approving, thought it ought not to be given to the young. *The Times* decided that 'there is nothing here to give offence to those who approach the subject in a proper way.' Dr. Marion E. Mackenzie, in an enthusiastic article in *The Yorkshire Evening News,* had no reservations. 'Bravo! Mr. Weatherhead, you have done a brave deed. "Even I dare not to have been so open" said a Professor of Psychology who took off his hat to him.' She recommended it as a book that all parents should read, adding 'personally I would broadcast the book to the whole British race.' *The Leeds Mercury* agreed, describing Weatherhead as

> the most compelling man who ever stood in a Leeds pulpit. He is eloquent. He is fearless. He is abreast of modern thought. He has written . . . the most candid, most revealing exposition of sex problems I have seen in English. . . . I should like to see this book sell by the hundred thousand. It will do a world of good.

Most of the reviews in the religious press were surprisingly favourable. Some were wholeheartedly approving. *The British Weekly* described it as 'one of the wisest and most sincere contributions to this subject we have read', and the *Presbyterian Messenger* called it 'the most complete treatment of the problems of sex which has yet appeared in English', though *The Christian World* disapproved of 'certain passages which . . . deal with obscure perversions of the sex instinct' which it thought should have been left out. Some of the strongest reservations came from Weatherhead's own denomination. A.J. Costain in the *Methodist Recorder* found the whole subject distasteful. 'As I am not among those who believe that there is virtue in much talking on these things, I am therefore not predisposed to a favourable verdict on the Rev. Leslie Weatherhead's book. But I am bound to say that I have been much impressed by his masterly handling of a difficult subject. . . . He is to be congratulated on a wise and brave book.' A longer review was contributed to the *Recorder* by J. Arundel Chapman, who was unstinting in his praise, but another friend, Eric Waterhouse, in the *Methodist Times*, questioned the 'desirability of an utterly frank and outspoken discussion of the most fundamental intimacies of life being broadcast to all and sundry.' He thought that it would do good if put into the hands of engaged couples before marriage, but harm if adolescents got hold of it. 'To put it bluntly, in some cases it will do great good but in others harm. Will the one outweigh the other?'

The *Methodist Times* (3 December 1931) printed a reply from Weatherhead, who said that though he deeply appreciated the kindly tone of the writer,

> I am not so foolish as to suppose that frankness is without any dangers at all. . . . But these are not nearly so serious as those incurred by ignorance,

and they never bring neurosis. Further, the hush-hush merchants have had their way for several hundred years. Let us give a new way a trial . . . let not all the frankness be shown by those who are hostile to the Christian way of looking at life. It is no characteristic of religion to be afraid to face facts, and I would go so far as to call it a crime that young people should be sent out into a world which shrieks sex at them without a knowledge of those facts which are relevant.

Waterhouse's article also produced a letter from a Mr. Joshua R. Sinfield, who 'deeply deplored' Weatherhead's book, and hoped that Waterhouse's comments would 'Counteract the harm this book may do. . . . There is much in the book that surely cannot be considered as the accepted views of the leaders of the Methodist Church. If such teaching is the result of psychology . . . then this particular school of psychology appears to me to be very dangerous.' Sinfield's distaste was shared by a significant group within Methodism – which included the autocratic and powerful Dr. J. Scott Lidgett – who considered that Weatherhead's writings on sex verged on indecency.

Waterhouse's article and Weatherhead's reply had been read by a contributor to *The Freethinker* (20 December 1931), who declared himself

hostile to the Christian way of looking at life. . . . One may add that the "hush-hush merchants" who had their ignorant and stupid way for several hundred years were all Christians; and their hush-hush policy was formulated from the Holy Bible. We gather that Mr. Weatherhead decided to be frank and write his book only because . . . he thinks that religion ought to make some sort of show of not lagging too far behind anti-Christian instruction. He is another dare devil of the Bishop Barnes breed. As for the latter portion of the above letter, it does no more than echo the reasons which anti-Christians gave years ago as grounds for enlightening Christian ignorance.

The book received considerable and on the whole favourable coverage in the medical press, though the *Lancet* thought it suffered from too much restraint imposed by its religious viewpoint: 'there is a constant qualification of psychological opinion, and the book is in some danger of giving a false and faulty shelter to those who have the symptoms of a disordered sex life.' The *Nursing Mirror* recommended it as 'the best we have yet come across' for helping men and women to overcome sex difficulties. The *St. Bartholomew's Hospital Journal* thought that young doctors, who had received little training in dealing with the sexual problems of their patients, and might themselves be nervous and timid in their own attitudes to sex, could well 'appreciate this remarkable book . . . only a few will be deterred by its religious undercurrent.' *Birth Control News* was enthusiastic, although it did think that the author had tried to cover too wide a field, and that 'in parts, the work seems to aim at making . . . a compendium of the whole question'. The *Guild of Health Review* and the *Eugenics Review* were also much in favour, though the latter reviewer preferred not to have his science mixed with religion. But he recommended the book: 'it deserves to sell by the ten thousand, and can do nothing but good. When one compares it with the sex treatises of the ascetic ecclesiastical sort one can only be thankful to see how far we have progressed.' The *Social Service Review* and the *Scouter* greeted the book as being very much needed. For the *Scouter*, it was 'an absolutely essential book for those who have the courage to face up to the facts and who wish at the same time to inspire high and lasting ideals on a deeply religious basis. . . . It may well be an epoch making book. . . . It is one of the cleanest and most spiritual books ever written.'

The book was also welcomed by the cinema industry, which was under attack for the sexual element and explicitness of many popular films, and found in Weatherhead an unexpected ally. Weatherhead had written that though there were some people such as 'the heavily repressed, the "idle rich," the highly sexed,' who were unduly excited sexually by some novels, plays and films, the system of censorship held the balance very well, and that the cinema was becoming a real asset to the community. He argued that the censor needed 'a deeper psychological insight' to recognize that 'suggestive dialogue is much more indecent than bare limbs in an artistic setting.'

The Cinema (23 March 1932) hailed Weatherhead as an ally from an unexpected quarter.

> It is so rare . . . to get an absolutely unprejudiced view from a pulpit that the *Cinema* has taken the opportunity to look further into the work that Mr. Weatherhead is doing. He has written a book which, for its refreshing sanity and recognition of the true facts of this "sex appeal" which is so often hysterically flung at the screen as a reproach, could not be bettered. . . . If the trade sets up its Defence Bureau, that Bureau should lose no time in enlisting Mr. Weatherhead; because we cannot have the help of too many right-thinking men.

There was wide coverage of the book abroad, especially in Australia and the United States. In the *Melbourne Herald*, (12 December 1931) a distinguished Australian Methodist, Irving Benson, described it as 'one of the very strongest, sanest and wisest books I have ever read on the subject. . . . If I were a millionaire I would give a copy of this book to every man and woman in Australia. To put it into the hands of young people would be to confer a blessing upon them for which they will be grateful as long as they live.' *The World*, (Sydney, 20 February 1932) said,

> If organised Christianity includes within its forces many such wise and temperate instructors as the author of *The Mastery of Sex*, the prospects of the withering away of that religion . . . are not nearly so clear as is feared. . . .
> One has read no book which deals quite so successfully with a subject made peculiarly delicate by the mucky and mincing attitudes which Anglo-Saxon society acquired by imitating the Good Queen.

Favourable reviews appeared in several other Australian papers, but the *Victorian Independent* (April 1932) was disapproving. Conceding that some parts of the book could be helpful, it described the book as 'the most bluntly plain description of sex relations we have seen.' It accused Weatherhead of not being concerned with morals, and of being so obsessed by the abnormal cases he had to deal with that he imagined that they represented the average. 'Of the honesty and ability of the author there is no question, but of the wisdom of his detailed description of sex organs and processes we are seriously in doubt. Indeed, they cannot do any good, morally or physically.'

American reviewers recognised the book as evidence that the churches in Britain were ahead of America in applying psychological knowledge to pastoral work. In the *Crozen Quarterly* (April 1932), Stewart G. Cole, the Professor of

Psychology at Crozen Theological Seminary in Chester, Pennsylvania, contrasted the attitude of religious writers to sex questions in America with those in England.

In the latter country such leaders as Gray, Shuter, Inge, Royden, Weatherhead and others have produced a scientific literature bearing on sex matters of which the church may be justly proud. Weatherhead's stricture against the church is particularly appropriate when applied to our own country, "the church has always been afraid of sex, and is stern in regard to sexual delinquency, and yet inconsistently indifferent to sexual hygiene and the prevention of disaster." The reviewer can think of only two types of persons who will not welcome this book: the ecclesiastically dominated Roman Catholic and the mid-Victorian-minded Protestant. It may shock many others, but shocks such as provided for in this book are required to move Westerners out of their ignorance and consequent social dangers.

To the *Bulletin* of the Hartford Seminary Foundation in Connecticut, Weatherhead symbolized 'the fact that the British clerical mind is more alert than the American to the implications of psychology for the pastor's work.' It suggested that one reason for this might be the wider prevalence of neuroticism in England due to the effects of the war. The New York *Churchman* stated:

We have learned to listen when Leslie Weatherhead speaks, and this volume is as fine as his *Psychology in the Service of the Soul.* It should be put at the top of the bibliography on marriage issued by the Department of Christian Social Service. . . . Spiritual insight, human sympathy, scientific knowledge, and practical experience are here combined in the best book of its kind yet produced.

The *American Church Month* wrote along similar lines commending it 'as the best book on the sex problem' the reviewer had read, providing 'the best medical and psychological knowledge of the day.'

Elsewhere, the *Friend* reported that the Friends' Centre in Paris had acquired the rights for a French edition of 'that most excellent book' and that '5,000 copies have been sold in Australia alone, and a Dutch edition is on the point of being published.' The book was very well received by the *Church of Ireland Gazette,* but the *Irish Times* reported that the Minister for Justice had made an Order prohibiting the sale and distribution of the book in the Free State, in a banned list which included such publications as *Midnight in the Place Pigalle* and *A Mistress of Terror,* and also D.H. Lawrence's *Lady Chatterley's Lover.* This listing points to a result of this book which was understandable but unwarranted. It gained Weatherhead a reputation as a 'liberal' in his attitude to sexual morals and behaviour which led later to his being asked to be a witness for the defence in the *Lady Chatterley* trial in 1960. When approached, Weatherhead said that he had not read the book, and would give his decision when he had done so. Penguin sent him a copy, which, having read, he immediately burnt. He then wrote to Penguin's solicitors saying that he could not support their case because

In spite of the literary merits of the book, it would get into the wrong hands, sell in millions and do immense harm both to young people and to many frustrated older people also. . . . I should myself vote against the publication of the book in our country where already sexual immorality is at a danger level. [Publishing the book] would be an anti-social act.

In spite of the descriptions of the physical and medical aspects of sex in his book, his attacks on Victorian attitudes and taboos, and his tolerance and understanding of people and their sexual drives and temptations, Weatherhead was still, with regard to the morals of sexual behaviour, a Victorian Nonconformist at heart. He stood for information, education and enlightenment, not license. His own word was 'healthy-mindedness.' He strongly disapproved of sexual relationships outside marriage, and no doubt one of his objections to *Lady Chatterley* was that her 'Lover' was not her husband. His son says of him, 'He was not, that is to say, permissive; he believed very strongly in self-control, continence before marriage, chastity and monogamy – the whole works.'

The Mastery of Sex brought him a greatly increased correspondence; much of it was abusive, though much more was deeply appreciative. According to Kingsley Weatherhead, 'None of my father's books, I believe, met with such demand on the one hand and such animosity on the other. Many were the letters of gratitude he received from the kind of people for whom the book was written.' This added enormously to his pastoral load, as bishops, doctors, ministers, teachers and individuals from all over the world read the book, and then wrote to him asking his help, detailing their most private thoughts and personal experiences, feeling that here was someone, perhaps even the only one, who understood what their needs and problems were. An article in the *Epworth Review* of September 1990 on 'The Experience of Gay Ministers in the Methodist Church', gives an example of this, from a fellow minister:

I phoned him up in some distress in 1966, and he invited me down to London to meet him. . . . We had a long and most wonderful talk and he urged me to carry on. I came with sudden feelings of great guilt. Only 23 years ago, and isn't it a terrible and sad commentary on our times that I couldn't go to any colleagues in the District, let alone the Circuit? But I did know Leslie Weatherhead personally from F.K. Swanwick, and he was most kind and helpful.

As the book went on selling, so this correspondence continued, particularly during the Second World War, when lonely wives and the men separated from them by the war for long periods wrote to ask for his advice in dealing with their sexual frustrations and temptations. He made a point of replying to them all. A doctor who was also a Sunday School superintendent wrote to him from Australia to say that the parson who had married him had told a friend not to touch Weatherhead's works, and that *The Mastery of Sex* was not kept on the open shelves of the libraries in South Australia, but had to be asked for and returned to the librarian after reading. Yet he had heard other ministers refer to Weatherhead as one of those 'who are prepared to face the facts of life and speak their minds.'

The book included a chapter on the sublimation of the sex instinct which was particularly appreciated. The slaughter of young men in the First World War had made thousands of young women widows, and left thousands of others with no chance of finding a life partner. Weatherhead spoke with genuine sympathy and insight to these, explaining how it was possible to re-direct sexual energy usefully into different and creative non-sexual outlets. The Rev. Elsie Chamberlain, who was herself married to an Anglican Vicar, the Rev. J.L. St. C. Garrington, who was a trained psychotherapist, wrote:

As far as I know, L.D.W. was the first preacher to join Christianity and Psychology. People say he attracted women especially – so he did, just after the First World War, when girl friends and wives of the millions of dead men needed a specialised kind of help, and he taught them about the Christian sublimation of their instincts. What is more, he was a past-master of the art of communication. . . . He could talk psychology in simple terms with homely illustrations.[3]

The Mastery of Sex continued in print for well over thirty years, even after Weatherhead had retired, and well into the 1960s decade of the 'permissive society.' Weatherhead made a note on the fly-leaf of his own copy, 'Still selling in October 1968'. Paul Ferris, in a recent study, refers to Weatherhead's book as

not a sex guide but a remarkably frank assessment of the Christian dilemma. . . . Weatherhead gave honest examples of the difficulties that Christians could find themselves in, but the solutions had to be ethically correct, and he found it hard to exercise a compassionate modern ministry in the murky waters of sexual reality. . . . In the long term Weatherhead wanted better education to dispel ignorance, raising sex from the level of "grimy embarrassments and furtive practice." Many good men like Weatherhead trudged towards this mirage.[4]

1. Frank Cumbers: *Daily Readings from the works of Leslie D. Weatherhead* (Epworth 1968) p.2.
2. Jeffrey Weeks: *Sex, Politics and Society: The Regulations of Sexuality Since 1800* (Longman 1981) p.87.
3. Letter, 21 December 1985, Chamberlain to Travell.
4. Paul Ferris: *Sex and the British: A Twentieth Century History* (Michael Joseph 1993) p.131f.

7. Weatherhead's Christology: The Oxford Groups

'I much doubt whether a complete adjustment to life is ever made,
or complete psychological health ever reached, without some
relation of the ego with God.'

Several books and publications followed *The Mastery of Sex*, a number of which were broadcast talks. In 1932 Weatherhead returned to the theme of *Jesus and Ourselves* with another well-received book, *His Life and Ours*, which he described as an attempt to explore the significance of Jesus for individuals in the twentieth-century. This owed much to Arundel Chapman, who was then Professor of Theology at Headingley Methodist College, Leeds. Chapman had given him 'a vastly deeper conception of the person of Christ, and he has shown me the inadequacy of the views I previously held.' Another considerable influence was C.J. Cadoux. Weatherhead's 1927 notebook contains notes from Cadoux on the life and significance of Jesus that provided much of the basis for the thought and the plan of the book.

His Life and Ours is mainly a series of sermons on this theme. Each of the chapters deals with a stage in the life of Christ, within which Weatherhead reveals his own approach to many of the traditional doctrines of the Church. He sets 'on one side' the Virgin Birth as offering no evidence of any importance in deciding the divinity of Christ. The doctrine of the Trinity he considers 'unsatisfactory', though he allows that 'the rich complex nature of God may be less erroneously described as containing two or more persons than as containing one.' In a statement which amounts to a personal creed he says,

> I find no difficulty in worshipping Christ. . . . I do not identify Jesus with God the Father, for that would make nonsense of Jesus' prayers to God. I note the subordination of the Son to the Father. But for me Christ has all the values of God. He is the perfect revelation of God, revealing as much of the mind and heart of God as human nature can reveal on the one hand or apprehend on the other. [p.51]

He understands the message of Jesus as 'the good news . . . that God was Father and all men His sons.' Jesus changed the picture of God from the 'fierce, jealous, avenging Deity' of much of the Old Testament, to the loving, compassionate and forgiving Father depicted in the story of the Prodigal Son. This revelation of the true nature of God was

> Good news indeed! What incentive to change your way of looking at life and thus enter into a fellowship with all God's sons and daughters, and living the life of fellowship, bring in the reign of God, the Kingdom of right relationships. [p.138]

This way of referring to the Kingdom he acknowledges in a footnote as having been borrowed 'from *The Stories of the Kingdom* by my friend G.R.H. Shafto', and it became a favourite and much used phrase of Weatherhead himself.

Many of the healing miracles of Jesus he considers were 'psychogenic'. Jesus was not able to cure all illnesses; 'To suppose that Jesus, in a few moments, could heal a broken leg or a suppurating appendix, would demand a very different conception of the nature of physical laws from that which at present holds the field.' Noting that Jesus depended 'to some extent' on the faith of those seeking to be cured, he argues that for any healing to take place today, the faith required was in methods consistent with modern science. There was no future therefore for spiritual healing, 'apart from scientific methods', since this was the only way 'to produce in the mind of the modern sufferer belief in the method employed.' Great advances could be made if the doctor, the psychologically trained minister and the psychotherapist would co-operate and put spiritual healing 'on a firm scientific basis.' Arguing for a recognition of the importance of forgiveness in spiritual and psychological health, and for recognition of the value and effectiveness of prayer, he insists that the minister of religion has a vital contribution to make.

> In these cases authority in religion is as necessary as a good knowledge of psychology, and no lay-psychotherapist is likely to avail. . . . I much doubt whether a complete adjustment to life is ever made, or complete psychological health ever reached, without some relation of the ego with God. [p.165]

Discussing the meaning and symbolism of the sacraments, he says that the bread and wine which Jesus took and gave to his disciples at the Last Supper, did not, in any sense, become his body and blood, but were 'symbols of that uttermost self-giving which He contemplated so soon.' The sacrament is 'pre-eminently the Christian's means of access to the Eternal', it is the 'central act of Christian worship . . . a repetition of the supreme act of Calvary. But it is also a present breaking of the body of Christ' in which the individual worshipper is one with the whole universal Church: 'when I kneel at His table, I, as part of His Church, His body, am offering myself to God in complete surrender.'

Weatherhead was frequently attacked for having an inadequate view of the Atonement. His immediate influence was Russell Maltby, but he followed a trend in Methodism that rejected substitutionary and legalistic theories and interpreted the Cross as being the supreme revelation of the nature of divine love. He states 'all legal relationships between God and man are foreign to the mind of Jesus. God is our Father we are His children.' Neither is sin 'a debt which somebody else can pay.' The Cross reveals 'the nature of God's love and of eternal values . . . we are shown a Divine deed of cosmic significance . . . the Divine method of conquering the world is that of loving man to the uttermost with a love that goes on loving whatever pride or fear or hate can do.' Only such total, unlimited love has power to save. The Cross reveals 'the eternal attitude of God to men.' It was also an act of dedication by Jesus himself to the whole human race. Heaven, for Jesus, 'does not mean escape from concern for humanity' since 'He will go on loving them and suffering for them until the last is gathered in.' At the same time, the Cross was more than the revelation of an eternal truth, 'it was a deed transcendent in its nature and cosmic in its range' in which Christ did 'something for us of infinite worth' which we could never do for ourselves. The Cross represents an impenetrable mystery:

> Some mighty deed in the realms of the supernatural, something done "once and for all" was achieved by the death of Jesus' which has dealt with all human sin and made it possible for forgiven sinners to come into a new and restored relationship with God.

Weatherhead draws on the findings of the Society for Psychical Research to put forward a theory of the Resurrection which relies heavily on what he calls 'psychical science' to give a possible explanation of what happened to Christ's physical body, and the nature of the 'body' in which he was seen after his death by his disciples. He suggests there was 'an evanescent metamorphosis' effected by the powerful spirit of Christ, which then appeared to the disciples in an 'etheric' 'Resurrection body . . . perceptible to the senses but spiritual in its essence.' He draws again on Maltby for his views on the significance of the Resurrection and the Ascension. The Resurrection does not prove the immortality of all men, since Jesus is a unique personality. Its true significance is that 'Jesus lives for ever, is for ever available to us, and that the power manifested in His Resurrection is the power at our disposal.' The meaning of the Ascension he finds in the Resurrection appearances which preceded it, by which the disciples were taught to realise that Christ was with them always, whether they could see him or not. The Ascension marked the completion of this ministry, 'in which Jesus successfully aimed at carrying the sense of His presence beyond the need of the senses, so that without seeing, or hearing, or touching, they knew Him to be near them for ever.' Weatherhead does not believe in a physical Second Coming, since the prophecies of Christ's coming again had been fulfilled in the coming of his Spirit at Pentecost

:we feel that heaven is all round us, and though there may well be in the future a worthy climax to all human history, Christ will come to men as often as they open their hearts to Him, and while there is a sense in which He is coming, there is a more true sense in which He is here. [p.328]

The final chapter, on 'Enthronement', was first produced as a broadcast talk on 22 May, 1932. In it he deals with the New Testament passages that present Christ, glorified, exalted and enthroned. This leads him to ask how far this picture represents reality, in a world where people live in crowded slums and where 'all through our national and international life there are elements of bitter and unforgiving hostility.' Even so, in these years before the outbreak of the Second World War, he sees signs of hope and of the progress of the Kingdom: in international relations through the establishment of the League of Nations, in improving social and industrial relations. Quoting Maltby's assertion that 'life will only work one way, and that is God's way,' he sets out what amounts to his personal philosophy:

by the application of His Spirit I believe we shall solve all our problems, and I believe there is no other solution. . . . Christ's is the only way which will, in the long run, work. However high we carry our heads they will be bowed before Him at last. [p.346f.]

The book contains a Questionary which was also published separately, to facilitate the use of the book by fellowship groups. Weatherhead had a great faith in such groups for strengthening the devotional life of individuals, and in his final chapter, on 'Accessibility', he lists 'Come into the Fellowship' as one of the three most important ways of entering into the experience of the living Christ.

During this period he was very taken with the Oxford Group Movement, founded by Frank Buchman, an American ex-Lutheran pastor, who, after a conversion experience at a Keswick Convention, visited Oxford in 1920 with a group of Cambridge undergraduates. The Movement developed from this visit, becoming known as the 'Oxford Group' during a visit by Buchman and his followers to South Africa in 1929. The Movement became very influential not only in Britain but also in South Africa, Canada and the United States. Weatherhead was attracted to the Group because it was active among the young university students he was happiest working with himself. It focused on the individual's relationship with God, and believed that individuals must be changed before the world could be. It also expressed a moral and social concern. John Vickers, whose family were leading members of the Roscoe Place Chapel in Chapeltown Road, Leeds, in the Brunswick Circuit, recalls Weatherhead's interest in learning about the Group's influence on him.

> I vividly remember the "after Service meeting" at 8.0 p.m. one Sunday evening in July 1933, when LDW invited three generations of my family – My Grandmother Mrs. Anne Elizabeth Vickers, my Father Mr. W. Farrar Vickers, and myself to give our witness and tell what we had found, after we all returned from that summer's Oxford Group conference held in Oxford.[1]

William Farrar Vickers was the Managing Director of the family oil business, and Weatherhead was a good friend. Vickers' new realisation of the practical nature of faith through the Oxford Groups led him to institute radical changes and improvements in the working conditions and business methods of his firm. Weatherhead was keenly interested in the effect of Christian faith on a businessman's working practices and controlling ethic. He counted many businessmen among his friends, and regularly included prayers for them in his services.

In July 1933, the *British Weekly* produced a special Oxford Group Supplement, which contained eight pages of appreciation and tributes to the Movement. The Group's most enthusiastic advocate was Canon L.W. Grensted, Oriel Professor of the Philosophy of the Christian Religion at Oxford University, who had been involved with the Movement from the beginning, but many tributes came from a wide variety of churchmen, scholars, politicians, lawyers, business men and leaders of the armed forces, including the Canadian Prime Minister, the Leader of the Parliamentary Bar at Westminster, and the Brigadier Commanding Catterick Camp. Edgar H. Brooks, the Professor of Political Science at Pretoria University, wrote 'To me the Oxford Group Movement represents the turning point of my life'. The Moderator of the Church of Canada, George C. Pigeon, called it, 'By all odds the greatest spiritual movement in the history of Canada, which has set fire to the whole country and brought to fruition the work of the Church.' In a later article, the Methodist, Dr. Leslie Church wrote, 'No student of religious life today can afford to ignore the Oxford Group Movement.'

In 1934, at the height of the Oxford Groups' success, Weatherhead produced a book, *Discipleship*, which owed a great deal of its inspiration and style to the Movement. It was based on a series of lectures he had given the previous year to the Methodist Whit-week Missionary Summer School at Swanwick. He believed that the Oxford Group Movement was making 'the greatest contribution to the reunion of the churches in our generation' through the way it was attracting to its House Parties thousands of young people from all denominations,

> gathered together at the feet of Christ, seeking the new life that He offers and concerned to pass it on, and unconcerned . . . with theology, the

consideration of orders, and the differences in their creeds. [p.67]
Weatherhead goes on to give his own testimony to the effect that the Oxford
Groups had on him;

> When I was first challenged by the Oxford Groups I went away into Wales
> on a holiday, and having had time there for meditation and prayer, a great
> sense of personal failure came over me. My church was full, the collections
> were increasing, every branch of the church seemed flourishing, and I could
> not think of any person with whom my relationships were wrong, but I felt
> that these things were being said by the devil; that although people's lives
> were being changed at least every month, my life was becoming self-satisfied
> and egocentric and that big chunks of my work were being done with very
> mixed motives. I wrote to a saintly doctor I know, who had been changed by
> the Oxford Group Movement, and he made a considerable journey to meet
> me in a Liverpool hotel. I poured out to him all the unrest and dissatisfaction
> and sense of sin which possessed me. I am not ashamed to add that this
> was not done without emotion which had been bottled up and which had
> been part of the cause of my unrest. In that Liverpool hotel I made a new
> surrender of my life to God and came back to the most wonderful twelve
> months I have ever known in my ministry. [p.37]

In spite of this, he came to develop increasing reservations about the Movement.
After the Oxford Group had visited Aberdeen, the Provost, Erskine Hill, produced
a laudatory pamphlet in which he appealed to the Group's critics to 'adopt the
attitude of Gamaliel to the early Christians.' Weatherhead marked the comment
in his copy in a way which indicates his agreement with it, but he also noted the
criticisms that were being made of the Movement, especially by psychiatrists,
which he could not ignore. A Canadian Psychiatrist, Dr. G.H. Stevenson, in an
article for the Toronto magazine, *New Outlook*, listed features of the Movement
that he considered were 'definitely harmful' to mental health. These included
centring the individual's thoughts on sin, inculcating morbid introspection,
'emotional orgies dealing with sex', insistence on listening to voices, which was
an 'invitation to frank mental disorder', and a 'sustained indulgence in
emotionalism' which would result in the warping of the personality of the
individual.

The *Christian World* (9 November, 1933) reported a lecture given by Dr. William
Browne, Wilde Reader in Mental Philosophy at Christ Church, Oxford, to his
students in which he criticised it on psychological grounds, saying that although
it showed great sincerity, it did not go deep enough. He argued that

> their four points – absolute honesty, unselfishness, purity and love – could
> be reached by no-one without analysis. If in place of such careful analysis. . .a
> great movement urged people to confess their sins and promised that they
> would get well at once it was fallacious.

The *British Weekly's* regular correspondent, 'Ilico' (Dr. Nathaniel Micklem),
attacked what he considered the arrogant attitude of 'Groupers' towards other
Christians, in ignoring the validity of the experiences of those outside the Groups.
He accused them of 'pride and censoriousness' and of denying that the 'new
vision, the new divine life' could come through any other channels but their
own: 'testimony to Christ is not the one thing with which they are concerned; it
is testimony to Christ and to the Groups.'

Weatherhead became finally disaffected with the Group through his impatience with their over-earnestness and inability to appreciate his sense of humour. Attending a house party on behalf of the *British Weekly*, in which the sexes having been segregated, each person in turn confessed his major sin, he reported that 'he had found the sessions valuable because by the time it got round to his turn to bare his soul he had learned two new actual sins and a handful of temptations. Frank Buchman never forgave him for this.'[2]

Yet Weatherhead continued to retain some respect and appreciation for what the Groups had achieved. More than twenty years later, in a sermon on 20 February, 1955, which attracted the attention of the national press, he protested that a report to the Church Assembly of the Church of England's Social and Industrial Council which had been highly critical of the Oxford Group Movement, (by then known as Moral Re-Armament) came from a committee which was heavily weighted with men known to be hostile to the movement. He repeated his defence in his Presidential address to the Methodist Conference later the same year, stating that 'some of the finest people in my church have found their way to Christ through the gateway of the group.'

1. Letter, 1 March 1992, John Vickers to Travell.
2. K. Weatherhead, op. cit., p.71f.

8. Speaking, Writing, Broadcasting

'Health is correspondence with environment. If man is, as most would agree,
body, mind and spirit, then the health of the spirit is correspondence
with its environment, and the name of that environment is God.'

From the mid-1920s Weatherhead was becoming the best-known and most-publicised Methodist in the country. Almost every week there were articles either by him or about him in the Methodist press. At a time when Nonconformity as a whole was seriously losing confidence, Weatherhead, young, dynamic, charismatic and deeply committed, drew crowds of mostly young people to hear him.

In March, 1930, he represented the Free Churches at the Naval Disarmament Service in Westminster Abbey, where he and the Bishop of Winchester each gave an address. When, to coincide with the opening of the Disarmament Conference in Geneva in February, 1932, a great public meeting was held in the Royal Albert Hall, he shared the platform with Lloyd George, William Temple and the Archbishop of Canterbury, and from the accounts, was the one who was listened to with the greatest attention and enthusiasm. *The Methodist Recorder* reported, 'When Mr. Weatherhead closed the audience gave him the cheer of the evening.'

Standing in the line of the great preachers of the past who filled city centre churches, he encouraged the belief that this ministry was still very much alive. Yet his image was disturbingly modern. *The Methodist Recorder* issue of 18 February 1932, conveys the impression Weatherhead was making, including on those who were not enamoured of him.

There are readers who have been very cross with Mr. Leslie Weatherhead, and I can hear some of them saying, "Oh, that terrible young man! What will he say next?" Say what you like about Mr. Weatherhead's daring and unorthodoxy, his normal congregation is one of the most remarkable in Methodism. Elderly people are sometimes a bit suspicious of him. Young people from colleges, schools, shops, offices hurry to Brunswick about an hour before the service to hear him. "The Churches are empty" somebody tells you. Tell him about Brunswick in a dull neighbourhood, not easy to find, a big old sanctuary on an island surrounded by gloomy buildings. . . . Brunswick must be quoted everywhere as one of the very bright and shining lights in a day in which too many bewail the darkness. . . . Mr. Weatherhead will pursue his own line, and his aim is really no different from that of the most fervent Cliff evangelist. I know he makes his young people fall in love with Christ. I know his freshness, his sincerity, and his challenge fill a great Church that might be half-empty. I know the beauty of the worship sends the people away feeling that they have been in the presence of God.

The Yorkshire Evening News featured a long article by a London journalist, Jane Doe, who described arriving in Leeds on a wet Sunday evening, and finding the streets deserted and all the pubs and cinemas closed. Meeting a local policeman she asked him what people do in Leeds on a wet Sunday. He told her to 'Go and hear Weatherhead at the Brunswick Methodist Church', adding, 'But you'd better hurry. They queue up an hour before the service starts.' Although not a regular church-goer, she stayed for the whole service which she described in detail. Weatherhead, she thought, seemed 'a very kindly man', and his voice 'curiously simple and curiously young. A bit too childish at times. . . We want virility in the Church as well as gentleness'. He impressed her as 'a sort of spiritual mixture of the late Gerald du Maurier and Franchot Tone', and concluded,

> My Leeds Sunday evening had been a success after all. I'd even say that, for one who's not a regular church-goer, it was an absorbing and spiritually refreshing one. If there were more Leslie Weatherheads in the Church there'd be less Clarke Gable devoteeism, at least on Sunday nights!

The Methodists celebrated the Reunion of their denomination in September 1932. During the years after Wesley, the Methodist movement had fragmented into a number of different denominational groups. In the second half of the nineteenth century their were several attempts to bring these groups closer together. Eventually a scheme of union was successfully drawn up in 1918, between the Wesleyans, the United Methodists and the Primitive Methodists, and the Methodist Church Bill was passed in 1929. A Uniting Conference was held on September 20, 1932, in the Royal Albert Hall, attended by the Duke and Duchess of York, in which the Deed of Union was signed.

The union was generally received with much enthusiasm, especially among younger Methodists, with whom Weatherhead, although he was then just a month short of his fortieth birthday, was particularly identified. As part of the celebrations a great youth rally was held in the Albert Hall at which Weatherhead was one of three chosen speakers, the others being the then Wimbledon Women's Singles champion, Dorothy Round, and the England cricketer, Harold Larwood. *The Methodist Recorder* reported that when Weatherhead stood up to speak he was received with

> a great round of applause, and delivered a moving and masterly address on "The Church". . . . Referring to the new Union he said, 'If they asked, "Has Methodism a future?" would they misunderstand him if he answered, "I hope not"? That week they had dropped the words "Wesleyan," "Primitive," and "United, . . . " He hoped that the Union was the forerunner of a wider union in which what we were saying in Methodism should be said in a greater Church, and the wounds in the Body of Christ should be healed.

He was also much in demand as a speaker to organisations outside Methodism. In 1929, he addressed the Rotary Annual Conference in Bournemouth, where he spoke on 'The Contribution of Rotary to Modern Civilisation.' *The Yorkshire Evening News* reported that,

> Rev. Leslie Weatherhead of Leeds made far and away the profoundest impression on the Rotary audience. . . One delegate asserts that speech to have been the finest he had ever heard in his life. "Why," he said, "There were even men in tears, so moved were they."

Another delegate wrote to Mrs. Weatherhead from the Conference,

> Just a few lines from another of your husband's admirers. We know full well how proud you are of him. You would have been prouder than ever this morning if you could have heard him speak. After he finished the whole

audience stood up in silence & then shouted L.E.S.L.I.E. Leslie! In our opinion his masterly address was the finest bit of the Conference. We are looking well after him. . . .

Yours sincerely,

Arthur Barrett.

Soon after going to Leeds Weatherhead began writing regularly for several different newspapers. During April and May 1927, he produced a series of six articles for *The Methodist Times* on 'The Defeat of Pain.' In August, 1933, he started a weekly page for *The Leeds Mercury* which continued throughout the rest of his time in Leeds. In a later note in his cuttings diary he commented, 'I got £5 a week for this. Poor now but in those days a help as my salary was only £340 per year with three kiddies to keep.'

He dealt with all manner of subjects, mostly with a psychological content, but ranging widely on themes as diverse as the taking of holidays, nervous breakdowns and the rising tensions in Europe with – in November 1934 – 'If War Breaks out, What Then?' During 1934, he wrote a series of articles for the *Mercury* on the problem of pain, based on a series of lectures he was giving at the same time on Tuesday evenings at the Leeds Y.M.C.A. Then, in February 1936, he undertook a weekly advice column for the *Yorkshire Evening News,* and in March 1936 he began a similar column for the *Methodist Times and Leader* which continued until November 1937, when the paper ceased publication after being incorporated with the *Methodist Recorder.*

In an article for the *Leeds Mercury* on 5 October 1934, he provoked a storm of protest from teachers by condemning the use of corporal punishment in schools. This was a subject he felt very strongly about, as he made plain in the most forthright language. His memories of his own miserable schooldays, when, he said, 'I came in for innumerable beatings', had made him particularly sensitive to and indignant at any violence against children. He argued that 'the whipped child has it thrust deeply into his mind that power and force are the same thing', and incensed members of the teaching profession by saying 'How can you condemn Hitler's methods of rule by violence when you rule your class or your home by exactly the same methods?' But what caused the greatest cries of outrage was his accusation of sadism and a statement that 'The strongest argument against corporal punishment . . . is that sexual perversion is likely to be set up by it, either in the administrator, the victim or the onlooker.' This produced a flood of letters of protest and personal abuse from school teachers, who accused him of attacking their profession, and even held a protest meeting against him. The enraged feelings of some found another outlet for expression. Coming out of a meeting late one evening, with some distance to drive home, he found that the air had been let out of all the tyres of his car.

In 1932, the Weatherheads looked forward to a further addition to their family, but the child, a boy, was born dead. Leslie took the body gently into his study, and read the baptism service, naming the child 'David'. The friendly Anglican vicar of Moor Allerton Parish Church readily agreed to the child being buried in his churchyard, and the following day conducted the funeral for him. Leslie placed a card on the body, on which he had written, 'David Leslie, Darling Son of Leslie and Evelyn Weatherhead. Safe in the arms of Jesus.' He mourned the child as if he had been a living member of the family, and believed that he continued to live as a real personality, somewhere, in another existence, and that they would eventually come to meet and know each other, in God's good providence.

The family were now better housed in Leeds than they had been in Manchester, but the church manse was still dark, and once again in a poor neighbourhood. With the increase of income he was receiving from the sale of his books, Weatherhead bought a cottage on the Sussex coast, which he called 'Rowanwood', after the house of the friends he had lodged with during his brief ministry at Farnham. The three children went away to school; to the Methodist establishments of Kingswood, in Bath, for the boys, and Margaret to the girls' school of Queenswood, in Hatfield, Hertfordshire. The family came together for the holidays, spending them at 'Rowanwood.' The cottage provided Weatherhead with precious space in which to relax in private with his family, and a vital means of escape from the pressure of his hectic public life.

In November 1934 Weatherhead produced *Psychology and Life*, which became an immediate best-seller and had a considerable influence. Several chapters had first appeared as articles in the *Leeds Mercury*. In his Preface he explained that it had been his ambition to write a technical text-book of psychology and its relation to religion, but that he had never reached the point where he felt competent to do this. His intention in writing was to save people from 'so-called "nervous breakdown"' and to show those suffering from mental and emotional conflicts, fears, worries and repressions 'that there is a path through the wilderness and enough light by which to see at least the next stretch in the road.'

The book included two forewords written by eminent representatives of the medical and psychological professions. The first was Sir Henry B. Brackenbury, then Vice-President and later Chairman of the Council of the British Medical Association, and also Chairman of the Council of the Institute of Medical Psychology and Vice-President of the Central Association for Mental Welfare. Brackenbury stated that 'As an exposition for thoughtful and non-technical readers of the modern outlook and method of psychology in relation to conduct it would be difficult to better it.' The other foreword was by Dr. William Browne, who commended Weatherhead as 'a sound psychologist, with a wide experience of the practical applications of the science.'

The book offers practical advice to ordinary people to give them some understanding of their own psychology and so help them to cope with their problems, and argues once again for the need for religious insights to be recognised, alongside the findings of the psychologists and doctors, in the healing process. In the first chapter, which bears the title of his later major thesis, *Psychology, Religion and Healing,* Weatherhead explains that the book is written to help those people who 'are suffering from all kinds of torture, mental and physical', but which 'it is no one's specialised province to treat adequately.' He has particularly in mind those whose physical symptoms are due to a psychological and spiritual disharmony which only a qualified psychotherapist with 'a healthy religious life of his own' was capable of helping:

> experience shows me that religion in the broadest sense, is an absolute essential. Health is correspondence with environment. If man is, as most would agree, body, mind and spirit, then the health of the spirit is correspondence with its environment, and the name of that environment is God. [p.24f]

He acknowledges that religion without psychology can also be inadequate. To tell a patient, at the first interview, to have faith, or surrender his fears to Christ, would, he says, 'have been as cruel as to tell the victim of a suppurating appendix to surrender it to Christ. Scientific help is as necessary in the one case as in the other.' Considering the future of healing, he forecasts that the development of 'non-material' methods of healing will eventually take over and supersede the physical, so that both modern surgery, which 'will seem a kind of carpentry', and the use of drugs will have almost no place left in medicine; instead there will be 'immense energies, some of them resident in personality itself, and others able, under certain conditions, to sweep through the personality from some source outside it which I cannot name otherwise than divine', which will cure not only functional disorders, but those which, though apparently organic, are due to psychological or even spiritual disharmony. He describes 'religious psychology' as 'the science likely to prove of supreme importance' since this would not only deal with psychological conditions but would also investigate 'the conditions of mind under which prayer and faith and trust are effective.' Saying that he has seen cases in which confidence or faith 'has actually altered cell formation in physical tissues', he argues that 'we must investigate by what psychological or religious methods such a valuable mental condition can be brought about.'

He calls for ministers to receive 'a far more adequate training in modern psychology,' not in order to practice psychotherapy, but because a minister's task involved daily dealing with people, so the 'science of human behaviour' was of 'paramount importance . . . second only to theology.' A minister so trained, would, as he visited people in their homes, be able to detect early signs of neuroses, he could co-operate with the medical psychotherapist as well as with the medical practitioner and know when to refer a person to them for treatment. He would be able to speak on psychological subjects and in his sermons show

> how marvellously almost all that is of value in the new psychology is already offered in the New Testament. Religion and psychology are inevitably wedded. Psychological troubles are mainly due to a faulty adjustment to life and reality. Religion offers a perfect adjustment. [p.41f.]

The book proceeds to discuss and explain, as far as possible in non-technical language, the nature of psychology and its subject matter, with chapters on 'The Levels of the Mind', 'The Importance of the Unconscious', 'Repression and Self-Control', 'The Inferiority Complex', 'The Mind of a Child', 'Fear, Anxiety, Phobia and Worry', and 'Depression and Irritability'. Weatherhead makes no claim to be presenting any original psychological theories of his own, or to be making any significant contribution to the development of psychology as a science. He presents a synthesis of the ideas of Freud, Adler and Jung without claiming to belong to or to prefer any one school, but simply as he had found them helpful. The one claim he makes is that religion has a necessary and vital part to play in the healing process, which the other disciplines of medicine and psychology should not dismiss or ignore. This is particularly so in the case of repressed guilt, where there is a deep need to receive forgiveness.

> Buried sins for which a person has never had any real sense of forgiveness are the cause of many a breakdown. . . . The best psychology in the world cannot say more than that simple word of the Master, "Repent".

Even in this book he advocates the healing and restoring power of the 'transforming friendship' of Jesus Christ, 'the greatest transforming power the world has ever known', saying that there is no advice from a psychologist which has the same power within personality as the experience of conversion.

> I can only set down my own convinced opinion after a great many years of psychological study and practice, and a Christian experience going back much further. It is that a real experience of Christ which follows surrender and loyalty to Him as far as one is able, is the most powerful force which the human personality ever knows and the greatest transforming energy the world has ever seen. [p.161f.]

The book was exceptionally well received. Canon Grensted, whose column was headed 'Wounded Spirits', reviewing it for *The British Weekly* (29 November 1934), wrote:

> Mr. Weatherhead occupies a very important position in that "No Man's Land," as he himself calls it, which lies between the field of the minister of religion and that of the professional psychologist . . . he is outstanding in his gift of simple and lucid exposition. He is a "popular" writer in the best sense . . . he is at the same time profoundly and sincerely religious, believing with all his heart that the faith of Jesus Christ is the key to every human problem, and that without that faith no system of psychotherapy, however skilful in technique, can meet the deepest needs of men. . . . The professional psychologist will recognise more fully than the general reader how considerable a store of psychological knowledge lies behind the easy paragraphs. When Mr. Weatherhead does his psychological reading it is difficult to say, but the reading is there. Even so it is clear that he has learned more from people than from books. And that is the best kind of knowledge, since it is tested against life.

W. Harold Beales, for *The Methodist Times and Leader*, was particularly enthusiastic:

> There is no need to plead for a large circulation for Mr. Weatherhead; for, whether in the British Isles or America, he gets it every time. . . . *Psychology and Life* . . . is unquestionably the best of his psychological books . . . here is an extension of the healing ministry of Christ.

Other reviewers were no less laudatory. *The Church of England Newspaper* declared 'his new volume . . . places the whole Church under a debt of gratitude to him.' *The Leicester Mercury* (7 December 1934), describing it as 'Mr. Leslie Weatherhead's great book', continued,

> though the adjective "great" may be considered to be superfluous or even presumptious when speaking of a book by one whose name and knowledge on this, the last-to-be-recognised of the Sciences, is International. . . . Mr. Weatherhead will make religion more real to you than most Clergymen to whom you have listened. Moreover he will make even the most hard-bitten modern realise that religion can be a complement to every day life.

The medical press was also complimentary. *The Lancet* regarded the book as 'one of the best of those by non-medical authors which would . . . satisfy the demand for concrete examples and for advice applicable to personal problems to an extent unusual in books of this kind'. *The Psychologist* described it as 'the kind of book for which many persons have been searching. . . . The writer deals with his subject in a way which will appeal to all who need a work on practical psychology which does not overlook religion.'

A Church of Scotland minister, writing in the *Glasgow Evening Citizen* (9 March 1935) was one of several who were impressed by Weatherhead's extraordinary capacity for work, asking 'How does Mr. Leslie Weatherhead do it? . . . That it is not merely done but done well, there can be little dispute so far as this book is concerned.' He went on to regret that

> when the theological curriculum in Scotland was being overhauled no specific Chair or Lectureship was devoted to the study of psychology in its bearing upon the problems of practical life . . . in this first-rate piece of pioneering work Mr. Weatherhead has certainly given all who are concerned with the training of the ministry a great deal to think about, the more so as he is himself a preacher of the first rank and a stirring evangelist, all of whose utterances are marked by a steadfast loyalty to the faith.

The Church of Scotland was however, slow to respond to this prompting. It was not until 1944 that it appointed a committee to consider training in psychology for its ministers.

Weatherhead's own local paper, the *Leeds Mercury* (29 November 1934), took some proprietorial pride in its association with him, and gave considerable space to its review, though its reviewer, "W.L.A.", acknowledged that Weatherhead was not without his critics:

> it is a well-balanced symmetrical, and lucid series of studies of psychology, health and religion. Through them all shines a strong and yet gentle personality, that of a physician of souls. I am aware that when I speak of him thus some readers grow restive and think such praise sentimental. Very well then; let us keep to the facts and use these to deal with any doubts or misgivings readers may have. First, what are Weatherhead's qualifications for dealing with psychology? It has been suggested that his knowledge of the subject is shallow and bookish. Those are not the terms used, but that is what some of the recent attacks upon him in Leeds amount to.

The writer then recounts Weatherhead's qualifications and quotes the two forewords by Sir Henry Brackenbury and Dr. William Browne, which, he pointed out

> supply a further answer to the questions raised by hostile critics. . . . These two extracts bear the testimony of men of the highest standing . . . in *Psychology and Life* you will find (unless you are very prejudiced indeed) help, sincerity and insight. Mr. Weatherhead, like other tender-hearted idealists, has his imperfections, but how glorious are his words of healing!

Psychology and Life confirmed Weatherhead's standing as the foremost exponent of the use of psychology as an aid to ministry, and considerably added to his reputation. According to Smart,

> Although only four years divide the publication of *Psychology in Service of the Soul* and *Psychology and Life*, the latter represents a considerable advance . . . this book established Weatherhead's position as Britain's leading authority in this field. In this field, at least, he was without peer.[1]

A laudatory review of the book in the magazine of the Oxford Group Movement gives some indication of the extraordinary, and even glamorous, reputation Weatherhead had gained by this time. It began with a report of a conversation overheard at the Group's holiday party at Oberammergau:

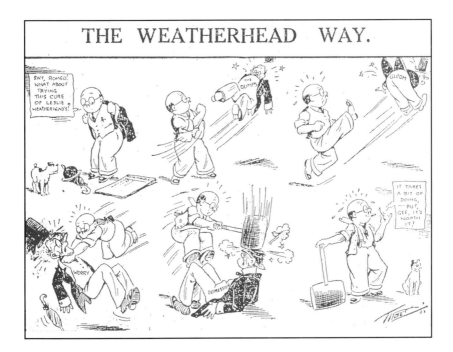

'Grouper: Have you heard that Leslie Weatherhead is here?

Stranger: Leslie Weatherhead? Let me see, he's a film star isn't he?

The article continued,

> There is no need to contradict such an impertinent rumour in the pages of this magazine as Mr. Weatherhead is known not only as one of our contributors, but as a Methodist minister who is the most popular religious writer of our day. And his popularity is very different from that of a film star, for it would be quite impossible to estimate the amount of good Mr. Weatherhead has been able to do to countless people of our generation through his spoken and written words. For not only is he a writer with a real message; he also has a happy style which both interests and convinces his readers.[2]

Following the First World War, the two new and extremely popular forms of mass entertainment and information, radio and film, had made broadcasters and performers known to millions, turning them into household names overnight and giving them a special fame and glamour as 'stars.' As Asa Briggs commented in his *History of the BBC,*

> Listeners had not become hardened to routine listening, and they opened their hearts to a number of successful broadcasters, including clergymen, popular educators, singers, talkers, story-tellers, and comedians.'[3]

Weatherhead had begun broadcasting remarkably early, and his regular wireless appearances made him known to millions who otherwise might not have heard of him. Norman Hillson, who produced a series of articles for the *Daily Mail* on his visits to different churches during 1938, referring to the enormous fame that came to Dick Sheppard through broadcasting, wrote:

> Today there are several other preachers who also enjoy wide fame through their addresses on the wireless altogether apart from their other literary and

parochial work. There are Pat MacCormick, also of St. Martin's-in-the-Fields, Leslie Weatherhead of the City Temple: and thirdly the Rev. W.H. Elliott of St. Michael's, Chester Square.

The B.B.C. was established in November 1922, and its first religious broadcast was given by the Rector of Whitechapel, the Rev. J.A. Mayo, on Christmas Eve that same year. Weatherhead began his broadcasting career in a religious series from Manchester in 1923.

John Reith, then General Manager of the B.B.C., and a Scottish Presbyterian of strong religious views, set up a religious broadcasting committee with representatives of the main churches in May, 1923, which suggested names for speakers. 'Reith looked for a good broadcaster and the excellent music of a "national shrine". . . . Nonconformists were not so suitable as they had too many words and not enough music.'[4] The first regular services began from St. Martin's-in-the-Fields on 6 January 1924. The representatives of the Nonconformist churches pressed for a share of Sunday services and asked whether some of the central Nonconformist churches could also be wired up for broadcasting. The Bishop of London, A.F. Winnington-Ingram, had readily given his approval for Free Churchmen to preach from St. Martin's. When Weatherhead moved to Leeds in 1925, he was immediately invited to become a member of the B.B.C. Northern Region Committee, and he remained a member until he left Leeds for London in 1936.

In July 1933, F.A. Iremonger, an Anglican, and former editor of the Church of England newspaper, *The Guardian,* was appointed Religious Director of the B.B.C. Popular clergy such as the Methodists, Donald Soper and Leslie Weatherhead, the Church of Scotland minister, George MacLeod, the Congregationalist J.S. Whale, and the Anglicans William Temple and W.R. Matthews, were given wider scope, publicity and popularity in broadcasting. Iremonger pursued the idea of instituting a Sunday morning service.

> Iremonger asked the regions to suggest central churches with a congregation of two to three hundred and 'a man of some personality". He wanted a man who could talk well for ten minutes. . . . In the north, the Methodists were particularly keen and the North Region Director assured Iremonger of Leslie Weatherhead's value as a star preacher. Unfortunately he was not a regular attender at the Northern RAC, and was earning the jealous feelings of other Nonconformists who felt he was succeeding rather too speedily in gaining support for a Northern equivalent of St. Martin's.[6]

Weatherhead, with his intimate, conversational style and exceptional communication gifts, was a natural for radio. Writing in 1935, in an article on religious broadcasting for the *Methodist Recorder*, the Rev. R.B. Shapland wrote:

> There are two outstanding Methodist broadcasters: Rev. Leslie Weatherhead and Dr. Donald Soper. One of them seems to me the perfect broadcaster and the other nearly perfect. I will not say which is which. . . . I might say of Leslie Weatherhead that he took his place at the microphone and the delightful talk simply happened. It sounds as if Dr. Soper had a microphone in his nursery and had lisped in studios.

Iremonger described Weatherhead in 1935 as

> one of the most appreciated of our morning preachers. . . . He wanted more "stars" of Weatherhead's calibre. . . . Iremonger . . . suggested bringing the

best personalities, whatever the denomination, to the microphone, and sometimes, as in the case of Weatherhead, Soper, Matthews, Hugh Martin, George
MacLeod and F.A. Cockin, keeping them there regularly. . . . Iremonger had
fought to maintain the central influence of Broadcasting House and CRAC
(Central Religious Advisory Committee) over urges in the regions to have
their own local "pulpit talent" brought to the microphone, and sometimes
the whole country. That is certainly how men such as Leslie Weatherhead
became even more popular in the nation than they were in their own regions.[7]

In May, 1935, Weatherhead gave an account of his broadcasting experiences in
an article for the *Leeds Mercury,* prompted by the occasion of King George V's
Jubilee broadcast. He had been surprised by the number of letters that he received
following a broadcast. Nearly four hundred came after his first, and he answered
each one himself. One came from two young men who happened to listen by
chance and were converted.

It told of two lads who had been out on a cycling tour of Northern Scotland.
They got caught in a shower of rain and went into a village 'pub' to find
shelter. While they were waiting they noticed a radio set in the room and
asked the landlord if they might switch it on. . . . At the close of the service
something happened which they describe best in their own words. 'We
decided we were a couple of wasters,' the letter ran, 'so we knelt down there
and then and gave our hearts to God.' There is no minister in England who
would not be thrilled to receive such a message.

He regarded broadcasting as 'the greatest privilege which is ever offered to me,
but it is the greatest responsibility I am ever likely to have.' Weatherhead
continued to broadcast regularly during the next forty years. During his time at
the City Temple, when one broadcast was over, a date was fixed for the next. The
Epworth Press regularly published his broadcast talks, and they sold by the
thousand. During the Second World War his World Service broadcasts
commanded attention in America and Australia and were heard appreciatively
by those in the forces serving overseas who wrote him hundreds of letters from
all over the world. A ship's captain, who gave his address as 'somewhere at
sea', wrote:

I was busily on the job of writing home, prior to getting into port, when you
of the City Temple were announced. . . . I listened – I stopped my writing
and listened to you more closely. I thank you sir. Your words were to me – a
sailor in command of a ship – a positive inspiration. I do not know if it was
the inference of your words, the tone of your deliverance or just the plain
straightforward way in which you spoke that held me. I imagine the latter,
for all sailors like straight speaking – anyhow, I feel somehow easier in heart
and mind at listening to your words.

Another letter came from a member of Parliament, Waldron Smithers, who said,
We should like to thank you for your broadcasts this week, and especially
for the one about Fear and Sickness this morning. When on Monday morning
you were announced to speak, my wife said to me, 'I am so glad – he is an
old friend'.

A Harley Street doctor also wrote to thank him for a broadcast, saying, 'Your
deep understanding and high courage I believe gave strength to all who heard.'

In 1955, Robert Silvey, the B.B.C.'s analyst of audience statistics, produced a survey of the audiences for religious broadcasting which 'threw up just a few names of specific broadcasters such as Soper, Cuthbert Bardsley of Croydon, Leslie Weatherhead and Ronald Selby-Wright – all to be found on the People's Service or Silver Lining.'[8] Weatherhead broadcast for the last time in a personal interview on 13 April, 1975, ending a career in broadcasting which had lasted for fifty-two years.

1. *Miracles of Achievement, op.cit.*, p.151.
2. *Groups* January 1935.
3. Asa Briggs: *The BBC. The First Fifty Years* (Oxford 1985) p.60.
4. Kenneth Wolfe: *Churches and the British Broadcasting Corporation 1922-1956* (SCM. 1984) p.7f.
5. *ibid.*, p.64.
6. *ibid.*, p.77.
7. *ibid.*, p.128.
8. *ibid.*, p.474.

9. From Leeds to London

'they wanted me to sign that I believed in the V.B. etc. etc. I told
them I did not know or respect anyone who would sign such a
document. The C.T. attracted me because it was SUPRA
Denominational & a world pulpit & I could remain a
Methodist Minister while I was its minister.'

At the beginning of 1934, Weatherhead was invited by a Leeds businessman friend, Ernest Appleyard, to join him and his family on a visit to the Holy Land. The insights gained on this tour, together with his already considerable knowledge of the culture and customs of the Middle East acquired during his war service among the Arabs, enabled him to bring the Bible imaginatively to life in his books and sermons. He produced a series of articles on his visit for the *Leeds Mercury* and the *Methodist Recorder*, which he expanded into two books, *It Happened in Palestine* (1936) and *A Shepherd Remembers* (1937).

Most of the extensive reviews, which were generally favourable, mentioned that there had been a number of travel books recently published about visits to Palestine, most notably, H.V. Morton's *In The Steps of the Master*, which topped the *Bookseller's* list for Christmas 1936, outstripping *Gone With the Wind* which came second. Weatherhead's book was well up the list, ahead of works by such well-known authors as H.E. Bates, Phillip Gibbs and Maurice Baring. *It Happened in Palestine* was greeted as not just another travel book, but as 'a practical examination of the Gospel history with a view to understanding and appreciation by the realisation of close contact.'

Foyle's chose it as its 'Religious Book of the Month' as did the Religious Book Club. The reviewer in the *Manchester Guardian* (15 December 1936) wrote:

This book will help to explain Mr. Weatherhead's extraordinary popularity as a preacher. He has the gift of conveying, with simplicity and directness to reader or to hearer, his own vivid and vital self. For my own part, I laid down this book with profound thankfulness that the man who at this moment is reaching a larger number of his fellows than any other living preacher can write so winningly and with such glowing sincerity, of Jesus Christ.

Weatherhead attracted criticism for his dismissal of the Old Testament, which he confessed to rarely reading, his psychological interpretation of the healing miracles of Jesus and rational explanations of the nature miracles, and for his emphasis on the human personality of Jesus, with the use of such phrases about him as 'elder brother' and 'best friend'. Roger Lloyd, in a generally favourable review in the *Observer,* objected to his use of such terms as 'fun and good-fellowship' in referring to Jesus, and calling him 'the first gentleman' (the title of a popular play at the time), which Lloyd considered was lacking a proper reverence and homage towards 'the High and Holy One that inhabiteth Eternity.' The most hostile review came from an unnamed reviewer in the *Congregational Quarterly* who objected that 'Weatherhead writes as a psycho-therapist' and that he 'always gets in front of his subject . . . we cannot forget him in the

Garden of Gethsemane or on the road to Jericho.' He dismissed the book as 'obviously quickly written' and as such would make no 'lasting impression.' The book went into twelve impressions by 1948, and Hodders produced a new edition in 1956.

During 1934 Weatherhead had given a series of lectures on the problem of pain to the Leeds Y.M.C.A. and produced articles on this topic for the *Leeds Mercury*. From this came another book, *Why Do Men Suffer?* (1935). The problem of pain was one that acutely troubled him. He was exceptionally sensitive to suffering in any creature, and actively supported the League for the Prohibition of Cruel Sports, writing articles supporting its policies in the *Leeds Mercury*. He was invited to speak on its behalf at a meeting at the Royal Albert Hall in November 1933. Only another engagement prevented him from doing so. He did however send a telegram expressing his sympathy with the cause and his good wishes for the success of the meeting. He also supported the work of the R.S.P.C.A., arguing that not only was it always wrong to inflict suffering wantonly, but that the effect was 'worse for the inflictor than the victim' because it was 'debasing and brutalising'. He attacked fox hunting as 'degrading' and 'giving run to primitive and savage blood lust', and hoped that it would be made illegal.

His hatred of unnecessary suffering also made him an active member of the Euthanasia Society, and though this brought him much criticism, he frequently spoke out in favour of allowing those who were incurably ill and suffering from excruciating pain to have their suffering terminated and to die with dignity instead of in agony. The *Methodist Times and Leader* (12 March 1936) included an article by him headed: 'The Right to Die'. In this he describes visiting a man in hospital who had a cancerous growth behind the eye.

I used to sit on his bed and he used to grip my hand until, literally he drove his nails through my flesh as wave after wave of anguish rolled over him. He twisted about in the bed in an agony that could not have been exceeded during the tortures of the Spanish Inquisition. At the foot of the bed stood or sat a slim young woman whose face I shall never forget. It seemed possible, day after day, to watch her wilt and fade . . . until at last, when merciful death released her husband, the spectacle of his sufferings had almost killed her too. The experience made me a firm believer in euthanasia.

After he had retired, he was invited by the Oxford Union to speak at a debate opposing the motion 'That this House believes that under no circumstances should euthanasia be permitted.' The leading speaker in favour was the distinguished Jesuit, Father Thomas Corbishley. The University magazine, *Isis,* described the debate as 'Excellent – certainly the best debate of the term and probably the best for a long time'. Weatherhead's address was 'A most moving speech, full of humanity and compassion, delivered without sentimentality or sensationalism.' Weatherhead was so successfully persuasive that the Union rejected the motion, voting 264 against to 178 in favour.

He dedicated the book, *Why Do Men Suffer?* to the memory of his mother and his sister Muriel, both of whom died painfully of cancer. He explains,

The subject of pain has haunted my thinking ever since I began to think for myself at all. My mind has followed every gleam which promised light on so dark a problem. . . . I have studied and pondered and prayed. [p.9]

As he was writing the book, in June, 1935, a severe earthquake occurred in

Quetta, the capital of Baluchistan, and several thousand people were either killed or made homeless. He recognises the effect that such disasters have on people's faith in the existence of a good and loving God, and in reply explains that earthquakes and volcanic eruptions are necessary to the survival of the planet, adding that the damage done by such natural events is often made worse by human folly, ignorance and stupidity. Much suffering is prevented when lessons are learned from the tragedies that occur, and the knowledge gained makes it possible for future disasters to be avoided or mitigated in their effects. For God to intervene would mean that the orderly rule of law which governed the universe would be arbitrarily broken, and could not be depended upon, and mankind would never acquire the knowledge to overcome disease or calamity on any permanent basis.

Weatherhead is convinced that God's attitude to suffering is not the detached indifference of a remote transcendent Being. God is intimately involved with every part of his universe, and with every one of his creatures. Such is the nature of this involvement, that he himself suffers at every level according to the degree in which the particular 'medium of His expression' is injured and prevented from fully expressing his purpose for it. The suffering which God endures through his immanence in and sympathy with all his creatures is therefore infinite and awe-inspiring in its extent:

> when we petulantly ask of any human tragedy, "Why does God allow this to happen?" we ought to complete the question and ask, "Why does God allow this to happen to Himself?" [p.143f.]

In the chapter, 'Is the Universe Justifiable?' he repeats an argument published first in a previous booklet, *Guarded Universe* (1932). 'No scientist could discover anything unless God revealed it; and progress in scientific research might equally accurately be called the progressive revelation of God'. In other words, God controls the release of knowledge, and so protects mankind from making discoveries which would be devastating to his reason and beyond his abilities to control or use; although Weatherhead still expresses concern that scientific discoveries are outstripping mankind's spiritual and moral growth. This need for God to protect mankind applies to the 'psychical sphere' which Weatherhead believes is equally part of the universe with the physical. In a section which indicates Weatherhead's interest in the paranormal and the existence of psychic phenomena, he says,

> there is a psychic universe just beyond the one we know. It is a universe we could not bear in plenitude, but it is there. . . . The wall between the universe that we can bear and the universe we could not bear is very thin, but it is there. [p.220]

Since this is 'a guarded universe. God has put sentries round it. Nothing can come in unless it passes them', even what seems a calamity to us is 'the measure of God's trust in us to use our resources, and less than the measure of the gain that may be won from it. "The calamity would not be allowed to break through unless this were true." This means that nothing finally has power to 'destroy the purpose of our lives. There is a limit set to suffering, and He will not ask from us more than we are able to bear.' Weatherhead's certainty that the universe is rational convinces him that even death is not the final calamity we suppose, but that since death is 'the ordinance of God' which must happen to everyone in

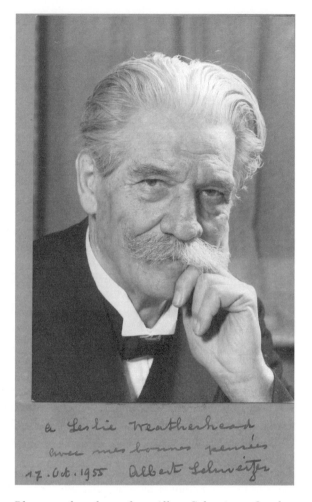

Photograph and note from Albert Schweitzer, October 1935

time, then it is natural to suppose that in the experience of dying each person must find themselves cared for as they were when they were born.

Throughout his time in Leeds, Weatherhead spoke out frequently on topical, social and national issues. He supported the Save Our Sunday campaign against the pressure for Sunday sport and Sunday opening of cinemas, believing that the traditional English Sunday was vitally necessary for safe-guarding the spiritual health of the nation.

International matters also troubled him. In 1929 he had been a member of a group led by the Bishop of Ripon which visted Germany as part of the World Alliance for the Promotion of International Friendship through the Churches. He made a number of friends there, and gained an awareness of what was going on in that country. He continued to watch developments there with increasing anxiety, especially after the rise of Hitler to power in 1933. He was earlier than most in realising the possibility of another war with Germany, and gave public expression to his fears in his regular articles for the *Leeds Mercury:* 'Can We

Save Europe?' (November 1933) 'If War Breaks Out What Then'(November 1934) and 'Abyssinia and the League of Nations' (September 1935).

In October, 1935, Albert Schweitzer, who was much admired by Weatherhead, and regarded by many as the greatest and most truly good man then living, visited Leeds as the Weatherhead's guest. Schweitzer spoke at an afternoon meeting at Silcoates School, and in the evening gave a lantern lecture at Brunswick on his work at Lamberene. The Weatherheads were greatly impressed by his warmth and friendliness, and especially struck by his humility and total lack of self-importance.

When the Methodist Conference for 1935 met in Bristol a great deal of attention was attracted to it by a proposal from Weatherhead that the Conference should appoint a special committee to examine the question of spiritual healing and to report to the Conference the following year. Weatherhead said there were many people whose illnesses were not physical or mental but spiritual in origin, and who could not be adequately treated by physical medicine. He proposed that a committee should be formed of doctors, ministers and laymen to collect evidence and to see in what way co-operation could be secured between the ministerial and the medical professions. Dr. Eric Waterhouse supported Weatherhead by seconding the proposal which was carried unanimously.

During his eleven years in Leeds Weatherhead had produced a dozen books which had given him an international reputation, both as a writer of popular devotional works, and as a leading advocate of the use of psychology in the pastoral ministry and of closer co-operation between members of the healing professions. He had become a national figure on radio and drawn crowds to his Brunswick Church, but his liberal theology, attacks on orthodoxy, and imaginative speculations in his preaching, (a typical sermon was 'Did Jesus go to College? – owing more to his imagination than to serious scholarship) attracted much criticism. In particular, his controversial use of hypnotism, his frank attack on sexual ignorance in *The Mastery of Sex*, and his interest in the paranormal had aroused hostility to him in influential circles within Methodism.

Weatherhead's increasing reputation had brought him attractive offers from outside his own denomination, but such was his love for Methodism and for his people at Brunswick that he chose to stay where he was. As early as 1931 *The Leeds Mercury* reported that he had refused three invitations offering a thousand pounds a year. Two were from Canada: to be Professor of Homiletics and Psychology at McGill University in Montreal, and to be minister of the Metropolitan Church, Toronto. The third was from a famous London Congregational church – Christ Church, Westminster Bridge Road, Lambeth. In 1932 he also declined an invitation from the Hampstead Garden Suburb Free Church.

He had been in his Leeds church longer than it was normal for a Methodist minister to stay in a pastorate, and the Methodist Conference now considered his next appointment. He had long cherished a sentimental ambition to become minister of Wesley's Chapel in City Road, London – world Methodism's central shrine and the place where his parents had met. This was being given favourable support when the autocratic Dr. Scott Lidgett objected, saying that he would not agree to a psychologist going to Wesley's pulpit. Lidgett's opposition forced Conference to take a vote – something rarely done on the question of appointments. The result was 157 in favour and 401 against. J.W. Lightly, the Principal of Headingly College, Leeds, had also, but in a more kindly way, suggested that Weatherhead was not the right person for Wesley's Chapel, since he would be required to be the warden of Wesley's House as well. But it was Lidgett's intervention that effectively blocked the appointment, and Weatherhead's long-held ambition was denied. He was bitterly disappointed, and this refusal continued to rankle with him. Several years later, in June 1941, after the City Temple had been destroyed and he was being offered the generous hospitality of St. Sepulchre's Anglican church, he contrasted his treatment by the Anglicans with the way he had been treated by members of his own denomination, referring to himself as a Methodist Minister 'deprived six years ago by the prejudice of a Methodist from regularly ministering from Wesley's pulpit in the historic chapel where his parents met and were married.'

As Conference was making this decision, two important London Congregational churches were seeking a new minister. The first of these was Christ Church, Westminster Bridge Road, which now approached him once again. Christ Church had been founded in 1785 by the evangelical, Rowland Hill, and there the Baptist, Dr. F.B. Meyer, had exercised a famous ministry. Weatherhead was attracted to the building, which was a vast, cathedral-like, gothic structure, but discovered that some of the deacons disapproved of his modernist views, particularly regarding the Virgin Birth and the miracles of Christ. He was further put off by the church's Trust Deeds, which laid down a strictly conservative creed for the church. Unable to subscribe to this, he once again declined the call.

The other church was the City Temple, which was seeking a successor to its distinguished Australian Baptist minister, F.W. Norwood. Weatherhead was already well known to the Temple congregation, having first preached there in 1928, and lectured annually to the church's Literary Society in the following years. He was not however the church's first choice. There was a strong feeling that it was time the church found a minister from within its own tradition, since it had not had a Congregationalist as its minister since R.J. Campbell resigned from the pastorate in 1915. The church had therefore approached Dr. John S. Whale, then President of Cheshunt College, Cambridge, and only when he declined did they turn again to someone outside their denomination, and invite Weatherhead.

The Methodist Conference unanimously agreed to his accepting the call (although Maltby had done his best to persuade him not to). In their letter officially confirming this approval, the President of the Conference, C. Ensor Walters, and the Conference Secretary, Robert Bond, wrote to him,

> In granting you permission to become Minister of the City Temple, the Conference wishes to express its deep sense of the noble service you have rendered to Methodism abroad and at home, and to assure you of its earnest prayer that your ministry in the great historic London centre may be crowned with God's richest blessing, and may bring life and joy to hosts of those who will look to you for spiritual guidance. We are confident God Himself will be with you.

Walter Armstrong, a Methodist minister friend of Weatherhead's, who had spoken out strongly in favour of his going to Wesley's Chapel, addressing the

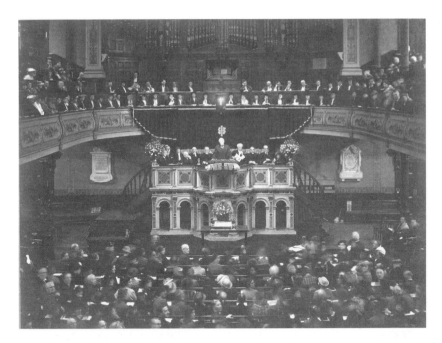

'The last Interruption', inside the old City Temple.

public meeting held at the City Temple to welcome its new minister, described the Conference as it considered the City Temple's invitation:

I have seen the Methodist Conference in strange moods, – but seldom have I seen it so hearty and enthused as it was when . . . with splendid acclamation, that great Conference gave its unanimous assent. I think it did this for two reasons. First, because of the really remarkable affection and esteem in which Mr. Weatherhead is held by us. For he is not a soul that dwells apart. He is not like some great mountain peak towering above all others, and looking down upon them. Mr. Weatherhead is greatly loved and greatly liked, because he has made himself like unto his brethren . . . there is a charm about his fellowship as well as a charm about his preaching which many of us greatly rejoice in. . . . The second reason was that Conference really did appreciate the very high honour you paid the Methodist Church by asking Mr. Leslie Weatherhead to be the Minister of this historic sanctuary – surely the greatest Free Church pulpit in the whole world.

Weatherhead had made a request to Conference that he might be allowed to remain within the Methodist ministry, and this was readily accepted by the Methodist authorities and also by the City Temple. He was staunchly Methodist at heart, in spite of his independent views and impatience with authority, and, such was his reputation, that during his time at the City Temple, the fact that he was a Methodist tended to be more widely known than the fact that his church was not.

Weatherhead had been attracted to both Christ Church and the City Temple because of what he termed their 'supra-denominational' character, as he explained in a letter,

I was invited to be minister of Xt Church & it was because it was supra-denominational that I was attracted & came down from Leeds & preached &

met the deacons but in those days they wanted me to sign that I believed in the V.B. etc etc. I told them I did not know or respect anyone who would sign such a document. The C.T. attracted me because it was SUPRA Denominational & a world pulpit & I could remain a Methodist Minister while I was its minister. (It hasn't had a Congregationalist for 50 years!)[1]

Although he respected the Congregationalism of the City Temple and was genuinely proud to be invited to so famous a pulpit, denominational allegiances mattered very little to him, and he was apparently indifferent to the fact that it was the Congregational character of both churches which enabled them to be above denomination in the way that he felt they were. (Although Dr. Sidney Berry, the General Secretary of the Congregational Union, had made this point in his speech of welcome.)

Weatherhead's decision to go to a church of another denomination brought him considerable criticism from among Methodists, some of whom accused him of deserting Methodism, and never forgave him for it. Yet it is difficult to see where else he could have gone within Methodism after Brunswick if Wesley's Chapel was barred to him. In London, the young Donald Soper had just begun his long and distinguished ministry at Kingsway, and Dinsdale Young was still exercising his at the Westminster Central Hall. The Central Halls were Methodism's main preaching platforms, but their ethos and style were too unchurch-like for Weatherhead to be comfortable in them. The visual surroundings of a beautiful building meant a great deal to him, and he always sought to create an atmosphere of quiet and reverence in worship. Noisy tip-up seats and Moody and Sankey hymns did not fit well with his gentler, conversational style of preaching and his thoughtful and penetrating prayers. Nevertheless, as was later admitted, Weatherhead's subsequent career in a church of another denomination caused

Many of an older generation of Methodists wistfully [to] speculate on what might have happened if Leslie had been allowed to accept the invitation to Wesley's Chapel.[2]

This failure to find a place for Weatherhead within Methodism was greatly regretted by those who felt that an opportunity had been missed when he was denied the pulpit he coveted, and this remains still one of the great 'might-have-beens' of modern Methodism.

1. Letter 22 November 1967. Weatherhead to Travell.
2. *The Methodist Recorder* Editorial, 8 January 1976.

10. The City Temple.

> 'where there is a live man with a live message who can talk to
> people simply and lovingly about God, a man whose experience is
> vital, infectious and radiant, as well as a man who can preach. . . .
> People go to worship. The church is alive. First things are kept
> first and all else falls into place.'

Weatherhead's appointment to the City Temple attracted considerable interest. He was now among the best-known religious personalities not only in England, but throughout the English speaking world, so that his going to the City Temple, regarded as the most prestigious Free Church pulpit in the country, seemed to many a natural progression. Welcoming him to the city, the Literary Superintendent of the British and Foreign Bible Society, John A. Patten, wrote:

It is in the fitness of things that Mr. Weatherhead should become minister of the City Temple. I well remember talking over church questions with a friend several years ago, and when we discussed who should succeed Dr. Norwood when he laid down his great ministry we agreed upon Mr. Weatherhead. It did not require great prescience to venture that prophecy, for the young Methodist preacher was even then making his reputation. The City Temple pulpit is not everybody's – in fact it is hardly anybody's. Only a man of certain outstanding and peculiar gifts is fitted to hold that stronghold of Nonconformity, and it is no reflection upon the Congregational ministry that it has failed to produce the required man at the required moment. Few Churches could produce him, and it is to the honour of Methodism that it has been able to do so.

The *Star* newspaper, which had immediately engaged Weatherhead to write a weekly series, in an introductory article by Wilson Midgley headed 'A New Voice in London' (7 October 1936), described the City Temple as 'the greatest English Free Church pulpit' and said of Weatherhead:

His books, his sermons and his scientific approach to the problems of life have made him an out-standing figure. When the vacancy at the City Temple occurred there was hardly anyone else to be considered.

The City Temple dated its history from the ministry of Thomas Goodwin, in 1640. Goodwin was a member of the Westminster Assembly of Divines and appointed Chaplain to the Council of State under Oliver Cromwell. In 1869 it called Dr. Joseph Parker to become its minister, and built a new home on Holborn Viaduct, which Parker christened 'The City Temple.' The church's links with the City were acknowledged by the City's gift of a magnificent marble pulpit, and the attendance in state at the opening on 19 May 1874, of the Lord Mayor and Sheriffs of the City of London. Because of its size, the church quickly became the venue for major Free Church gatherings: it was regularly used for meetings of the National Free Church Council, the Brotherhood Movement, and many other similar causes.

Parker rapidly became one of the major preaching attractions of Victorian

London. His congregations regularly totalled 3,500 every Sunday, and he established a Thursday lunchtime service which also drew large numbers. An American connection was formed when in 1886 Parker invited the famous American preacher, Henry Ward Beecher, to preach, and the church became an accepted place for Americans to worship in when visiting London. Parker himself was awarded a Doctor of Divinity degree by the University of Chicago. In 1902 he was followed by his own chosen successor, R.J. Campbell, whose style and personality were very different from Parker's and closer to Weatherhead's. As a student Weatherhead frequently went to hear Campbell and was deeply impressed by him. Weatherhead said that Campbell inspired him with a 'deeper sense of the wonder and dignity of the Christian ministry', and a 'determination to put into my own ministry those ideals which so vividly characterised Dr. Campbell's.'

Campbell not only continued to draw the crowds but also to attract controversy to the City Temple. The novelist, G.K. Chesterton, declared in a letter to the *Daily News* that he had always admired Dr. Campbell, 'if only for his happy knack of getting into a row!' Campbell joined the Passive Resistance Movement against Balfour's Education Act of 1902, and became closely involved with the Labour Movement, which resulted in a book, *Christianity and Social Order*. He preached a theological liberalism which, when published in another book, *The New Theology*, provoked an on-going and bitter argument in the religious and national press. The Congregational theologian P.T.Forsyth, in an article in *The British Weekly* said it was the greatest peril to the church since the Gnosticism of the second-century. This theology was Christocentric, emphasising the humanity of Jesus and the immanence of God, rather at the expense of his transcendence. After thirteen years Campbell resigned his ministry, and turned away from Nonconformity to the Anglicanism which had always attracted him.

Campbell was succeeded by an American, Dr. Joseph Fort Newton, then minister of the Liberal Christian Church in Cedar Rapids, Iowa, who served during the latter part of the First World War. His assistant was Maude Royden, a gifted Anglican, who, because she was a woman, was not permitted to preach in churches of her own tradition. Fort Newton returned to America in 1919, and the church then invited Weatherhead's immediate predecessor, Dr. F.W. Norwood, an Australian Baptist who was chaplain to the Australian forces. He built up a reputation as an outstanding preacher with a world perspective, concerned for the major issues of the day.

Norwood came to the City Temple at a difficult time. The war years had taken their toll. The church was no longer attracting the crowds that had flocked to hear Parker and Campbell, and as a result, the church's finances had diminished while the cost of maintaining the building and the organisation had increased. There was a depressed sense of discouragement and pessimism pervading the fellowship, affecting all but a small determined and faithful few.

For some years Norwood battled successfully against the general decline in church-going brought about by the effect of the war on people's religious beliefs and changes in social attitudes and behaviour. When, in 1924, the City Temple celebrated its Jubilee on Holborn Viaduct, it recorded that the membership of the church, which had been less than 100 at Parker's death in 1902, had, during the four years of Norwood's ministry, more than doubled, from 250 to over 500.

During the 1920s the regular seat-holders alone exceeded a thousand subscribers.' But then, 'during the early 1930s. . . . Attendances at the Sunday services fell ominously.' The effects of the world-wide economic depression were particularly felt by the City Temple, which had always depended on large numbers of visitors, a great many of whom came from overseas, to maintain its finances. The numbers fell away to the point where there were few strangers and the congregation was reduced to the nucleus of church members and regular adherents.

The loss of income became critical, and was made worse when some seat-holders cancelled their subscriptions on the grounds that there was no longer any need for them to reserve their seats. Norwood responded by launching a bold scheme for modernising the building at a cost of £20,000. Then, in 1933, he went on a fifteen month world tour, returning to resume his ministry in October 1934. Attendances at the services briefly improved, but then again began to fall away and the church's financial deficit steadily increased. Norwood was seriously considering resigning from the church when the National Free Church Council, of which he was President, approached him to lead a national crusade of evangelism. Norwood's interests were always wider than the City Temple: he had not only served as Chairman of the Congregational Union of England and Wales in 1930-31, but also stood at the General Election in 1929 as a Liberal Parliamentary candidate for Stoke Newington, in which he was narrowly defeated.

Norwood announced his resignation to the congregation at a service on 19 January 1936, expressing his disappointed hopes for the church:

To make that resolve has not been easy for me. There was a time when I dreamed that the City Temple might be the strong base which would spread its influence abroad into every corner of the land. But I found that my efforts to carry her influence afar involved a slackening and failure on my part at the base. . . . There was also a time when I dreamed of a great building scheme which would have consolidated this place, and made it self-supporting, given it some revenue of its own, enabled one to have a colleague in the ministry who would do the necessary work at home while one carried out his work abroad. But that dream did not materialise. Part of it did. A great deal of work has been done.[1]

The City Temple depended heavily on the income it received through the offertory plate each Sunday, and this laid a great burden on the minister, since it was his reputation and ability to attract the crowds which produced the church's income. If for any reason the congregations declined, then the minister at the time was bound to feel he was failing the church. Weatherhead's successor, Leonard Griffith, felt this to be an intolerable and unreasonable burden, as did Norwood:

I know of no other church where so much depends upon the Minister's personal character and resources. There is so little that can compensate for any personal deficiencies. The defences supplied by organisation are at a minimum. . . . It is still true, as I said to you at my own acceptance of the task, that the City Temple may either "make" a man or "break" him.[2]

At the Annual Church Meeting on 7 February, the Church Secretary, Alexander Miller, stated in his Report that the Minister and Church Council had been concerned by the evidence of smaller congregations in recent years, which he attributed to 'the prevailing apathy in matters of religion.' Norwood in his address to the same meeting said,

> Let me remind you that the City Temple is a very difficult church. . . . If this church is to maintain its national ministry, it requires a certain order of gifts. Indeed, I question if this church can maintain itself unless the man in its pulpit is of significance in the eyes of the country in general. I question if a preacher, however faithful or eloquent, could hold this place together if the general public were not interested in him.[3]

The social changes taking place between the wars affected the churches as the nation divided between the growing numbers of unemployed – mostly in the North – and the South, where those in work were enjoying rising standards of living and greater freedoms and opportunities than they had known before. The growth of suburbia led to a move away from the centres of the big towns, and those who previously had found in the churches their main source of education, inspiration, entertainment and social life, were discovering a whole range of new and different possibilities. Churches contracted as youth hostels, holiday camps and cinemas opened and flourished. Hiking and cycling had already for decades been replacing churchgoing as a regular Sunday activity. The great Nonconformist churches in the city centres were particularly vulnerable. The Free Churches had depended for their leadership on the power of the pulpit, and rested their authority on the Bible. The radical questioning of the Higher Criticism undermined the authority of the Bible as the given Word of God, and as a consequence also the authority of the pulpit. Following the war, people were generally more sceptical and less susceptible to the persuasive power of oratory and rhetoric. The growth of broadcasting meant that people had access to the best minds and could listen to the finest speakers in the comfort of their own homes. The old style of public speaking had gone out of fashion, since broadcasting required a more conversational and less dramatic approach. According to Kenneth Slack 'This had a profound effect upon the Free Churches, whose leaders had been the great pulpit orators . . . men seemed to turn more readily for religious enlightenment to the paperback than the pulpit.'[4] It was in this climate that Norwood spent the latter part of his ministry at the City Temple, and in which Weatherhead began his.

It had already been arranged for Weatherhead to preach on 12 July before his name was put forward for consideration as the church's next minister. When the Church Council discovered that he was due to broadcast from St. Martin's-in-the-Fields on 14 June, it held a hasty evening meeting and unanimously agreed to send a deputation of church officers to offer him the pastorate. A special Church Meeting was called for 2 July at which the members voted, with four against, to accept the recommendation of the Council to call Weatherhead to the church. When he preached on 12 July the church was packed at both services. Among those in the congregation was the former Prime Minister, David Lloyd George, who had turned up with a party of seven.

Weatherhead's ministry began officially on 4 October, and the 21st was set aside as a Day of Recognition. A 'Welcome Luncheon' was held in the Holborn Restaurant, with R.J. Campbell presiding over a large number of guests and official representatives from all denominations, and a letter of greeting was received from Lloyd George. In his speech of welcome, referring to the generosity of the Methodist Church in permitting Weatherhead to go the City Temple,

Campbell said his appointment was a 'significant gesture', a 'portent' and an example of practical Christian unity. Harold Roberts, then Professor of Theology at Headingley, Leeds, wrote on behalf of Methodism,

> Mr. Weatherhead's call to the City Temple has given great satisfaction to many of his friends. While we can ill afford to lose him, we realise that the pulpit which he occupies belongs in a real sense to all the Churches. Incidentally, the gracious consent to his request to remain on the roll of Methodist Ministers is deeply appreciated by us, since, among other things, it symbolises an attitude of mind that has transcended the limitations of denominationalism.

Weatherhead saw it this way also. Unity was a cause he advocated at every opportunity. At the Albert Hall Rally in 1932, celebrating Methodist Reunion, he had expressed the hope that 'it might be the forerunner of a wider union', and in an article on 'Christian Reunion' he had declared that he would welcome reunion with the Church of England, and was even willing to be re-ordained, 'not because I believe my own "orders" to be "invalid" . . . but as an outward and visible sign of entry into a wider sphere of usefulness and as a symbol of my sincerity in desiring to see the wounds in the body of Christ healed.' This enthusiasm was welcomed by his new church, and the article was reprinted in the October issue of the *City Temple Tidings* with the comment 'Events will probably prove Mr. Weatherhead a persistent and persuasive champion of Christian Reunion. Denominational barriers have no place in his outlook as a Minister of Christ.'

For years Weatherhead had been a welcome preacher in the churches of most of the major denominations, including the Church of England, and he counted ministers of all denominations among his friends. Soon after going to the City Temple, he wrote to the *Congregationalist* calling for Methodists and Congregationalists to unite. Commenting on the friendly way in which the paper reported the activities of Methodists, and the 'brotherly welcome' he had received from Congregational ministers, he said 'I dream of a great United Free Church of England. Its power and influence would be enormous in the life of the nation.'

This letter created a considerable amount of interest and correspondence, including a supportive letter from Donald Soper, who felt that 'such a proposal ought to commend itself to everybody who has the Kingdom of God at heart.' Several writers saw difficulties arising from differences of Church structure and organisation – especially the Methodists, who were still sorting out the practical problems arising from their own recent Union. Weatherhead always treated such problems lightly, and in any case was much less affected by them than most of his ministerial colleagues, since he was himself now in practice free from the restraints of denominational control. He retained his enthusiasm for Church Unity throughout his life, and was particularly proud to be President of the Methodist Conference when it initiated Conversations with the Church of England in 1955, although, in a private letter, some time after he had retired, he said

> I wd not support Meth-Anglican union if it spoilt the union between Meths and other Free Church denominations, and secretly I'm glad in a cowardly way that Meth-Ang Union wont come till long after I'm dead. I certainly would refuse to deny communion to a person because they had not been

confirmed. . . . About Meth-Anglican union I feel that Methm would not introduce an element more divisive than exists already in the C of E. (EG. Angl Cath & Low Evangelical). Also John Wesley longed for Methm to remain in the CofE & also Methm could be just the yeast that altered the whole heavy lump of present Anglicanism.[5]

Speaking at both the luncheon and at the evening meeting, Norwood welcomed Weatherhead generously. Referring to his 'magnificent qualities', he was, he said, 'Profoundly thankful that Mr. Weatherhead has begun his ministry in the City Temple.' But there was also an unhappy, even bitter note in Norwood's speech. He contrasted the welcome for Weatherhead with his own reception when he came to the church.

I never had a welcome meeting. I have not yet been inducted. . . . I did not know five people in the British Isles at that time outside the camps of the Australian soldiers. . . . I never had any laudatory press notices. . . . I can only remember one letter of welcome that was sent to me by anyone in England at that time. . . . It was from the late Dr. Jowett. I treasure it because the first year or two of my life as Minister of this Church were the loneliest I have ever spent. . . . Your experience Mr. Weatherhead, will begin from a different altitude than mine. You come on a wave of great and well-deserved popularity. I had to fight my way through misunderstanding and suspicion. . . . This Church is a church that will take all you have got and would take more if they could find it. This old City of London is a very impersonal kind of place, it will squeeze a man dry, and it will not be over-much concerned about him when he is dry . . . and when they have drained you dry, they may begin to say that you really have not got much to say after all. . . . This place will make or break you. Keep your soul my brother. Nothing else matters.[6]

Dick Sheppard, and the Editor of the *British Weekly*, John A. .Hutton, both warned about the temptations and dangers of popular preaching. Hutton especially said;

There is this tragic thing: you can get anything you want. If you are out for a cheap, popular, triumphant career, you can have it. . . . Any man with your kind of gifts can fill the City Temple night and morning if he cares to. . . . There is a higher and a lower road of life. . . . It would be dreadful if the cult of mere popularity were to be made much of by the Church.[7]

Weatherhead replied, 'Would you believe me if I said I am not out for cheap popularity, I am not out to win cheap applause: I hate it.'

In June, he had written two articles for the *Methodist Times and Leader* on 'Preaching' and on 'Popular Preaching'. Before he began his ministry at the City Temple he repeated the second of these in the September issue of the *City Temple Tidings*. His success in attracting crowds when churches in general were facing emptying pews prompted criticisms that he was deliberately courting popularity and preaching a watered-down version of the gospel to achieve it. He was sensitive to such criticism and hurt by it. He was intensely serious about his preaching, and worked extremely hard at it. He wrote an article for the *Methodist Times and Leader*, (16 April 1936) 'On Making Sermons', in reply to a request from a local preacher, in which he described his attitude to preaching and his methods. In this he said that nothing draws people to church more than preaching, which should leave them looking at Christ, not admiring the preacher. The sermon was important, but not the most important thing in a service; the Free Churches had given it a greater prominence than it ought to have, so that worship had suffered, because services had become centred on the ability of man rather than the worship of God. But

> where there is a live man with a live message who can talk to people simply and lovingly about God, a man whose experience is vital, infectious and radiant, as well as a man who can preach then there is no problem. People go to worship. The church is alive. First things are kept first and all else falls into place.

He went on to describe his own method of working, saying that he rarely made a sermon between one Sunday and the next. He liked to get his subject early, reducing it to its final form as late as the day before it was preached. He always wrote out his sermons, often several times, aiming at simplicity so that the sermon would not be 'over the head' of anyone of fourteen. In every congregation there were broken hearts: 'if one poor soul before us sees a tiny glimpse of His glory and opens his heart to the living Christ, our sermon will have done its work, though text and sermon and preacher be forgotten.'

In a further article for the *Leader* (4 June 1936) replying to another local preacher who was critical of sermons being written out in full and then read word for word, Weatherhead compared writing a sermon with painting a picture.

> Just as a man who loves painting is not presumptuous because he takes pains to get exactly the right shade and exactly the right colour, so a man painting with words is not presumptuous if . . . he wants a sentence to carry not only clear meaning but a certain beauty, a certain tone. I have written and crossed out and re-written, and re-written again, and found an aesthetic delight when I have come to feel that a sentence conveys exactly the meaning I want it to carry . . . when words carry colour as well as meaning . . . it is . . . a deliberate insult to a congregation to . . . presume to deliver a message from the living God without the most careful intellectual preparation and especially a prayerful preparation of oneself.

He was strongly against the reading of sermons, saying that although he always had his full manuscript with him in case of emergency, for ten years after leaving college he preached without using any notes, until a friend told him he was putting too great a strain on his memory. After that he used brief notes which he consulted as little as possible.

> In the delivery of the sermon the less one consults one's notes the better. One may forget to say something one intended to say, but one will gain more than one loses by remaining en rapport with the congregation which fact is absolutely essential in all speaking.

Weatherhead deplored the way the phrase, 'a popular preacher' was 'used as an insult' implying that 'the preacher has attained his popularity in an unworthy way' by courting publicity and playing to the gallery, and that such preaching is the opposite of 'intellectual preaching.'

> To put popular preaching over against intellectual preaching is another unfair and misleading comparison. If I dress my sermon out in long theological words; if I show that I have a knowledge of the philosophical problems of the schoolmen; if I quote Thomas Aquinas, and Bergson, and Otto, and

Dibelius, someone is sure to think it is a clever sermon, and intellectual preaching. If, having paid studious regard to all I can learn from such masters. . . . I take pains to write simply and illustrate in a homely way and clear away doubts and beat out a track so that a boy of fifteen or a char-woman, or a miner, or a university professor can equally easily find their way to God, then my effort is damned by some highbrow in his first year at theological college by the label "popular".

A preacher should be his natural self. He should not
throttle down or suppress his personality . . . or offer to God a wooden service when he is really a vivid personality. . . . If God has given us a warm, emotional nature we are not to be icebergs in the pulpit. If God has given us a ready sense of humour, we are not to look as miserable as possible lest some jealous idiot says we are 'playing to the gallery.'

Weatherhead greatly resented the personal attacks and criticisms which he himself had suffered because of his success, and in this article he lets his indignation at the unfairness of so much of it boil over, describing the 'enemies of the popular preacher' as 'narrow-minded and censorious. . . . Unpopular themselves' they are 'the greatest liability to any ministry and one of the greatest hindrances to the spread of true religion.'

Popular preaching is preaching to which people respond, preaching which grips them . . . all preaching ought to aim at being "popular." It ought to aim at bringing the "people" into vital contact with Jesus Christ. . . . Let that message be delivered with all the winning charm, with all the glowing fire, with all the simplicity, and, if natural and spontaneous, the bright humour of which the preacher is capable.

That Weatherhead was himself an outstandingly popular preacher was quickly demonstrated by the queues which began to form outside the City Temple for every service immediately he began his ministry there, and which continued to form, whenever he preached, throughout the whole of his ministry, and even years after he had retired.

The impact of his ministry on the City Temple was immediate, and remarkable in the speed with which his plans for the church began to take effect. Within the first month, the City Temple Psychological Clinic had been started, a lodge of the Samaritan League had been formed – with one hundred and twenty five men attending its first meeting on 16 November, following an appeal by the minister on the previous evening – and sixteen new members had joined the church – a figure which grew to well over one hundred before he had completed his first six months. Plans were also in hand to start a Friday Fellowship, described by Weatherhead as 'the strongest spiritual force' in his last church.

Weatherhead's ministry also brought about an immediate improvement in the Temple's finances. The Sunday collections increased considerably as the congregations increased. Two friends from Leeds provided him with a house of his own, which meant that the church was not required to provide a manse, and so benefited by some £3,400. In addition, the royalties from all his books sold on the church bookstall were given to the church.

Norwood had wished that the church had been able to provide him with a colleague in the ministry who would do the necessary work at home while he carried out his work abroad. In May, after Norwood had announced his resignation, but before Weatherhead had been invited, the church had appointed two 'Lady Ministrants' 'for whole-time service in various branches of our Church work.' This meant that Weatherhead had the help of these two assistants, Miss Nettie Agnew and Miss Winifred Barton, from the start. They did a great deal of home and hospital visiting, interviewed people for membership and baptisms, and dealt with much of the normal pastoral work of the church. Miss Barton had been a missionary in the Kashmir, and then, with Miss Agnew, had spent three years in medical missionary work in Islington before going to the City Temple. Miss Agnew died early in 1937, only a few months after her appointment, but Winifred Barton continued as pastoral assistant with Weatherhead throughout the rest of his ministry.

The forming of the Psychological Clinic fulfilled Weatherhead's long-held dream that such a clinic should be a normal part of the church's pastoral ministry. In July, he had presented to the Methodist Conference a well-received report from the Committee on Spiritual Healing, which clearly represented his own views and influence. In it he recommended that psychology might be included in the training of theological students, and that there should be established a 'centre to which people may come for treatment and advice.' At the City Temple he seized the opportunity to create such a centre himself. He advertised for committed Christian doctors with medical and psychological qualifications to work with him at the church, making it possible to combine the different disciplines and insights of medicine, psychology and religion. He was immediately joined by Dr. Alfred Torrie, whom he had known previously in Yorkshire as a general practitioner. Weatherhead had encouraged Torrie to take a post-graduate course in psychology and move to London, where he had successfully established himself in Harley Street. Torrie was one of the first to become a member of the City Temple after Weatherhead began his ministry there. In his December letter Weatherhead was able to say that the Psychological Clinic had been started, and that they were being embarrassed by applications to help. He stated that no fees would be charged by either himself or the medical staff, although donations to the church would be welcomed: 'the aim of the clinic is to provide psychological help for the poor.'

For Weatherhead, the church context of the Clinic was of real importance, since he believed that the church itself could provide a healing fellowship. He encouraged those who sought his help to attend worship and to join the church's fellowship groups, where they would find necessary acceptance and friendship. His eagerness to establish these groups as quickly as possible reflected this, and eighteen groups were soon meeting every Friday evening. He invited people to offer for discussion 'those problems which beset people, old and young, in various walks of life', saying, 'better than pure theological problems are the personal problems, the solving of which helps us to live more adequately the Christian life.'

His move to London brought him to the centre of national life and established him as a national figure. *The Times Review of the Year* (1 January 1937) for 1936 included his going to the City Temple in its list of important Church appointments made during the year – the only non-Anglican to warrant a mention.

It was a time of the most serious events, both nationally and internationally. The previous October, Mussolini had invaded Abyssinia and by July 1936

Abyssinian resistance was overcome. The British and French attempted to appease Mussolini by offering him two-thirds of Ethiopia and part of British Somaliland, but Mussolini had no interest in such deals. In May, the Abyssinian Emperor, Haile Selassie, was driven into exile. After addressing the League of Nations in Geneva, he journeyed to England and settled in Bath.

Weatherhead met Haile Selassie on at least two occasions in 1936: informally, on the day of his Recognition Meeting in October, and at a luncheon given for the Emperor at the City Temple by the London Free Church Federation on 24 November. The previous September, Weatherhead had contributed an article for the *Leeds Mercury* (30 September 1935) headed 'Abyssinia and the League: What Should Britain Do?', written in response to a letter he had received from a member of Parliament who had said that 'knowing my interest in World Peace, he would value my views on the present situation.' Weatherhead dismissed the fear that Italy's act of aggression could lead to the end of the League of Nations, but argued that if Britain alone decided to apply sanctions against Italy, this would not only be 'interpreted as an act of unfriendliness', but would also represent the sheerest hypocrisy, for Italy after all

> is only pursuing the very policy which gave Britain some of the most desirable parts of her Empire . . . how can we reproach Italy for her intention toward Abyssinia when we remember how we ourselves got India and the Soudan? . . . With all our horror of what Italy is doing there must be an understanding of Italy's problem. . . . Britain has not the moral authority to judge the nations. . . . Her past history forbids it, and her present interest in Egypt forbids it too.

He proposed 'as an act of national penitence' that Britain should offer some of her territories in Africa to Italy to satisfy 'her legitimate desire for expansion'. He hoped that 'some of the proposals I have made might lead to a United States of Europe' and so be 'a stepping stone towards world understanding and brotherhood.'

In his attempt to be fair to Fascist Italy Weatherhead overlooked the interests of the people of Abyssinia, and of Somalia, the other territory he was offering to Mussolini. His article stirred much comment and protest, though his ideas – which suggest some political naivety – were not so different from those of others who shared his horror at becoming embroiled in another war, nor that far off (except in motive) from the squalid deal Hoare and Laval had proposed. Mussolini's propaganda about his need for the economic resources provided by colonies persuaded others beside Weatherhead that his demands were reasonable. Dr. Alfred Salter, a Wesleyan who became an agnostic, but was then was re-converted by Scott Lidgett and eventually became a Quaker, wrote, in February 1936:

> Can it be expected in view of this unequal and unfair distribution of the world's resources that these virile, energetic and spirited nations will continue to sit quiet, restricted in self-development, deprived of necessities and comforts, and starved or semi-starved, while other nations, notably ourselves, have everything we need? Why have we full supplies? Just because we were first into the field in seizing all the delectable and exploitable parts of the earth.[8]

Italy's invasion of Abyssinia altered Weatherhead's views. In a later article in the *Leader*, (21 May 1936) he expressed his horror and indignation at the methods Mussolini's forces were using to conquer the Abyssinians. Possibly because of the reactions to his previous suggestions, and an awareness that in his new situation in London he needed to be more careful in making statements on public issues, Weatherhead now said that he had no intention of giving advice to the British government about what it should do:

> Not only am I entirely incompetent to offer political advice, but such advice is not the business of the pulpit to offer. Matters of Government. . . are not the sphere of the Christian Minister. Yet there are occasions when the pulpit should speak out and do so boldly and immediately, even at the risk of speaking foolishly from the point of view of the counsels of men. The pulpit must speak out if, in any situation, the law of Christ is being broken or the loving purposes of God are, in that situation, being obscured or apparently defeated.

He referred to Abyssinia again, in his very first sermon preached as minister of the City Temple, on the morning of 4 October 1936. His theme was 'The Humility of God', and he contrasted the way God acts with the way men behave:

> Badoglio [Mussolini's son-in-law and commander of the Italian air force] knowing that all things had been delivered unto him through the might of Italian soldiers who fought a half-civilised people with tanks and bombing planes and mustard gas, proceeded to enter a capital in pomp and glory and demand the surrender of all arms and of every native. Jesus, knowing that all things had been delivered unto Him by His Father . . . removed His robe, took a towel . . . and began to wash His disciples feet.

This was typical of the way Weatherhead would use current topics and events in his sermons. He occasionally preached 'topical' sermons, when he felt strongly that some happening had been of such importance that it warranted dealing with from the pulpit and it was justifiable to devote a whole sermon to the event – as he did when the King, Edward VIII, abdicated in December that year – but his usual way was to relate his religious theme to what was going on in the world at that time, and to the things that were uppermost in people's minds. He was concerned to avoid what he described in his articles on preaching as 'topical preaching which never goes deeper than the topic; never gets down to some deep message of God for the people.'

The City Temple held its first Annual Church Meeting of Weatherhead's ministry on 22 February 1937. This was his first direct experience of the Congregational system, in which the Church Meeting, under the Lordship of Christ, is the highest authority in governing each autonomous local church. Coming from the more hierarchical Methodism he was very happy to have the greater freedom and independence which the Congregational system gave him. He had justified his move to the City Temple on the grounds that it was 'not a Congregational Church in the ordinary sense of the term', and even Congregationalists, often disapprovingly, acknowledged that this was so. The City Temple's emphasis on the importance of the man in the pulpit meant that the minister, at least since the days of the autocratic Joseph Parker, could to a large extent – given the acquiescence of the Church Secretary and Council – impose his own wishes and personality on the way the church was run and on what it decided to do. This was an important factor in the speed with which Weatherhead was able to get so many of his ideas accepted and implemented by the church. He was also 'Through the powers conferred upon me as Minister' able to co-opt his own choices on to the Church Council, and he took full advantage of this. The City Temple did not have the customary Congregational monthly church meeting where all important decisions should be made. There were the Annual Church Meeting, and Quarterly Church Suppers, which were mainly social events at which new members were welcomed and some reports of organisations and activities occasionally received. Throughout Weatherhead's ministry the members for the most part were happy to follow wherever he led. According to Ronald Ward, who was a young member of the City Temple during the first months of Weatherhead's ministry, and the first from that ministry to become ordained,

> The Church Meeting did not loom very large in the life of the C.T. in those days. So far as I remember, he never attended May Meetings . . . and he was stoutly loyal to his Methodism. One has to remember that he was the C.T. then, in himself. I don't think any of us thought of the C.T. in denominational terms at all. . . . His ministry was such an extraordinary phenomenon that people were drawn to the church exclusively by the minister and never thought of it apart from him.[9]

Weatherhead was thus remarkably free to introduce his own methods, as Cyril Dewey, who was a leading member of the church in those days, recalls:

> He knew what had proved successful at Brunswick before he came to the C.T. . . and when he proposed that a similar scheme be started at the C.T. Church members gave wholehearted support. In other words, the 'authority' of the Church Meeting was a mere formality.[10]

At the February meeting, the Church Secretary, Alexander Miller, reported that the new organisations and activities introduced by Weatherhead 'had made the City Temple a centre of throbbing interest night by night during each week.' The success of these activities had also greatly increased the need to modernise the Temple's meeting rooms and ancillary premises; the church therefore agreed to press on with raising the £20,000 necessary to implement the rebuilding scheme which had been advocated by Norwood.

Calls for Weatherhead's services increased from beyond the City Temple. On 17 January he preached the Edinburgh University sermon in St. Giles's Cathedral. During one week in May he spoke on three successive nights: at the Albert Hall, the City Temple and the Queen's Hall, 'to well over fifteen thousand people' gathered for the Congregational Assembly and important Methodist meetings. At the Albert Hall he addressed the Methodist Annual Missionary Rally. The *Methodist Recorder* (6 May 1937) attributed the greatly increased numbers of young people present to his being there:

> The audience I should say was considerably larger than last year's. . . . One thing is quite certain – this audience was a very youthful one. The presence on the platform of a minister who has a remarkable sway over the minds and hearts of young people may have accounted for this.

Weatherhead still retained the passion for Missions which had led him to go to India in 1916, and during his ministry at the City Temple the London Missionary Society and the Colonial Missionary Society received his vigorous support. In his address in the Albert Hall he not only spoke from his experience in India but challenged the audience to include the people of Europe in their missionary concern. The visit to Germany he had made in 1929 had brought him contacts with German Christians and he learnt at first-hand from them what the current situation was in that country. Saying that there 'were hundreds of splendid young men and women' in Germany and Italy who were trying to find their way to Christ he suggested that 'perhaps the peace of Europe depends on whether the missionary spirit is strong enough to hold those who love Christ together against whatever forces may be reared against them.'

In March, he had been presented to the King and Queen and other members of the royal family at Buckingham Palace, and in April he gave a broadcast interview to Howard Marshall which was reported in *The Listener*. Marshall wanted to know about the work of the City Temple. Weatherhead stressed the appeal to youth, saying that the average age of the congregation was around thirty and that attendance overflowed into the pulpit and the lower hall, and though this meant it was possible to accommodate some 3,000 people, many others had to be turned away. The greater part of the interview was taken up with the work of the Psychological Clinic, which no doubt interested Marshall because of its novelty, but this led Weatherhead to express some disappointment that it had omitted all reference to the worship and devotional life of the church. He felt also that the broadcast had been too egotistical, focusing too much on himself rather than on the church as a whole.

He continued to put emphasis on building up the fellowship. He appealed for fifty people to form a 'look-out committee' who would look for strangers in the pews in front of them and invite them to other church activities, befriend them and encourage them to consider membership. Describing the congregation at this time, Ronald Ward says,

> those attending were almost exclusively middle class and upper middle class, with a number who were highly successful in various professions. Leslie could always count on the strong personalities who gathered round him, and of course there was never any lack of money. Many young people, nurses, teachers etc. were attracted by the preaching, which was of course what really mattered. However the C.T. had an inner core which formed a genuine church, and it was more than an audience. Weeknight activities, such as the Samaritan League and the Friday Fellowship, were well attended. The Friday Fellowship was very popular, because it provided an opportunity to meet the minister, and to take part in discussion. I do not remember any Bible Study, and there was no interest in abstract theological questions. Very few working class people attended. Leslie challenged an educated congregation to think about the faith, and everything was geared to the problems of everyday life. Superficially, one might have concluded that the appeal was intellectual, though not academic, as there was a good deal of questioning of traditional views and attitudes. In reality, however, an emotional magnetism was generated in the carefully planned services, and it was this which held people more than they realised.

In July Weatherhead was invited to take part in the Silver Jubilee celebration of the theological colleges affiliated to the McGill University of Montreal. A broadcast service on the B.B.C. World Service on 4 July brought him correspondence from a missionary in China, and from Australia, New Zealand, Canada and many parts of the United States. He attended the Methodist Conference in Bradford and presented the report of the Committee on Spiritual Healing, which had been set up following his proposals to the Conference in 1935, and which had appointed him as the Convenor. The Conference agreed to his proposals to establish experimental clinics similar to the one at the City Temple, where ministers and doctors could co-operate; to include psychology in the training of ministers, and to 'press upon ministers the value of intercession in case of illness.'

He supported this last proposal by giving accounts of cases of recovery following prayer which had occurred during his ministry at the City Temple. As a regular part of the evening service he had instituted 'the Fellowship of Silence', during which he asked for prayers on behalf of people in trouble. His method was usually to give their Christian name and say a little about their condition. He avoided giving information that was too personal, or that might produce a negative reaction in the minds of the congregation, such as naming a distressing disease regarded as incurable. He would ask the congregation to focus their thoughts on the one prayed for, explaining that prayer was a way of co-operating with God and providing a channel for his healing energies. Writing in the April Tidings he had given details of some of these cases and quoted several letters he had received from those who had been prayed for and who had recovered. This again brought him to the attention of the press and the publicity added considerably to his correspondence.

He sailed to America on 15 September, where his first engagement was to address a special meeting of American ministers in the Fifth Avenue Presbyterian Church in New York, on behalf of the Federal Council of Churches of Christ in America. As his ship, the Queen Mary, arrived late he had to go straight to the church where he found over a thousand ministers of all denominations waiting to hear him. Weatherhead spoke on the theme of the minister's work 'in connection with the direct appeal he must make to men and women in the name of the Gospel of Jesus Christ.' Writing to the Editor of the *City Temple Tidings* (November 1937) the Dean of the Drew Theological Seminary, Dr. Lynn Harold Hough, described the meeting as

> the finest gathering of ministers of many communions which had been seen in New York for many years . . . he captured his audience from the very first sentence. . . . It is not too much to say that the great group of ministers of many communions was most profoundly impressed. Every man felt that Mr. Weatherhead searched his soul and that he had a right to do this because he had searched his own soul first of all.

Immediately after this Weatherhead went straight on to a luncheon meeting arranged in his honour by his American publishers, the Abingdon Press, the oldest religious publishing house in America. Having given another address which was equally well received, he then took the night train to Canada where his first lecture was delivered the following evening, and he went on to give five further addresses in four days at the McGill University Divinity School. He was again invited to stay in Canada and teach psychology but once more he declined, telling his church, 'though I was honoured by the suggestion, I would rather preach the Gospel in London.'

Returning to London, he was overwhelmed by the enthusiasm of his welcome home. On his first Sunday back, which was also the first anniversary of his ministry, the church was crowded morning and evening, the overflow hall was packed and over a thousand people had to be turned away. This was followed by a 'Welcome Home' church supper the following Tuesday, which again was crowded to capacity, so that Weatherhead asked the Church Council to consider how they could accommodate more people for these quarterly church gatherings.

He at once resumed his heavy workload and schedule of engagements, travelling to Bristol to give two lunchtime addresses on successive days to the Congregational Union Autumn Assembly. He told his church that he could not accept one tenth of the invitations he was receiving, and that he was getting some sixty letters a day, 'not a few of them lengthy epistles requiring well-considered replies'. His weekly articles in the *Star* and the *Methodist Times and Leader* generated further correspondence, so that at one time he was having to deal with an average of a hundred letters a day, often running to forty or fifty pages – one letter was of ninety pages – and going into intimate detail of the writer's most personal and private problems. To respect their privacy, he attempted to answer them all himself, writing in the green ink which became his distinctive trade mark, from the time he had discovered a large cheap bottle of it in an Indian market. Many of the letters he would deal with late at night, when he felt he had time to think and was less likely to be interrupted by visitors or the telephone. Inevitably, their problems were of such a nature that they could not easily be set aside when he needed to sleep.

Although the church was attracting increasingly large numbers of people, and its organisations were thriving, there were also some unhappy undercurrents. Weatherhead was stung by criticisms which suggested that through his many engagements elsewhere, the sale of his books and his frequent broadcasts, he was making a great deal of money. He felt compelled to defend himself concerning fees and the selling of his books in the church porch. He explained that he did not accept a fee for taking services, but only travelling expenses, though lectures to literary societies were in a different category. No fees were charged by the Psychological Clinic: 'I have never even thought of the practice of Psychology as a means of making money.' He pointed out that all the royalties from his books sold at the church went to church funds, and that no fees were ever paid by the B.B.C. for broadcasting a religious service.

At a Friday Fellowship meeting Weatherhead challenged the discontented directly by asking the groups to discuss 'What are the things that most harm our church life at the City Temple?' The groups responded by placing gossip at the top of the list. Weatherhead took this so seriously that he made it the theme of an address, which he also had printed in *Tidings*. He regarded malicious gossip as one of the most evil and destructive influences in undermining the spirit of fellowship within the church, and he was aware that he was the subject of some ill-informed 'treacherous and disloyal' underhand remarks himself. Obviously resenting this, and feeling the need to defend himself, in his Minister's letter for February, 1938, he again returns to the subject of his heavy work load, setting out in detail the way he spent 'a typical day.'

This was the Wednesday of the week in which I am writing these notes. Most of the morning was spent in preparing the service paper for the following Sunday and planning out a course of sermons on "False Deductions from Christian Truths." This included preliminary reading on the general subject and the dictaphoning of the most urgent letters. After lunch the interviewing of people in spiritual and psychological trouble. When one has spent over two hours with people in deep distress and often in tears, one is ready as any woman could be for a cup of tea! Then more interviews, a brief appearance at a meeting in our hall below, an appearance at the induction service of the Rector of St. Andrew's, our next-door church, an appearance at another meeting in our own church and then a call to a hospital in North London, the fifth hospital visit since noon on Monday. . . . The day ended after midnight with a call on the relatives of the dear one who was so ill . . . and a tiny note for them to pick up in the hall at break-fast time telling them that at midnight she was sleeping peacefully.

He insists he is not grumbling, 'To me this is the finest work in the world, and I think I must be the happiest man in London', yet the pressure of all that he had to do, and the feeling that no matter how hard he worked, there were those who still criticised him for not doing the things they felt he ought to have been doing, or paying sufficient attention to what interested them, was having a serious affect on him.

That same month, his health gave way. His doctor, Lord Horder, told him that at his 'present rate of living' he would give him two years to live. At the Annual Church Meeting in February the church accepted a statement from the Church Secretary that in future the minister's programme of work and duties would have to be considerably curtailed. This breakdown of health seriously undermined his self-confidence, leading to periods of deep depression and a keen sense of failure. As the weeks passed he fretted at being away from the church and at the length of time his recovery was taking. In April he wrote to the church, 'I am just weary to be back amongst you all and once more to take up the work I love.' He refers to 'long days and weeks of weariness and pain' saying, even so, that

I am really the luckiest man in the world. I have a loving wife – my best chum – splendid doctors, devoted friends, a praying and patient people, and above all and under all, a God whose meanings shine through every experience, whose loving care is endless, and who does not desert, in the hour of need, even those idiots who think they can work from 15 to 16 hours out of every 24 without damage to the delicate machinery which He devised!

Although it was not until his second anniversary Sunday in October that he was able to take up his ministry again, he returned briefly to the church to chair the Church Supper on 7 July, and then to his pulpit for the evening service on 10 July, still far from well. He was glad to be back, but more than usually nervous. He knew, however, that not only were many friends and various groups through-out the country praying for him, but that one minister friend had promised to lock himself in his study and remain there in prayer for the whole length of the service. 'Standing there in the pulpit I felt as though waves of power and love were coming up to me . . . so that the service I had dreaded became one of the happiest I had ever known.'

The previous year he had produced a series of sermons and articles for the *Methodist Times and Leader* (October/November 1937) on 'Religion and Nervous Breakdown'. In these he rejected the term 'nervous breakdown' and substituted the word 'neurosis', which he defined as 'a faulty adaptation to life', so that the sufferer was 'torn by conflicts he cannot understand or comprehend . . . depressed by a sense of fear and guilt, the cause of which he cannot discover.' Whatever the causes, 'Every nervous breakdown . . . means that the patient's self-esteem was threatened.' Religion, he argued, through giving a sense of belonging to God, 'empowers us to draw life from our fellowship with Him, to find a peace and serenity which a busy life full of distracting duties cannot impair', and provides, 'in the love of God, the only satisfactory basis for self-esteem', which, because 'it is a basis outside ourselves' is 'invulnerable'. Therefore 'that esteem which the breakdown seeks to maintain at such terrible cost will not even be threatened.'

His own dark suffering forced him to modify his views, though he insisted that 'no spiritual – or indeed, psychological – principle to which I held has been disproved by the experiences through which I have passed', and came to protest indignantly against those who asserted that no true Christian should ever suffer from a breakdown such as his, since to do so indicated a lack of faith. Yet, as he later admitted, he had tended to take physical health and vitality for granted, and regarded good spirits as the outcome of his faith and belief.

In an article for the *Star* (21 October 1937) he had stated that as long as there was no mental conflict, 'Nervous breakdown through overwork, I would hazard the opinion, has never happened.' He continued to insist that 'nobody breaks down through overwork', but admitted to having 'learnt many lessons', promising that 'one day I shall preach on "the treasures of darkness".' He believed that his experience had brought him to see his own weaknesses more clearly and to have a deeper sympathy and understanding for others. Prayer too 'means more to me now than it ever did.' It was not until many years later that he devoted a whole book to the subject, with *Prescription for Anxiety* (1956) and the tone is markedly different from his earlier books of practical psychology. He is no longer the confident expert sharing his professional knowledge and advice, however sympathetically, with those who seek it. He writes instead as a fellow-sufferer, able to speak directly from his own dark ordeal and with the new understanding and authority this gives him:

> The writer knows by experience what this feels like, and he would be happy to think that anything he had learned about coping with mental distress was of help to others who usually are entirely misunderstood by those who have never been through this particular hell of human misery. [p.14f.]

He resumed his ministry at the end of September. He was still under doctor's orders to limit his activities, and the church, recognizing the importance of conserving his health and energy, appointed the Rev. Dorothy Wilson to be his Pulpit Associate, a post which she agreed to fill for one year. Dorothy Wilson was originally a Presbyterian, and had trained at Westhill College, Selly Oak to work with Presbyterian Sunday Schools. As her own denomination did not then have women ministers she entered the Congregational ministry and trained at Mansfield College, Oxford, where she was the first woman to gain the Oxford University diploma in Theology. The thesis for her B.Litt. degree, on *Child Psychology and Religious Education* was published and made her widely known. She was ordained at Carrs Lane, Birmingham, and served as assistant there, and then became minister of Hest Bank Congregational Church in Lancaster. After only a brief time there she developed arthritis of the spine and this forced her to give up her ministry. Needing a more favourable climate, she travelled widely abroad in warmer countries, and gained a considerable reputation as a preacher, speaker and writer. Weatherhead welcomed her as the ideal colleague and for the next few months they shared the Sunday services, which relieved him from the burden and responsibility of having to preach twice every week.

1. *City Temple Tidings,* No.159. February 1936. p.74.
2. *City Temple Tidings,* No.160. March 1936. Minister's Notes.
3. *City Temple Tidings, ibid.,* p.112.
4. K. Slack: *The British Churches Today* (S.C.M. 1961) p.72f. .
5. Letter, 22 November 1967, Weatherhead to Travell.
6. *City Temple Tidings,* No.168. November 1936, p.347f.
7. *City Temple Tidings, ibid.,* p.335.
8. Martin Ceadel: *Pacifism in Britain 1914-1945* (OUP 1980) p.188.
9. Letter: Rev. Ronald Ward to Travell, 20 November 1992.
10. Letter: Cyril Dewey to Travell, 14 November 1992.

11. The Approach of War

'God has given us our lives and our property, and the lives of our
loved ones, but never let us forget that the Czech people are
paying part of the price of our peace'

On 29 September the Prime Minister, Neville Chamberlain, flew to Munich to
negotiate with Hitler. That same day the City Temple held its Church Supper, and
inevitably the tension of the international situation and the imminent threat of
war had an oppressive effect on the meeting. A guest speaker was the Rev. T.
Hunter Boyd, who had only two days before returned by air from Prague where
he had been serving in a summer pastorate. In his address Boyd spoke with
strong emotion about the effect of Chamberlain's negotiations with Hitler on the
people of Czechoslovakia:

> During the last six weeks he had visited Vienna on five occasions. He had
> seen Jews in their own homes, and knew at first hand something of the
> agony which these people were going through. The thought that part at
> least of Czechoslovakia might have to bear the same tyranny was too terri-
> ble to contemplate . . . he was in a room with a number of prominent Czechs
> when the news came through that Britain and France could not offer any
> help. Tears filled the eyes of those men, but no resentment or anger was
> expressed: they seemed stunned by the shock. "I wept and prayed with
> those people." For his part he could not merely pray: "O God, prevent war!"
> but we must pray with equal fervour that right might be done. He concluded
> an eloquent plea with the words: "Remember these people!"[1]

Chamberlain's return from Munich proclaiming 'peace in our time' was greeted
with relief and rejoicing by most of the country, and Sunday October 2 was
declared a national day of Thanksgiving for Peace. The B.B.C. had arranged to
broadcast from the City Temple following the evening service. Weatherhead
prepared his address, and as the tension built up during the preceding week,
revised it several times in response to the political situation. Almost at the last
moment the B.B.C. decided that the national crisis was of such importance that
only the Archbishop of Canterbury should speak to the nation and empire. The
City Temple broadcast was therefore postponed until 6 November.

That October Sunday Weatherhead preached at the morning service, which
marked not only his return to the pulpit but also his second anniversary as
minister of the church. Munich however took precedence over these more
personal and pastoral concerns. He told the congregation:

> Let us not forget the Czechs, it is no day of rejoicing for them. . . . God has
> given us our lives and our property, and the lives of our loved ones, but
> never let us forget that the Czech people are paying part of the price of our
> peace. . . . I do not know whether you share with me a rather uneasy feeling.
> Do you feel just a little as though you had made friends with a burglar, on
> condition that if he took nothing more from you, or your immediate friends,
> you would not do anything about his taking anything from anyone else? I

YOUTH LOOKS AT EUROPE.

13

By the Rev. Leslie Weatherhead.

eighteen months at Geneva who could say that our spokesmen came with a constructive plan which they hoped to see adopted.

Their attitude has been more like that of the two British Ministers, one of whom in moving the Naval Estimates said that he hoped they would never be so low again, and the other of whom, speaking of aerial disarmament, said that if certain proposals were carried out we should have to rely on international goodwill for our security and prosperity, "*a thing quite inacceptable when alternative measures are available.*"

* * *

I CONFESS that a short experience of Parliamentary Debating has a singularly depressing effect on the mind. The listener thinks that he has got some encouraging fact, only to discover afterwards that it is half a fact, or that it is greatly modified by other facts which are kept from him.

is deaf to all appeals to throw all weapons away and live together in unity and Godly love and find the plenty that God has provided for all who will share. It is a picture, not exaggerated, I think, of the Europe of the politicians.

* * *

BUT not of youth. Youth finds it hard to hate. Youth doesn't want to kill and destroy. Youth has few suspicions and distrusts.

Youth is large-hearted and generous in understanding. Youth wants big helpings of good fellowship, mutual service, sport and work. We must work with youth. We must make habit tracks deeper and deeper which lead the mind to thoughts and deeds of peace. By habit tracks I mean those imaginary grooves cut deep in the mind by repeated thinking along which rush our mental activities as soon as the initial stimulus is given.

that Hitler again and again has told us that he wants peace, and when I remember that he spent four years at the front I believe him. Remember that he actually fought in the Great War. He was at the front for four years.

The Rev. Leslie Weatherhead.

Hitler.

I WANT to take this opportunity of developing the theme opened up last week, and if possible of answering some objections. I hope I did not seem unfair to statesmen. I accept the view that they are trustees and are doing their best within the limits imposed upon

Weatherhead's article on disarmament. 17 November 1933.

hope the "burglar" has been converted. Let us believe in the conversion, but let us not forget the Czech people in our prayers.[2]

The postponed broadcast was heard in South Africa and the United States, and with particular interest in Germany. With the threat of war in mind, Weatherhead called his address, 'Think Before You Fight'. He argued against war as an instrument of policy, denying that he was a pacifist, since he recognised that there were some circumstances, such as the defence of the helpless, in which to fight was a lesser evil than doing nothing. He called on 'idealistic youth' who would be expected to fight and be killed in another war to demand from politicians the right to hold their own conference for peace. He believed there were far more people in every country who wanted peace than who wanted war; that what united ordinary people everywhere was far greater than the things that divided them. He called for all Christian people to put their loyalty to Christ before their allegiance to any nation and to support every organisation and practical means to preserve peace.

The broadcast prompted over a thousand letters, including many from Germany. During the broadcast he had spoken sympathetically of the German people, mentioning attending an Armistice Service in Berlin, in which he had stood next to a grieving German war widow, and meeting in Hamburg a young German minister, exactly his own age, with whom he found many things in common, and who had been fighting on the opposite side in Mesopotamia at the same time that Weatherhead himself was there. From the time of his visit to Germany in 1929 he took an increasingly concerned interest in what was happening in that country. In November 1933, the year Adolf Hitler came to power, the *Leeds Mercury* printed Weatherhead's picture opposite that of Hitler, heading an article by Weatherhead: 'Youth Looks at Europe'. In this he commented on the disarmament debate going on at the time, pleading that disarmament should be taken seriously, and that only by getting rid of the weapons of war could peace be secured. He expressed little confidence in politicians and an idealistic faith in 'youth', who, he believed, were totally opposed to war. He was prepared to believe the best about Hitler, and to credit him with good motives and good intentions in spite of his having 'made ghastly mistakes, of which the persecution of the Jews was the greatest.'

In a previous article headed 'Can We Save Europe?' Weatherhead had proposed that the Christian leaders of Europe should form a European party that would put aside party politics and national ideals and 'in the spirit of prayer . . . quest for the mind of Christ in regard to modern Europe.' They should then seek election in their own countries under the banner of 'International Christian.' In time they might even have a 'United States of Europe.' He believed that if the Christians of Europe had been adequately represented in 1914, that war could have been prevented, and that 'some such method is the only way to prevent war in the future.'

He was encouraged 'by the scores of letters, some in the press and some private' in response to his articles, and by being 'quoted, with approval, in the House of Commons by the Member for Barnsley, and when the Bishop of this diocese expressed general agreement', to return to the theme again in January 1934. Asking, 'what more can WE DO for peace in Europe?' he put forward six suggestions based on each individual's sphere of influence. He called for parents to teach their children to treat others with Christian kindness and love, and for them not to buy toy soldiers and toy guns and tanks which led to children associating war with games of pleasure and enjoyment. He wanted parents to refuse to send their children to schools which ran Officers' Training Corps, and the teaching of history not to glorify winning battles as a sign of the greatness of a nation. War films and plays and novels should be 'carefully censored' and 'any section of the press that is harming the cause of peace' should be boycotted. He appealed to his readers to join one of the peace movements, commending 'as one in which I am particularly interested, the World Alliance for the promotion of International Friendship Through the Churches.' He also commended the Fellowship of Reconciliation, as well as the No More War Movement and the League of Nations Union. He called for everyone to write to their Member of Parliament, asking to know not only their views on peace and disarmament, but their personal policy on 'the suppression of the private manufacture of armaments in this country.'

Weatherhead was appalled by the possibility of another war which would repeat the awful suffering and millions of casualties of the previous war, as well as reviving the hatred and the propaganda lies. Even more terribly, according to every authority he had consulted, it would be a war in which London could be destroyed in three hours, and which would involve the mass deaths of civilians, and which would finally achieve nothing except the possible ending 'of what was once a great civilisation.' In another article for the *Leeds Mercury* (16 November 1934) he expressed disappointment that his proposal that an international Christian party should be formed

> had been dismissed as impracticable, after it had been printed by many provincial papers, aired in Berlin, printed in Paris, and quoted in the House of Commons. . . . I was informed that Mr. MacDonald and Mr. Baldwin were already international Christian statesmen; that the statesmen of Europe would never agree to such a proposal, and in a word, that the suggestion was foolish. . . . I could get no one to advance it in high quarters where, alone. it could become effective.

In October, 1934, Dick Sheppard had launched his Peace Pledge Union with a nation-wide appeal for postcard declarations of support for pacifist principles. Sheppard was the leading figure in the pacifist movement which had its origins in the First World War. Christian and Socialist pacifist organisations were formed when the war began in 1914, and the movement became a political issue when conscription was introduced in 1916. Weatherhead admitted that it was not until after the war, when he returned to England in 1922, that he had begun to think seriously about the problem of war. He became a strong advocate for disarmament, arguing in his address at the big disarmament meeting in the Royal Albert Hall in February, 1932, that this was the only way to prevent war in the future. His friendship with Sheppard and another leading pacifist, Donald Soper, led him to be influenced by them for a time, and also by the pacifist writings of Beverly Nichols, A.A. Milne and the Congregationalist, Leyton Richards.

Weatherhead was delighted when the Methodist Conference in 1934 committed itself to disarmament, and stated that 'war should be condemned as a crime against humanity and repudiated as a method of settling international disputes.' Dick Sheppard had visited him in Leeds, and he had been impressed by his arguments for pacificism and readily signed his peace manifesto, saying, 'I have definitely finished with war.' In October 1937, a group of the pacifist Fellowship of Reconciliation, which as one of its basic principles stated that 'as Christians we are forbidden to wage war', was formed at the City Temple. But although he came close to the pacifist position, Weatherhead was finally unable to accept it in spite of Sheppard's efforts to persuade him. The pacifist formula, 'War is beastly. Have nothing to do with it!' was too simple: 'it seemed sound. But the more I thought, the more I felt that it was not going to be nearly as easy as that. My pacifism would have been a refusal to think. . . . I tore up my "Peace Pledge" avowal. I began to think again.'

On 7 November 1938, the day following the broadcast service from the City Temple, Ernst Von Rath, the Third Secretary of the German embassy in Paris, was assassinated by a seventeen-year-old Jew. Two days later the Jews in Germany suffered the terrors of the Kristallnacht in which scores of them were attacked and murdered, thousands arrested, shops and businesses looted and destroyed, and 119 synagogues set alight in a campaign deliberately orchestrated by Hitler's Nazi government. Many in Britain who had previously made excuses for Hitler now turned against him. During the morning service the following Sunday Weatherhead felt compelled to protest, saying that although the pulpit should not be used to pronounce on political matters,

> when a moral issue arises, a great historic pulpit like this must not remain silent. It would be weak, cowardly and shameful to let the matter pass as though it were irrelevant to the cause of true religion. I am referring of course, to the treatment meted out to our Jewish brothers and sisters in Germany. Perhaps the greatest service we can render them is to pray for them and their persecutors. And this we shall do. We must not slip into mere condemnation, or warm ourselves in the moral glow produced by denouncing others, particularly when we ourselves are safe from the concentration camp. There is a real danger of setting up bitter feeling against the whole German people, at a time when we greatly desire to increase friendly feeling, forgetting that there must be tens of thousands of Germans who loathe this cam-

paign of hate and torture as much as we do. At the same time it must be said that nothing could have so strained our sincere desire for friendship with Germany as this ferocious and unmerited orgy of cruelty, officially planned and systematically carried out against men and women and even little children whose only offence is their religion and race. When we think of them robbed of their possessions, hunted from their homes, beaten, insulted, degraded. . . . We see revealed the ethics of the pit, the morals of primeval slime. We can only pray that the Christians in Germany may have the courage to protest against this monstrous iniquity, and that the persecutors will see quickly how inevitably they are alienating themselves, not only from all the Christian people in the world, but how every civilised humanitarian heart is disgusted and revolted at a brutal display of sadistic bestiality scarcely exceeded in the days of Nero.[3]

Arriving at the church on Sunday evening, 11 December, Weatherhead was surprised and delighted to find in the congregation Dr. Stanley Jones, the distinguished American missionary and author of *The Christ of the India Road* Weatherhead invited him to speak to the congregation, and in his address Dr. Jones paid generous tribute to Weatherhead's fame and influence. Weatherhead was greatly moved and comforted when Jones referred to his own similar breakdown in health several years before. He went on to tell how once, on board ship, he had made contact with a fellow-passenger who was spiritually hungry. Jones had lent him one of his own books, but the passenger had given it back to him saying 'I can't read this, its too hectic!' Jones then lent him Weatherhead's *The Transforming friendship. This* had made such a profound impression on the man that after reading it, he surrendered his life to God. Jones went on to say that at one time he had found that he was becoming jealous of Weatherhead's fame, and the wide influence of his books in every part of the world.

I recognised in my own heart that evil thing we call envy. I knew I must stamp it out somehow. So I hit on the plan wherever I went of recommending people to read his books. Then I found myself rejoicing in his influence, and I have come tonight, as you have done to hear him preach.[4]

Weatherhead's health was still not good. On Lord Horder's insistence, he again took leave from the church, and with his eldest son Dixon, and two friends from the City Temple, Mr. and Mrs. Robert Allen, he left Southampton on 28 December for a cruise to South America, returning on 6 February. On one Sunday in Buenos Aires, he broadcast twice; from St. Andrew's Church of Scotland in the morning, and at the request of the Cathedral authorities, from a broadcasting studio in the evening. On his return he presided over the Annual Church Meeting on 21 February. He felt the spirit of the meeting 'was simply splendid' but that 'It was a bitter pill to swallow when I realised that but for my illness our debt would have gone by now. The depreciation in collections during my absence amounted to nearly a thousand pounds.' He was cheered by the report that in spite of his absence, 90 new members had joined the church, 75 on confession of faith, and that the membership was now 620, the highest level in the history of the church.

During March, together with representatives of all the major denominations, he attended the House of Commons to present a peace petition to the Prime Minister, Neville Chamberlain. The petition stated the belief that permanent peace could not be secured by competitive armaments, nor by sacrifices imposed upon small nations, and urged that 'a new peace conference should be held open to all nations and directed towards remedying the economic and political conditions likely to lead to war.' Weatherhead, speaking on behalf of the Free Churches, assured the Prime Minister that he was prayed for daily by members of all the churches, who thanked God that 'he so earnestly desired peace through consultation', and appealed to him not to give up the approach of good-will.

Between the drawing-up and the presentation of the petition it was overtaken by events. On 15 March, Hitler's troops occupied Bohemia and Moravia, and he himself entered Prague. He then began to threaten Poland. Chamberlain entered into an alliance with Poland promising that if Polish independence was threatened Britain and France 'would lend them all the support in their power.'

Weatherhead continued to hope that war might still be prevented, and convinced that there were many ordinary people in Germany who did not want war, he began his own peace campaign to maintain contacts with German citizens. During his sermon on 'Munich Sunday', 2 October, he had offered to put anyone who wrote to him in touch with someone in Germany that they could correspond with and maintain links of friendship. He now appealed for volunteers from the members of his congregation to visit Germany to offer friendship and good will. He was delighted with the response, not only from the members of his church, but from Germany itself:

> We have had a letter of warm invitation from the Mayor of Dusseldorf, one
> of our centres. Last Sunday a young German minister was lyrical in praise of
> the scheme. An American pastor in Berlin assures me of the good that can
> thus be done, and on all hands hopes are high. The scheme has been
> mentioned to Mr. Chamberlain and to Sir John Simon.[5]

When the 'goodwill invasion' began in July over 150 people had volunteered to go. They were instructed to avoid becoming involved in political discussion, and 'especially to refrain from destructive criticism of the Nazi regime.' It was Weatherhead's hope that other churches might follow his lead. After Munich, the Peace Pledge Union had also sought to encourage 'personal acts of reconciliation on a mass scale' suggesting that its members should invite German visitors to stay with them. On 29 August, the former Cabinet Secretary, Maurice Hankey, wrote to *The Times* suggesting that '"the innumerable bodies of all kinds in this country which have established contacts with some corresponding body in Germany" should send letters to their opposite numbers urging a peaceful solution to the Danzig crisis.' Weatherhead planned to lead the last party from the City Temple himself, but at the end of August he received a telegram from the Foreign Office telling him to cancel his visit and to bring his people home.

The church-life of the City Temple continued to develop. The Annual General Meeting in February considered a draft of a revised Constitution presented by the church Council. This was meant to bring together and codify resolutions which had been passed at Church Meetings during the previous twenty years. The City Temple's Constitution was based on the Congregational Model Trust Deed as recommended by the Congregational Union. Authority in the church was vested in the Church Council, presided over by the minister, whose approval was necessary before any nominations to the Council were accepted. He also had the power to make his own nominations for co-option on to the Council, though these had to be confirmed by the members of the church at the next Annual Church Meeting, which was the only regular meeting of members laid down in the Constitution. Special meetings could be convened by the Council, or at the request of one fifth (or one hundred, whichever was the less) of the members of the church. Associate Membership was provided for members of other churches temporarily residing in London, and Honorary Membership for church members who had moved away. Such members were entitled to attend all church meetings, but not to vote or to accept nomination for the Church Council. The officers of all church organisations were required to be members of the church, and the Council was empowered to appoint one or more of its own members to the meetings and committees of all such organisations.

The desirability of having a children's church had been suggested at a discussion in the Friday Fellowship in December 1937. Weatherhead's easy way of talking to children had been an appreciated feature of his services in Leeds, where, unusually for that time, he would leave the pulpit and go down to where the children were, to speak to them directly. The City Temple had a graded Sunday school, meeting in the afternoon, which catered for children from the local Holborn area, but there was a need also to provide for the children of church members, most of whom lived well away from the church. The Children's Church was introduced at the beginning of 1939. For the first time the City Temple was providing something for the children of its own people, since it was not a practicable proposition to bring in children from the suburbs to the afternoon Sunday School.

At the request of the B.B.C. Weatherhead broadcast a series of talks on 'The Mystery of Pain' during May and June. These were fully published in *Tidings*, which immediately sold out, so that it was necessary to re-print them in a sixpenny booklet. In June also, Dorothy Wilson, whose one year term as Associate Minister came to an end in September, made a contribution of her own towards keeping the name and controversial nature of the City Temple before the wider public, with a broadcast talk on 'Women and the Ministry'. The Literary Society flourished and had to close its books at its maximum membership of 2,200. The annual meeting of the City Temple's Home of Service reported in June that during the year over 9,000 meals had been provided, holidays arranged for needy families, and clubs for boys and girls run for young people living in sordid and squalid surroundings.

International events continued to affect and overshadow the life of the church. In April Mussolini attacked and occupied Albania. At the service on Easter Sunday evening Weatherhead asked the congregation to stand to signify approval of a telegram which he had sent to the Pope imploring him 'to protest in the name of Christ against the invasion of Albania.' Although no reply was received, Weatherhead felt 'good was done. The electric response of the congregation revealed its feeling on the issue and the Church made its act of witness as, indeed, I think all Churches should do on any major question of morality.'

In May, during the processing of the Compulsory Military Service Bill through Parliament, a member of the Friday Fellowship drew Weatherhead's attention to the fact that the Bill was so worded that an objector could only take a solicitor or trade union official to support him at a tribunal. With memories of the previous war and the harsh treatment of conscientious objectors in mind, Weatherhead persuaded Sidney Berry to join him in sending a letter to the Minister of Labour, Ernest Brown. As a result, the Bill was amended to allow a minister of religion or other friend to accompany a conscientious objector to a tribunal and to speak in his defence.

Weatherhead received an invitation from Sir John Simon, the Chancellor of the Exchequer, who was himself the son of a Congregational minister, to lunch with the Prime Minister in Downing Street. Chamberlain gave them a full account of his trip to Munich, and expounded on the international situation 'with the lucidity one associates with Mr. Chamberlain.' Weatherhead took the opportunity to press once again his belief that the common people of Germany had no grievance against the ordinary folk of Britain. He reported to *Tidings* (June 1939)

> I asked the Prime Minister whether he did not think it possible to open up other channels besides those opened up by diplomatic relationship. You can imagine how I felt when Mr. Chamberlain said: "What Mr. Weatherhead has said is exactly my own opinion. . . . We are being driven to this measure, not by any hostility towards or from the German people, but solely on account of the Government of that country. . . . I shall strive for peace as long as I possibly can, and even if Government negotiations broke down I should realise how many of the German people really desired to live in peace with us." [p.207]

By this time Weatherhead had ceased to have any illusions about the nature of Hitler's regime. In May he produced an article as a special supplement to *Tidings*, headed 'For Such a Time as This.' In it he sought to explain Nazism on the basis of Hitler's personal psychology. He considered that the Nazi movement was the extension of a diseased personality, and that the source of all that was deplorable and contemptible in Nazism was at least as much pathological as it was crudely and brutally political. In another article for the *Methodist Recorder* in June, headed, 'To a Young Man Liable for Military Service', he set out the growing list of Hitler's brutal acts, and, recognising that there was now little possibility left for peaceful negotiation, he stressed the necessity of restraining evil, even if this meant war.

Hitler's troops invaded Poland on 1 September, and on Sunday, 3 September, Neville Chamberlain declared that the nation was at war with Germany. The City Temple congregation listened to the broadcast from a radio receiver fixed in the pulpit. Twenty minutes later, the first air-raid siren sounded. Weatherhead immediately directed the congregation to the quickest and safest way to reach the hall below the church. Then, turning to the choir, he said, 'You are in uniform and are on duty. You will go on singing hymns until the church has been vacated and you will then follow the congregation.' In spite of the interruption, the service continued in the hall.

1. *City Temple Tidings,* Vol. XVI. No.192. November 1938. p.341.
2. K. Weatherhead, *Leslie Weatherhead, A Personal Portrait* (H&S), p.115f.
3. *City Temple Tidings,* December 1938, p.25.
4. *City Temple Tidings,* January 1939, p.67f.
5. *City Temple Tidings,* June 1939, p.206.

12. The Impact of War

*'it is not sound to have such a superior ethic that it saves you
from assisting your country in her greatest need, that is, if she
is to remain your country, and the ties which bind you to
her are really precious.'*

Although that first air-raid warning of the war turned out to have been a false alarm, and it was to be some months before the serious raids began, the war had an immediate effect on the life of the city and of the church. Weatherhead was at once offered a chaplaincy in the R.A.F., but this he declined, feeling that he must stay with his congregation. The introduction of the blackout meant that the time of the evening service had to be changed from 7.0 p.m. to 4.0 p.m. *The Times*, which conducted a survey of the city churches on the Sunday following the outbreak of war, reported that the City Temple congregation that day was 1,200 in the morning and 1,500 in the afternoon. Weatherhead thought that this estimate was on the high side and was concerned that it marked a serious drop in numbers which had previously been over 2,000. He was worried over the financial loss involved, especially as the church was so near to clearing its deficit. In his October letter he assured those who were staying away that there was a fine shelter in Shoe Lane only a few yards from the church, and that the City Temple basement was well below pavement level, and therefore reasonably safe.

His sermon on the morning of 10 September was headed 'The Christian Dilemma'. In it he asked what the church should do now that 'evil unprecedented, horror immeasurable, have been released into the world.' He said that the church must not enter into the political arena 'and dilate on what diplomatic moves might have been made to avert war. Let us leave being wise after the event to others.' Nor should they indulge in diatribes against Hitler and his satellites, which would only stir up bitterness and the desire for revenge. He repeated his assertion that pacifism and war were both wrong. He was strongly opposed to narrow nationalism, but

> I am sure that logically, and indeed spiritually, it is not sound to have such a superior ethic that it saves you from assisting your country in her greatest need, that is, if she is to remain your country, and if the ties which bind you to her are really precious.

He described England and France as 'the world's policemen' who were seeking to 'arrest the cruel bully' who might end the independence of the free nations of Europe and train their children 'in the doctrines of godless tyranny.'

Yet, even after war had been declared, he still clung to the hope that a conference might be called which could solve the conflict by peaceful means. During the early period of the 'phoney war', when little seemed to be happening, others too shared his belief that this might still be a possibility. A conference of Free Church ministers which he attended sent a declaration to the Prime Minister which, while it recognised the necessity of redressing the wrongs inflicted on Poland and Czechoslovakia, expressed the hope that an international conference

Leslie Weatherhead, 1940

might be convened which would 'do away with the recurrent fear of aggression and war . . . and may lay firmly the foundations of a new international order on a federal basis.' He was encouraged when *The Times* of 23 October reported a speech by Lloyd George which presented a similar argument. If war was necessary, Weatherhead felt, 'then the Church should be the last to admit it and the first to accept the better way of the council table.'

In October, the S.C.M. Press produced a book of the sermons he had preached since arriving at the City Temple, under the title *The Eternal Voice*. The book included a Bible reading and a prayer with each sermon, and a questionary at the back to facilitate use in discussion groups and class meetings. This was followed in December by *Thinking aloud in Wartime*, in which he gathered together the ideas on peace and war which he had been expressing over several years and set them in the perspective of the war now begun. In this he continued to argue for the holding of a peace conference, and pleaded that instead of bitterness there should be an attempt to 'understand the enemy'. The book immediately sold out, went into several reprints throughout 1940, and continued to be reprinted throughout the war.

The tercentenary of the City Temple fell in 1940. The planned celebrations were clouded by the uncertainties of the war, yet, during the first months of 1940, as far as the civilian population was concerned, very little seemed to be happening. Families who on the outbreak of war had been evacuated to the country began to trickle back to the cities. The City Temple moved its Sunday evening service back to the later time of 6.0 p.m. The Children's Church, which had been abandoned for safety's sake and as children had been moved away from London, recommenced as they began to return, though still in small numbers. Attendances at church services, which had fallen off at the beginning, began to improve. At the end of 1939 the church membership stood at 722 – an increase of 102 during the year. Increasing business demands caused the resignation of the Church Secretary, Alexander Miller, and J.H.J. Dewey, whose family had been associated with the City Temple since the days of Joseph Parker, was appointed in his place. Weatherhead preached a series of sermons on 'Is it Courage We Need?' which were published as a small book. During the bitter winter of 1940 the weather was apparently more of a worry than the war. In his March minister's letter, Weatherhead wrote:

> Probably no-one has ever endured worse weather in England. . . . Sunday after Sunday I thought to myself, "Few will venture out today, and who can blame them?" But out you came in amazing numbers. . . . It almost seems as if the joyous old days will return, if only Hitler will leave us alone.

The 'phoney war' came to a sudden end on 8 April, when German forces overran Denmark and invaded Norway. British forces were withdrawn from Norway on May 2. Chamberlain's government was coming under increasing criticism for its conduct of the war. Yet, in spite of the critical war situation, both the Prime Minister and Lord Simon, who was now Lord Chancellor, found time to address the Assembly of the Free Church Council from the pulpit of the City Temple on April 16. But Chamberlain's days in office were now numbered. On 10 May he was forced to resign and Winston Churchill became Prime Minister. That same day, Hitler invaded Holland and Belgium. Both were quickly overrun. The Dutch army surrendered on 15 May. The day before, the Germans had broken through into Northern France and by the 19th they reached the sea at Abbeville. The British Army retreated, and on 27 May began to evacuate from the beaches of Dunkirk.

The City Temple's Tercentenary celebrations began on Sunday, 26 May. Dr. John Whale preached at both the morning and evening services on 'Our Puritan Heritage'. The King had asked that 26 May should be observed as a National Day of Prayer. The B.B.C. chose the City Temple to represent the Free Churches, and broadcast the additional special morning service from the church at which Weatherhead preached. *The British Weekly* (30 May 1940) reported:

> An early morning congregation, vast in numbers, had reached the City Temple on Sunday for the service at 9.25 a.m. . . . The Rev. Leslie Weatherhead's sermon on the power of prayer must have carried comfort and hope to listeners everywhere. . . . Mr. Weatherhead spoke in a quiet voice, and did not raise his eyes from his manuscript, but there were moments in which he himself, as he faced the microphone, seemed to draw help and inspiration from his own words. He conveyed his firm belief in the idea that

Neville Chamberlain addressing the Assembly of the Free Church Council from the pulpit of the City Temple, 16 April 1940.

without a shadow of doubt, our cause and the morale of our fighting forces depend on the spiritual power exercised by the people at home. Some things, he emphasised, are contingent on man's doing, and some things are contingent on man's praying. God leaves both to us.

A celebration lunch was held at the Holborn Restaurant the following Wednesday. That afternoon the Lord Mayor and the City Sheriffs attended a special service conducted by Dr. James Black, a former Moderator of the Church of Scotland, and the same evening a Public Thanksgiving Meeting was held, presided over by Viscount Simon. The shadow of events in France affected all the speakers, not least Lord Simon, who as a member of the Government was most aware of the seriousness of the situation. *The Times* (30 April 1940) made the occasion the subject of an Editorial in which it reviewed the history of the church, declaring that 'At such a moment as this the influence of this great Christian power in the City of London at the heart of the Empire has a value beyond reckoning.' For its article, *The Times* relied heavily on a new history of the City Temple written to mark the tercentenary by the church's treasurer, Albert Clare.

The minister's pastoral letter for the July *Tidings* contrasted sharply with those of the preceding months. The fall of France, the desperate evacuation of the British army from Dunkirk and the opportunist entry of Italy into the war on the side of Germany impressed the threatening reality of the war with a new seriousness upon the people at home. Weatherhead wrote: 'Things look black indeed. . . . What can we now say to our people? The question was asked me several times in a week by ministers.' That month, the German air-force launched full-scale bombing raids on South East England, and the Battle of Britain began in earnest.

The first raids produced fewer casualties than expected. Weatherhead happily quoted two verses by the humorist A.P. Herbert, called 'Siren Time':

We waste our sleep in gazing at the blue;
The rumbling bombers blindly drop their loads,
A few men die; – but more have died from 'flu
And many more are killed in crossing roads.

So let us do as we are told to do;
But let no sky-hog make a mug of us.
The Heinkel's not as nasty as the 'flu,
The bomber is less deadly than the bus.

Weatherhead commented, 'The facts bear out the rhyme. . . . So far, Hitler's bombers have been less than half as deadly as the British motor-car! Your chance of escaping a bomb is higher than your chance of escaping a 'bus.'

Within a month, the situation had terribly changed. The Battle of Britain reached its climax on 15 September, but before then, the blitz on the capital had begun. The Germans bombed London every night from 7 September to 2 November, when they switched their attack to the industrial centres in the provinces. The service on Sunday evening, 15 September, was interrupted by a raid, and the congregation was forced to take shelter under the Viaduct, where the service was continued. Weatherhead's pastoral letter for October had a far more sombre note.

Parts of this great city . . . look as if an earthquake had visited it. Between three and four hundred civilians have been killed, and between one and two thousand seriously injured, and thousands rendered homeless. . . . The tubes are filled with people who spend all night in them.

A bomb had fallen within a hundred feet of the church and smashed all the windows on one side of the building. Although so far none of the church members had been killed or injured, some, including the Minister's Assistant, Winifred Barton, had been made homeless. The situation was now so dangerous that the church was having to consider abandoning its services altogether.

October marked the fourth anniversary of Weatherhead's ministry, but it was no month for celebration. In his November minister's letter he described for his members the round of suffering and tragedy his pastoral visiting had now become.

The month of October . . . has been the saddest month of any I have known. . . . A score of our families have been bombed out of their homes. In one afternoon I visited members in three different hospitals. I wonder what Hitler would have said if he could have come with me to visit a girl who in one night, had all her family killed save a sister who was a nurse on night duty and who came home in the morning to find her home a heap of rubble. The girl I visited was trapped by heavy masonry falling on her feet. . . . Today I have been to see a heroine whom we are proud to think of and pray for as one of ourselves. Last Sunday she worshipped with us in the morning. At night she was on duty at an A.R.P. post when an anti-aircraft shell exploded near her and wounded her so terribly that her left arm has been amputated. . . . She greeted me in the ward with a courage and a cheerfulness that made a lump come into my throat. . . . With seven thousand people killed by bombs in one month, and over ten thousand injured, seven hundred of the killed and an equal number of the wounded being children under sixteen, it is a matter of thankfulness that the proportion amongst our own people is not higher.

St. Paul's was damaged in a raid, and the Council of the City Temple sent a message of deepest sympathy 'to our Parish Church round the corner.' The Church Treasurer, Albert Clare, had two narrow escapes when a daylight raider machine-gunned people in the street near his home and a time-bomb partially destroyed his house. Many more church members had lost their homes and the extreme demands of visiting and caring for his congregation in these circumstances inevitably caused Weatherhead considerable strain.

My visiting literally leaves me trembling in every fibre of my body to think of the sorrow and suffering some of you are called upon to bear. One day last week I just felt I could not go on any longer. I just couldn't bear to hear one more story or to see one more sufferer. But I am so very proud of you. No one who has not been continuously in London can know, or will ever know, what the experience has been day after day, night after night. . . . It is one long horror. Every day and night tragedy descends on some home. Some life is desolated. Some heart is broken.

At the request of his publishers, who wanted a follow-up to *Thinking aloud in Wartime*, Weatherhead produced *This is the Victory* for which he rewrote and expanded some of his sermons preached at the City Temple during the previous few months. In his Preface he set out the background of the book by describing the conditions in London during the autumn of that year. His graphic picture of living through the Blitz, with the growing numbers of victims, made a considerable impact when the book was published abroad, and served to arouse sympathy for Britain and especially for the people of London.

The book is in three sections: 'Our Faith', 'Some of Faith's Allies', 'Faith's Forward Look.' It ends with a chapter, 'Faith in the New World', in which Weatherhead looks ahead beyond the end of the war, and considers some suggestions given to him by a member of the City Temple's Friday Fellowship, in response to Weatherhead's asking 'what he would like to see in the new world.' Many of the suggestions reflect the current of ideas which led to the 1942 Beveridge Report and the Welfare State. Weatherhead prints them without comment, but omits the 'political suggestions which I do not think are worth printing'. Among these were the abolition of the House of Lords, a reduction of allowances to the Royal Family and Proportional Representation. With this reservation, he is clearly in sympathy with many of the ideas put forward. These included the abolition of national sovereignty and the setting up of a federal government in Europe, the main duty of which 'would be to break the financial ring that now allows one section of the world to starve while food rots in another in order that the price may be kept up'; the state ownership of all public interests and resources, a five day week, shorter working hours and holidays with pay; decent housing for all, all hospitals to be state financed with free medicine available to all, the school-leaving age to be raised to sixteen, and all children to be taught two languages in addition to their own.

Weatherhead expressed further ideas for social reform in two articles for the *British Weekly*, written at the Editor's request, on 'The New Age', which had been the subject of an Oxford Union debate in which he had been invited to speak. Stating that 'there is literally no hope without God', since without God 'Every programme of social reform breaks down . . . always on the same rock, human selfishness', he said that the Church should 'press the claims of the unemployed' and oppose: the 'private ownership of slum property' and 'of the resources which God meant all His children to share', as well as the 'the dependence of hospitals on charity', the punishment of crime 'without psychological enquiry and treatment', the 'inequality of educational opportunity', blood sports and all capital and corporal punishment.

This is the Victory gained appreciative comments from journals in South Africa and America, which were still far removed from the war; their reviewers were clearly moved by Weatherhead's account of life in London during that terrible year. In America it topped the list of best-selling religious publications. *The Richmond Times* (23 March 1941) described it as 'a book that should be read by every person who feels burdened in "this unmatched hour of man's despair." ' *The Rand Daily Mail* (26 April 1941) declared 'This preacher has faced reality'.

Although, as 1941 began, the raids continued, and in January a building next door to the church was destroyed, it was decided in March to re-start the second Sunday service at 4.0 p.m. and to revive the Fellowship Groups on alternate Saturday afternoons. On 23 February 1941, a message of greetings and support was brought to the church by the Rev. Edgar H.S. Chandler, who had arrived in England as the special representative of the American Section of the World Council of Churches, of the Federal Council of the Churches, and of the General Council of Congregational Churches in the United States. He had been sent to discover what practical help the American churches could give to the British churches which had sustained serious damage and loss of property because of the bombing. He assured the church,

> there is increasingly the realisation in America, of our common aims, our common purpose; a growing resolve to work to give, if need be fight with you, for those values which we count dearer than life itself.

Weatherhead responded by saying,

> We desire our American friends to feel the urgency of the situation, as they undoubtedly would if Canada were in the hands of the Nazis, as we feel it with the Nazi menace, which has already subjugated Austria, Czechoslovakia, Memel, Poland, Norway, Denmark, Holland, Belgium and France, massed in force not a hundred miles from where we are now gathered.

The 'Minister's Notes' for April began with an excited statement: 'THE DEBT ON THE CITY TEMPLE HAS BEEN CLEARED!' An anonymous donor, a member of the church, had proposed to buy off the City Temple's debt, a sum of £1,113.3.1d. For the first time since the outbreak of war in 1914, the church was free of debt. Weatherhead, who had particularly felt the burden of the financial worries of the church which had increased because of the smaller congregations and fewer services brought about by the war, was relieved and delighted by this news, declaring it 'exhilarating and encouraging.' There were other reasons for encouragement also: though the income from offertories, the self-assessment scheme and pew subscriptions were down, the Gift Day Appeal in October had

Remains of the City Temple after its destruction by incendiary bombs on 16th April 1941. The bust of Joseph Parker, upright and still in one piece is in the foreground.

produced £530.16s.11d., nearly double the amount of the previous year. In spite of everything, the church's membership had continued to increase, and now stood at 766. April therefore began happily and optimistically. The evening service was moved once more to the later time of 6.0 p.m.

Then, at 2.30 on the morning of the Thursday after Easter, 16 April, fire from incendiary bombs destroyed the church. Weatherhead got to the building while the fires were still burning. All that remained of the church were the tower, some pillars and the bare walls. The famous great white marble pulpit was a heap of rubble. Although there had been several firewatchers stationed in the building (as there had been since the war started), when the incendiaries fell, the first firewatcher had stumbled on the roof and been injured. By the time he had been taken to safety, the roof had caught fire in three places. Pieces from the burning roof fell on to the wooden pews below, and in a few minutes the whole place was ablaze.

As Weatherhead made his way to the front entrance, he saw a young woman in tears looking through the gates which opened on to the Viaduct. Together they stood and looked at the devastation. In the centre, they saw the bust of Joseph Parker, which had been thrown from its pedestal, but was still upright, still apparently defying the forces of darkness which had destroyed his Temple.

Albert Clare greeted Weatherhead that morning with the words, 'Le City Temple est mort: Vive le City Temple!' A City Temple Reconstruction Fund was immediately opened.

Such was the reputation of this church and its minister that probably the destruction of almost no other church in Britain, apart from one of the great cathedrals, would have been received with such world wide shock and sorrow as the City Temple. The shock was the greater, coming, as it did, so soon after the publication abroad of *This is the Victory*, which had contributed significantly to the awareness of people in America and elsewhere of what Londoners were enduring. The news brought messages of sympathy and regret pouring in from all over Britain and from abroad. Dr. Albert Peel wrote on behalf of the Congregational Union of England and Wales of which he was Chairman, and Sidney Berry sent a personal message, immediately offering the use of the Memorial Hall in Farringdon Street, so that the worship of the church was able to be continued there without a break.

The Dean of Johannesburg, Dr. William N. Palmer, wrote, recalling having attended the City Temple on Armistice Sunday night in 1936, 'when I waited for over an hour in the rain to get in.' He thanked Weatherhead for all his books, saying that 'They are widely read in South Africa. . . . God bless you richly and have you in His care and keeping, for many need your inspiration and witness at this hour.' The President of the Baptist World Alliance sent a message of sympathy 'on behalf of the Baptist Communion throughout the world.' A Canadian minister, David A. MacLennan, of the Timothy Eaton Memorial Church, Toronto, wrote that the news that the City Temple had been destroyed 'was for multitudes of Canadians like receiving news of the death of a dear and honoured friend,' and that the United Church of Canada had launched a campaign to raise funds for British Churches. Dean Lynn Harold Hough wrote from America, 'deeply distressed and profoundly moved' and enclosed a cheque for the rebuilding fund. Dr. H. E. Fosdick also wrote to say that his Riverside Church had taken an Easter offering 'a considerable part of which went to Britain, and I hope some of it went to help the repair of churches that have partly been put out of commission.' John D. Rockefeller Jr. wrote, recalling his visit to the City Temple the day Weatherhead began his ministry there, and expressing his 'deep sorrow' at the destruction of 'one of the great religious centres of England'.

Before the end of April, Weatherhead received a letter from G.H. Salter, the Vicar of the Temple's near neighbour, St. Sepulchre's, at the other end of Holborn Viaduct. The letter, which Weatherhead said, 'has moved us to the very depths', was an invitation, given with the full consent of the Bishop of London, for the City Temple congregation to have the full and unconditional use of this Anglican church for their Sunday Services. Salter said, 'I should wish you to feel as completely at home (if that were possible) in my Church as you would in your own.' Weatherhead considered this was not only a remarkably generous offer but one which expressed 'our essential unity in Christ which may well mark the beginning of a new epoch in the life of all the Churches.' The City Temple Council accepted the offer 'with unanimous and enthusiastic eagerness', and the first service at St. Sepulchre's was arranged for Whitsunday, June 1. Although this was the largest of the City churches, it was still necessary to take up the offer from St. Paul's Cathedral of the loan of six hundred chairs to increase the accommodation.

Before the City Temple congregation could move to its new sanctuary, on May 10, London suffered its worst night of the blitz. The House of Commons was destroyed and many other famous buildings seriously damaged, among them Westminster Abbey, Westminster Hall, Lambeth Palace and the British Museum. One of the younger members of the City Temple Council, Ivor Gundry, was killed while taking fire-watching duty on behalf of someone else. St. Sepulchre's was also hit: all its windows were blown out and its ancient watch-house demolished. Salter however insisted that the planned service should go ahead, and the City Temple moved to the old church which, apart from a few weeks in 1944, was to be its home until the war ended in 1945.

13. St. Sepulchre's

'Not since the earlier days of John Clayton (minister from 1805 to 1845) has
the City Temple had a Minister who to anything like the same
extent has devoted himself to the service of the Church as has done Mr.
Weatherhead, throughout a period with which no comparison exists in
our annals. He has proved himself not only a Minister but also a pastor,
and he certainly knows his people extraordinarily well, individually.'

The City Temple was but one of 15,000 churches of all denominations which
were either seriously damaged or destroyed by the War. By January 1941, 115
churches in the London Congregational Union had been damaged and 20
destroyed, and during the last year of the war six more were hit by flying bombs.
Among the other denominations, 2,600 Methodist Churches were damaged, 800
beyond repair, of which one third were in London. The Baptists had 700 churches
damaged, and 66 totally destroyed, including Spurgeon's Metropolitan
Tabernacle at the Elephant and Castle.

In September, Weatherhead was informed by the Government that a 'very
strong invitation' had come from the Federal Council of Churches in America
and the World Alliance for International Friendship through the Churches, for
him to visit America 'in the interests of British-American understanding'. The
previous month, Winston Churchill had made the first of his visits to President
Roosevelt, desperate to gain American assistance following the German invasion
of Russia in June. The British Government regarded the strengthening of the
relationship between Britain and America as of the greatest importance, and
they were keen for him to accept, but Weatherhead, whose wife had just had a
serious operation, was reluctant to leave the church and his family. The Church
Council felt that as this was a matter of national importance he should go,
though they were still anxious about his health. But when he saw the itinerary
and the programme of speaking engagements, lectures and broadcasts that he
was being asked to undertake, and that he was expected to be away for at least
four months, he realised that his physical health was not robust enough for
such a demanding journey. His medical adviser, Lord Horder, strongly advised
him not to go, and so the visit was cancelled, though it was hoped that he would
make it at a later date. Before another such visit could be arranged, the Japanese
bombed Pearl Harbour, America was brought into the war and the need for such
goodwill visits was gone. The cancellation of the visit was greeted with some
relief by the City Temple, though many ministers and others in America wrote to
express their disappointment at not seeing and hearing him there.

The generosity of the Anglicans in offering St. Sepulchre's had solved the
City Temple's most immediate need of somewhere to worship. The *Star*
newspaper, noting this exceptional act of hospitality, reported 'Two sets of
worshippers, each following a distinctive type of service, are now using St.
Sepulchre's. Cynics recording the more unexpected results of this war will write
that in 1941 even Christians of different sorts were kind to one another.'

There was still the acute problem of finding meeting places for all the Temple's various organisations – essential if the church was to continue to function and to hold its members together. Once again, the Anglicans came to the rescue: the Vicar of Holy Trinity, Kingsway, offered rooms for the use of the Women's Meeting, the Ladies Working Guild, and the Social Circle. St. Bride's Church, Fleet Street, readily offered its schoolroom for the use of the Children's Church. Other organisations were meeting in various parts of London. The London Missionary Society allowed the church to hold the meetings of the Fellowship groups and its periodic 'At Homes' there. Weatherhead continued his private pastoral and psychological interviews with individuals at his own home in Finchley, and at the rooms of Dr. Edith Hudgell, one of the City Temple Clinic staff in Harley Street. In May, 1943, the Congregational Union, to coincide with its annual May Meetings, mounted an exhibition at Westminster Chapel of photographs and relics of bombed churches. This was opened by Lady Louis Mountbatten, and the City Temple was prominently featured. Weatherhead took the opportunity to ask Dr. Martyn Lloyd-Jones, then co-pastor of Westminster Chapel with Dr. Campbell Morgan, if the City Temple might share some of their accommodation. Reporting the result of this conversation in his July Minister's Letter, Weatherhead told the church that Lloyd-Jones

> listened to me with cordial sympathy. . . . But since we talked, the matter has been discussed at Westminster, and we are told that no offer of the temporary use of the premises can be made. We are disappointed but not downhearted and we understand the situation.

The 'situation' was that Weatherhead's psychology and his liberal theology were unacceptable to Lloyd-Jones and the conservative members of Westminster Chapel. Lloyd-Jones' biographer, Iain H. Murray, repeatedly contrasts his preaching with Weatherhead's:

> The standpoint of the two men could hardly be further apart. . . .[1] The younger generation of Free Church Ministers (and a number of the older) were certainly not in favour of any return to the old message. Weatherhead and Soper were united in the conviction that it was "stern views" of God which were the supreme reason for the alienation of the people from Christianity and they were ready to blame "bibliolatry" for the existence of such wrong ideas about God.[2]

In March 1941, The *British Weekly* had printed an article by Weatherhead on 'Why the Church has lost its grip on people'. That same month, Lloyd-Jones was in Edinburgh delivering three addresses at the Free Church College on 'The Tragedy of Modern Man', in which he attacked the ideas of the liberals, saying, 'The more the Church has accommodated its message to suit the palate of the people, the greater has been the decline in attendance at places of worship.' Since Lloyd-Jones, Weatherhead and Soper, with William Sangster, were the best known and most popular Free Church preachers in London during the whole of the war, and, in spite of the destruction of the City Temple, even Hitler's bombs could not deter people from crowding to hear each of them in their respective places of worship, the charge that any of them was responsible for emptying churches seems peculiarly without foundation.

The City Temple congregation settled into worshipping at St. Sepulchre's remarkably quickly, in spite of the strangeness of the surroundings and the practical difficulties involved in adapting to the borrowed building. From the first Sunday morning queues of people gathered to crowd into the church, and several hundred had to be turned away. The loyalty of the congregation was severely tested throughout the following bitterly cold winter, when most of the windows had been blown out by the bombing. Undeterred, people turned up with extra coats and rugs, braving the weather as well as the blitz. Weatherhead particularly appreciated the building's architecture, finding it not only aesthetically pleasing but a positive aid to worship. He told the Annual General Meeting in March, 1942, that he had never enjoyed taking services more.

The City Temple's plans for the reconstruction and modernising of its premises, first initiated by Dr. Norwood, had been set aside when the war started, but the destruction of the church immediately resulted, not just in a revival of these plans, but in a determination to rebuild as quickly as possible, and better than before. A Rebuilding Committee was formed, with the resolution to rebuild on the same site, and as quickly as war-time conditions would permit. Sidney Berry seized an early opportunity to suggest that the new building might also provide the headquarters for the Congregational Union: a proposal that was warmly received by both the church and representatives of the C.U. In October, a letter appeared in *The British Weekly* from Mr. E. Foster Jeffrey, suggesting that the new building should be 'a cathedral for all Free Churchmen rather than a church for the Congregational denomination only.' Weatherhead responded,

this is indeed the vision which we hope to translate into fact. The City Temple has never been noted for its narrow denominationalism. . . . I feel I owe a debt of deep gratitude to Congregationalism for its hospitality and to Methodism for all that it has been to me, and I carry all the officials of the City Temple with me when I say that nothing would please us better than to think that the new City Temple of our dreams may prove to be a Free Church Cathedral and symbol of a United Free Church of England.

The news of the destruction of the Temple had already brought in donations towards re-building from many parts of the world, so that when Albert Clare launched 'An Appeal to Friends of the City Temple Everywhere' in June, he was able to announce that together with the balance of the Reconstruction account, the Rebuilding Fund already stood at nearly £2,000. When Weatherhead visited his former church in Leeds in July, to his delight the Brunswick congregation contributed a further £70. towards the fund. In December, a lavish 48 page illustrated brochure, *Rebuilding the City Temple,* written by Weatherhead and selling for a minimum of a shilling, was produced, giving an account of the church and the bombing, and appealing for funds.

Weatherhead continued to broadcast frequently from St.Sepulchre's as he had from the City Temple. During the week 9 to 14 June he gave the daily morning talks on the 'Lift Up Your Hearts' programme, and then, on 3 August, he returned again to the theme of 'The New Age' with an address on 'The New Order'. (The terms seem to have been interchangeable.) In spite of the immediate demands of the war, there was a widespread and world-wide consensus of concern and opinion on the kind of world society that should be created when the war was over. Even President Roosevelt's speech, delivered in January 1941, proclaiming the 'Four Freedoms' – of speech, of worship, and from fear and want – contributed to this common mood, setting out idealistically the things that the allies wanted to believe they were fighting for, rather than confining itself to condemning the human enemy they were actually fighting against.

There was a feeling, which Weatherhead shared and expressed, that the war was 'a symptom of a widespread disease, and when the symptom is dealt with, the disease, unless we deal with it, will remain.' Many who had served in the previous war felt that there had been a failure, at the end of that conflict, to build a better society and create the conditions which would have secured a lasting peace and prevented such a calamity breaking out again.

Early in the war, a government minister, Lord Macmillan, who was himself a son of the manse, invited church leaders to issue a statement on their attitude to the war. This was published in *The Times* on 21 December 1940 and signed by the Archbishops of Canterbury and York, the Cardinal Archbishop of Westminster, and the Moderator of the recently formed Free Church Federal Council. This was later issued as a separate leaflet headed 'Foundations for Peace: A Christian Basis: Agreement among the Churches.' It said:

> No permanent peace is possible in Europe unless the principles of the Christian religion are made the foundation of national policy and of all social life. This involves regarding all nations as members of one family under the Fatherhood of God.

The statement referred to the 'Five Peace Points' which had been issued by Pope Pius XII, stating the right of all nations to life and independence, and calling for 'mutually agreed organic progressive disarmament, spiritual as well as material,' with 'some juridical institution' to oversee and safeguard these rights. It listed five 'standards by which economic situations and proposals may be tested.' These were: the abolition of extreme inequality in wealth and possessions, equal opportunities for every child to develop their abilities, safeguarding the family as a social unit, restoring sense of divine vocation to a man's daily work, and the recognition of the earth's resources as 'God's gift to the whole human race'. Behind these proposals were statements of principles agreed at an international Conference of Life and Work held in Oxford in 1937 on 'Church, Community and State', and subsequently published that same year in a book, *The Churches Survey their Task*.

Weatherhead justifiably claimed that these things that were now being so widely debated because of the war, he had been interested in and spoken about for years. Once the war had begun, there were many who were articulating a desire to bring about radical changes in the ordering of society as soon as the war was won. Weatherhead expressed the fear that 'post-war weariness' might cause people to slip back into their old attitudes and ways as they had after the previous war in 1918. Giving his own list of 'five things that the church must do to promote, encourage and establish the new order', he repeated much of previous statement by the Church leaders, adding that the Church must win the individual for Christ, expose evil, encourage reform, prepare the public mind to receive reforms, and emphasise the world-scope of the new order. The order of priorities indicates Weatherhead's strong evangelicalism. He held that

> The church's main task . . . is to change the individual. . . . It is better to try to convert a Foreign Secretary than to write to the Prime Minister suggesting what our foreign policy should be. . . . If we really want Christian Government we must put in Christian men and women.[3]

The Church should expose the social evils: the misuse of wealth, the disparity in private possession between rich and poor, the unequal distribution of the earth's resources, the bad social conditions which affect the health and happiness of the poor, and the neglect of religious education. He regarded as 'one of the most terrible evils of the present time' the fact that the country was becoming 'rapidly pagan. . . . Unless this matter is put right, in three generations we shall have gone a long way to producing a pagan country.' The Church should press for essential legislation, since without legislation 'reform remains a dream instead of a fact. . . . People must be made to do that which the community at its best sees as best, or else they will never do it.' In this he agrees with Donald Soper, who held that 'There must be economic and political action before the kingdom of this world could be made into the Kingdom of God.'[4] Weatherhead adds that the Church must work to influence public opinion, which he regarded as about the most powerful force in society, using the openings provided by wireless, publishing and the press as well as the pulpit, to 'prepare the public mind to receive reforms.' Following the statement by the four Church leaders, he says that 'the church must emphasise the world scope of the new order' and that every nation 'must come to regard itself as a member of . . . one great family of nations under the Fatherhood of God.' Only in this way could the enmity between nations, which produced wars, be prevented. 'No new order can be a final solution anywhere unless all men everywhere are included in its scope.' But the role of the church was to provide 'a compass' rather than 'a map', not to draw up the legislation, but 'to hold up the vision of the City of God.'

Weatherhead was encouraged by the response to his broadcast and the correspondence it produced. One Anglican listener wrote, 'I have been waiting for years to hear a clergyman preach that particular sermon, and say those precise things.' This and similar reactions persuaded him to revive his idea for an International Christian Movement which he had first proposed at a meeting in the Albert Hall in 1937. At a meeting of the Fellowship Groups in February, 1942, and in a sermon at St. Sepulchre's the following Sunday, he outlined his hopes and plans for this organisation. He justified his call for such a movement by saying that there was as vital a need to prepare for peace as there had been a need to prepare for war. This must include not merely a consideration of social, economic and other problems, but a recognition of the need to foster the right spirit to bring about the necessary and beneficial changes and to bring Christian insights and values to bear. The aim of this Movement would be to seek friendship and co-operation between Christians of all religious traditions as well as nations, including the many German Christians for whom their faith in Christ was more important than their nationality. The movement would also by-pass denominational differences, and encourage Christians to co-operate together no matter what their differences of belief and practice might be. He was impatient with repeated conferences on Church Union which

> have given the world the impression that we are more concerned with our own particular denominational emphasis than on winning the war against evil. . . . This movement is not hostile to any denominational witness, but it would seek to gather all who love Christ and try to show forth his spirit in a witness undimmed by denominational emphasis, and it would make its members more vital, more spiritually dynamic, more Christ-centred in their own churches. This, not another denomination, is its aim.[5]

The movement would form groups 'to discuss and study social, as well as devotional, problems', though not with the intention of trying to produce a precise social programme, 'a blue-print of a new age.' Rather it would encourage reform 'by giving publicity to its necessity, helping reformers, pressing for legislation, and encouraging Christians who have the qualifications to take up the tasks of Government.'

Weatherhead's vision for this movement extended much wider even than a Christian campaign for a worldwide improvement in social conditions for all. He saw it as spearheading the way towards a vision of Christianity as the 'final religion', transcending all the current denominational forms it had taken, and widening its horizons to include truths and insights from non-Western cultures and other major religions:

> the Christianity that must spread, is something bigger than we in the West have ever even glimpsed. Chinese thought, and that of Africa and India have a positive contribution to make without which a true view of Christ is impossible. . . . He is not the fulfilment of Judaism only but of Hinduism, Mohammedanism, Buddhism, and He is the crown of every religion, fulfilling all that was true in them all.[6]

He invited people to join the movement by signing six pledges which included, a commitment to Jesus Christ, to spending time in Christian meditation, to meeting and co-operating with other Christians in order to extend Christ's kingdom, and to promoting

> that truly international Christianity which is enriched by the thought of other nations and in which Christ is put first, above all the barriers that divide men, whether of race, colour, social position, creed, intellectual ability or wealth.

Weatherhead's 'essay on the Movement' was published as a threepenny pamphlet obtainable at the church bookstall. Response to it was slow, but Weatherhead remarked that he was relieved rather than disheartened, 'I dreaded anything in the nature of a rush.' In fact, he was not the only one thinking along these lines. A member of Parliament, Sir Richard Acland, had issued a similar pamphlet, following a conference of Anglican clergy and laity in Malvern in January, 1941, presided over by William Temple. When Weatherhead preached at the London City church of St. Mary Woolnoth's in May he found that Canon Scott Holland had instituted a movement there he called 'The Christian Legion.' Recognising the similarity of their ideas, Weatherhead suggested that they should explore the possibilities of drawing their two movements together, though he felt that it was still too early in the existence of his own movement for this to be considered.

Weatherhead also considered combining with the 'Commission of the Churches for International Friendship and Social Responsibility' which had been organising 'Religion and Life Weeks' throughout the country. But again he felt that the time was not yet ripe, since the Commission had not published its basis of membership or obligations. However, Weatherhead was ready to concede that if they discovered that the two movements were 'out for the same thing', then they should merge, since there was no point in duplicating movements to unite the Churches in action. He took part in a number of the 'Religion and Life Weeks', speaking at various meetings in different parts of the country, and helped to plan and then addressed a 'Religion and Life' meeting at the Mansion House in the City of London.

In spite of Weatherhead's initial enthusiasm in launching his International Christian Movement, it aroused no great response. The truth was that he was not able to give the time and single-minded attention to organising, publicising and leading it, which it really needed if it were ever to become significant. Over the following months, though he continued to refer from time to time to the 'new order', and repeated his views of what was necessary in order to establish a better society after the war, the scheme faded from view, overtaken by events and more successful enterprises elsewhere. It was not that he was out of tune with the times, or that his plans for the International Christian Movement were impractical or irrelevant. Rather, the opposite was the case. Others in stronger and more influential positions were in different ways pursuing similar goals, and were more effective in establishing organisations and means to bring them about. In November 1942, Sir William Beveridge published his Government-sponsored *Report on Social Insurance and Allied Services,* which became the basis for the post-war Welfare State. Sir Richard Acland had formed his Common Wealth Party in 1942, which succeeded in winning by-elections in April 1943 and January 1944. Acland was one of the key speakers who addressed a crowded Oxford Town Hall meeting in December 1945, on the theme of the involvement of Christians in post-war politics, which resulted in the formation of Christian Action under the leadership of a former R.A.F. chaplain, Canon John Collins. Weatherhead's wider hopes were also pre-empted, and to some extent fulfilled, by the inauguration of the British Council of Churches in 1942, and the improving relationships between churches internationally, which led to the founding of the World Council of Churches in 1948.

Weatherhead was also prevented from applying himself more actively to the cause of his Movement, apart from all the obvious demands of his ministry, by the fact that his health was still causing concern. He had never fully regained the vigour and zest for life he had enjoyed before his breakdown in 1938. The additional pressures and strains of the war were increasingly telling on him, when, during the particularly harsh winter of February, 1942, he was laid low with a severe attack of influenza. Albert Clare, in his report as Secretary and Treasurer to the Annual General Meeting on 19 March 1942, paying tribute to his minister, said

> Not since the earlier days of John Clayton (minister from 1805 to 1845) has the City Temple had a Minister who to anything like the same extent has devoted himself to the service of the Church as has done Mr. Weatherhead, throughout a period with which no comparison exists in our annals. He has proved himself not only a Minister but also a pastor, and he certainly knows his people extraordinarily well, individually.[7]

Such dedication was costly. Sharing daily in the sufferings and griefs of his people he identified with those to whom he ministered, and found it impossible to detach himself from their problems. He suffered from a constant, debilitating migraine, which he described as being like a tight iron band around his skull. He turned for help to J.A. Hadfield, and submitted himself to a sustained psychoanalysis of over 200 hours. This was the first time that Weatherhead had undergone such treatment himself, although by this time he had been a practising psychologist for more than twenty years. Allowing himself to be analysed now relieved some of the pressures from which he was suffering, and gave him a deeper insight into the treatment of his patients. Moreover, as a prolonged analysis was regarded as the essential method of training for Freudian analysts, it also served to answer those of his critics who, in spite of his considerable reputation and his writings on the subject, had refused to take his qualifications as a psychologist seriously.

In time for Lent, 1942, he produced a new book, *Personalities of the Passion*, which was based on a series of Lenten addresses, and sub-titled, 'A Devotional Study of the characters who played a part in the drama of Christ's Passion and Resurrection.' In this Weatherhead combined his experience of Palestine and the Middle East with his psychological knowledge and insights, to describe and explain the key personalities involved in the crucifixion of Christ. His radical and unorthodox conclusions, and especially his interpretation of the character and motives of Judas, whom he described as 'one of the most tragic personalities in history, and one of the most misunderstood', aroused much adverse comment and criticism.

Weatherhead's way of explaining – and even excusing – Judas, indicates an important element in the appeal of his preaching. He made ordinary people feel that whatever they might have done, however ashamed and worthless they felt themselves to be, there was still some good in them, because there was something of God in them. To use the American phrase, he encouraged them to 'feel good about themselves.' One member of his congregation (Mrs. Keith Rankine) used to say jokingly, but with justification, 'He makes you feel that you are really rather nice and that God is really very very nice.' In *Jesus and Ourselves* (1930) he heads a chapter, 'Jesus's Concern for Our Self-Respect', citing the stories of the woman taken in adultery, the prostitute in the house of Simon the Pharisee, and Zaccheus, to argue that Jesus always recognised the good in people, and would 'stop at nothing to give a man back his self-respect', which Weatherhead defines as 'belief in one's own worth – worth to God and worth to man.' When the disgraced cabinet minister, John Profumo, was forced out of office in 1963, Weatherhead publicly spoke up for him from the pulpit of City Temple, without condoning or excusing his adultery, but praising him for his outstanding social work in the East End of London through the Toynbee Hall Settlement.

The reviews of *Personalities of the Passion* were generally favourable, most finding it speaking to the contemporary war situation. It attracted such comments as that of the *Lincoln and Stanford Mercury* 'Mr. Weatherhead has a genius for investing familiar themes with a new and thrilling interest. These character studies bring out the relevance of the Gospel for this dark hour.' It was warmly received by American papers. *The Christian Science Monitor* (20 March 1943) said that

Out of his wide experience and a deeply spiritual outlook, he has written of the Easter event in a manner so tender, so understanding, as to bring to each reader a clearer concept of the inner meanings of that most significant week.

During Weatherhead's vacation, from 26 July to 13 September, the ministry of the church was supplied by an old friend from America, Dean Lynn Harold Hough, of the Drew Theological Seminary, Madison, New Jersey, who had been a regular summer visitor since he first preached at the City Temple as an American army chaplain in 1918. This visit was the outcome of a request from the Federal

Council of Churches in America to the State Department in Washington. Urging that he should be granted special travel facilities, they said,

America could have no finer representative in England than Dean Hough. The City Temple is such a prominent centre of Christian life and thought in England that the opportunity which such a visit would offer is really unrivalled. His mission is so important that we are confident that there will be no difficulty in securing transportation on the Atlantic Clipper.[8]

The State Department responded by finding Hough a seat in the Flying Ace service. He was given a very warm welcome on his arrival at the City Temple, and delighted both Weatherhead and the Treasurer, Albert Clare, by insisting on donating the whole of his summer fees of 100 guineas to the church's Rebuilding Fund.

1. Iain H. Murray: *The Fight of Faith 1939-1981* (Banner of Truth Trust 1990) p.22.
2. *ibid.,* p.61.
3. *City Temple Tidings* September 1941, p.202.
4. *op. cit.,* p.108.
5. *City Temple Tidings* April 1942, p.55.
6. *ibid.,* p.60.
7. *ibid.,* p.64.
8. *City Temple Tidings* August 1942, p.133.

14. On Being a Minister

He stressed first 'the absolute necessity of devotional discipline', which he
said was of such importance that 'the value of all the other work you will ever
be called upon to do depends upon its reality and its sincerity.'

To mark the beginning of Weatherhead's seventh year as minister of the City
Temple, in October, 1942, Albert Clare asked him to write an account of his work
as minister of the church for *Tidings*. Clare probably expected a description of
activities which indicated the status of the church and its minister: lunching at
Downing Street, attending the royal garden party, the broadcasts, speaking and
lecturing at important gatherings throughout the country and abroad. Instead
Weatherhead wrote a personal account of the burdens and pressures, and gave
an insight into his understanding of the ministry, which he described as 'one of
the most fascinating and absorbing jobs in the world.'

His approach is essentially pastoral. He puts 'a love for men and women . . .
enough to want to help them', as the most important qualification, before
academic education, psychological or pastoral training or business efficiency.
He tells frankly of the demands, difficulties, frustrations and disappointments
during his six years at the church. He describes the circumstances which led to
his breakdown in 1938, and the sense of failure, shame and humiliation this
produced in him.

Dr. William Kyle, the founder and Director of the Westminster Pastoral
Foundation, wrote of Weatherhead (the *Methodist Recorder* 8 January 1976):
'He had a capacity lacking in many apparently great people – he was able to
trust some of his friends with the innermost depths of his thoughts and emotions.'
Weatherhead's sermons and particularly his monthly 'Minister's Notes'
frequently contained the kind of personal information which most other ministers
would consider too revealing of themselves to include, and is usual only in
correspondence between friends who know and trust each other very well. This
was partly due to his deliberate policy of showing his own human weakness,
'letting people see your feet of clay', as he put it. He sought to counteract the
desire of many in his admiring congregations to put him on an impossible pedestal.
It also added to his appeal, since it indicated that he regarded his church members
as being among his personal friends whom he could trust with his own feelings
and worries. He would write also to complete strangers in the same intimate and
friendly way. It was part of his attraction and charm that he seemed to lack much
of the personal reserve about himself in talking to others which most people
have.

Weatherhead seized the opportunity to express his feelings about 'the
nightmare that the work of the City Temple Minister can become.' He said that
he 'made a great mistake' when he first came, by ignoring advice to 'regard the
Temple as a preaching centre' and instead making it his ambition to build up the
living church in a closer fellowship. After the strain of meeting the demands of
the pulpit, as the first priority, 'the great strain comes in the sorrows and difficulties

of individuals.' Arguing that 'Christ would never turn anyone away' he had tried to help everyone who sought his aid, including 'perfect strangers . . . some even from overseas.' The afternoons spent in psychological interviews he found drained him emotionally, nervously and spiritually. He added to this strain by attempting to open all his own letters, which during 1937 were arriving at the rate of a hundred a day. He felt he must treat them with the absolute confidentiality of the confessional and keep all their intimate personal details to himself. He had kept up his preaching and lecturing 'at least once or twice a week in other parts of the country' as well as writing weekly articles for the *Methodist Recorder*, the London *Star* and the Yorkshire papers.' Thus it came to pass in 1938 that I was living a mad life.'

He paid tribute to the way much of the administration of the City Temple was shouldered by Albert Clare, and to the help he received from his Pastoral Assistant, Winifred Barton, and Winifred Haddon, who had left an important government post in the Treasury to become his personal secretary in June 1941. He commented that an Anglican church with a comparable congregation would probably have several curates. This was an old cry from City Temple ministers.

In October 1943, he gave the ordination charge in St. Sepulchre's to one of his own proteges, Ronald Ward, a member of the City Temple, who, after training at New College, had been appointed as a chaplain to the forces. In this address, Weatherhead further revealed his idea of the ministry. He stressed first 'the absolute necessity of devotional discipline', which he said was of such importance that 'the value of all the other work you will ever be called upon to do depends upon its reality and its sincerity.'

The daily discipline of time spent in prayer before the day began was for Weatherhead the essential preparation enabling him to meet the considerable demands of his day. But in 'devotional discipline' he also included the strict and efficient use of time and 'being busy with important things.' He warned about being careless of one's physical health, speaking from the lessons of his own experience. Yet the minister, he said, 'must have a head for business', able to understand the financial affairs of the church, since he must spend time in raising money. He must keep in touch with the civic affairs of the town where he works, and 'be awake to local evils and sympathetic with the good work being done'. Additionally 'he ought to be a trained psychologist' and also at home with child-psychology, 'for his work in the Sunday School and amongst Boy Scouts and Girl Guides makes this essential.' He should be 'well up in all movements for social improvement, understand the philosophy of Karl Marx and the details of the Beveridge Plan and the history of every movement in between.' He must be widely read: not only must the latest works of theology be mastered as they are published, but 'Astronomy and biology, essays, biography, and poetry must not be missed.' He should also be up on the latest novel, since 'How can a minister understand his people if he doesn't read what they read?' In addition, he must be a good organizer, efficient 'in running fellowship groups, boys' and girls' clubs, institutions, and guilds.' 'No young man should enter the ministry who is not a good open-air preacher. It is useful if he can play the piano!'

This list of qualifications and requirements is so daunting that it was no doubt partly tongue-in cheek, but it must also be said that Weatherhead did in fact fulfil them all himself – including playing the piano – and was simply passing on his own experience of the ministry as he himself practised it. He warned about the impossibility of fulfilling everyone's expectations, and therefore being prepared for criticism, 'for it will surely come, whatever you do.' With evident personal feeling, he talked about being criticised for being a 'popular preacher', though 'an unpopular preacher is criticised even more'.

In April 1934, Weatherhead had produced an article for the *Leeds Mercury* on 'The Minister of the Future.' In this he recognised that social changes had affected church attendance and the status and role of the minister. He anticipated the end of the traditional Sunday of 'two stereotyped services of hymns and prayers and lessons and sermons' and suggested instead that one of these should be scrapped in favour of group discussions 'of vital questions related to both religion and life'. He speculated on the different kinds of specialised ministries that he wished he could have in his own church, in addition to the two full-time helpers he already had (a deaconess and a personal secretary), picturing a kind of group ministry which would share the tasks of visiting, preaching and youth work. He included 'a trained psychologist who had specialised in child-psychology who would take in hand all my Sunday-school work'. Most of the article was devoted to arguing the case for the minister of the future being trained in 'religious psychology' sufficiently to recognise neurotic symptoms before a victim 'reaches a condition in which it will take an analyst eighteen months to cure him.'

In October 1966, the fiftieth anniversary of his ordination, he was invited to give a lecture on this topic at the Selly Oak Colleges, Birmingham, *On Being a Minister*. The comparative calm of retirement had by then replaced the sense of strain evident in the wartime years; he was no longer pre-occupied with the personal burdens and pressures he had felt then, but his understanding of the role of the minister had changed very little. His approach was still pastoral and traditional. He divides the lecture into sections which would have been recognised and accepted as the appropriate ones by those who trained and ordained him fifty years before, discussing the 'Call', 'Training', 'In the Study', 'In the Pulpit', 'In the Home', 'In the Vestry', 'The Qualifications of the Minister', and 'the Minister's Reward.' Apart from one reference to 'worker-priests', which he equated with Methodist local preachers, he spoke wholly in terms of the minister as one who is ordained and appointed to serve as preacher and pastor to a particular church and congregation. He did not discuss, and showed little interest in, any other possible models of ministry, or the changing needs of the churches which required different kinds of ministry, both auxiliary and lay, which were then beginning to be seriously debated and introduced. Nor did he consider any changes that might take place in the concept of ministry through the movement to unite the different denominations and the call for the Free Churches 'to take episcopacy into their systems', although he was the President of the Methodist Conference when it began Conversations with the Church of England on the possibility of uniting and had spoken strongly in favour of doing so.

In his lecture he argued that the theological colleges should spend more time on teaching psychology and 'the art of preaching' than on Greek and Hebrew, and less time also on 'a subject like Hinduism.' It might be expected that Weatherhead with his experience in India and the Middle East, as well as his passion for Christian missions, would be in favour of theological students learning about other religions. In 1966, when this lecture was given, the study of other religions as a university subject was just beginning to grow rapidly in popularity, but the full impact of the changing nature of British society into its present multi-cultural, multi-ethnic and multi-religious mix had not yet been felt, and it was still thought that only those who were intending to serve as missionaries abroad needed to know anything about other religions.

Among the necessary qualifications for the ministry, after a love for people and 'a firm conviction that Christ and His message are relevant to to every man's need', Weatherhead added a sense of humour, which he saw as an essential antidote to nervous strain and as preventing a minister taking himself too seriously. Weatherhead possessed a very quick and lively sense of humour, he enjoyed a funny story, and would frequently use one to convey a point in a sermon or deliberately to relax his audience and to recapture their attention. Preaching about the '*Honest to God*' debate during the 'sixties, he came out with:

A equals B and B equals C.
C equals D and D equals E.
Hush, hush, whisper who dares,
The Bishop of Woolwich is saying his prayers!

He believed that humour was a divine gift, and that it had a therapeutic, and also a spiritual value. During the worst days of the war, he would deliberately include humorous anecdotes in his Minister's Notes in the *City Temple Tidings*. His son remembers that once, he leant over the pulpit and said with some urgency, 'If you know a funny story, for God's sake go and tell it to someone.' He would tease those he thought could take it without offence, although sometimes his wit could be sharp. According to a close friend, Binstead Griffiths, who was treasurer of the City Temple for over thirteen years, 'His sheer enthusiasm for and interest in people and their well-being was infectious, but it could be scathing, and often very wittily so, when he thought the need arose: he hated pomposity.'

The November *Tidings* included a sermon on 'The City Temple at Worship', in which he explained his approach and his desire to make the services of the church 'richer and more fruitful.' Free Church worship, he said, 'has a peculiar danger, the danger of slovenliness.' Since there is no set liturgy or particular ritual required, there is a risk of 'disorderliness'. 'Freedom can become licence.' He said,

for years I have laboured, in consultation with others, to make [our services] so beautiful and so satisfying that, whatever may be the mood in which a worshipper enters the church, some part of the service will alter his mood sufficiently to open his being to God.

The concept of beauty was very important to him. He believed with Keats that 'Beauty is truth, truth beauty,' and that God was both and the creator of both. Beauty was therefore of the utmost spiritual value, and one of the most direct and important avenues to God. He held that someone who had 'rested in beauty' would be more dedicated in combating evil. 'You will work the harder to make the world a place where all men can be happy and all things come into harmony with the Eternal Mind.' In his delight in the supreme value of beauty and its effect on human character, he failed to consider those whose characters combined a fine aesthetic appreciation of beautiful things with considerable moral deficiencies, including even extreme cruelty – as became evident when the horrors of Hitler's extermination camps were later exposed. When he was writing, the accounts of brutal guards, after their deadly day's work, going home to their families and listening to Beethoven and Mozart were still to come. But beauty, as a vital element in worship, manifested through the architecture and in the music, mattered a great deal to him.

For Weatherhead the most important element in worship was prayer. He explained the different forms of prayer, from Anglican Collects to the silence of the Quakers', that he felt free to use and included in the services, and his habit of always writing out his own prayers beforehand, rather than praying extemporaneously: a practice he criticised because it tended to be 'expressed in the same phrases Sunday after Sunday, and when it is offered, inevitably part of the energy of the mind is used up in making English sentences.' He discussed intercessory prayer, saying that 'When you pray you are adding your prayers to the mass of prayer going up all over the world, prayer for a righteous, just and lasting peace and for the enduring liberty of all peoples.' He explains his practice of praying for sick individuals by name:

> Prayer can't "cure" any more than the doctor "cures" . . . the doctor opens every door he can for the healing power of God. . . . Prayer does not overcome a divine reluctance to help us. Prayer takes hold of the divine willingness to help us, and co-operates accordingly. . . . We are beginning to learn the immense importance of the mental and spiritual powers within mankind. A buoyant soul, a courageous attitude to life, a belief in recovery, a stronger grasp on health, a radiant hope, are factors of immense importance in recovery. Supposing prayer calls them into being, as I believe it does, and suppose it can do so via the unconscious part of the patient's mind, then the calling into being of such things as hope, courage, optimism, serenity, might well be the deciding factors which determine the recovery of the patient.

Tidings included a sample 'Order of Worship' showing the usual form used at the City Temple. This began with an organ prelude and an introit, and included four hymns, three brief periods for silent fellowship and meditation, a poetry reading, as well as the Bible reading, anthem, prayers, offertory and sermon. This order is very little different from the one he set out as the ideal in his army notebook in 1918, and it is representative of the formal, dignified approach to worship which many Nonconformist churches aspired to then, and which now appears to be more common in the United States than in England. It expresses an approach to worship which emphasises reverence, dignity, and order, and depends on the musical capabilities of the choir and organist, as well as the personality and gifts of the minister, to create the desired atmosphere conducive to worship. It is a concept which depends on an educated middle-class culture, and contrasts with the now current, and less ordered and more casual approach to worship made popular by the charismatic movement, in which short repeated choruses, electric guitars, and free expression predominate.

In November, 1943, Darkin Williams, the editor of *The Quiver* magazine, printed an article criticising church services, in which he said 'There is no fellowship and people do not get to know one another' and that 'The sermon varies between harmless homily and an indefinite essay.' Weatherhead responded by challenging him to attend a service at St. Sepulchre's. Williams accepted the invitation, and wrote a long account of his visit in the February 1944 edition. In this he said that his father had been a member of the City Temple and the choir in Dr. Parker's time, 'and, with church meetings once a year, and congregations gathered from all parts of London – nay, of the world – there was no social fellowship.' Williams described the service in detail, impressed with the packed church, the predominance of young people, the atmosphere of reverence. He was startled by the second reading which was from Oscar Wilde, and full of admiration for the sermon, on 'Jealousy', the first of a series on 'Sickness of the Soul', which he said, fitted 'the lives of one hundred per cent of the congregation.' He ended by saying

> that November article would never have been written if all preachers spoke to men and women as the pastor of the City Temple talks to them. Neither would we have empty pews in our churches.

Saying that 'I did not know there was any corporate fellowship in the City Temple', he accepted Weatherhead's invitation to attend a Friday Fellowship meeting in an Anglican church hall off New Bridge Street. He went on 'a soaking wet day', an air raid started as they gathered and the sound of anti-aircraft guns continued throughout the whole time they met. Yet, Williams reported, the hall was full of people, mostly young, and he 'noticed that Mr. Weatherhead knew his audience, and in almost every case called the girls who spoke by their Christian names.' He conceded Weatherhead's point that there was genuine fellowship at the City Temple but concluded, 'It is up to readers to write and tell me this sort of thing is general in all the churches. Then I will withdraw my November article and apologise handsomely.'

The quality of the services that Weatherhead led at St. Sepulchre's was known and appreciated in other places also. In February, 1944, a hundred and forty American soldiers joined the congregation for a service. This was the result of discussions they had been having with their chaplain in which they too had criticised church services. In answer the chaplain brought them to the City Temple, although it was over fifty miles from where they were stationed.

15. The Final Years of War

'a symbol in stone of the worship of God: a cathedral which is a symbol of what I hope will soon be a fact, the union of all the Nonconformist denominations into a United Free Church of England.'

On 4 December, 1942, *The Times*, in an article headed 'Deliberate Plan for Extermination', made the British public aware for the first time of the extent of the Nazis' systematic persecution of the Jews. This brought an immediate response from William Temple, and the Allies made a joint declaration of condemnation on 17 December. The Foreign Secretary, Anthony Eden, made a speech in Parliament which 'deeply impressed the House of Commons. . . . The whole House stood in silent protest.'

Referring to this in his February pastoral letter, Weatherhead declared that 'though the Government has moved it has not moved far enough or done all it might have done.' In newspaper articles as early as 1933, Weatherhead had spoken out against Hitler's treatment of the Jews, and in October, 1938, the City Temple group of the Fellowship of Reconciliation together with the Youth Council on Jewish and Christian Relationships had entertained Jewish refugees at a 'Hospitality Social'. The contacts made then ensured that the members of the church were aware of the plight of the Jews and had a continuing concern for them. In November, 1938, Weatherhead had interrupted his morning service to condemn Nazi actions. He now criticised Eden for promising only to take action after the war. Stating that 'Of the six million Jews living in occupied Europe at the outbreak of war, between one and two million have been murdered by the Nazis'. He insisted that 'some plan of rescue, by the exchange of Jews for interned Germans, by action on the part of neutrals . . . should be put in hand by the United Nations at once.' He urged the readers of *Tidings* to lobby their Members of Parliament to get something done. He was pleased to report in the following issue that two members of the church had written to their M.P.s enclosing Weatherhead's article, with the result that both Members of Parliament had replied promising that they would see that the matter was speedily raised in the House.

On 21 March a Service of Anglo-American Friendship was held. After a short service at St. Sepulchre's, the congregation processed along Holborn Viaduct led by the band of the Grenadier Guards. Among those sharing in the service, together with Weatherhead and the Vicar of St. Sepulchre's, were the Senior Chaplain to the American Forces in Britain, Dr. Blakeney, and Dr. Daniel Poling, Minister of the Baptist Temple in Philadelphia, who gave the address. The American Ambassador had intended to be present but at the last minute he was required to accompany Anthony Eden to Washington. He was represented instead by an American naval officer. During the service, which was broadcast to America, the flags of Great Britain and the United States were presented and exchanged as 'a reaffirmation of British and American Unity.'[1] In his address, Dr. Poling read messages from President Roosevelt, Lord Halifax and the American Ambassador.

Service of Anglo American Unity, 21st March 1942.

The previous day, the church's Annual General Meeting had heard that church membership had increased by over fifty new members, and now stood at 792. The church was financially in credit, and for the first time since the beginning of the war, entirely free from debt. A resolution was passed allowing ex-members of the Church Council who had served for twenty years and over in the church to attend Council meetings, 'in the capacity of Members Emeritus ... such Councillors would not possess the right to vote on Resolutions submitted.' In February, Weatherhead was delighted to report that a member of the church, Lord Leathers, formerly Mr. Fred Leathers, whom he had received into the church with his family in 1937, and who had become Minister of War Transport in May, 1941, had been made a Companion of Honour. Lord Leathers was responsible for combining the two departments of transport and shipping, and overcoming the considerable difficulties caused through having four separate and rival railway systems, by building new marshalling yards and linking lines enabling through trains to travel freely across the different systems.

In 1943, the tide of the war was at last beginning to turn. Following the victory at El Alamein in November 1942, the Germans and Italians had been driven out of Africa, and by the summer of 1943 the vital battle against the U boats in the Atlantic had also been won. Italy had been invaded and finally surrendered on September 7. There was a general lifting of spirits at home which Weatherhead shared, although he warned in his October letter that there was still a hard road ahead, and much grim fighting still to be done. He urged his people to make sure of their spiritual resources, which would be needed as greatly as ever.

October marked not only the completion of Weatherhead's seventh year at the City Temple, but also his fiftieth birthday. On 10 October, his anniversary Sunday, he preached on 'The City Temple of Tomorrow', sharing with the congregation his vision for the future of the church. He wanted the building, he said,

> to be a symbol in stone of the worship of God: a cathedral which is a symbol of what I hope will soon be a fact, the union of all the Nonconformist denominations into a United Free Church of England. . . . It must be the kind of building that compels worship. By its very architecture it must induce that sense of numinous awe which is one of the means through which the august presence of God is mediated to men and women.

Instead of a large central pulpit he wanted the pulpit moved to one side, and the central focal point to be a holy table with a large crucifix either on it or above it, a stained glass window, and an open Bible on the table. He wanted the building to be always open, day and night, with a rest room providing refreshments, and a 'very beautiful children's church' which he hoped someone would donate, where the children could share in a service 'which perfectly meets their need and in which they take a definite part.' He anticipates that the church's dozen organisations would return to their pre-war strength, and would need accommodation, and he wanted the Literary Society to have a Christian education role, 'to offer serious lectures on theology, economics and psychology'. The demands on the Psychological Clinic were such that there was a need for double the number of doctors that staffed it before the war. There must also be accommodation for a 'choir four times as big and as fine in spirit' and also an orchestra 'so that the great musical compositions can be more adequately offered to those who, like myself, find so much inspiration in the ministry of sacred music.' He criticises the kind of church youth clubs which offer billiards, whist drives, drama and dances but 'which are no part of the living organism of the church. . . . If young people only want to enjoy themselves on church premises we are not interested.' He wanted 'a ministerial colleague who is a specialist in young people's work' and a 'Hospitality Club, so that when lonely people come to church on Sunday morning I can tell them that Mr. and Mrs. Jones are expecting them for lunch.'

The picture is of a new City Temple, closer in style – and with a crucifix – to a traditional Anglican or Roman Catholic church, but continuing, though with more resources and greater involvement of members of the church, the same activities and concerns that it had before the war. Weatherhead does not anticipate any postwar changes in social needs, conditions and attitudes that would seriously affect and alter the role of the inner city church. His continuing concern is with the lonely and needy individual, friendless and searching for warmth and meaning in the city. 'We have something to offer that can end their loneliness, lighten their burdens and transform their lives.'

When the new City Temple was eventually opened, in 1958, the pulpit was to one side, but was so unusual that it continued to be a dominant feature in the sanctuary. There was a Holy Table, on which the Bible was placed, standing within the apse, but this was so heavy and cumbersome that it was not practical to use for the Communion, and another table was placed in front of it whenever the sacrament was celebrated. Weatherhead got his stained glass window, but instead of a crucifix there was a beautifully shaped cross, lit from behind, which though aesthetically pleasing, was nothing like the rugged representation of the crucifixion which he had in mind. There were, however, purpose-built interview rooms for the Clinic's doctors to use, and better accommodation for the organisations, which continued to flourish, so that by the very end of Weatherhead's ministry, it seemed that most of his hopes for the City Temple had been achieved.

In December 1943 a new book of his sermons was published, *In Quest of A Kingdom*, a title which indicates the influence of the Fellowship of the Kingdom. The book included much of his thinking on the post-war 'New Age.' It was dedicated to the Vicar of St.Sepulchre's, George Salter, and was 'an attempt to help the reader understand what Jesus meant by the phrase "the kingdom of heaven", or "the kingdom of God", and more importantly, to enter it.'

There was a remarkable consensus of opinion among the religious papers, including *The Christian World, The Expository Times* and the *British Weekly*, that this was 'the best thing he has yet given us', though the critic in The *Daily Sketch* (23 December 1943) took him to task for saying that 'He believes most fervently in Hell Fire – I do not share that belief. . . . I find the statement that Hell Fire is "one of the results of love" paradoxical and unacceptable.' Two things in particular appealed to the reviewers. The first was his concern for the end of the war. The *Birmingham Post* (1 January 1944) quoted approvingly Weatherhead's warning against repeating the mistakes that followed the ending of the previous war, when

> the whole nation was exhausted, spiritually, emotionally, physically, financially, and we sat back and let things happen through sheer inertia. . . .
> We were so relieved that the long strain of war was at an end that we did not realise the moment of victory was the moment of a new beginning of opportunities that had never come before.

The other was his expository skill in explaining the parables of Jesus. Said the *British Weekly*, 'Mr. Weatherhead, who has himself the gift of telling stories, has been extraordinarily successful in his exposition', while the *Expository Times* (June 1944) declared, 'these sermons are examples of the finest evangelical preaching. . . . Psychology, though a useful handmaiden, is no longer mistress of the writer's thought.' John Sutherland Bonnell, of the Fifth Avenue Presbyterian Church, New York, reviewing the book for the American magazine, *Religion in Life*, decided that it was 'not a work of scholarship such as the studies of A.B. Bruce, Buttrick and others who have written standard books in this field', and that the style was 'reminiscent of the devotional literature of last century'. Even so he found it 'stimulating, informative and replete with inspiration for minister and layman alike.'

On 9 February, the Bishop of Chichester, George Bell, spoke out in the House of Lords against the policy of obliteration bombing raids on German cities. Commenting on Bell's speech in the April *Tidings* Weatherhead felt that Bell's 'brave speech . . . ought not to be passed over in silence.' He praised Bell's 'great sincerity and courage', and his recalling 'the danger of sinking all moral questions in our desire to crush the enemy.' But while agreeing with Bell that it was wrong to bomb civilian targets as retaliation for the German's bombing of cities -'since when was it our policy to do what they have done?' – yet, he could not totally agree with Bell, since 'if the measures adopted shorten the war, and while destroying many lives, save the lives of yet more of our own men; if this dreadful severity is in the end the truest mercy, then given war, it seems justifiable.' He accepted the official Government claim that, for example, 'the bombing of Hamburg meant the loss of four hundred million man hours of work in the ensuing three months', stating that 'if this be true the bombing could be justified as a military measure.'

Weatherhead's argument in support of the bombing campaign is the same as that later used to justify the dropping of the atomic bombs on Hiroshima and Nagasaki. He did recognise that along with the rest of the population, he was in the hands of the press and the statements of the military for any information concerning the effectiveness of the bombing. Bell, on the other hand, 'was regularly better informed than his opponents and his sights were higher.'[2]

That spring London was again under attack from renewed night-time raids. Coming so late in the war, when the hope of victory was strongly in the air, this new blitz had a more serious effect on morale than that of 1940, as Weatherhead realized: 'war-strain borne for five winters doesn't equip us for these midnight raids. We were fresher in 1940.' His health was again causing anxiety and he was advised by his doctor to take his holiday early. His old enemy, insomnia, had returned and he was suffering from nervous exhaustion. In spite of this, he felt able to tell the A.G.M. in March, 'it's a happy Church. I don't know a happier . . . the fellowship of the Church is as healthy as I have ever known it in the eight years of my ministry.'

The long-awaited Allied invasion of the continent on 6 June brought an excited lift of spirits to war-weary Britain, but on 13 June the first of Hitler's flying bombs fell on London. In July St. Sepulchre's was seriously damaged and once again the City Temple was temporarily homeless. For the first time since the war began, Weatherhead openly questioned whether it was wise to continue to meet for worship.

> In the three hundred years of the life of the City Temple, it is safe to say that services have never been held under such conditions . . . we can find no building with a safe shelter wherein to hold our services . . . it becomes a matter of serious concern whether the lives of the people should be risked by holding the services at all.

The services were continued, at the Polytechnic Hall in Regent Street, but week-night organizations were suspended. In his autumn Gift Day Appeal Weatherhead wrote:

> It is little wonder that our congregations went down in number and in size. Those who attended the services ran a grave risk of injury or even death, and any strangers willing to take the risk of worshipping with us found it difficult to discover just where we were on any particular Sunday. On one Sunday, indeed, our collection totalled £4.

The flying bomb menace lasted for some 80 days, but by August, 80 per cent of them were being destroyed. On 7 September, Duncan Sandys, the minister responsible for the defence of the city, announced that 'The Battle of London is over.' But the very next day, the first V2 rockets fell on London. There was no civilian shelter possible against these weapons which came without warning and caused considerable devastation when they exploded. No defence was found against them and they continued until almost the very end of the war, the last rocket landing on Orpington on 27 March 1945.

Weatherhead had personal worries which added to the strain he was feeling.

In September, his younger son, Kingsley, left Cambridge and entered the navy. His daughter Margaret's school, where she was now head girl, had been bombed five times, and the Weatherhead family home had been damaged three times. Dixon, his elder son, was a medical student at St. Bartholomew's Hospital, almost next door to St. Sepulchre's.

St. Sepulchre's was sufficiently repaired for Weatherhead to be able to return there in time for the opening of the ninth year of his ministry, when he preached on 'Preparing for Peace.' The rebuilding plans for the new City Temple were going forward, and in October he was able to announce that he had received the complete architect's plans for the new building. He expressed himself delighted

> at the way the architect – whose name I will reveal when the plans are passed – has contrived to fit all the accommodation we want into the space at his disposal and also has caught my vision of the spiritual meaning and significance of the City Temple and enriched it by his own interpretive genius.

He told the Church in December that the architect was Mr. Frederic Lawrence, F.R.I.B.A., of Bournemouth, and explained that when he was lecturing in Bournemouth he had been shown the plans of the new Methodist Punshon Memorial Church and had been so impressed by them that he had asked to meet the architect. Like Weatherhead, Lawrence had an interest in mysticism. In *The Shining Brother*, he had written an account of having a mystical association with St. Francis of Assisi. A psychic medium in 1924, and another in 1932, told him that he would be a builder of churches. Until that time he had built a thousand houses and several municipal buildings but only one church. From 1932 onwards he received mainly commissions for churches, so that, at the time of the writing of his book, he had designed 17 churches, carried out alterations on 15, and was involved in plans for another 18. His book describes his contacts with 17 psychics; among them was Geraldine Cummins, whom he had first met in 1936. Cummins was later in correspondence with Weatherhead and his friend, Raynor Johnson. Although there is no evidence to indicate it, Weatherhead must have been aware of their shared interests. He was naturally drawn to Lawrence, and felt a special harmony with him and his approach to the design for the new sanctuary.

The Church suffered a severe blow on 11 November, with the death of Albert Clare at the age of 62. His illness had caused him to resign in September from his posts as Secretary and Treasurer of the Church, and as the Editor of *Tidings*. Weatherhead missed him and his friendship acutely. No one could have given him more encouragement and whole-hearted support. The fact that Clare had held at the same time three of the most important lay offices in the church had caused Weatherhead serious concern, since he recognised how unwise it was to give one person so much responsibilty. J.H. Dewey was appointed Church Secretary, and the editorship of the magazine was taken over by Miss Alice Head, who was a distinguished professional journalist and Editor of the *Good Housekeeping* magazine. She had been the personal secretary to Oscar Wilde's one-time friend, Lord Alfred Douglas, and was the personal financial representative in Great Britain of the American newspaper magnate, William Randolph Hearst.

A series of five sermons on 'The Will of God', which Weatherhead had preached at the beginning of the year, became the basis of broadcast addresses he gave in October for the B.B.C. 'Lift Up Your Hearts' programme and were subsequently published as a small book. The correspondence resulting from the broadcasts was 'greater than ever before.' The book sold ten thousand copies in the first month and immediately went into a second edition. It was aimed at helping people suffering from the confusions and disasters of war to understand and to trust the will of God as eternally loving, wise and good. Weatherhead opposed the fatalistic belief that everything that happens, including the cruel deaths of children and loved ones in wartime, is the inevitable and inscrutable will of God. Instead, using the crucifixion of Jesus as his example, he distinguished between what God intends and what God allows. He argued that the Cross was not God's intentional – his ideal – will for Jesus, since this must have been that Jesus should succeed in his mission of winning all mankind into the kingdom of God. The Cross was the will of the evil men who resisted Jesus and wanted to destroy him. It was something that God allowed, but did not intend. God's circumstantial will was that Jesus should accept the Cross and not run away from it, since only by facing his death with courage could Jesus show that their was no limit to his love. God's ultimate will was unalterable and could not be defeated by circumstances or any opposition of evil. He was able to take the Cross, which was against his will, and turn it into the supreme instrument of his will in fulfilling his ultimate purpose.

The book received a wide and favourable press coverage, apart, almost exclusively, from the *Church Times* (24 November 1944), whose anonymous reviewer chose to compare the book unfavourably with one published at the same time by C.S. Lewis, *Beyond Personality*, which was much more to his doctrinal taste. After praising Lewis for 'another dazzling exposition of the Catholic faith', which, while containing nothing original, 'is brimful of excellent theology', he dismisses Weatherhead as 'small beer after Mr. Lewis.' The sermons, he says,

> are elementary enough, and will probably do good. But the underlying doctrine is not very profound, and there is a sentimental strain which will repel many readers, even if it is acceptable to those who listened to the sermons.'

Most reviewers recognised the purpose of the book, and those for whom it was intended, and found it particularly helpful. The *Edinburgh Evening News* extracted several quotations from it for its 'Thoughts for Today' column. The American reviewers were impressed, recognising that it was written by a minister who knew at first hand the terrible experiences of war. Dr. James A. Wagner, Minister of St. Peter's Evangelical and Reformed Church, Lancaster, writing for his local journal, the *Lancaster Advertiser* (31 May 1945), said,

> If I should name one pastor who, it seems to me, more than any other has understood and ministered to the mood and need of people in our war-torn times, it would be the Rev. Leslie D. Weatherhead. . . . Here is a pastor who has been living not "in a house by the side of the road" but right down in the road "where the race of men go by."

He urged that the book should be bought and given whenever 'some friend is afflicted with a long illness or a great grief, in circumstances when one's wits and faith are tried to the uttermost, send a copy of this little book instead of one of the stereotyped "sorry you're ill and get well soon" cards.'

The Will of God was published in America by the Abingdon Press, who continue to keep it in print. By the mid-seventies, it had sold over 300,000 copies in the United States alone. Among those who read the book and sent a message of appreciation to the author was Albert Schweitzer, who wrote that he was 'impressed by the simplicity and profundity of his thoughts and the vivid manner with which he treated this subject so full of anguish. . . .'

In February 1945, a new book of sermons, *A Plain Man Looks at The Cross*, was published. This was sub-titled: 'An attempt to explain in simple language for the modern man, the significance of the death of Christ.' Weatherhead said that the sermons which made up the book were the result of

a line of thought which I have hammered out through many years, and goes back to my own dissatisfaction with explanations of the Atonement given to me at College. Not that the explanations were really inadequate or untrue, but the form in which they were stated did not win that kind of response in the mind which is necessary before truth can be of value to personality.

Weatherhead considers that the typical attitude of the ordinary person to the Cross is an indifference and incomprehension due to ignorance of its significance for them and their lives. This lack of comprehension is serious, because 'the Cross of Christ is the clue to both understanding and releasing into our lives that saving power' by which alone the nature of man might be changed and brought into a right and dynamic relationship with God, without which all mankind's plans and hopes for a 'new world order' will go for nothing. He acknowledges the influence of W. Russell Maltby, and the help of Vincent Taylor, then Principal of Wesley College, Headingley, Leeds, whose books Weatherhead had studied, and who had given him his personal advice in the preparation of the book.

Weatherhead argues that to talk about the Cross using the language and metaphors of St. Paul and the Apostles, who, as first-century Jews, used the symbols and thought-forms of their own time, is little help when trying to convey the meaning and unique importance of the Cross to modern individuals. It needs to be expressed in different and more understandable terms. The use of blood symbolism based on Jewish Temple sacrifices is not helpful, but repugnant to the modern mind. He seeks to explain the meaning of the Cross without using the technical language of theology, taking as his starting point the things that Jesus himself said about his Cross and his perception of his mission. From this he says

the eternal Christ, the Son of God, committed Himself to a mighty task of world-wide significance, costly to himself beyond human imagination, and effecting for men a deliverance beyond their power to achieve. [p.9]

He examines the historical theories of the Atonement, together with more modern ones, 'in order to gather, as we pass, the truth in them all.' But he rejects the use of such terms as 'propitiation' since they have so changed their meaning that they now obscure the truth instead of revealing it.

Taking his stand on his belief in the nature of God as the infinitely loving Father, and using his knowledge of human psychology, as well as theology, he rejects all forensic and substitutionary interpretations of the Cross, on the grounds that the guilt of one person cannot be transferred to another, and that to punish an innocent person for the wrongs committed by another is a denial of justice. He says instead that the pre-requisite for understanding the Cross and what was achieved by it is 'the Divine Nature of Christ who gave up His equality with God, and became *what he still is for our sakes*, a human Person while yet remaining divine.' Rejecting the symbolism of blood sacrifice, he adopts instead the image of the Bridegroom, which Jesus Himself used, and interprets the Last Supper as the entering into of an eternal covenant:

> Christ as Bridegroom, betrothed to the human race never to be divorced from it, in order that through His union with it He may at last present mankind as a spotless Bride to God. . . . His death is regarded as His marriage with humanity. The Cross is like the symbol of the wedding ring; the sign of endless devotion. [p.10]

Weatherhead's critics predictably divided between those who recognised and approved of what he was seeking to do, and those who disapproved of him because he did not accept their doctrinal position or conservative biblical theology. The *Yorkshire Evening News* (26 February 1945) praised him, saying

> however profound his theme, he never fails in clarity of thought or simplicity of language. His books like his sermons, have a charm of their own. . . .
> There is no suggestion of New Theology about the book, it is a reasoned and refreshing re-statement of the old.

The *Times Literary Supplement* reviewer found Weatherhead's concern to deal with the language of evangelical religion strange to him, and judged that while the book might be welcomed by those brought up in that tradition, it would not have 'the same appeal to those who have never been brought into contact with these particular traditions.' The *Baptist Times* thought the book might be useful as an aid to devotion, but it could 'scarcely be regarded as a serious contribution to the theology of the Atonement.' The *Christian World* accused him of presenting 'the *fruits* of salvation, but not its *genius*.' It objected to Weatherhead's statement that guilt could not be transferred, saying that this was 'contrary to the experience of a multitude which no man can number . . . in this century and in every century since the day of Christ.' The *Church Times* was, as usual, dismissive, disliking Weatherhead's use of psychology in his interpretation of the Cross, but the American *Churchman* (15 May 1945) took the opposite view, finding the book

> exciting; full of new light and unexpected vistas . . . this book bears out a theory which this reviewer [Joseph H. Titus] has long maintained; that only a person who is soundly grounded in psychology – who understands human motivation – is qualified to interpret theology . . . the science of divine motivation. And of course, few, if any, theologians are as well equipped as the author for this.

The book became another best-seller, going into several editions, including nine reprints and 33,000 copies in the United States, where it remained in print until 1968. Weatherhead himself thought that this book was instrumental in his being awarded an honorary Doctorate of Divinity by Edinburgh University in 1948.

In March, the National Peace Council, of which Weatherhead was a vice-president, launched a national 'Be Kind to the Germans' campaign. This Council had been established in 1908 as a federation of national societies concerned with the promotion of peace and the development of international goodwill and co-operation. Among its member societies were the Student Christian Movement, the Methodist Social Welfare Department, the Free Church Federal Council, and several trade unions and professional associations. The Council sought support for a petition setting out what it believed was necessary for a 'constructive peace.' These included a refusal to blame one nation or group of nations for the war and the ending of military occupation and the transfer of responsibility to 'free German agencies' as early as possible after the end of hostilities. Weatherhead was among a number of well-known people who supported the Council and signed the petition. Other signatories included Professor Harold Laski, Dr. Maude Royden, Dame Sybil Thorndike, Augustus John, the Dean of Canterbury, Cardinal Macrory of Armagh and several members of Parliament.

The war in Europe ended on 8 May. In a repetition of the way he had greeted the Armistice in Basra in 1918, Weatherhead had arranged that the moment the end of the war was declared, St. Sepulchre's would be opened, and as soon as the church was full, a service of thanksgiving would be held for which an order of service had already been printed. 13 May was declared 'Victory Sunday'. Weatherhead preached at both the morning and evening services to packed congregations, with people sitting in the porch and even on the pulpit steps. During the afternoon, at the invitation of the Dean, he joined the procession of clergy at St. Paul's for the National Service of Thanksgiving attended by the King and Queen and the Prime Minister, with members of the cabinet and representatives of every area of national life. Weatherhead was the only non-Anglican minister included in the service, although the leaders of the different denominations had been invited to attend. The fact that the Free Churches were practically excluded yet again from participating in the nation's thanksgiving, as they had been in 1918, after another war in which so many members of their churches had fought, suffered and died, brought letters of protest to *The Times* expressing 'deep disappointment' from the Chairman and the Secretary of the Congregational Union, A.M. Chirgwin and Sidney Berry. The explanation given by the Canon-in-Residence, V.A. Demant – that the service was 'not a national but a State occasion' and therefore only members of the established Church could properly take part – failed to satisfy them, since, as Dr. Chirgwin pointed out, every public reference to the event, including the printed order of service, referred to it as a 'national thanksgiving.'

In an article for the *Sunday Graphic* (6 May 1945) headed 'Let us give thanks today', Weatherhead said that although there was great relief at the war coming to its end , it was not a time for high spirits. 'We have suffered too long and too terribly.' He said he would only celebrate

when the killing is over in the Far East, as well as in Europe, when San Francisco or a subsequent conference reveals a plan which will effectively prevent a gang of psychopathic criminals from turning God's earth into a satanic lunatic asylum.

It is possible to argue that in terms of war service there was nothing exceptional about Weatherhead's wartime ministry. He did not, for example, like W.E. Sangster, take responsibility for the shelter and safety of hundreds of people night after night throughout the war. (Weatherhead had generously described and praised Sangster's great shelter ministry in an article for the *Sunday Graphic* in September, 1941.) Nor did he, like Donald Soper, organise food kitchens for people sheltering in the underground. He took on no extra or specifically war-related role or responsibility. Turning down the offer of a chaplaincy in the R.A.F., he continued to exercise his preaching and pastoral ministry as hundreds of other ministers in London and the rest of wartime Britain were doing, although he attracted attention because of his position, reputation and his writing and broadcasting. What was exceptional was the nature and quality of his preaching and ministry. His preaching, which had always been directed towards his hearers' lives and personal situations, took on a new depth and urgency as he responded to their fears and anxieties, their religious doubts, their uncertainties, their questions about good and evil, faith and belief, which total war inevitably raised.

During the first months of the war he preached frequently on war-related themes, but by no means all of Weatherhead's sermons throughout the war years were on this theme. Even a sermon preached in answer to a soldier's letter asking how to become a Christian makes no mention of the war at all, but speaks instead wholly about Jesus and the power of his transforming friendship. The sermons he selected for publication were the ones he believed were of a more general and lasting application because they did not deal with the specific circumstances of the war during which they were written. In its review of *The Significance of Silence* (1945), written at the beginning of 1946, *The Christian World* said,

> This is preaching with a capital P and perhaps the greatest tribute to Mr. Weatherhead's ministry is to be found in the fact, that now, when the war is over, the themes with which the author deals are seen to be just as relevant as they were at the time of their exposition. Which is to say that Mr. Weatherhead's war-time preaching kept to the great basic, unchanging realities of life. The second observation which springs to the mind of the reviewer is the breadth and depth of Mr. Weatherhead's ministry. It runs all the way and covers all the field that lies between the religious conception of time, and a straight evangelical appeal to the spiritually discouraged.

In an article on 'Preaching in Wartime Britain' written for the Chicago *Christian Century*, (19 May 1943) Weatherhead said that the wartime preaching that was most needed was preaching aimed at what he described as

> this evil cult which has more and more possessed men's minds during the past fifty years – this cult which holds that in man, unaided by any supernatural power, are all the qualities necessary to make a new world.

He regarded the war as the strongest argument against this fallacy – which he labelled 'humanism' – at a time when all the science, wealth and resources of the most advanced nations had not only been unable to prevent the catastrophe, but had hugely contributed to it. Yet, although people were frightened, the war had not affected their thinking deeply enough to make them change their ways and realise their need of God. 'If peace came tomorrow most people would slip back into their old grooves. Indifference to the very name of God.' Preaching about the war he said, was not common, and the kind of jingoistic patriotic preaching which was prevalent during the previous war was 'fortunately as dead as a dodo.' He outlined three kinds of war preaching which met varying needs. First was answering people's questions and bewilderment, second, dealing with their secret worries, and third – but by far the most important – was helping men to see that:

without God life is doomed to disaster, individually and nationally. The necessity of God – that is what we have got to preach . . . individually, socially, industrially, nationally, internationally – this must be, in my view, the line of our wartime preaching. The relevance of religion, Christ's offer of power, the interpretation of religion in terms of daily life in all its phases. [*ibid*]

The conservative evangelical preacher of Westminster Chapel, Dr. Martyn Lloyd-Jones, declared that, when the war broke out, Weatherhead (with Donald Soper) was 'among those who have temporarily lost their message . . . having long used the pulpit as a platform for the giving of political advice to governments.'[3] Lloyd-Jones regarded the war as the stern judgment of God on the sinfulness of mankind. In his preaching he increased his emphasis on judgment and the wrath of God. But what Lloyd-Jones regarded as a temporary loss of their message by Weatherhead and others was, in Weatherhead's case at least, due more to an appalled awareness of the catastrophe that had befallen the world, and, with clear memories of the earlier war, a deep sorrow at the terrible suffering that the war would inevitably bring.

The week after war was declared, Weatherhead preached on 'The Christian Dilemma', in which he tackled the immediate questions he felt needed answering, as well as the attitudes that he insisted should be avoided. He argued, for example, that the Church should not 'enter the political arena and dilate on what diplomatic moves might have been made to avert the war.' Diatribes against Hitler and his satellites should be not be indulged in, remembering that there were many Christians in Germany 'who hate war and long for peace as much as we do.' He sets out his pacificist argument that though war is a terrible evil yet 'We cannot escape, however we may wish to do so, from being implicated in whatever the State may do.' He argues that one's duty to the State means that having taken 'all its benefits' one should be prepared to 'come to its assistance' when it is in danger. It was impossible to reconcile war with Christianity. There was no such thing as a righteous war. 'Our choice once more is between two black evils. . . . If a man is confronted by two evils, one of which he *must* do, he will not be held guilty of personal sin in doing the lesser.' They should not pray for 'victory of arms, but the speedy cessation of the conflict, and the prevailing of righteousness and justice without further bloodshed.' This provoked criticism in *The Christian World* which reported Weatherhead as saying it was not possible to pray about the war. He replied that there were some prayers that should be made, such as for the wounded and dying on both sides, for those who risk their lives and those who mourn and suffer, for German friends, and for the leaders of Germany and other nations as well as our own, but he could not pray

some such prayer as this: "O God, help me to shoot straight, to kill or maim my brother German. . . . Help me to drop my bombs accurately and kill as many as possible of my brothers for whom Christ died. . . . To me that seems blasphemy. . . . The Church lost prestige in 1914 because she talked of "a righteous war." A man who can equate bomb-dropping with the service of Christ would seem to me to have lost his spiritual vision.

Early in 1940 he preached a series of sermons on the nature of courage, subsequently published as *Is It Courage We Need?* (1940) and later preached a series of sermons 'On Our Need of God', in which he makes a distinction between calling on God to bless a human programme and seeking to know what God's will is and concentrating all one's human energies and powers to carry it out:

> The fact that this war has meant for many a spiritual collapse shows that the real "God" we believed in was man. We had so trusted man's ability that when man failed we had no other God to fall back on. . . . Man has dominated the stage. And the result is hell.

Other sermon titles such as 'Is Our Faith Adequate for These Days?' indicate the way he dealt with the down-to-earth questions which went to the heart of people's anxieties, doubts and fears. In November 1940, preaching on 'The Peacemakers', he expressed optimism that the war would be won, but also the concern 'that we should win the peace.' Accusing politicians of selling the peace after the previous war by the terms they imposed, he asked, 'is there enough Christian goodwill about to make a Christian peace?. . . Shall we in one, two or three years time be bursting with Christian charity to treat the Germans as our brothers?' In a sermon on 'Barabbas' in March 1941, he said,

> The thought I want to leave with you is that the *same government which restrained Barabbas crucified Christ* . . . however justifiable it is to resort to violence to restrain international criminals . . . no nation can carry on a war like this without a threat to its own soul. . . . You cannot adopt over a long period the methods necessary to deal with gangsters without threat to the capacity to practise gentleness, humility, forbearance, pity and love. When the war is over a new war will begin as important as this; the inner war to purge our hearts of war's methods and war's effects on our own souls.

One of the last sermons he preached at the City Temple, just before the building was destroyed, raised the question 'God and War: Is God on Our Side?' which he called 'the hardest question of all.' He began by warning his congregation that they might feel definitely hostile to his point of view. He described visiting Germany just before the war, and meeting pastor Bodelschwingh, famous for his work among epileptics. Bodelschwingh was in charge of a great mental hospital at Bethel which held 6,000 inmates. He later became famous for refusing to permit the Nazi authorities to carry out their policy of liquidation of all the insane and mentally deficient at his hospital, saying they would have to kill him first. Such was his reputation throughout Germany for his devoted work among these people that the Nazis gave way. The hospital had been hit by British bombs. Weatherhead said,

> God is only on our side to the extent to which we do His will. . . . God loves Hitler . . . as much as He loves King George, hating the things that Hitler does, wounded in another Calvary by everything that is evil which goes on. . . . He never ceases to love the essential soul of the evildoer.

Quoting Abraham Lincoln as saying, 'It does not matter whether God is on our side; what matters is whether we are on His', Weatherhead said that he refused to 'equate a British victory with God's victory' for 'what are you going to say to a devout Norwegian who equated the victory of his country with that of God and then found Germany over-running his land?'

Preaching at a stage in the war when Germany was winning all the battles, he raised the possibility of a German victory, but said that even this would not be a defeat for God, any more than the Cross was a defeat for God's purposes.

I am not going to be too ready to say God is on our side if you mean that God is a kind of pro-British deity who can only regard all Germans with horror. . . . Do not let us think of God in terms of sides but in terms of a world purpose He is working out, and let us pray that, if it be His will, we may, through His victory, make His Kingdom come nearer, and just leave it there. . . . The only thing that matters is the victory of God throughout the world.

He returned to the theme of God's inevitable victory, no matter what happened in the conflict of arms, soon after the destruction of his church, and it was a constant note in his preaching throughout the war. In July 1940, at almost the worst period of the war, just after the fall of France and the evacuation of Dunkirk, he had written in his Minister's Notes,

God will win, whether we win or lose. . . . If God can do more with a defeated nation that is penitent, than with a victorious nation that is aggressive, we must bow to His way with men, for he has taken it before. . . . God can make the "wrath of men to praise Him," and his glory matters more than either victory or defeat.

In May 1943, he preached on the text, 'Thou Shalt Love Thine Enemy', recognising that it was a difficult and even dangerous theme to take since it might be thought 'likely to undermine the morale of our people.' But, he said, it was sheer cowardice to put this saying of Jesus into cold storage until the war was over, when it might be easier to love the people of hostile nations. 'We shall not fight any better by hating. Hate is an emotion which would disturb cool judgment and blur good motives.' Love cannot mean 'like,' no-one could expect to like the typical Nazi, nor does loving the enemy mean letting him off the proper punishment for his evil actions. Love meant acting 'in a spirit of good-will.' Weatherhead said they must be ready to believe that 'the enemy is not expressing his real self in the foul deeds that he does'; evil teaching had made him accept false ideals, the defeat in 1918 had given him a sense of inferiority and a desire for vengeance. It was necessary to believe that Germany was capable of making 'a contribution to the family of nations which is of immense value.'

Because of his specialist interest in psychology, Weatherhead was frequently labelled as a 'psychological preacher', and dismissed as such by his critics, who suggested that in his preaching psychology took precedence over theology, though a study of his printed sermons shows that his use of psychology was always subservient to the exposition of his chosen religious theme. But, particularly during the war, he drew on his knowledge of psychology to give practical help and advice to his hearers, so that they might be better able to understand their own feelings, fears and reactions to their abnormal circumstances, and better able to cope with them. At the height of the blitz, in the summer of 1941, he preached on the theme of 'Endurance', out of concern for the psychological effects of the continual bombing. Weatherhead's plea was that people should hold on to faith in God:

Endurance is the word for these days, not physical and mental – though I know those are demanded – but that spiritual endurance that hangs on to the thought that Jesus was right about God, that endurance that maintains the inner citadel of the spirit inviolate unto the end.

His psychological insights were not just detached clinical observations, but expressions of his own feelings and reactions to the strains of the war, in which he identified himself closely with his listeners. He explained the exhaustion that comes from the breaking of routine by the exceptional demands and decisions forced by the war, the way anxiety and fear bring fatigue, and cause irritability and depression. More frequently he introduced psychological counselling into his monthly Minister's Notes in the *City Temple Tidings*, which were pastoral letters in a real and practical sense. In August, 1940, he advised those who could to take some sort of holiday, especially for the sake of their children, saying that since an adult's temperament depends on his childhood, they should do their best, in spite of the war, to make children's lives as happy and sanguine as possible, and since children were very sensitive to atmosphere, to avoid passing their feelings of fear on to them. His letter for February 1942, on the nature of 'war-strain,' which he says 'is a strange thing and takes strange forms,' shows the way his psychological advice was always combined with a strong insistence on the importance of faith in God:

> With some extroverts it is largely physical and comes out in rheumatisms or neuralgia or neuritis or headache or indigestion or sciatica or asthma or acidosis. With some introverts it is largely emotional and comes out in tension, worry, temper, tears, tantrums and general "hard-to-get-on-with-ness". It hardly passes anyone by, especially between the ages of forty and sixty. We must guard the fortress of the soul from invasion. We can do this partly by keeping some time of silence each day when we drink in energy and fill up reservoirs of quietude from a contemplation of the timeless things, the eternal values that war cannot touch . . . partly by leaving the responsibility – so long as we have followed His signposts day by day – to Him. For nothing can happen to us that He does not allow, and nothing that he allows can finally defeat his purposes.

Weatherhead did not try to avoid talking about the dark effects of the war on people and sought to help his readers understand and face up to their own feelings, fears and re-actions, believing that only by so doing could they maintain their health of body and mind. At the same time, he clearly identified closely with them, doing the same thing for himself. But always, if psychology provided the analysis, the comfort and encouragement came from faith. Often he shared with his readers some of the sad letters he received, sometimes as many as a hundred a week, especially after a broadcast. One man wrote to him saying that his wife had died in 1938, and then his son of twenty-one was killed in action. The man ended his letter, 'All that I loved has been taken and in my grief I say – "Why should it be me?" All is gone and my life is in ashes.' Commenting on the suffering so many of them described, Weatherhead wrote:

> What a dreadful thing life would be if there were no answer to such agony!. . .
> I don't think I should have the heart to wade through them unless I knew that in the Christian Message there is an answer to the need underlying them all.

During the last months of the war, the random attacks on London by flying bombs and then rockets affected the morale of the population even more than the blitz had done. He recognised the sense of depression which resulted from the delayed victory as the bombs continued to fall. He spoke about the positive things that had come out of the evil of war, which might not otherwise have been gained, and which pointed forward to a better society when peace finally came, mentioning the Education Act, the new concern over national health, and the Beveridge Report, the possibility of 'Full employment in a free society.' In March, 1945, with victory approaching, he spoke more about the 'kind of terms a Christian nation should impose on the Germans', saying,

> The choice is revenge or peace. Peace only follows the restoration of self-respect. . . . European civilization is too sick already to stand much more. . . .
> The Government of the world by Britain, America, Russia and China is a monstrous idea, so proud in its arrogance that it would most certainly ride quickly to a catastrophic fall. Yet another "balance of power" is too risky to be tried again. There is only one other possible way. It is really to try out what has been called a vain dream, but to which practical politics must come speedily, namely, an organized, world-wide federation, a family of nations.

There should be an international police force, 'an international political instrument' taking care of the welfare of smaller nations. Unless this happened, he said, 'we shall be slipping down the perilous slope to world-war number three.'

Towards the end of the war he returned more frequently in his preaching to the Christian hope of life after death, and the possibility of meeting loved ones again in the after life, knowing as he did from his experiences in the previous war, how acutely their loss and suffering were felt by those who had been bereaved, particularly as war ended and the survivors came home. He once more sought to offer comfort through the belief that life continued beyond death, and therefore those who had lost loved ones might eventually be re-united with them.

When the war in Europe finally ended, Weatherhead shared the general joy, but he refused simply to thank God for the victory, saying again that victory was not a sign that God was on the side of the victors. He said that if they had been defeated, he would have told them not to lose their faith in God, and that such a defeat would have been no evidence that God had deserted them. He therefore refused to claim the victory as evidence that God was specially supporting them.

> The rightness of a crusade does not inevitably mean victory for the crusaders. Poland knew this in 1939, and subsequently Czechoslovakia, Belgium, Denmark, Holland and Norway. . . . I am not so eager that we should thank God for this victory, for I should put it down to the sacrifice of our men, and to the help of America and Russia. . . . I am much more eager that we should offer this victory to God, asking that we may know His will as to how we may take next step and use this victory to the highest advantage. If Germany would offer her defeat to God and ask the same question, then God could use both victory and defeat to fulfil His purposes . . . *spiritually* victory is more dangerous than defeat . . . and a comfort we can . . . offer to German Christians, to say that God can use a defeated nation that is penitent . . . more valuably than . . . a conquering nation if it became proud, intolerant and unbrotherly.

Throughout the war Weatherhead continually repeated his belief in the German people, refusing to encourage any campaign of hatred against the German nation as a whole, though aware that this was hard to take for people who night after night were on the receiving end of German bombs. Though, as Wilkinson records, 'In England ordinary people often displayed an extraordinary capacity for forgiving their enemies.'[4] Weatherhead also persisted in saying that Germany was not entirely to blame for the war, insisting that the seeds of this second war had been sown by the harsh terms imposed on the Germans at the end of the First. These, he held, had deprived the Germans of their dignity and self-respect as a nation, and had created an atmosphere of resentment and grievance which brought Hitler to power and which he was able to exploit. He constantly warned against making the same mistake again, and spoke out strongly against the repetition of a policy of 'Germany must pay' when the current war ended. Alan Wilkinson points out that at least from the arrest of Niemoller in 1937, the resistance of some Christians to Hitler had become known throughout the world. 'Thereafter not all Germans could be regarded as Nazis.' But in any case, Weatherhead, through the contacts he made in Germany when he first visited there in 1929, and which he maintained closely from then on, was well aware of Christians in Germany, and had a personal sympathy for them which not all in his congregations would have readily shared. In a series of broadcasts towards the end of 1940, Lord Vansittart, the Government's chief Diplomatic Adviser, had argued that the Germans had always been brutal warmongers. But there were other significant Christians, most notably William Temple, Cyril Garbett the Archbishop of York, and Bishop George Bell, who voiced views similar to Weatherhead.

The dominant theme of Weatherhead's preaching throughout the war was the 'necessity of God'. In every sermon and pastoral letter he stressed his conviction that the war itself was due to the failure to heed the things of God during the years before, and that there could be no prospect of real progress in the future or of a good and lasting peace when the fighting finally stopped, without a return to Christian values and faith, that is until religion once again became a dominant influence in the lives of individuals, societies and nations.

Weatherhead sought to be ruthlessly honest and vigorous in facing up to the realities of the war and its effect on people's lives. He courageously confronted the hard questions, and though one of the oft-repeated criticisms of him is that of sentimentality, there is very little in his war-time sermons and pastoral letters of a maudlin and sentimental nature. His intelligent perception of the important issues and his way of analysing them was sharp and keen, and he placed his ideas about the war, and his views on the policies that he thought should be pursued after the war, always in the context of an insistence on the necessity for a firm and positive faith in God. As a consequence he attracted and held the attention of large congregations, among whom were men and women – such as Lord Stamp, Lord Leathers and Alice Head – of great responsibility, education and high intelligence, with wide knowledge and experience of life. As well as crowds of ordinary people who regularly braved the dangers of the blitz, the flying bombs and the difficulties of the journey to attend the worship he led, which they found was never unrelated to their lives and circumstances, never a mere means of brief escape, but a strengthening and uplifting experience which sustained and upheld them, in faith, courage and hope, though at great cost to himself. Alice Head, writing in January 1941, during the darkest period of the war, spoke for very many when she paid her own tribute to him:

I doubt if there is a single member of the City Temple congregation who has not felt (in common with myself) that the overwhelming burden of ordinary, everyday living simply could not be sustained in these calamitous days without the help, comfort and inspiration of the Rev. Leslie Weatherhead's pulpit message, Sunday by Sunday. On leaving the Church, Thursday and Sunday mornings, I have often had some fellow-worshipper whisper to me, "Well, that has set me up for the week. Now I feel I can go on." A tremendous responsibility rests on Mr. Weatherhead: and how nobly he bears it!

During the long years of war, Weatherhead refused to offer an easy, superficial, cosy and comfortable message which would not have stood up to the harsh experiences of wartime living. He persistently confronted the realities of the present in all their stark horror, without trying to minimise them or pretend they were other than they were. He believed that the only way to help people come to terms with the shocks and strains of war and to survive through them, was by encouraging them to face the truth about their bleak circumstances, however awful, frightening and depressing they might be. At the same time, he always pointed forward to the future, preparing his people during the worst days of the war to face even the possibility of defeat, without loss of courage or faith, persuading them to hold on to the belief that God's good and loving purposes could never be finally overcome. And when the tide had turned towards victory, though the end of the war was still a long way off, he constantly directed their thoughts to the kind of world that might be possible when the war was finally won, embracing the Beveridge Report's plans for a new ordering of society, but repeatedly stressing that this would come to nothing unless there was a new turning to God. Even when his church was destroyed he refused to dwell on the past but spoke instead about his hopes for the future and the fresh opportunities that lay ahead, not only for a new and finer building but for a stronger fellowship, more inspiring worship and greater and more effective means of service.

1. For many years these hung together in the entrance to the rebuilt City Temple.
2. Adrian Hastings: *A History of English Christianity 1920-1990* (SCM, 1991)
3. The Fight of Faith, *op. cit.*, p.21.
4. Dissent or Conform? *op. cit.*, p.278. Wilkinson quotes a bereaved father saying of the German who dropped the fatal bomb, 'He didn't know what he was doing'.

16. The Immediate Post-War Years

'The Church of the future must no longer boggle about organic unity
with other branches of the Christian Church. . . . There must be,
rather, unity in social endeavour. . . . Rather than see, in any one
town, a conference of the Anglican, Congregational, Presbyterian, Methodist,
Baptist, Quaker, Salvationist, and other branches of the
Church, meeting together to discuss theological doctrines, I would
see them engaged in a conference as to how the slums and other
evils which curse their town could be abolished.'

The abrupt ending of the Japanese war in August 1945, through the dropping of
atomic bombs on Hiroshima and Nagasaki, brought peace at last; but introduced
a new and more terrible fear to the world than anything known before. The
massive killing of Japanese civilians showed how far the world had moved from
the first months of the war in 1939, when the use of bombs against civilians was
regarded as the worst of war crimes. Weatherhead was appalled by this new
weapon. He found it impossible to praise the atomic bomb, and regarded the
justification that the war was thereby shortened as 'a specious argument . . . we
have now reached a point where all "decent" warfare is superseded if it ever
existed'. Along with a number of other speakers, including C.E.M. Joad, Vera
Brittain and Victor Gollancz, he addressed a packed meeting at the Westminster
Central Hall on the theme, 'Real Peace This Time!' Successful though the meeting was, he felt depressed by it and doubted that much worthwhile had been
achieved.

He was still writing regular articles for the national press and in February,
1945, took over a weekly column from the Anglican Canon G.H. Elliott in the
Sunday Graphic. In December Epworth brought out a new book of his sermons,
The Significance of Silence. In his Preface he recounts the wartime circumstances
in which the sermons were preached, and describes his church and congregation,
saying that his 'parish' extended 'more than twenty miles in every direction
from the City Temple' and beyond – at one time there were seat-holders who
attended regularly from as far away as Liverpool, Southampton, Birmingham
and Harrogate. He was proud of the fact that the church included members of
the Cabinet, senior civil-servants, peers of the realm, Harley Street doctors,
academics, lawyers and business men, as well as students and nurses, 'clerks,
typists, young business men and women, postmen and policemen.'

The book attracted an unusual amount of attention, largely because of the
extended preface, which the magazine, *Public Opinion*, thought many would
find 'as interesting and inspiring' as the sermons. In the United States the
wartime provenance of the sermons attracted particular interest. The sermons
drew a great deal of favourable comment, even in the usually more unfriendly
publications. *Life of Faith*, while saying that it had little use for Weatherhead,
found this book more acceptable, since 'less dogmatic' than his earlier 'ephemeral
books', discerning a 'sensitive maturity formerly not experienced.' The *Sunday*

School Chronicle had no reservations: 'here is preaching at its best, with length and breadth and depth and height about it. . . . He is undoubtedly one of the prophets to his day and generation.' The *British Weekly* (17 January 1946), looking back nostalgically to the expository style and genius of Joseph Parker, nevertheless stated,

> This is in some respects his most important book, in that he gives himself so intimately and personally to his own big family, the City Temple congregation, whose vicissitudes during the war seem only to have deepened the family spirit. Not only does he point the way to other preachers as to the type of sermons which the world needs today: but to other congregations as to how they should cultivate the family spirit.

It thought that the book marked

> a stage further along the road to a new kind of preaching . . . the form of the sermon is indicative of a new time. He cannot presume on the former knowledge of the Bible and his preaching is more on subjects and on questions. . . . It is personal preaching of the highest quality, the preaching of a man who is in close rapport with his time, so full of spiritually discouraged and seeking souls. . . . His message is Christ-centred and burning.

Some of the English critics deplored the personal and autobiographical element in these sermons as intrusive, but this aspect of Weatherhead's style met with much approval in the American reviews. The Chicago *Christian Century* (1 May 1946) valued the sermons particularly for this: 'We want to feel that the sermon proceeds from the life experience of the preacher, that it is not the result of theoretical day dreaming in the armchair, but that it comes from the preacher's encounter with life.' The Professor of Practical Theology at Drew University, Hazen G. Werner, was impressed, as others were, by what the book revealed of the life of the City Temple, the range of its activities and the strength of its fellowship during the traumatic war years. The book was chosen by the *New York Sun* as its selection for the Religious Book Club.

With the war over, the Anglicans, who understandably wanted to have St. Sepulchre's returned to them, began to exert friendly but firm pressure for the City Temple to vacate the building. A year after the war had ended, a polite but official notice of ejection from St. Sepulchre's was received from the Anglican authorities. Once again, The City Temple congregation needed urgently to find a new home. As a temporary measure, the Friends' Meeting House in Euston generously accommodated them, though this could only be a very short-term arrangement. Weatherhead approached Wesley's Chapel in City Road, very much hoping that a move there might be the answer. But this proved impracticable. The church was not large enough for the City Temple congregation, nor could it be available for more than one service a Sunday. Then, early in 1947, an invitation came from the Presbyterian Church in George Street, Marylebone, which was thankfully accepted. Weatherhead was to minister to his City Temple congregation there longer than anywhere else, and several years longer than he was ever able to at Holborn Viaduct.

The church in George Street, which seated some fifteen hundred people, was similar in design to the old City Temple, with a high central pulpit and a circular gallery running round three sides. The Presbyterian authorities were very generous in the terms of their offer. The minister of Marylebone, Dr. P.B. Hawkridge, had recently left the pastorate, so the Session Clerk, A.C. Adam, wrote to Weatherhead extending the invitation, saying, 'As we are at present without a minister the basis of the arrangement would be that you conduct the services on three Sundays out of four and we be responsible for the fourth.' Some of the members of the church wanted to call their own minister to be appointed on terms of an equal ministry with Weatherhead, with the services shared equally between them, but Weatherhead insisted he could only come on the original terms, and not on terms of equal ministry. The Presbytery readily agreed to this, saying it could not feel justified in agreeing to the appointment of another minister to the Presbyterian congregation at the present time. It proposed instead that a young assistant minister should be appointed who would watch the interests of their congregation.

The City Temple moved to Marylebone, and Weatherhead began his ministry there on Palm Sunday, 30 March 1947. It was some months before the Presbyterians could provide an assistant for him, but eventually a Canadian Presbyterian, W.G. Onions, was appointed for one year, from May, 1948. Weatherhead was greatly relieved by the appointment, saying that the burden of the church was becoming more than he could carry alone.

> The Sunday services leave me so exhausted that I find it hard to recover for the following Sunday, in view of the many interviews, endless letters, the numerous Committees, and the details of our administration which are a perpetual demand. I am sure you will be patient if I withdraw from some things that I have done for years, and let a younger man really share the burden.

The long war years had taken their toll of his nervous and physical resources, and he was suffering from considerable strain. On 18 April he wrote to John Dewey, the Church Secretary,

> I saw the specialist, Dr. Geoffrey Evans, last evening. He gave me an hour and a half's examination and said though there was nothing organically wrong I am worn out. Pulse 54 instead of 72 and blood pressure &c indicating that the reserve of nervous energy is nil. He thought it urgent for me to take three months off. But I am to see him again on April 26th. So I don't propose to do anything or announce anything till then. If I can get over this bad patch without all the public sensation of cancelling engagements I should like to do so but I could see he was concerned. If you care to ring him O.K. but don't advertise it to the world. I'm not dead yet, though I am very exhausted.

He took an early holiday in May, but was back taking both services on 30 May.

From the beginning of 1949, Weatherhead altered the previous arrangement for the services and began to share more of both the conduct of worship and the preaching with his assistant, explaining, 'During the last year I have felt the strain of preparing and preaching two sermons on the same day to such large congregations.' He thereafter limited himself to preaching at both services on one Sunday only each month. Both ministers preached at one service only on the other Sundays, apart from the originally agreed Presbyterian Sunday, when Onions preached at both services. Although he appealed to the congregation to maintain the numbers regardless of who was preaching, and Onions was a very acceptable preacher, inevitably, numbers (and income) dropped whenever Weatherhead was not occupying the pulpit himself.

The life of the church progressed. An Evangelical Team was formed in July, 1945, which travelled to many parts of the country, conducting services and campaigns, often in co-operation with Donald Soper's newly formed Order of Christian Witness. A Junior Council was formed to make it possible for the ideas and enthusiam of younger members of the church, for whom Weatherhead always had a special regard, to play a part in influencing church policy.

In October 1947, he tried an experimental service which caused a great deal of comment in the press, as well as misunderstanding through the way it was reported. The service was divided into four parts with breaks between each, during which people could leave and return as they wished. The first twenty-five minutes were devotional, with hymns, prayers and an anthem. This was followed by a sermon on 'Can Christian Faith live in a Scientific World?' Part three consisted of a question and answer session, during which members of the congregation were invited to write down questions to be handed to the minister for him to answer, leading to a general discussion. The evening was concluded with a social hour and refreshments and closed with family prayers at 9.0 p.m. Weatherhead said he obtained the idea from a church in Berlin in 1922 and had always wanted to try it out.

The event proved embarrassingly successful. It attracted considerable advance notice in the secular press and drew so many people to attend that the church was full long before the service started, with many standing and others sitting on the dais around the pulpit. The presence of several journalists and others whom Weatherhead referred to as 'onlookers' made the atmosphere of the occasion, he felt, 'mildly sensational'. Too many questions – more than fifty – were sent up to be answered, and in spite of having been in church for over three hours, far more people wanted to attend the social hour than the hall could accommodate. There were further reports in the press, with much comment about members of the congregation being encouraged to go outside for a cup of tea and a cigarette during the service. One popular newspaper displayed the headline, 'Pop out of church to get a drink, then come and answer back.' This was copied with adverse comments by newspapers as far away as South Africa, and led to Weatherhead receiving several critical letters asking him not to degrade religion in this way. Even so, he was sufficiently encouraged to continue the experiment in a modified form the following month, and subsequently, question and answer services became a regular feature of his ministry.

The Annual General Meeting in April, 1948, approved the setting up of a new organisation, 'The Friends of the City Temple' which it was hoped (with the rebuilding in mind) would

> crystallize the immense volume of goodwill for the City Temple, which is almost world wide, and . . . would increase the revenue of the Church because its members would lay it upon themselves as an obligation to help along the work and witness of the City Temple.

This proved an effective and supportive organisation, with branches established amongst sympathetic visitors and adherents not only in Britain but also in many other parts of the world, particularly in Australia, following a highly successful visit there by Weatherhead in 1951.

Wider issues exercised him. He had made no reference in his monthly letter to the Labour landslide in the election of July 1945, possibly because he was out of the country at the time. But the depressed state of the nation gave him concern. The Butler Education Act was implemented in 1947 but the economy was in ruins. Stafford Cripps who became Chancellor in 1947, imposed a strict period of austerity. Taxes remained at the high level they had reached in wartime, and rationing not only continued, but was widened to include bread and potatoes for the first time, and the worst winter in living memory in 1947 brought power cuts and coal shortages. Weatherhead's broadcasts were affected by electricity cuts, and he took an increasingly jaundiced view of the state of the nation and of the Labour government.

In a sermon, 'Is Britain Becoming Decadent?' he attacked the dockers for striking in order to get more pay for less work, saying that he found 'that employers of labour have a higher ethic than employees', and criticised the high level of income tax. In August, he preached on 'National Crisis', saying that 'a mood of disillusionment and depression, and in some cases, cynicism, has befallen us.' Deploring the low spiritual state of the nation, he declared that 'The way in which the present Government has misused the American loan is a sin which stinks to high heaven,' and that the Trade Unions were 'committing sin' in compelling workers to produce less than they were capable of doing. He accused the Government of putting party interests before the good of the whole nation, saying 'The confusion, the sense of frustration, the bewilderment, the darkness that is upon us are the moral judgments of God.' Although he insisted that 'no one can discern my political colour because I do not know it myself. I cannot find any political party saying what I want saying', he was evidently out of sympathy with the policies of the Labour Government and its attempts to solve the problems of an almost bankrupt and exhausted nation. Taking tea in Downing Street with Prime Minister Attlee in May did not increase his faith in the government. '"Politicians," our host said modestly, "could not do everything." I felt that his modesty was justified.'

In November, 1946, the Anglican Church Assembly had passed a resolution appealing to the British Government 'to do its utmost' to enable the German people to 'rebuild their lives on sound foundations, without danger to the peace of the world', adding, 'This Assembly is deeply concerned with reports of hunger in the British Zone of Germany and will support His Majesty's Government in any measure it may adopt to avert the threatened famine.' Two days later Weatherhead asked his congregation at the evening service to stand and indicate their support for this resolution: 'the great congregation immediately rose without apparently a single dissentient.' He believed that the harsh and humiliating treatment of Germany in 1918 had produced in the German people a deep resentment and sense of grievance which had been an important factor in enabling Hitler to seize power and led to the Second World War. Every effort therefore needed to be made to help the Germans rebuild their nation and to establish a democratic and civilised regime as quickly as possible.

The City Temple early began to organise food-aid and re-established the contacts it had made previously with German Christians. Weatherhead was moved by a letter from a German schoolmaster friend with whom he had stayed in Berlin after the First War. This described conditions in Germany and criticised the way the Occupying Powers were carrying out their administration, saying they 'do not seem able to grasp the psychological condition of a nation that has gone through the greatest political and moral catastrophe in its history.'

Weatherhead was particularly concerned that over two years after the war had ended German prisoners of war had still not been repatriated. He backed Victor Gollancz's 'Save Europe Now' campaign and joined in signing a memorial to the Prime Minister, stating the 'gravest concern' at the slow rate of repatriation. It set out the desperate need in Germany for the men to rejoin their families and restore their homes and country, and begged 'most urgently that the rate of repatriation should be speeded up.' In his reply, Attlee said,

> Our general attitude on this whole question is that we wish to arrange for the return of all prisoners of war to Germany as soon as this is possible. . . .
> I sympathise with the human considerations which are put forward in the memorial, but I cannot share the view that the retention of German prisoners of war in foreign countries for labour purposes is inequitable, when it is recalled that this is one of the only practical means by which Germany can make any reparation for the loss and destruction which German aggression has brought on so many countries of Europe. I need not emphasize the importance of the work being carried out by German prisoners of war in the United Kingdom, particularly in agriculture. And other reasons apart, difficulties of transport would in any event have made it impossible to achieve a much higher rate of repatriation.[1]

Weatherhead visited Germany himself during the summer of 1950 at the invitation of the Senior Chaplain to the Forces. He was appalled by the apathy he found among the ordinary soldiers, and at the amount of devastation still evident, but was impressed by the facilities being provided for the troops, and by the unaggressive and polite way the British forces were behaving towards the German people.

On 23 November 1946, the Archbishop of Canterbury, Geoffrey Fisher, in a sermon in Cambridge on Church Union, said that the Free Churches should 'take episcopacy into their system.' This sermon provoked a considerable and fierce debate, and stimulated a serious dialogue about ways to achieve organic union which continued without much success for the next three decades. Weatherhead was an enthusiast for union, though from his independent position outside the mainstream of officialdom and responsibility he could take a sweeping attitude to union which ignored all the theological and practical difficulties. Commenting on Fisher's sermon in his Minister's Notes, Weatherhead said 'I would gladly submit to Episcopal reordination.' (Donald Soper also expressed a willingness to accept Anglican ordination, which led to remarks that 'Weatherhead and Soper want to become bishops!')

Weatherhead did not seem to see, or to take seriously, the fact that the Anglicans would not be impressed by his willingness to accept reordination without believing in it, and that it still left the theological difficulties unsettled. Following the publication of one of his own sermons on union with the Anglicans, Weatherhead received a letter in response from Fisher who said he was 'grateful for the welcoming spirit which it showed' and repeated that his own suggestion about union 'did not contemplate absorption.'

In spite of the impetus that his sermon had given to the union movement,

Fisher himself was a strict, authoritarian Anglican, inflexible in his rejection of anything which he felt was against the interests and the status of the established Church. A few months before the Cambridge sermon, the Air Minister, Lord Stansgate, who was a Congregationalist, had appointed the Rev. Elsie Chamberlain as the first ever woman chaplain to the forces. Fisher wrote Stansgate an angry letter objecting to her being described officially as Chaplain, and demanded an assurance that she would 'not be permitted to exercise her ministry or take services for Church of England personnel' and to know 'what steps will be taken to secure that all Church of England personnel are strictly warned that under no conditions must they either intentionally or by inadvertance attend services at which she administers the sacraments.'[2]

The 1940s were a significant period for the movement towards church unity. The Church of South India was formed in 1947, bringing together, in one episcopal system, Anglicans, Congregationalists, Methodists and Presbyterians. Since the non-Anglican clergy were not required to be re-ordained, this caused considerable dissension in Anglican circles in Britain over the question of inter-communion between the Church of England and the newly created hybrid. Weatherhead, with his strong Indian associations, took a keen interest in the United Church, and was outspokenly critical of Anglican attitudes towards it. He had himself, he said, prophesied as long ago as 1922 that the Church Union in India would be a tremendous success and that its methods should be adopted in Britain. He was disgusted with the statement by the Archbishop of Canterbury in an 'Open Letter to Bishop Stephen Neill' that

> The Indian Church will not be in full communion with the Church of England
> . . . the Church of England has no official relation to or communion with, the
> South India Church as such, it has a great concern for it, if only because it
> contains a very large ex-Anglican element.[3]

In his November Minister's Letter Weatherhead attacked this as 'shameful and disgraceful', saying that 'it torpedoes the whole scheme. Any thoughtful Indian in the South India Church must feel himself unchurched.' He went on to declare his 'passionate conviction that the Anglican Church will never achieve its true purpose in the land until the Anglo-Catholic section is separated from it. Until that happens any talk of union with the Free Churches except in action is a waste of time.'

Although Weatherhead actively supported the setting up of the Anglican and Methodist Conversations when he was the Methodist President in 1955, the Anglican attitude to the Church of South India had made him sceptical about the success of attempts to unite any of the Free Churches with the Church of England, and he argued instead for a united Free Church of England as a more realistic goal. At the beginning of 1946, he preached a series of sermons on 'The Free Churches and the New World', in which he said

> the Church of the future must no longer boggle about organic unity with
> other branches of the Christian Church. . . . There must be, rather, unity in
> social endeavour. . . . Rather than see, in any one town, a conference of the
> Anglican, Congregational, Presbyterian, Methodist, Baptist, Quaker,
> Salvationist, and other branches of the Church, meeting together to discuss
> theological doctrines, I would see them engaged in a conference as to how
> the slums and other evils which curse their town could be abolished.

Congregationalists and Presbyterians had begun a series of talks about union in 1932. Although by 1935 it was agreed that this could not be proceeded with, they did result in the development of closer relationships and new ways of practical co-operation between them. With the end of the war, the Presbyterians initiated a new series of talks in 1945, which produced a *Report of the Joint Conference* which was presented to the Congregational Assembly in May 1947. This caused lively debate but failed to get the united support of the Congregational Union. It was decided to receive the Report and to send it to the churches and County Unions for them to consider. The members of the City Temple debated the Report at a special Church Meeting the following February. Chairing the meeting, Weatherhead expressed the hope that 'the City Temple, when given the opportunity, will come into this scheme as strongly as possible.' He went on to say that he very strongly desired that the Methodist Church should also be invited to join such a union, and that there could then be a United Free Church of England.

Weatherhead's international reputation and appeal to members of all churches was indicated by the appearance in his congregation that summer (1948) of five bishops attending the Lambeth Conference, and many others from abroad who had come to London to watch the Olympic Games. He received further recognition when he was awarded an Honorary Doctorate of Divinity by Edinburgh University. He was chosen to speak on behalf of all those receiving honorary divinity degrees, and in his address insisted on the necessity of associating culture with God. He said, 'All great culture had had its origin in religion, and if it be divorced from its spiritual force it cannot live.'

Confirmation of Weatherhead's public standing came also from an unexpected quarter. At the time of the General Election in 1949, when Lord Elton, a former Labour candidate and Independent peer, in an article for the *Yorkshire Observer* (17 October 1949), argued that the economic plight of the nation was so desperate that there was a need to put party politics aside and elect a National Government made up of the best minds in the country. He suggested that there was a lot to be said for reverting to the medieval tradition of putting a great Churchman into office, and he proposed 'the Archbishop of York or Dr. Leslie Weatherhead.'

In April, a series of five broadcast addresses were published in book form as *The Resurrection and the Life.* These repeated the themes of Weatherhead's earlier books about Jesus, presenting the risen Christ as a living and available presence, and included sections on the afterlife and a speculative note on physical resurrection, which he said he did not believe in. He put forward instead, following St. Paul, the possibility of a spiritual body, using psychology, psychical research and scientific ideas to speculate on what happened to the body of Christ in the tomb, and the nature of the resurrection body in which he appears to his followers after his death. The *British Weekly* (6 May 1948) together with other reviewers, noted Weatherhead's 'infectious enthusiasm for the future life; it is a subject to which Mr. Weatherhead appears to be giving special attention.' Even the conservative *Life of Faith* (12 May 1948) found that 'Evangelical believers need have no cause for misgivings from this book,' and that it 'could be used to real advantage to rouse ordinary, unthinking people to face the challenge of Christianity's central message.'

Another book, *When the Lamp Flickers,* followed in December. This was a series of twenty-one sermons based on questions originally handed in at the question and answer services and preached under the general heading, 'What did Jesus Really Mean?' Mervyn Stockwood – a High Anglican with left-wing political views – writing in the *Church of England Newspaper*, thought that Anglicans would welcome the book, which gave 'interesting and helpful answers to the questions which are frequently asked at religious discussion circles', but he felt that Weatherhead accepted too easily the social status quo, and missed explaining the relevance and importance of the sacramental aspects of faith. W. Bardsley Brash, in *The Methodist Recorder* (9 December 1948) recalled a remark made to himself:

> Many years ago, Dr. C.J. Cadoux, one of the most learned men I have ever known, said to me: "I have often heard Leslie Weatherhead, and he is always well prepared and always shows intellectual strength". These words were verified as I read this book. . . . It reveals a mind in close touch with the questions of the age, with a great gift of answering modern difficulties.

From the time when he had first arrived at the City Temple, Weatherhead had regularly sought the advice of a small number of distinguished friends who had been attracted to the church by his ministry. With the agreement of the Church Council, these were formally constituted into an Advisory Committee. Their names were printed under those of the members of the Council in each month's *Tidings*. The first members of this group were Colonel George Crosfield, who was the National Chairman of the British Legion; Sir Robert Evans; Lord Leathers of Purfleet, who had been Minister of War Transport; Lady Lennard, who served on the Church Council, and had run a hostel for women in the services during the war; Dr. J. Burnett Rae; General Sir John Shea, who had been Governor of Jerusalem and then Adjutant General of India, and Lord Stamp. They were unelected, and entirely chosen by the minister. He explained that,

> either individually or meeting together, [they] could be called in consultation by the Council when critical decisions had to be made in the life and policy of the church. This is in no sense a slight on the ability of the Council to make its own decisions, and in any case, the Advisory Committee would not have any executive power at all. But for a long time it has seemed to me a pity that we neither acknowledge nor use the immense and influential ability of a number of very distinguished people who regularly attend our services.

Although they had no official authority within the church, their influence was bound to be of some weight, as was demonstrated later in the debate over where the church should be rebuilt.

Weatherhead's Presbyterian colleague, W.G. Onions, completed his year and returned to Canada in June 1949. In his place the Presbyterian authorities appointed the Rev. Herbert T. Lewis as minister to their congregation at Marylebone. Although Lewis had none of Weatherhead's charismatic personality or preaching abilities, he was a wise and exceptional pastor, and the two, who had known each other for several years, became the closest of friends.

1. *Tidings,* November 1947. p.241.
2. Janette Williams: *First Lady of the Pulpit: A Biography of Elsie Chamberlain* (The Book Guild 1993) p.30.
3. 'Open Letter to Bishop Stephen Neill' (Church House 1947)

17. Plans for Rebuilding: Debate, Delays and Frustration

'for the sake of those who came after him, an immense "white elephant"
church should not be built which would be hard to fill and hard to
finance, and . . . they should not sacrifice the beauty and spiritual
appeal of Mr. Lawrence's plans in order to gaze upon empty seats.'

As soon as the war ended, Weatherhead was keen to get on with the rebuilding
of the City Temple. In December, 1945, a special meeting was held to discuss the
architect's plans with the members and to receive their approval of them. At this
meeting, the Church Secretary, J.H. Dewey, in presenting the plans, made a
strong plea for the church to be rebuilt on its old site in Holborn, insisting that
in spite of predictions that the 'centre of gravity' of London would continue to
move westward, the City Temple had a duty to maintain its witness as the only
Free Church within the square mile of the City.

The size of the proposed new building caused considerable debate. Since
modern requirements meant that more space had to be allowed for each person,
the total seating capacity would have to be several hundred seats less than the
former church. Some members argued that the financial needs of the church
made it essential that the church should be able to accommodate as many people
as possible, but Weatherhead warned that, especially if they remained in Holborn,
they could not expect to go on attracting large numbers indefinitely. Arguing
that 1,300 seats would be adequate for the future, he said that:

for the sake of those who came after him, an immense "white elephant"
church should not be built which would be hard to fill and hard to finance,
and that they should not sacrifice the beauty and spiritual appeal of Mr.
Lawrence's plans in order to gaze upon empty seats.

Eager as the church was to get on with re-building and to return to a sanctuary of its
own, it was to know many years of frustration before that dream was finally realised.

Weatherhead and the members of the Church Council met with the Labour
Minister of Works, George Tomlinson, to present the case for rebuilding. A
Freechurchman himself, he was sympathetic, but told them that resources were
extremely scarce, and priority had to be given to houses before churches, even
ones as famous as the City Temple. The church was keen to secure the services
as an Appeals Organiser of the Rev. John Smith, minister of Streatham
Congregational Church, who had considerable experience and success as a
professional fund raiser, but Smith turned the invitation down, although he did
agree to join the Rebuilding Committee.

Weatherhead was becoming increasingly frustrated with the delay and the
many unforeseen obstacles preventing the rebuilding of the City Temple. The
most serious blow occured in May 1948, with the sudden death of the architect,
Frederic Lawrence. Weatherhead, who had been so impressed by Lawrence,
and enthusiastic over his designs for the new sanctuary, felt his loss keenly.
Lawrence's death meant that his plans could no longer be used and another
architect needed to be found, so that even the little progress that had been made

towards the rebuilding was now lost. Weatherhead chafed at the continuing building restrictions imposed by the government and seized delightedly on a speech made by Princess Elizabeth, when she laid the foundation stone for a new parish church at Bromley, in which she had said that it would be 'altogether wrong to neglect the rebuilding of our churches on the silent assumption that our material comfort is more important than our spiritual welfare.'

The following March *Tidings* was published as a 'Special Rebuilding Number.' In his Minister's Letter, written to be read before the Annual Church Meeting later that month, Weatherhead argued strongly against the church being rebuilt at Holborn. The Church Council was divided, but the members of the Advisory Panel were unanimously against returning to Holborn. They had stressed that with so many people homeless and a continuing acute shortage of building materials it would be 'iniquitous' to divert labour and materials to provide a building for a church which was as adequately housed as theirs was at Marylebone. They argued that the cost of rebuilding on the old site, which they estimated at over £180,000, would require the church to raise, even with grants from the War Damages Claims, at least £80,000, and in addition there would be the considerable cost of running such a building.

Weatherhead made it clear that he had no intention of absenting himself from the church for an extended period (as Norwood had done) in order to try and raise the necessary funds, asking, 'what would happen to the congregation in the meantime?' There was also the problem of the nature of the site at Holborn, which he had been professionally informed was likely to be affected by water from a tributary of the Fleet river, and therefore providing adequate foundations would increase the estimated cost by some £40,000. He insisted they should stay in Marylebone, where they had successfully established themselves, drawing big congregations, in an area which attracted thousands of people to it at the weekends. To rebuild on the old site just for the sake of tradition, when so few people were in the area on Sundays would be quite wrong, and every ministerial friend he had consulted had told him the same. He feared that a building in Holborn would rapidly become a white-elephant. The days when city-centre churches attracted massed congregations were past, and increasing transport costs and the general drift away from church going convinced him that it was unrealistic to imagine that if the City Temple returned to Holborn it could again attract such crowds as it had before the war – and without big congregations the City Temple could not pay its way.

Among the alternatives, the Rebuilding Committee had considered moving to the King's Weigh House Church near Grosvenor Square. Weatherhead was much attracted to this building and its situation. He had a great admiration for its former minister, W.E. Orchard, who had been a considerable influence on him and on his approach to prayer and worship. Such associations meant a great deal to Weatherhead, and the whole design and style of the building, with its central aisle, chancel and side pulpit, as well as its excellent acoustics, strongly appealed to him. But in spite of all its advantages, Weatherhead reluctantly concluded that, much as he wished otherwise, the King's Weigh House Church was not the answer. The architects had advised them that it was impossible to increase the capacity of the church to more than a thousand people, which meant that every Sunday evening they would have to turn over five hundred away. This he could not to agree to do, and although there were those who thought that the time would come when the congregations had diminished to the extent that accommodation for a thousand would be sufficient, he felt it was too soon to accept that situation.

He considered there was no better alternative than to co-operate with the Marylebone Presbyterians in exploring every possibility of uniting fully with them and eventually rebuilding a united church on the Marylebone site. The idea of such a united Congregational and Presbyterian church was highly attractive to him, as pointing the way forward to the wider union of the two denominations. It would also mean that they could carry on the work of the church, which was growing so successfully at Marylebone, without once more having to uproot themselves and begin all over again somewhere else. This suggestion was warmly welcomed by the Session of the Marylebone Presbyterian Church, who responded by passing a resolution saying that they 'would welcome any suggestions whereby our co-operation could be strengthened and placed on a more permanent basis.'

The Annual General Meeting on 21 March was mainly taken up with where the new church should be built. The members of the Rebuilding Committee, with the exception of John Dewey, who was the most passionate advocate for the church to return to its historic City site, supported remaining in Marylebone, as did all the members of the Advisory Panel. Weatherhead was concerned that the differences of opinion should not cause disunity within the fellowship. He was anxious to make clear that although the advice of the unelected Advisory Panel 'which had no executive power' had been accepted, 'The Church Council was not set aside by this body', and the views of the Council had not been disregarded.

> He felt however, that he knew the views of all the members of the Council, and that they could not get much further by endless discussion. . . . It was not for him to teach a Congregational Church the nature of Congregationalism, but he might remind them that the meeting of Church Members was the supreme court, and could, in fact, do almost anything.

E.H. Jeffs, the Editor of the *Christian World*, invited correspondence from readers on the future of the City Temple. Weatherhead immediately responded with a letter in which he proposed that the Congregational bodies housed in the Memorial Hall might come together with the City Temple to erect a building comparable to the Methodist Central Hall, which would house all the Congregational offices and departments in one centre, together with the church hall for its assemblies and meetings. The Holborn site was not big enough for this, but he thought another site might be found, possibly within the City boundaries. The advantages – especially to the City Temple – of this joint venture were that 'an appeal for a licence would have stronger backing, and that the financial burden would be lightened.'

Only after he had sent the letter did Weatherhead seek the approval of the Church Council, but this was given without dissension. His chief concern was to overcome the division within the congregation over where the new church should be built, and by suggesting that this could still be in the City, though not on the old site, he successfully met the wishes of the traditionalists, led by John Dewey, though not without giving way on the argument for staying and uniting with the Presbyterians in Marylebone.

18. Travels Abroad

'We are very orthodox people. I have read your books and note that you
are always orthodox at the end, though shockingly heretical at the beginning.
So when you speak to us, please begin close to the end.'

With the ending of the war, Weatherhead was again free to travel abroad, and
found himself much in demand. In June 1945, at the request of the Methodist
Conference, he accompanied the then President, Dr. A.W. Harrison, on an official
visit to Ireland. The next year he travelled to the Channel Islands, to Ireland
again, and then to Sweden, Norway and Switzerland. One person who heard him
in Ireland was an American journalist, Roy L. Smith, Editor of the *Christian
Advocate*, the official paper of the Methodist Church in the United States. Smith
reported his impressions of Weatherhead's preaching under the heading, 'I
heard Leslie Weatherhead.' Describing him as 'Britain's most famous preacher',
he was impressed by his personality, his humour and the persuasiveness of his
style:

It's his eyes that fascinate you. At one moment they are searching you out,
as though they might have some weird power of piercing walls and time.
Then at other times they flash with a merry light which is born of his persistent
humour, for he is capable of being excruciatingly funny if he chooses to be.
When he does turn humorous, however, it is entirely unstudied and un-
planned. . . . There is a radiance about his very presence when he is preaching . . . and a strange sense of divine presence is felt by the listener. . . . He
depends upon persuasion, rather than upon vigour, to carry his point . . .
the deepest impression left upon me, as upon all others, was "Did not our
hearts burn within us as he talked with us by the way?" Leslie Weatherhead
has a remarkable ability to hide behind himself while he is preaching, so that
God may speak to the people.[1]

In June 1946 Weatherhead flew to Norway and then to Sweden, where he
addressed the Swedish Methodist Conference. Also with him was the Rev. W.J.
Smart, who was reporting the Conference for the *Methodist Recorder* (4 July
1946). Smart reported,

He [Weatherhead] had flown from England the day before to address two
meetings in Stockholm at which the total attendance was seven thousand
people. Bishop Arvidson introduced him to the Conference and he was
given a standing welcome. He spoke through an interpreter for over an hour
on the subject of Healing and captured his audience from his opening
sentences and held it to the last. Mr. Weatherhead is here for the first time
but his books have been best sellers here for many years. One felt proud to
be an Englishman in Sweden with Leslie Weatherhead around.

Smart, who had not known Weatherhead personally before this visit, was
impressed by his 'genius' for individual friendships. Booked into the same
hotel, and in adjacent rooms, they met every day, often beginning conversations
before breakfast and continuing them after supper. At the end of the week,

Weatherhead returned to England while Smart went on to Norway, Finland and Denmark. Immediately on his return, Weatherhead wrote to Smart's wife to explain how they had met, and to let her know how her husband was. This simple act of kindness was much appreciated by both Smart and his wife, and left a deep impression on them of Weatherhead's thoughtfulness and care for individuals.

Shortly after his return, he was involved in a car accident which caused him serious concussion. Attempting to return to work too soon, he brought on a condition which he said he had never heard of before, 'post-traumatic headache and depression', which left him feeling seriously weakened and depleted of energy for some considerable time.

Three years later, Weatherhead was delighted to visit the United States again, when he was invited to give the Lyman Beecher Lectures at Yale University during April, 1949. He had planned to speak on 'The Place of Healing in the Modern Church', but he was asked, 'rather late in the day' to change his subject. Not having time to produce a new manuscript, he spoke from notes, on 'The Minister's Responsibilities to His People in Worship, Counselling, Preaching and Healing'. The lectures were relayed to two overflow halls, enabling him to speak to audiences of over 900 at each lecture. The Dean, L.A. Weigle, told him that his lectures were 'the best attended and commanded more general interest than any other that I can remember.' He went on to preach and lecture at the Union Theological Seminary, New York, at the Fifth Avenue Presbyterian Church and at St. Bartholomew's Church. During his stay of sixteen days he spoke fourteen times, and met with many leading American ministers and theologians, including Reinhold and Richard Niebuhr. He was particularly pleased to visit Dr. H.E. Fosdick in his own home.

That summer, he made another visit to Sweden where he had been invited by the Methodist Bishop of Scandinavia, Bishop Arvidson, to be guest preacher at the Swedish Methodist Conference. In his invitation, the Bishop wrote,

We are very orthodox people. I have read your books and note that you are always orthodox at the end, though shockingly heretical at the beginning.

So when you speak to us, please begin close to the end.

In Sweden he gave seven addresses in seven days and immediately on his return went on to Liverpool where he was one of the preachers at the Methodist Conference.

In May, he fulfilled a long-standing ambition to visit the Catholic pilgrimage centre at Lourdes with his elder son, Dixon, who was now fully qualified in medicine and psychiatry. They applied to the Catholic authorities for permission to travel as pilgrims and to study their records, and were given every opportunity they wished to see for themselves and to learn everything they could. Weatherhead was impressed by the care which the Catholic authorities took, and their reluctance to make claims for cures, declaring that the purpose of the pilgrimage was to deepen the spiritual life of the pilgrim and to strengthen his faith in Christ and his Church. He concluded that some inexplicable cures did take place, but that these were extremely rare. Though there were ten thousand pilgrims in Lourdes during the week they were there, not one claimed to be cured. He acknowledged that to visit Lourdes could be a powerful religious experience, but he was greatly saddened by the obvious disappointment and hopelessness of the unhealed pilgrims on the way home, and felt that their faith had taken a severe blow.

Preaching soon after the General Election in March 1950, on 'The Christian Contribution to the National Situation', he suggested that the international tension might be eased and understanding improved if Princess Elizabeth and her husband, Prince Phillip, were to visit Russia as good will ambassadors. He repeated this the following week at a City Temple Literary Society Meeting in response to a remark made by the lecturer, Dr. Charles Hill, 'The Radio Doctor', that 'perpetual fear of Russian intentions' was preying on people's minds. This was favourably reported in the national press, but Lord Vansittart, in a debate in the House of Lords on March 29, denounced several members of the Church as communists, and then attacked Weatherhead for his suggestion, which he described as 'impertinent and ignoble.' The newspapers gave the impression that Vansittart had also denounced Weatherhead as a communist. Weatherhead protested, 'I am blue, not Red', but Vansittart's attack caused him considerable embarrassment. The day of the report, he was due to broadcast one of a series of talks in the B.B.C. Silver Lining programme, and there were immediate demands that he should be taken off the air. The story and the charge were also widely reported by the American and the Australian press.

Weatherhead had accepted an invitation to visit Australia the following year, and was anxious that this furore should not prevent him being allowed entry into that country which was then going through a strong anti-communist phase. The Australian Prime Minister, Sir Robert Menzies, had succeeded in presenting a Bill in Parliament dissolving the Australian Communist Party. The Bill was enacted, but later declared invalid by the Australian High Court. The Australian papers had included Weatherhead's name as one of those on what they referred to as 'Lord Vansittart's black list.' The Methodist Church Press and Information Officer, Tom Goodall, who worked hard to repair the damage to Weatherhead's reputation, arranged a press conference for him with the representatives of the Australian and New Zealand papers. He pointed out, as did others, that in *When the Lamp Flickers* (1948) Weatherhead had included a chapter showing that Christianity and Communism were not only different creeds but incompatible, and Weatherhead repeated this again in a later seasonal sermon on 'The Christmas Challenge to Communism.'

When Vansittart was made aware of the effect of his remarks on Weatherhead he invited him to lunch and issued a press statement correcting the mis-reports, and later sent him a personal letter:

> I am shocked to hear that you have received letters reproaching you with Communist leanings. That of course is quite fantastic. I knew your record too well to suppose for a minute that there could be a vestige of truth in such a notion. I happened to dissent from a suggestion which you made some while ago, but that in no way whatever impairs my high regard which I have, and ought to have, for you. I should be most unhappy if a mere episode in our relations were misused in any attempt to hinder the good work which you constantly strive to do among your fellow men.

This relieved the situation by providing him with a document that cleared his name with the Australian authorities and enabled his visit to take place.

The planned itinerary took him away from the country for six months. With his daughter, Margaret, he left London by ship on 1 February, 1951, stopping at Colombo, Ceylon, on the 17th. He was due to give a lecture in the Church, but the demand for tickets was so great that the Town Hall, holding 1,500, was booked instead. Even so, the hall was packed and the audience overflowed into the gardens outside. One of the purposes of his tour was to investigate the possibility of raising an international fund for the rebuilding of the City Temple. From the collection taken at this meeting the church subsequently received a cheque for £50. After the meeting he visited the local hospital to see a girl suffering from a nervous breakdown, and later that same night spoke to a gathering of Indian ministers and British missionaries.

Arriving at Perth on 27 February, he preached at a midday service, 'crowded out, with people standing at the doors', before going on to Adelaide where he spoke at an evening meeting in the Town Hall on 'The Illusion of Humanism.' They reached Melbourne on 3 March, where they stayed at the University with his old friend, the Master of Queen's College, Dr. Raynor Johnson.

The invitation to visit Australia had come from Dr. Irving Benson, minister of the Wesley Methodist Church in Melbourne, and also from the Rev. Gordon Powell, minister of the Collins Street Congregational Church. It was arranged that Weatherhead should preach once a Sunday alternately in the Congregational and Methodist churches and 'each Wednesday evening to give a lecture to the Congregationalists on "Psychology" and to the Methodists on "Religion."' 1951 was being celebrated as the Victorian Commemoration Year, marking the Centenary of Government in Victoria, and the Jubilee of the Commonwealth of Australia. Weatherhead's visit was welcomed as part of the special events connected with these celebrations.

The three months Weatherhead spent in Australia demonstrate the impact his personality and speaking had on those who heard him. Since his reputation preceded him, it was to be expected that, at least to begin with, he would attract crowds of the curious who had never before had the opportunity to hear or to see him, but the longer he stayed there, the greater the crowds grew, until even the largest halls available were not big enough to hold all those who wanted to hear him.

Weatherhead was thrilled with his reception. In his May letter he told the church:

> I do not think I have ever had a greater honour done to me than has been done at Melbourne, for I have had accorded to me a Public Welcome in the Town Hall. It was filled with nearly three thousand people last Friday night, all of whom paid either two shillings or five shillings to come in. The Lord Mayor presided, and the Governor of the State and also the Archbishop of Melbourne were present on the platform. I spoke for nearly an hour on "The Relevance of Religion in the Modern World", and at the end, had the unusual experience, for a speaker, of receiving an encore. They went on clapping and I just did not know what to do until an official told me to get up and bow, which I did, feeling a cross between a fool and a film-star, but it was all very kind and we received unending kindness from everybody.

In addition to his public speaking engagements he was also providing several hours of psychological counselling to individuals, as well as giving interviews and answering a considerable correspondence. To his great relief he was given a small committee who organised the details of his timetable for him, and all invitations to speak and lecture were handled by them. As these amounted to far more than he could possibly accept, he was glad to be spared the embarrassment of making refusals himself. He was relieved also that the committee provided him with protection from the inevitable nuisances who otherwise would have pestered him.

In Canberra, the Prime Minister gave a luncheon in his honour, to which all the members of the Cabinet were invited. He made a flying visit to Tasmania to address a meeting in Hobart Town Hall, and to Brisbane for another Town Hall meeting, where he spoke to an audience of 2,500. The crowds in Melbourne continued to grow, with people arriving at 4.30 for an 8.0 o'clock evening lecture which was relayed to four different venues. For his last meeting, his hosts booked the Exhibition Hall, the largest hall in the city, with a seating capacity of 8,000.

Throughout Australia Weatherhead's visit was front-page news. His host, Dr. Irving Benson, wrote enthusiastically to the City Temple:

No church on the continent is large enough to hold the crowds that flock to hear him – his sermons have been relayed to adjoining halls and other churches, and still people are turned away. . . . We expected a prince of preachers, a master of the human heart, with the answer to the aching need of men's lives, but we did not know until he came that he is a great evangelist. People have been changed, men and women have surrendered their lives to Christ and set out on the high road of discipleship . . . his infectious love of the Bible has set people searching the scriptures with new zest. . . .

The supreme glory of his preaching is not that Dr. Weatherhead is a pulpit giant, but that men and women go home saying, "Isn't Christ wonderful!"

The Australian papers gave full coverage to each of his appearances and addresses, many of which were regarded as highly controversial. *The Age*, referred to the size of his audiences as 'phenomenal', saying 'Nothing quite so frank and forthright has been heard from an Australian pulpit for a long time.' The Melbourne *Advertiser* 17 May 1951) reported,

No guest speaker has so caught the imagination of the Melbourne public. . . . Literally thousands of people have been turned away from his crowded meetings. What is more, the interest increases the longer he stays. . . . Through his books Leslie Weatherhead has become a household name in thousands of Melbourne homes and many have come out of curiosity to see a well-known author. Without exception, they have been captivated by his personality and it is common to hear people say 'I'm not going to miss a meeting.' Around the city conversation is frequently opened with the question, 'Have you heard Weatherhead yet?' The following is a typical tribute from one of his thousands of Australian admirers, . . . 'I feel he has stirred us up and begun a revival in our midst. There has hardly been a service from which I have not gone away thinking "That hit home and I've got to see what I can do about it."' That is what Melbourne is saying about the visit of Dr. Leslie Weatherhead.

There were some critical and dissentient voices. Weatherhead's remark that much of the Bible should be 'blue-pencilled' attracted a great deal of coverage and comment in the newspapers, and particularly upset the more conservative, who held two meetings of their own to protest publicly at Weatherhead's more provocative statements, which they declared to be un-Scriptural and contrary to Christian teaching.

The attendance at the last two meetings arranged by the Collins Street Church totalled 11,000. On one occasion the lecture was relayed into the Scots Presbyterian Church opposite and into the Independent Church Hall as well. Even then a fourth hall was needed to contain the crowds. On Weatherhead's final Sunday, he preached in the morning at Wesley Church and then in the afternoon gave a broadcast address in which he appealed for funds for the new City Temple. According to Gordon Powell,

> The power of Dr. Weatherhead's appeal was such that the radio announcer said that he had been moved so much that he intended to send a donation and he hoped many others would too – a thing I have never heard before on the air.

The service that evening was at Collins Street which was hopelessly inadequate since it seated only 1,400. The Town Hall holding 3,000 was booked again, and then the minister of the Scots Church asked if the service could be relayed to his congregation also. In spite of very unpleasant weather, the people began to gather at 4.0 p.m. and the crowd became so great that the police were called to control it. The Town Hall was filled within ten minutes and the crowd then overflowed into the other two buildings, packing them both. Powell reported that the collection at the final lecture was £575 and at the Town Hall service £600 with an additional £500 collected by Miss Gladys Opie, a former worshipper at the City Temple, whom Weatherhead had appointed as Secretary of the Friends of the City Temple in Australia, and who acted as secretary of the rebuilding fund.

Leaving Melbourne at the end of May, the Weatherheads spent one night in Sydney, where he preached at another crowded church, before going on to Auckland, to spend a month in New Zealand. He preached at the Beresford Street Congregational Church, and at the Pitt Street Methodist Church, the service from which was relayed to four other churches. He went to Wellington to preach and to speak at the University, and to Christchurch, where he preached twice at the Methodist Church before going to Dunedin and then back to Auckland. From there they flew to Fiji, where some ninety per cent of the population were Methodists. Here they stayed for nine days, during which he visited and preached at the various Mission Stations, before going on to Canada, to preach and lecture in St. Andrew's Church and at the Minister's Conference at Union College in Vancouver.

Both Weatherhead's sons had moved to the United States in 1950 and 1951. He seized the opportunity to stay with his younger son in Tacoma, Washington, where Kingsley had taken a post as Professor of English Literature at the College of Puget Sound. From there he went on to give one lecture in Winnipeg. Here he was met by his elder son, Dick, who drove with him to Toronto where he preached at both the Deer Park Church and the Timothy Eaton Memorial Church on 22 July, before leaving for home on the Queen Elizabeth from New York, arriving in time to take both services at the City Temple on August 5. He followed this exhausting itinerary by preaching at both services each Sunday throughout the rest of the month. Everywhere he went collections were taken for the Rebuilding

Fund, so that he was able to report on his return home that a sum of £4,006 had been raised towards the new church, with further gifts promised.

1. *Tidings* August 1946. p.190f.

19. Psychology, Religion and Healing

'To say nowadays, then, in the light of psychosomatic medicine, that
religion has no relation to physical illness is more than ever absurd. . . .
Guilt, repressed or conscious, is most certainly a fruitful cause of both
physical and psychological, as obviously of spiritual, illness. Unless
the physician can deal with guilt . . . he cannot effect a radical cure. It
is not usual for the physician or the psychologist to say, "Thy sins
ar e forgiven thee." Has not religion then a vital part to play in the
cure of certain kinds of illness such as those caused by guilt?'

In October 1950, Weatherhead had been awarded a London Ph.D. for a thesis on
'The Place of Psychology in the Integration of Personality with special reference
to the field of Religion.' He chose the wording of this title reluctantly after his
preferred word 'healing' was rejected as being dubiously unscientific. The thesis
was expanded and published in September, 1951, under his chosen title,
Psychology, Religion and Healing. The book was immediately recognised as a
significant work in this field, and established his reputation as a leading authority
on psychosomatic diseases. Although there were others also writing about
psychology and ministry – most notably, the Congregationalist, Dr. Harry Guntrip,
whose book, *Psychology for Ministers and Social Workers* had appeared in
1949, and the Scottish Presbyterian, Dr. J.G. Mackenzie, whose *Nervous
Disorders and Religion* was published in the same month as *Psychology,
Religion and Healing* – Weatherhead was exceptional in bringing pastoral
psychology together with other non-material methods of treatment in a
comprehensive study, considering every aspect of the Church's ministry of
healing as a whole.

The wide range of subjects dealt with by Weatherhead, not only psychology
and hypnotism, but euthanasia, demon possession, Spiritualism, paranormal
phenomena and psychic research, were not for him disconnected hobby horses,
but logically related areas of enquiry stemming from a unified system of belief,
the central tenet of which was the loving goodness of God, whose ideal will for
all was total harmony and health of body, mind and spirit, in a loving relationship
with Himself. Weatherhead believed that since this was God's world, everything
that happened in it, however strange, could be a source of revelation and for the
discovery of new truth which might lead to a greater knowledge of God and
benefit mankind.

At the Methodist Conference in 1935, he had proposed the setting up of an
enquiry into every aspect of spiritual healing. This resulted in the appointment
of a Conference Committee with Weatherhead himself as its Convenor. He
presented the reports of this Committee each year to Conference, and its findings
inevitably owed a great deal to his own work and interest in the subject.
Psychology, Religion and Healing contains much of the thinking and
conclusions which, since 1935, had been presented in these reports. In 1946, as
an outcome of this Committee, the Methodist Society for Medical and Pastoral

Psychology was formed with Weatherhead and the psychologist, Dr. Percy Backus, as co-Presidents. Weatherhead set out the aim of his book as

> to review every known method of healing through the mind and spirit, to assess the place of psychology and religion in the field of non-physical healing, to pass a critical judgment on the methods used to attain health in this field, and to ascertain along which lines modern techniques might usefully proceed. [p. xv.]

The book's seven sections, following an introduction on the earliest known attempts at healing, cover the healing miracles of Christ and the early church, the earliest developments of psychological methods, to modern religious approaches, and the different modern schools of psychological medicine. The last three sections attempt an assessment and finally a synthesis of the religious and scientific approaches to healing and attempt to 'establish the view that the *complete* integration of personality can be achieved only by taking both psychology and religion into account.'

In the book, Weatherhead dismissed the idea that disease came into the world as a consequence of human sin, pointing out that fossil evidence shows that animals suffered before humans existed. He traced the origins of religious suggestion in healing from the ancient Egyptians, finding the sources of both religious healing and psychotherapy in the 'strange medley of superstition and magic' prevalent in the cultures of the ancient Middle East. The Old Testament contained prayers for health, and the belief that the cure of a disease was a sign of God's forgiveness. Jesus, he says, regarded disease as 'part of the kingdom of evil' and 'God's ideal purpose for every man as perfect health of body, mind and spirit.' The healing miracles of Jesus revealed that there were 'other healing powers available in the universe' in addition to those accessible to scientific research. Weatherhead argues that 'the most powerful curative factor in the world is spiritual' and that many diseases with physical symptoms arre due 'not merely to an inharmonious relationship between the mind and what might be called its secular environment . . . but between the soul and God.' He allows the possibility of demon possession, supporting this with examples from his time in India and the findings of Spiritualism, and even suggests that in cases of epilepsy 'light will be thrown . . . from research into psychic phenomena rather than the physical or psychological fields.'

Turning to 'Earlier Methods of Healing Through Psychology' he deals with the development and use of hypnotism, describing his own method of inducing hypnosis, and experiments in which he had been able to raise and lower the temperature of the body and to induce dreams and hallucinations. Reviewing 'Modern Methods of Healing Through Religion', he examines the laying on of hands, Lourdes, Christian Science, healing missions, psychic phenomena, intercessory prayer, and the work of several religious healing movements, including the Guild of Health, the Guild of Pastoral Psychology and the Methodist Society for Medical and Pastoral Practice.

He devotes an outspoken and critical chapter to Christian Science; approving its emphasis on the importance of spiritual and mental attitudes for health and well-being, and its denial of the belief that God deliberately sends disease as a punishment for sin, but rejecting its claim to be truly Christian, since it fails to take seriously the reality of human suffering and denies the incarnation and the agony of Christ. He describes its founder, Mary Baker Eddy, as highly neurotic, and her book *Science and Health,* on which Christian Science is based as a 'most involved hotch potch of vague and sometimes contradictory ideas.'

He is equally condemnatory of public healing missions, saying that in them the healers knows nothing of the causes and symptoms of those they invite forward, treat all patients alike, and put the onus for healing on the faith of the patient. He commends instead a service in which the aim is 'the unity of the worshipper with God' before which the minister has privately interviewed each person seeking healing, explaining the nature of faith and the purpose of the service, and ensuring that the consent of the patient's doctor had been obtained.

From the end of the First World War, when preparing his book, *After Death*, Weatherhead had made a study of the claims of Spiritualism, and this led him to investigate the whole field of psychic research. He attended seances, even holding them in his own home, met with mediums and all kinds of psychic practitioners, and conducted experiments of his own. He was an early and enthusiastic supporter of the Churches' Fellowship for Psychical and Spiritual Studies, and belonged to the Society for Psychical Research. He could therefore draw on a considerable fund of first-hand knowledge and experience. In *Psychology, Religion and Healing* he reaffirms his belief, set out in *After Death*, 'That through mediums, some kind of contact is sometimes made with an intelligence or intelligences on some other plane of being', but also warns that 'Spiritualism has not made a single definite, valuable or original contribution to Christian thought concerning the life after death.' He agrees there is a need for further enquiry, saying that not all spiritualism could be dismissed as 'fraudulent inventions', although some of the claims might be capable of alternative explanation.

In a chapter on the practice of intercession for the sick, he details his own methods and discoveries during his ministries in Leeds and at the City Temple over a period of 25 years, during which such intercessions were a regular part of the worship of these churches. Referring to other sources to show 'that the literature of the subject points to the same conclusions as my own', he insists that 'prayer has its laws and conditions' some of which 'seem to be slowly emerging', noting that a prayer for a child seemed to have more effect than one for an adult, and that where 'a patient is really loved . . . prayer seems more likely to be full of healing power'. He gives an account of the method he would use during a church service: this was to mention three or four names and ask the congregation to focus their minds on each in turn, explaining that such prayer was co-operating with God by providing a channel for his healing energies.

He argues that recent experiments with telepathy, particularly those carried out by J.B.Rhine, underlined the importance of Jung's theory of the Collective Unconscious, and that the evidence for telepathy provided some explanation of what happened when intercessions were offered for a particular individual in church. But he denies that such intercessions were 'merely telepathy', saying that telepathy is 'part of the machinery which God uses' but not an adequate description of the 'releasing of the divine energy'.

He examines the healing value of the theories of Freud, Adler, Jung, and McDougall, acknowledging Freud as the most important 'pioneer psychologist', but concluding that the 'fundamental weakness and condemnation of Freudian psycho-analysis is its entire lack of interest in a subsequent re-orientation or synthesis.' Weatherhead is more attracted to the ideas of Alfred Adler, who thought that Freud put too much emphasis on sex as the explanation for neurosis. He prefers Adler's technique of 'therapeutic conversation' to Freud's method of psycho-analysis since Adler's treatment offers 'a more loving and kindly relationship to the patient than Freud's cold scientific method obtained.' Adler's system was much closer to religion than Freud's because Adler's cure involved the patient doing something to change his way of life, but only religion was able, through the grace of God, to provide the power outside the patient himself, to make that transformation possible. Weatherhead held with Hadfield that 'the most potent causal factor of neurosis' was neither sexual repression nor the hunger for superiority and power, but

> the frustrated hunger to be loved, where love means more than the sentimental and erotic, namely the desire for approval, the longing to be appreciated, the basic need of being treated, at least by someone, with goodwill. If so religion . . . has a vital part to play in any thorough curative psychological treatment. [p.279]

Weatherhead himself was a disciple of no particular school. In his previous books on psychology, and in his newspaper articles and lectures, he applied ideas and methods gathered from all of them. His interest in psychology was practical rather than theoretical, since as a Christian minister and pastor he was looking for the most effective and beneficial ways of helping those who came to him with their troubles, and accepted anything from any system which he discovered worked in practice.

Having had some two hundred and fifty hours of analysis himself, with three different psychotherapists, and knowing well several others whose methods and techniques he had studied, he gives a detailed description of modern psychotherapeutic practice and explains his own way of conducting an analysis with a patient. This includes 'free association,' in which the patient is invited to say anything that comes into his mind about himself, without any guidance from the psychologist, the interpretation of dreams, Jung's method of word association to uncover the sub-conscious, and, in some cases, a careful use of hypnosis. He describes using such equipment as a microphone strapped over the patient's heart to monitor variation in heart beats to indicate emotional changes, and a galvanometer registering differences in resistance to electric current caused by perspiration – though he found that the use of such gadgets was apt to make patients self-conscious and therefore could be counter-productive.

He sums up 'The way of healing through modern psychological techniques' as:

> The discovery, with the skilled help of the psychologist, of those factors in the deep mind . . . which led the patient to adopt a faulty pattern of reaction to difficult situations. The recognition of the motives that led him to adopt that pattern. . . . The determination to substitute a true reaction for the faulty one, using all the aids open to him, such as auto-suggestion, positive thinking, the banishment of self-pity and the use of religious insight and faith. [p.310f.]

Defining 'health' as 'the complete and successful functioning of every part of the human being, in harmonious relationship with every other part and with the relevant environment', he explains that, 'Where the relationship with the relevant environment is cut off, a state of disease ensues.' This is true also for mental health, which 'depends in some measure on adjustment to the surroundings . . . and with the relevant environment which might be called the world of true ideas.' Since man is also a spiritual being,' The health of the spirit or soul depends on its harmonious relationship with the other parts of man's personality and its relevant environment, and for Christians, the name of that environment is the God whom Christ revealed.' Because the human being is 'a very closely-knit unity of body, mind and spirit,' disease or disharmony in one part affects the personality as a whole. Diseases of the soul, including 'jealousy, hate, malice, bad temper, resentment, worry, emotional rebellion and so on,' can cause distress in the other parts of the personality, resulting in the existence of diseases which are 'psychosomatic,' that is, physical disablement which has its origin not in the body, but in the psyche.

> To say nowadays, then, in the light of psychosomatic medicine, that religion has no relation to physical illness is more than ever absurd . . . guilt, repressed or conscious, is most certainly a fruitful cause of both physical and psychological, as obviously of spiritual, illness. Unless the physician can deal with guilt . . . he cannot effect a radical cure. It is not usual for the physician or the psychologist to say, 'Thy sins are forgiven thee.' Has not religion then a vital part to play in the cure of certain kinds of illnesses such as those caused by guilt? [p.318]

It was Weatherhead's particular insight to realise that in Freud's emphasis on the importance of repressed guilt in causing neurosis there was the possibility of a bridge between psychology and theology. Freud had shown that by analysis a patient could be helped to acknowledge guilt and so neutralise its effects, but the psychologist had no way of dealing with the guilt itself. Weatherhead recognised that this meant that there was a vital part for religion to play in the healing process, and that psychology could therefore be a means by which a soul could be open to receive the gospel. For, if healing were to be complete, the power of religion to offer forgiveness and absolution had also to be included, since this was something beyond the powers of the psychologist to provide. Weatherhead's psychological understanding, therefore, strongly confirms for him the necessity of the gospel, and makes him an even more convinced evangelist:

> The forgiveness of God, in my opinion, is the most powerful therapeutic idea in the world. If a person really believes that God has forgiven him, then the burden of guilt and the fear at the heart of it disappear [p.338f] . . . psychology, as such, has nothing to say about forgiveness and nothing to say about redemption. It is just at this point that the patient frequently feels an intolerable loneliness and helplessness. At this point he is ready for the good news of the gospel, for something to be done for him and in him which no one can do but God. . . . I have never, in thirty years, known a psychological treatment which, in this field of guilt, could by itself obtain freedom for the patient without recourse to all that the Christian religion offers. [p.348]

Christian worship which combined beauty, honest and relevant preaching, which showed that the Church was concerned for body, mind and spirit, and which emphasised 'God's unfailing, unconditional love' would 'take its place as one of the great integrating and healing factors in the life of the world.' Since love, even the love of God, had to be more than an idea, however, it was not enough to tell a patient, 'God loves you'. To be real it needed to be experienced. A church which had a welcoming fellowship, 'with a warm experience of God in their own hearts' would mediate the love of God through loving persons to the patient. At the City Temple the medical psychiatrists who helped at the Clinic often introduced patients to the Fellowship Groups in the belief that 'a group meeting for Christian fellowship, discussion and prayer, has a very high therapeutic value.'

Weatherhead's final section, 'The Modern Search for Healing Through Psychology and Religion', begins with 'The Needs of the Integrated Personality,' which he says is the goal at which the co-operation between psychology and religion aims. These needs are for the maximum physical, mental and spiritual health attainable. Since 'the primary will of God' is perfect bodily health, 'anything less is a temporary victory of evil.' The healthy body helps the mind to attain health, and the mind 'seems most healthy' when it feeds on beauty and truth, 'when it gets its full measure of affection and is believed in, and when goodwill towards others is practised as a constant habit, and goodwill from others is attracted by virtue of love.' He claims that, in spite of 'the healthy pagans' who never pray or meditate or worship 'no one can be completely healthy without some communion with God . . . maximum health of spirit demands some form of worship, and worship, when it is true communion with God, has again and again proved to have won, as a by-product, increased health for the worshipper.' Physical and psychological treatments on their own 'cannot of themselves integrate personality, for neither can relate it to reality.'

He advocates that ministers should be given some psychological training, and, guarding their own spiritual and mental health through proper spiritual and devotional self-discipline, should give priority in their ministry to the pastoral interview. But the minister should not be a practising psychotherapist. If more than half-a-dozen interviews is needed, the patient should be referred to a Christian medical psychiatrist. If the minister wishes to be more involved it would be better that he should qualify in psychology and medicine and take up this as his Christian vocation. All ministers should be trained to recognise 'psychopathological conditions.' Doctors should be willing to recognise the value of the minister's 'pastoral visit' both in hospital and to the home. Where an illness is psychogenic, the doctor and minister should be able to discuss the case, since there may be factors concerning the patient's home and private life which the minister knows, which have a bearing on the patient's outlook and health. All theological colleges should grant a Diploma in Pastoral Psychology to ordinands 'who successfully complete a reasonably stiff course of study.' The doctor should also be aware that 'a medical training does not make a psychiatrist,' and the minister may legitimately have some reservations about the doctor's ability. The Christian doctor should

> show the patient that he believes in religion. Let him join . . . a discussion
> group where there is co-operation between minister, doctor and patients
> who are well enough to attend. Let the doctor direct people to go to church

and get the fellowship and love which every live church offers. Both ministers and doctors should interest themselves in drawing up a panel of Christian medical psychotherapists and psychiatrists. [p.480f.]

In a chapter on 'The Church Psychological Clinic', Weatherhead describes his own work at the City Temple, in the hope that others will follow. He explains that all applications for assistance came through himself. Where the case could be adequately dealt with by 'psychotherapeutic conversations,' it was not necessary to refer the case to the clinic doctors. Such a 'conversation' needed to be far more than handing out advice:

> the conversation should be designed to spread out his whole problem before the patient with all its ramifications in such a way that the patient himself will see what ought to be done and himself make the decision to do it. Such action carries the patient's not the adviser's authority, and gives him confidence and the sense of being master of his soul. . . . I do not undertake anything worth calling a "treatment." The latter, I hold, is the province of the medically qualified psychotherapist. The doctor who undertakes the case sends me a brief report as to how the patient is progressing, and at the end of the treatment I frequently see the patient and again put before him the needs of the integrated personality and discuss with him how he may attain them. . . . By having the Clinic linked with the Church, we emphasise the place of religion in healing, and we can offer, in the fellowship of the Church, just that atmosphere of love and goodwill which a neurotic so badly needs. . . . In helping at this point the minister has a supernatural ally. . . . It is the desire of most men and women, deep down, to be good. It might be called the 'pull upward'. . . . There is an urge to perfection, a longing for integration, a passion for completeness in personality. On this the minister can always rely. [p.483f.]

He concludes that 'A religious interpretation of life on broad lines seems to me essential to a *complete* integration of personality, and thus to *complete* health.' Neither psychology nor material medicine are substitutes 'for the dynamic spiritual energy which the Church of the first century knew.' Nor are the activities of Lourdes, Christian Science or Spiritualism and Healing Missions. The Church must rediscover

> her lost . . . supernatural gift of healing. . . . The intercession of people united in love for Christ and living disciplined lives, and the laying on of hands, undertaken after prayer and self-discipline, by a priest or minister, or other person who is the contact point, so to speak, of a beloved, believing and united community standing behind him and supporting his ministration to a patient who has been taught to understand the true nature of Christian faith are clues well worth following up. [p.488]

Psychology, Religion and Healing received considerable and world-wide reviews, especially in America and in Australia, where Weatherhead's recent visit had made him particularly well known. Most reviewers, like the *Evening News* (29 September 1951) recognised the book as being of exceptional importance and as 'the first, full-length, authoritative and analytical treatment of its subject'. J. Stafford Wright, in *Life of Faith,* considered that 'There are probably less than half a dozen people in this country with the necessary knowledge, experience and sympathy to write a full-scale book on Healing. There may not be more than one man, and that man Leslie D. Weatherhead.' Gilbert Russell in *Theology* agreed, saying, 'the book is based on a wealth of experience possibly unmatched in any other contemporary religious writer.' The Chaplain of Guy's Hospital declared that it was 'one of the most important books of the year – if not of the century.' For the *South Australian Methodist* it was 'epoch making', and the American preacher and pastor Norman Vincent Peale, in the *New York Herald Tribune* (9 March 1952) considered it 'probably the most thorough book yet written showing the relationship of psychology and medicine to the Christian faith in the solution of personal problems.' The American *Pulpit Digest* judged it 'By far the most complete study of religion and healing that has ever been written.'

The medical press was generally welcoming, responding to Weatherhead's reference in the book to a statement by the Central Ethical Committee of the British Medical Association, following discussions with the Churches' Council of Healing, which had been published in the *British Medical Journal*, encouraging co-operation between Christian ministers and members of the medical profession. *The Lancet* (13 October 1951) strongly approved of Weatherhead's insistence 'that every patient must have all the help that medicine can give', but considered that his examples of cases whose cures were 'inexplicable except by a change in the patient's spiritual life' were not satisfactory evidence from a medical point of view since he had offered no pathological or radiological evidence for them. It concluded that while 'Some doctors will disagree with most of what he says, many with some of it, all should be able to subscribe to his main thesis – that some patients will recover more quickly and completely . . . if the priest is allowed to collaborate with the doctor and to reinforce his treatment with the ministrations of the Church.' Another medical journal, the *Medical Press* (30 April 1952) thought the book 'worthy of the highest commendation.' Although it questioned the status of some of the medical authorities Weatherhead had quoted, it was impressed by the scale of Weatherhead's achievement:

> The field of knowledge gathered together in this book is immense . . . a writer who has studied the psychiatric and psychoanalytical literature so thoroughly and yet maintained a balanced and practical and enlightened outlook as has Dr. Weatherhead, is unique in our time.

The eminent psychiatrist, William Sargant, in *The British Medical Journal*, agreed that 'Psychiatry might gain much from a more searching examination of why spiritual healing is often more successful than its own practices in helping some people in states of mental conflict', and in the *Nursing Times*, (22 December 1951) another well-known psychiatrist, David Stafford-Clark, said 'This is in every sense a very good book. Dr. Weatherhead has succeeded in writing one of the most important books to be produced by this generation of medical or religious writers.'

The religious reviewers were on the whole enthusiatic, none more so than E.H. Jeffs in the *Christian World* (27 December 1951) who compared the book to Columbus setting out on a great voyage of discovery, saying that it constitutes 'a call to the Churches, not to be resisted without peril, to fit out an expedition forthwith. . . . This book inspires us to believe that enough knowlege and faith – reasonable faith – are now available to us to justify, to demand, the launching of our ships on the great adventure'.

Weatherhead's theology – or, in the opinion of some, his lack of it – aroused considerable criticism in some of the more conservative and orthodox journals. The *Church Times* considered his treatment of the subject 'rather superficial at times . . . the author does not handle theological problems with that sureness of touch which he shows in matters of psychology'. Gilbert Russell, in *Theology*, found Weatherhead's 'demand . . . for a "non-sectarian Christianity". . . obsessional.' *The Universe* decided that it must be 'his Protestant training that prevents his finding at Lourdes the big-scale examples of the very truths he is concerned to expound.' The American *United Churchman* (28 February 1952) though it considered Weatherhead was possibly the 'pre-eminent authority' in this field, nevertheless stated 'The book breaks down where he tries to relate psychological and spiritual healing to theology. Dr. Weatherhead's interpretation of the Cross is one-sided. Theology is not his field and the position he upholds is dangerously out-dated. Otherwise this is an excellent book.' An even weightier American broadside came from *The Westminster Theological Journal* (May 1953) which declared that

> the "Christian religion" which Weatherhead firmly believes is so very relevant to the whole involved matter of health is not rooted in an adequate theology. It is not formed by a biblio-theological matrix . . . guilt is nowhere related to the law of God. . . . Weatherhead has no doctrine of original sin by which to explain the tragic character of fallen man . . . the want of an adequate theology robs Weatherhead of the opportunity to give objective character to forgiveness as an element in God's justification of the sinner. . . . Weatherhead . . . knows of no divinely ordered and divinely executed program of redemption in the Christ of Calvary. . . . We must conclude that Weatherhead cannot be regarded as our trusted and qualified mentor to direct us in the increasingly important work of integrating valid psychological insights with sound religion.

Canon C.E. Raven, in *John O'London's Weekly* (7 November 1951) described the book as 'popular rather than academic' and was critical of what he said was 'the lack of any adequate treatment of the place of suffering in the life of man and the purpose of God. The naive assumption that suffering is contrary to God's will . . . his book does not seem to show any very profound insight into the problem.' This provoked Weatherhead to protest that he had stated in the Preface that suffering was not the subject of the book, and that he had dealt with it at some length in his previous book, *Why Do Men Suffer?*

The previous week, in the same journal, Clifford Allen, author of *Modern Discoveries in Medical Psychology*, found Weatherhead's argument about the possibility of demon possession 'grossly fallacious', saying 'our knowledge of the cause of epilepsy is much greater than Weatherhead admits.' Weatherhead's claim to have experienced such psychic phenomena as ectoplasm, Allen says, shows that he 'fails to maintain a scientific outlook in many places in his book.' Allen refused to accept that religion had a place in the treatment of psychological illness: 'The only reason why it should have is that a great deal of neurosis is caused by a sense of guilt which, in itself, has been implanted by wrong types of religious teaching.'

Other reviewers were startled by the reference to ectoplasm, but though this aroused some reservations, they were impressed by the book as a whole. In *Pastoral Psychology* (February 1952), Seward Hiltner, Associate Professor of Pastoral Theology in the University of Chicago, thought that this demonstrated 'a courage to examine many things, for better or worse, which are usually tossed off with a sophisticated shrug.' In a generally favourable review, *Psychic News* thought that 'spiritualists will probably feel that the doctor's prejudices get in the way when he comes to consider their methods of healing.' Hiltner, on the basis of what Weatherhead had to say about Christian Science, judged that he was

> a broad and comprehensive, but not a deep scholar . . . in discussing Christian Science . . . he does not attempt to clarify the inner nature of the appeal of Christian Science to some people. For this kind of reason, none of his discussions may be considered the final and definitive treatments of his subjects.

Donald Soper, however, thought the opposite. In his obituary tribute to Weatherhead for the *Methodist Recorder* (15 January 1976) he wrote, 'To anyone who would disparage his scholarship. . . . Let me commend his masterly chapter on Christian Science in his book *Psychology, Religion and Healing*.'

Published in September, 1951, *Psychology, Religion and Healing* sold out 10,000 copies in the first three months. It was reprinted in December, and a second edition, revised and enlarged, appeared in 1952. It was reprinted with further revisions in 1955, 1959 and 1963.

The Rev.J. Vipond, who had reviewed the book favourably for the *Church of England Newspaper*, returned to it again nearly three years later (on 1 January 1954) saying that,

> its contents have had a widespread influence on the thought of our time. It came into the shops when the Church's revived interest in healing was at its peak, and preserved it from the enthusiasm of cranks. Its sanity brought the goodwill of the medical profession, and its cogent argument that unhealthy thinking and unspiritual attitudes of mind cause illness made a good case for the need of religion. It is a scholarly and well-written book which no thinking Christian can afford to neglect.

Psychology, Religion and Healing contained several appendices which gave detailed case studies of healings which had apparently taken place through prayer and worship. With these, Weatherhead had included both a complete form of service for the laying on of hands and a form 'for gathering information about a patient who seeks psychological help.' With Weatherhead's account of his own methods, the book provided a practical guide for anyone who wished to follow his lead, and this aroused a response. E.H. Jeffs' article in *The Christian World* brought a letter suggesting that 'accredited representatives of both Christian Science and Christian Spiritualism' should be invited to explain their theory and practice to the Congregational churches. The Methodist, Maldwyn Edwards, called for a much bolder approach to intercessions for the sick and for including 'a place in Church services for Prayer Fellowship in which two or three people are specifically mentioned', and for laymen as well as Christian ministers to 'know more of the laws which govern the health of mind and body.' Sydney Myers, minister of Princes Street Congregational Church, Norwich, in a review for the *Eastern Daily Press*, found the 'most important part of the book' was 'the reiterated plea for fuller co-operation between doctors, parsons, psychiatrists and others directly involved in ministering to the various ills of men and women.' He asked 'Is it possible . . . to effect closer team-work in Norwich and Norfolk between our doctors, parsons and psychiatrists. . . . Will anyone go forward here?'

In July 1952 Weatherhead presented to the Methodist Conference the report of the Committee on Spiritual Healing. In this he said that 'interest in spiritual healing was extending in all the churches.' He warned against Conference giving its sanction to 'so-called healing missions', saying that it was rare for anybody to be permanently healed at such a mission. He pleaded with Conference to direct that "healing," or the laying-on of hands with the intention of healing, should be done privately. Such meetings should consist only of the patient and a small group of friends, together with praying people who had thought their way through the problems involved. The Conference accepted the report and directed that persons attending services on church premises for the purpose of receiving the ministry of the laying-on of hands should have been prepared privately by their minister and should have the consent of their doctors.

This attracted considerable correspondence, which Weatherhead followed up in August with an article, 'How Can We Obey Christ's Behest to Heal the Sick?', which provoked even more letters, mainly concerned with his criticisms of healing missions. This continued well into October, ending with another article by Weatherhead, 'Methodism and Spiritual Healing', in which he replied to his critics and repeated his condemnation of healing missions.

Weatherhead's work had attracted considerable interest outside his own denomination and even outside the Church itself. The *Sunday Times* printed an article by a consultant psychiatrist on the subject of spiritual healing, which praised the work of the City Temple Clinic which it described in detail. In October, 1952, the Archbishop of York, Dr. Cyril Garbett, gave an address on spiritual healing that owed a great deal to Weatherhead's book. The *Sunday Graphic* invited him to write a response to Dr. Garbett. In this Weatherhead supported everything Garbett had said, and he further praised the Archbishop's address in the *Methodist Recorder*. This prompted a personal letter from Garbett in which he referred to Weatherhead's book as 'the fullest and clearest statement I know on the whole subject and I have been recommending it to those who wish to know more of the subject.'

Psychology, Religion and Healing established Weatherhead as the acknowledged authority on all non-physical methods of healing, and gave considerable impetus to the debate on spiritual healing. Weatherhead's own interest also moved increasingly in this direction. In January, 1952, at the Convocation of Canterbury, the Dean of Salisbury, H.C. Robins, proposed 'That this House commends to the sympathetic attention of the Church and particularly of parish priests the modern revival of spiritual healing.' Weatherhead was one of the signatories of a letter to *The Times* (31 January 1952) welcoming this move, which announced the setting up of an interdenominational centre by the Guild of Health, which had the backing of both the medical profession and the church, 'to enable clergy, doctors, psychologists and members of the nursing profession, to work together in furthering the cause of health and healing.'

20. Rebuilding: Thanks to Rockefeller

'they might raise a marvellous church at a cost of a quarter of a million
pounds and fail miserably in the eyes of God, unless in the members was
such a quality of life that others longed to possess it and who found
that the closer they got in fellowship with the City Temple Church,
the richer was their experience of Christ.'

To mark the eleventh anniversary of the destruction of the City Temple, a service was held in St. Sepulchre's and broadcast on the B.B.C. World Service. Weatherhead had wished that instead of rebuilding the City Temple, they could purchase St. Sepulchres from the Anglican authorities, enlarge it in the same architectural style, and carry on there. He had mentioned this to Archbishop Fisher, but received no response.

The problems surrounding the rebuilding of the church continued to be his major concern. It was finally decided, with Weatherhead's reluctant agreement, that to rebuild on the old Holborn site was the only practical option for the church. It was easier to obtain a building licence for the original site, and some money could be claimed from the War Damages Commission, at least for a plain substitute building. The Rebuilding Fund held only £25,000, but any appeal for funds was only possible when positive action towards rebuilding had been taken. The church had anticipated receiving a substantial amount from the Congregational Union Reconstruction Fund, but the claims which other churches had made on it ahead of the City Temple had considerably reduced the amount available. More delay inevitably meant that this would be reduced even further. Weatherhead made clear his regret at the decision, though accepting that there was now no practical alternative. He once again reviewed the arguments against going back to Holborn, 'where nobody goes on Sundays', at a time when church attendances generally were declining, and transport was becoming more difficult and expensive.

The Rebuilding Committee appointed Lord Mottistone and Mr. Paul Paget as their new architects. It was hoped that they would co-operate with Mr. Ronald Sims, who had taken over the practice of Frederic Lawrence, and so be able to use some of Lawrence's original plans. However, the question of the copyright of the plans proved awkward, since this was claimed by Sims. The church did not feel able to appoint Sims himself to continue what Lawrence had started, since Sims was only newly qualified, and he readily accepted that he was not a suitable choice for this particular commission. It became evident that the only way forward was to start afresh with completely new plans provided by Mottistone and Paget.

The new architects had a very different approach from that of Frederic Lawrence, and it seems that, after all the delays and setbacks, the church decided to go for someone safe, rather than adventurous, with a well-established reputation. Lord Mottistone was a principal architect for the Anglican establishment. He was the surveyor of fabric for St. Paul's Cathedral, and architect to St. George's Chapel, Windsor, and to Portsmouth Cathedral. He had been responsible for the reconstruction after war damage of Lambeth Palace, and the Deanery and Canons' Houses of Westminster Abbey. He had also designed the Chapel for the Order of the British Empire in St. Paul's. Among his other commissions were work at Eton College, Fulham Palace, the Charterhouse, London, and several churches, including St. Mary's, Islington and All Hallows by the Tower.

Mottistone quickly advised that the existing tower and facade should be kept, since this would make it easier for permission to be obtained from the War Claims Commission to rebuild. Weatherhead was delighted with the new plans. 'I have no word of criticism for any part of them. . . . To have listened to all our demands and to have incorporated them into a building of beauty and usefulness has been a work of sheer genius on the part of our architects.' There was the considerable problem of raising the necessary money, particularly as it was strongly felt that the new building should be opened entirely free from debt. The estimated cost of new building was put at approximately £250,000, and in addition they would need an Endowment fund of £50,000. The secretary of the Appeals Committee, John Dewey, with his connections in the City, was confident that substantial sums would be forthcoming from organisations within the City, and the rest from England and abroad. It was arranged for Weatherhead to spend some six months seeking to raise money in the United States, which he agreed to, without much confidence in his ability to achieve the hoped-for result.

A report in the British press that the German arms manufacturer, Alfred Krupp, had been awarded thirty million pounds to restore his industrial empire prompted Dewey to draft a letter which Weatherhead signed and sent to Krupp, suggesting that since the City Temple had been destroyed by German bombs, presumably made in his factories, Krupp might be willing to donate some of this money towards the rebuilding of the church. Herr Leonhard Lunk replied on behalf of Krupp, saying that the press reports were wrong, that Krupp had no large amounts to dispose of, and that he was therefore in no position to help.

Changes were taking place in the life of the church. In December, 1951, the Friday Fellowship, which had long been a distinctive feature of the church's activities, was re-organised by Miss Winifred Barton to become the Community Evening. The evening was planned to begin between six and seven o'clock with the providing of a 'substantial meal' and an opportunity for social fellowship. From 7 p.m. there were a variety of of 'sectional activities' which ranged from table tennis and Scottish dancing to prayer meetings, Bible study and serious debates. The evening concluded with an epilogue at 8.30 p.m. conducted by the members themselves. Weatherhead welcomed this initiative enthusiastically, hoping that it would go some way to solving the problem that the City Temple shared with other city centre churches, which, although they attracted considerable congregations, were not community based: that of enabling the members to meet and get to know each other socially. It also provided him with an opportunity, which he seized whenever he could, to get to know his church members better, and to enter into friendly conversation with them.

Weatherhead was much less happy when he found himself reluctantly forced to do something about the choir. For him, the quality of the music in worship was of considerable importance, since so much of the atmosphere of a service depended on it. But over a number of years the standard of the choir had deteriorated so much that he felt that this had become an increasing embarrassment which could no longer be ignored. Wanting to avoid having to pick out individuals, with all the hurt and unpleasantness that would involve, he finally decided, with the support of the Church Council, to sack the whole choir, with the exception of the four professional soloists, and then to invite anyone who wished to belong to audition for it. A stricter voice test was introduced, and a requirement that only those who could read music would be accepted. As far as possible he hoped that all choir members would be members of the church. A choir committee was also set up without whose approval no-one would be allowed to join the choir. To his considerable relief, this arrangement succeeded in producing a greatly improved choir, without any break in continuity, and allowed some of the older members to retire gracefully without too much pain – though not without some protest at the church meeting.

Weatherhead opened the new session of the Literary Society on 9 October with a lecture on 'Psychology and Psychiatry; Yesterday, Today and Tomorrow.' In this he defined Psychology as the science of behaviour, Psychotherapy as the art of healing the mind which has become neurotically or emotionally ill, and Psychiatry as the art which deals also with the mind that has become psychotic or insane.

> Because Psychology is the science of behaviour it is relevant to every problem in which behaviour is a factor in the total situation, so we had the introduction of psychology into the fields of industry, education, crime, marriage, child-welfare and religion, as well as into the field of healing.

Much of the lecture was a summary of *Psychology, Religion and Healing*, and stressed the importance of psychology in healing. He criticised the trend towards interpreting the 'phenomena in terms of the material', and the use of physical means, such as electric shock treatment, to remedy the sources of human behaviour.

> He was far from despising or condemning these methods but the philosophy which imagined that they proved the superiority of matter over mind was, he thought, as silly as supposing that you made a person non-musical in nature by taking away from him the musical instruments by which alone he could express his musical temperament. You had not altered his nature but limited or destroyed the instruments he used to express it.

In an article in January, 1953, the *Daily Sketch* asked its readers 'Do You Want a Brighter Sunday?' Weatherhead was delighted when from among 'the thousands' who responded, the *Daily Sketch* printed a letter from a 'Housewife, Beckenham', who wrote enthusiastically about the difference attending the City Temple each Sunday had made to her life. Yet, although all seemed to be going well with the church, Weatherhead was concerned that there was a lack of genuine fellowship and Christian spirit at the heart of the church's organisation, and he drew attention to this in his address to the Annual Church Meeting. He praised the newly formed Community evening as 'the outstanding development of the past year' and the Psychological Clinic and the members of the Prayer Circles who 'were doing their part in the healing ministry of the church.' But he went on to say that he thought that those who derived the greatest good from the church were those who attended the services but were furthest away from 'the grinding of the machinery' at the centre:

the Devil was quite ready to tell them that it was a successful church, that their finances were marvellous, and their congregations crowded, but let them remember that this was the kind of thing the Devil *would* say, and the truth was that the gossiping, pettiness, little-mindedness and excessive cliquing that went on in certain organizations which he could name, should remind them that they might raise a marvellous church at a cost of a quarter of a million pounds and fail miserably in the eyes of God, unless in the members was such a quality of life that others longed to possess it and who found that the closer they got in fellowship with the City Temple Church, the richer was their experience of Christ.

Weatherhead hated gossip, which he regarded as one of the most destructive and deadly poisons within a church and fellowship. The gulf between the ideal of the church which he wanted it to attain and the reality created by the all too fallible human beings who made up the membership must always have troubled him, though the City Temple was not necessarily, or noticeably, any worse than most churches, and no doubt a great deal better than many. But Weatherhead was an idealist and a perfectionist, who wanted the church to be the best it was capable of being, and he would not ever let it slide into complacency and pride because of its fame and success.

At the same meeting, one of the members, Mrs. Mines, drew attention to the fact that although the cost of living had trebled during Weatherhead's time at the church, the salaries of the City Temple staff had not been increased. Weatherhead had no warning that this matter of salaries was going to be raised, but he seized the opportunity to say that the four members of the staff were not adequately paid, and that this should be looked into, particularly since the church was showing a significant credit balance in its accounts. He went on to say, 'with great diffidence', that after 17 years service he was being paid less than his predecessor, Dr. Norwood, although when he began his ministry there, the church was between six and seven thousand pounds in debt, which had not only been wiped out but for ten years the accounts had been closed with a substantial credit balance, as well as having a substantial sum in the Reserve Fund. He proposed the appointment of a small committee to look into the matter and take such steps as were necessary, and he suggested that the meeting should authorize any necessary payment to be made from the Reserve Fund in this connection. This was received with 'great enthusiasm' by the meeting. As a result, the four members of staff were given increases in their salaries, retrospectively from 1 May. Weatherhead, with the agreement of his wife, refused to accept an increase, but he pointed out that when he eventually left, the church would have to find the money not only for a higher salary for the new minister but also for a manse as well, since the house in which he was living was his own.

On 17 May Weatherhead preached on Church Unity at the evening service in St. Paul's Cathedral. This had received advance publicity in the national press and the building was crowded, with people standing at the back. In his sermon he repeated many of his previous statements about unity and the Church of England, claiming that there was a far greater divergence of views within the Anglican Church than existed between all the Free Churches, and questioning the Thirty Nine Articles, saying that it was wrong to demand intellectual acceptance of theological propositions. He attacked the linking of the Church with the State, and the interpretation of episcopacy as depending for its validity on the apostolic succession through the physical act of the laying-on of hands, but repeated his willingness to be "re-ordained" by an Anglican Bishop which he would regard not as 'a repudiation of my previous ministry, but as a dedication to a wider ministry in the future. (Perhaps ordination, then, is not the word.)' He attacked as sinful the Anglican refusal to allow those attending Youth Conferences at Amsterdam, Oslo and Bangor to share in Communion with other Christians, and added, 'I think it is also a sin that if a young Indian Christian who is an Anglican joins the United Church of South India there, and then for some reason comes to this country, he finds that he has put himself out of communion with the Anglican Church here though that Church was part of the Union in India.' He argued that the way forward for unity was to unite in action against evil. He praised the way the Church's Council of Healing was bringing together members of all denominations to revive the ministry of healing, saying that there were 'a hundred great causes in which, in Christ's name, we could unite.' He called for a ten year ban on arguing in favour of doing. Through such unity in action, Christians of all persuasions would get to know one another better, and 'please God, love one another, and the unity of love is greater than the unity of intellect and far more convincing to the world.'

The *Christian World* printed the sermon in full. The *Daily Sketch* report focused on Weatherhead's willingness to be re-ordained with the headline, 'Sensation in St. Paul's.' But *The Church Times* (1 May 1953) was so offended by the use of the pulpit of St. Paul's by someone not episcopally ordained that it declared that it would 'discontinue, until further notice, the announcement of the names of preachers . . . in the said cathedral church.'

In October, Weatherhead opened the eighteenth year of his City Temple ministry with a lecture to the Literary Society on 'Some Unexplored Secrets of the Mind.' In this, he discussed the work of the Society for Psychical Research, of which he was a member, and argued that 'The idolatry of materialistic science was coming to an end and a new interest in non-material concepts and values was arising.' He insisted that 'The phenomena of psychical research were factual. . . . It was the explanations that needed exploring.'

The same month, Epworth produced his latest book, *That Immortal Sea*. This was another volume of sermons, produced at the instigation of Dr. Leslie Church and the Rev. Frank Cumbers, who was then the Managing Editor of the Epworth Press. The book includes a sermon on 'Christ's Unconventional Love.' Above the title of this in his own copy he wrote, 'The favourite, I think, of all my sermons; preached at M. Dec.3 1950 & broadcast in N.Y. in 1954'. This sermon is quintessential Weatherhead. In it he speaks in simple language about the way Jesus treated individuals, loving them unconditionally. He describes Jesus as being free from the 'conventional ecclesiasticism of His day' and expressing the most profound messages about God in simple terms that ordinary people could understand. Weatherhead presents the friendship of Jesus as a present reality, being offered at that moment to each of his hearers. He appeals to them to accept it, without dwelling on their sins or any sense of unworthiness, since it is freely offered, saying that to accept it is also to receive a joy which removes all meanness of spirit: 'Christ can so fill your heart with His joy that there will be no room left in it for anything but love.'

The reviewer in *The Methodist Recorder* (17 December 1953) was particularly moved by this sermon, saying that it 'stabs the conscience awake. I read and reread 'Christ's Unconventional Love' several times within two or three days.' *The British Weekly* described the book as 'Weatherhead at his effective best.' *John O'London's Weekly* (13 November 1953) referred to Weatherhead as 'a preacher who draws a congregation by main force, spiritual force', and praised his courage in dodging none of the main issues, adding, 'the book is almost worth the money for the quotations', picking out as an example his attack on science which disdains humanity, 'Hell is paved with good inventions.' Commenting on the fact that in this book Weatherhead says nothing about 'his wonderful work in blending healing psychology with religion,' the reviewer describes this as 'a modern Christian enterprise which may in future be seen to compare with the starting of medical hospitals by the medieval church.'

Other reviewers were equally enthusiastic – apart from the *The Church Times* which decided to ignore the book altogether. No previous book of Weatherhead's had received such universal praise and acceptance. Dr. Ryder Smith, in the *London Quarterly and Holborn Review* (January 1954) wrote his review in the form of a letter addressed directly to Weatherhead:

Dear W., I must just write you a line about your latest volume. It must be about fifteen years since I heard you preach, and do you know, you've improved. I should hardly have thought it possible, but there it is . . . you will expect me to disagree with you sometimes, and so I do. . . . I do not think your doctrine of 'luck' will hold water, and I'm not sure that you cover the whole ground about pain. . . . But 'What is this between thee and me?' You say that your purpose is to give people 'a glimpse of Jesus'. Well, old fellow, again and again in these sermons I've seen Him. So will other people, and that is the test of tests.

In spite of the fact that books of sermons had gone out of fashion, and were no longer thought to be popular, as most of his reviewers predicted, *That Immortal Sea* became an immediate best-seller.

The City Temple launched a World-Wide Appeal for its Rebuilding Fund with a luncheon at the Mansion House in February 1954. This was arranged by John Dewey and hosted by the Lord Mayor, Sir Noel Bowater. Among the guests were some of the most important and influential people in the City, including the Chairman of Lloyds, the Chairman of the Coal, Corn and Finance Committee of the City of London, the Chairman of the Stock Exchange, the President of the City of London Retail Traders' Association, the Marshal of the City of London and several former Lord Mayors. Weatherhead was not pleased with the way the press reported the event. He was particularly angered by the *Daily Mirror* whose criticism of his forthcoming trip to America to raise funds there was reproduced in Washington and New York, raising prejudices, he felt, against his visit before it began. He was also annoyed by the *Daily Mail* which 'reported nothing at all except a three-line flippancy because the Toast Master mispronounced my name.' Several other papers got the figures wrong, and he was only just in time to stop one of the most famous papers in the country reporting that we only wanted £3,000 and that the church would seat four hundred people! Since every reporter was provided with a brochure with all the facts and figures in it, it is unpardonable that responsible papers should send irresponsible reporters to a function of such importance.

He was somewhat mollified by being rung up by an old Methodist friend, Sir Leighton Seagar, who promised to pay the entire cost of the Lunch, and when the distinguished artist, Frank Salisbury, who was also present, and had now become a member of the City Temple, promised to paint his portrait if someone would pay £500 into the Rebuilding Fund.

It had been arranged for Weatherhead to spend ninety days in the United States from 12 March, returning in time to attend the Methodist Conference in July. He had mixed feelings about this trip. He did not enjoy appealing for money, and the letters he had been receiving from America about his prospects of raising any significant amount were discouraging. A friend who had recently made a similar visit found that he was only able to cover the cost of his passage through receiving a last-minute gift from an individual. Weatherhead remembered also that his predecessor, Dr. Norwood, had left the church for several months for a money-raising world tour, which had resulted in little money, and an emptier church when he returned. Generous gifts from North America had been made to help restore bomb-damaged churches in England: Canterbury Cathedral had received half-a-million dollars from Thomas W. Lamont of the J.P. Morgan Company in 1947, and in 1953 an anonymous Canadian gift of 100,000 dollars was made to Westminster Abbey. These no doubt encouraged the City Temple Council to hope that their church's appeal might attract a similar generous response, but the length of time from the ending of the war to the start of the rebuilding meant that the City Temple was very late in seeking to tap the sympathy and good will from America that the bonds of war had created.

Weatherhead was well aware that he could not go to America only to raise money, and that to attempt to do so would undoubtedly mean that the American authorities would refuse to allow him to enter their country. In order to visit America at all, he had to accept a host of invitations to preach and lecture which he had previously been turning down. In doing so, he failed to take account of the travelling times and distances involved, accepting appointments on consecutive days which were often in places several hundred miles apart.

The tour began with a reception in New York on 19 March attended by many prominent American ministers and laymen, under the auspices of the World Council of Churches. The host at this event and for his two weeks stay in the city was a friend from his former visits to America, Mr. O. Dickenson Street, who was largely responsible for the arrangements for this present visit. Street was a member of the Reformed Church, Bronxville, where Weatherhead had his first preaching engagement. With the minister, Dr. Russell Lowell Ditzen, who, as a student, had first heard Weatherhead preach some twenty years before, he had prepared a special brochure for the occasion, welcoming Weatherhead as 'one of the most inspiring, thought-provoking and helpful preachers of our time.'

This booklet, which included photographs and an account of the bombed City Temple (which it inaccurately described as 'the oldest non-Anglican church in England'), consisted of tributes to Weatherhead from prominent Americans in the different spheres of his interests. Among these, the one which no doubt gave Weatherhead the greatest pleasure was from Dr. Harry Emerson Fosdick, who wrote about his preaching, which he said was

notable for its vital relevance to every man's need. He knows human nature;

*Leslie Weatherhead saying goodbye to his wife before
leaving for a preaching and lecturing tour of the U.S.A.*

he has shared its problems in war and peace, and with insight and eloquence
he brings the Christian gospel to bear both on our intimate personal needs
and our public concern.

Dr. John Sutherland Bonnell, of the Fifth Avenue Presbyterian Church, described
him as 'one of the foremost pioneers in the English-speaking world in the
application of spiritual therapy to human problems'. The Book Editor of the
Methodist Church in America, Dr. Nolan B. Harmon, referred to him as 'an
author who has reached millions of people by his books. It has been said that he
is the best-known religious writer in the world.' The Professor of Preaching at
Yale Divinity School, Dr. Halford E. Luccock, wrote about the 'unique and
unforgettable experience' of hearing Weatherhead give the Beecher Lectures
on Preaching at Yale five years earlier.

To me, as to many others, it was a rare achievement in the communication of
mind and spirit to a large audience. . . . There is a quality about Dr.
Weatherhead's personality and speech which is his own, a rare combination
of deep-feeling clarity and pungency of expression and delightful sense of
humor which plays around his thought like heat lightning.

Dean Lynn Harold Hough added his own warm tribute, welcoming him as
one of England's most distinguished preachers. . . . The Reformed Church

of Bronxville will recognize at once the authentic quality of the word which Dr. Weatherhead speaks, and will feel the touch of magic in his personal charm.

In addition to the Brochure, Dr. Ditzen had written a personal letter to the minister of every church in America where Weatherhead was due to preach, commending the work of the City Temple. At Bronxville Weatherhead was greeted with crowded congregations and was much relieved to find that the day's collections, amounting to over 2,000 dollars, more than covered the whole of the cost of his passage to America and back.

During the following week he addressed a conference of psychiatrists and ministers. He found the programme 'rather tiring (at one session I answered questions for three hours).' The next Sunday morning he preached at Christ Church Methodist Church for Dr. Ralph Sockman. Here the collection for the City Temple amounted to £200. That evening he preached 'at the only Congregational Church which has invited me during the whole trip, namely Broadway Tabernacle on Broadway.' He was greatly disappointed at having so little welcome from the City Temple's fellow denominationalists, compared with the support he was receiving from the American Methodists. At the request of Helen Keller he recorded a reading of the whole of his book, *The Will of God*, for the John Milton Society for the Blind. Though he reported that he was 'very fit and happy', he was beginning to feel the considerable pressures of his heavy programme. He wrote home, 'The demands of a trip like this do throw one back on one's spiritual resources, and I have never realized before the truth of the saying, "Let him who would have an experience of God take on a job that is beyond his powers and then pray."'

The American multi-millionaire, John D. Rockefeller, who had attended the service at the Park Avenue Church, hosted a luncheon for him, then invited him to his home. He was shocked to learn of the heavy schedule that Weatherhead had taken on. He begged him to cancel some of his engagements, and insisted on giving him a tour manager, Mr. Harry Fish, an economist from the Rockefeller Foundation and a member of the Riverside Church, to look after him and handle all his hotel reservations and tour details. Weatherhead was particularly grateful that Fish also took over the keeping of the accounts of the tour which included not only Weatherhead's expenses, but all the various collections and donations from churches and individuals towards the Rebuilding Fund. But Rockefeller's generosity went further still. The following day, Weatherhead received a letter promising a gift of money which immediately provided most of what he was seeking to raise, so that the major burden and worry of his trip was lifted from him almost from the beginning.

Rockefeller was not the only generous business man in New York to help him. Mr. Stephen Clark, of the Singer Sewing Machine Company, sent him ten thousand dollars, and Mr. Myrom Taylor, who was the American representative to the Vatican, and who attended the City Temple whenever he was in London, sent him another five thousand. Weatherhead forwarded the money to the Treasurer, Alice Head, who immediately and profitably invested it, but both kept it a close secret until after Weatherhead had returned home.

From New York he travelled to Philadelphia, chauffered by Dickenson Street's son and daughter-in-law, who had given up their summer holiday to look after him. He was very appreciative of this, since they saved him from a great deal of the stress and fatigue of travelling long distances. In Philadelphia he was required to preach twice on the Sunday morning, at 9.30 a.m. and immediately afterwards at 11.0. a.m. Though both services were packed he greatly disliked doing this, since having preached his usual length of sermon, there was almost no time for a break between the first service and the next. From there he went on to Washington for two days, where he gave the address at a luncheon, gave a lecture, and felt much honoured to be invited to give the prayer at the opening of the Senate, where he met Vice-President Nixon. He preached at the Foundry Methodist Church, where he was delighted to find that the minister, Dr. Frederick Brown Harris, not only subscribed to the *City Temple Tidings*, but used one of Weatherhead's own prayers in his Baptism service.

The American papers were very interested in his views on the Billy Graham Crusade, then taking place in London. In England, somewhat unexpectedly to many people, Weatherhead had defended Graham against his critics, telling people to go and hear him, and describing him as a 'sincere, humble, genuine person. He has a great gift . . . for which we should thank God.' Weatherhead had attended a service at Harringay and said that he 'could not find anything in the whole service that was psychologically unsound.' There was no building up of emotion and the service was entirely free from the methods of the American hot gospellers. There was no sensationalism in Graham's preaching, which was 'very simple and very challenging.' Weatherhead described what Graham was doing as 'magnificent', and asked why people were so critical. Graham's theology might be fundamentalist, but the theology could be dealt with later. He praised the way Graham was reaching ordinary people, 'I wish I could do that sort of thing and bear that kind of witness. I am not going to be critical because somebody else can do what we have failed to do. I am going to pray for him and his converts, and I invite you to do the same.' He repeated this appreciation in

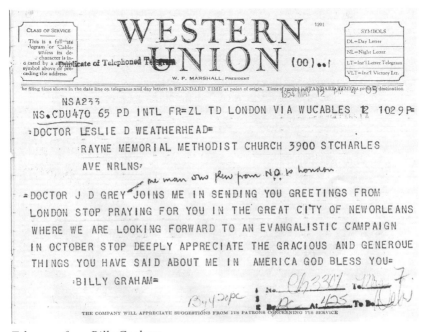

Telegram from Billy Graham

his interviews with the American press. In response, Graham sent him a telegram from London, 'Deeply appreciate the gracious and generous things you have said about me in America. God bless you. Billy Graham.'

Weatherhead repeated his defence shortly after his return to England in July, when he preached at Marylebone on 'The Gospel According to Billy Graham.' He argued that everyone must translate Christ's gospel into terms of their own personality. 'It does not become "my gospel" until I can do that. I cannot pass it on to another until I have made it my own.' Of Billy Graham he said, 'I made a resolution some time ago that as a Minister I would not criticise another Minister unless in my opinion he was doing definite harm. In my opinion this man has done immense good to an immeasurable number of people, and we should do well to thank God for him and seek to conserve and stabilize the results of his mission.' Having so often been on the receiving end of harsh, unjust and unkind criticism himself, Weatherhead knew how wounding it could be.

From Washington Weatherhead flew to Chicago, where he preached at the North-Western University, and in the evening spoke in a broadcast service at the Sunday Evening Club to an audience of 2,000. 'It was midnight before I got to bed, but it was worth it.' The following day he was relieved to be invited for a round of golf. 'I was hungry for fresh air and exercise. . . . I played badly as usual but it was good fun.'

He moved on to Cleveland, and then Detroit, where he preached at the Trumbull Avenue Presbyterian Church. From there he went to St. Louis and then to Wichita Falls in Texas where he gave the Perkins Lectures, which consisted of ten lectures in five days. By this time the considerable strain of his exhausting tour was seriously affecting him. He described this as 'the most demanding week I think

At Wichita Falls, Texas, April 1954.

I have ever lived through.' He spoke twice every day from Sunday to Thursday inclusively, and each address lasted an hour. After the Sunday morning service he felt so unwell that a doctor was called, who diagnosed that his endocrine system had collapsed. With the help of injections and a regular massage after each morning lecture he was able to get through the week. The temperature was over 85 degrees, and he was amazed at the way people turned up to hear him, with some 1,500 each morning and over 2,000 each evening. The strain of the tour was now so great that he even feared he would have to abandon it and return home. In some places he found that though he had accepted one engagement, when he arrived he was expected to fulfil several others. He was also unprepared for the considerable changes of temperature: leaving a cold winter climate in Detroit and next day finding himslef in the sub-tropical heat and humidity of St. Louis. He found it impossible to rest, and began to feel jaded and exhausted. He wrote to his congregation:

> I have been tremendously helped by your prayers. Please continue to help me. I need that help sometimes desperately. I have never been so thrown back on God for His sustaining power and grace as I have been on this trip and He has never failed me.

It was a relief to be able to visit in Memphis his eldest son Dick, a senior physician on the staff of a mental hospital there. Dick accompanied him to New Orleans, where he gave another series of lectures at the Rayne Memorial Church, and was made an honorary citizen of the city. Needing to cut down this impossible schedule, he cancelled his other engagements in Texas and flew to California, where he gave the Commencement Address at the Pacific School of Religion, Berkeley, and was awarded an Honorary Doctorate of Divinity. From there he flew to Tacoma in Washington State, to give the Graduation Address at the College of Puget Sound. Here he was given the Honorary degree of Doctor of Letters. In Tacoma he addressed the Methodist Conference of the Pacific North-West, and was delighted at being reunited with his second son, Kingsley, a professor of English Literature there. Having cancelled his engagements in Los Angeles and Arizona, he was able to spend a few days with his family, which gave him time to restore his health and recover from the sheer fatigue of his tour.

He returned to New York for his last engagement, which was to preach at the Riverside Drive church which had been built by Rockefeller for Harry Emerson Fosdick. That Sunday he was again a guest of John D. Rockefeller and his wife. He was much impressed to be be staying in the home of 'perhaps the richest man in the world. . . . Two more humble, lovable, unassertive and sincere Christian people I have never met.' Rockefeller initiated a discussion of the results of Weatherhead's trip, and he was overwhelmed when Mrs. Rockefeller, 'desired to to have a share in the heart-warming action of her husband. The amount she named brought me the knowledge in that moment that the burden was entirely lifted; the gap closed.'

He came home to an enormous welcome. 'The congregations on 11th July were amazing, and at night I fear many could not gain entrance and scores stood for the entire service. What a joyous day it was!' He spoke at length at both services about his American trip, and was able to begin by announcing that owing to the generosity of American friends, and especially Mr. and Mrs. J.D. Rockefeller, he had returned from America with gifts and promises amounting to

Rockefeller, he had returned from America with gifts and promises amounting to over half a million dollars, which meant that the total amount needed for the rebuilding of the church had now been raised, and they could look forward to opening the new building entirely free of debt.

21. President of the Methodist Conference

'I deeply love Methodism, and I owe everything to Methodism, and
I shall serve Methodism as well as I can.'

Weatherhead returned from the States in time to attend the Methodist Conference, which was meeting that year in London under the shock of the news that four Methodist workers had been murdered the previous week by members of the Mau Mau organisation in Kenya. The Conference elected him President-Designate, after two votes had been taken. Dr. Harold Roberts, whose name had appeared second in the ballot, withdrew, saying that he did not feel that he would be able to sustain the usual very heavy itinerary which had been planned for the President. In his view too much was demanded of the President in his year of office, and he felt that his own physical health would not be able to stand the pressure of these demands. Weatherhead, so soon after his exhausting tour of the United States, felt very much the same. He hesitated about accepting, but the honour meant a great deal to him, especially as his ministry was in a church outside Methodism.

The election did not come as a complete surprise, since his name had appeared on ballots in previous years. One senior Methodist described him at the Conference as the Prodigal Son of Methodism. This was no doubt meant kindly, but it was also unfair: he had not deserted Methodism, and was not therefore a repentant returning to the fold, but a greatly distinguished Methodist – probably the most famous Methodist minister in the world – with a huge reputation, who had earned the recognition of his church and peers. The press quoted a 'spokesman at the Conference' who said, 'This is the first time in our history that we have invited the minister of a Congregational Church to be our President', describing it as 'a remarkable gesture of Christian Unity.' This reaction suggests that Weatherhead was regarded by some as being now fully outside Methodism. *The Times* (8 July 1954) was nearer the truth when it reported,

> The fact that the Methodist Conference has asked Dr. Weatherhead to become President next year while serving as minister of the City Temple is a tribute to his outstanding personality. A "near precedent" to his election was stated by an official of the Conference yesterday to be the election of the late Dr. J.H. Ritson to the presidency of the Wesleyan conference in 1925 while serving as secretary of the British and Foreign Bible Society.

The Church Council of the City Temple passed a unanimous resolution recognising the honour done to their minister, saying they 'will be glad to set him free during that year for whatever duties the office demands.' As an expression of gratitude for the success of his American tour, they provided a Rover car for his use, though this remained the property of the church.

In November, Weatherhead made a nostalgic return to his old family church in Saxby Street, Leicester. In 1940, this church also, like the City Temple, had been destroyed by German bombs, and he was asked to launch the church's rebuilding fund. While in Leicester he lectured in the De Montfort Hall, the largest hall in the city, to over 1,700 people, on 'The Church's Ministry of Healing.'

Leslie Weatherhead's induction as President of the Methodist Conference, 1955.

He made his first appearance on television when he gave the close of the year epilogue on 31 December, 1954. He found TV more difficult than radio, finding the number of technicians involved very distracting. According to Edwin Robertson, who produced several of his religious programmes, Weatherhead was beginning to lose popularity in broadcasting after the war. Some criticised his voice as 'sing-song' and thought that he sounded 'too parsonic.' His persuasive style, which was so effective in the pulpit, was becoming unfashionable. However, he continued to broadcast regularly and effectively in the B.B.C. 'Silver Lining' programme which Robertson produced, and Weatherhead found he was 'overwhelmed' with letters in response to these broadcasts.

Margaret Knight, a well-known atheist, began a series of controversial broadcasts in January 1955 on 'Bible Myths' and 'Morals without Religion.' Robertson invited Weatherhead to reply to her in a dialogue on television which Robertson produced. In his view, Weatherhead was good, and had the answers to her attacks on religion, but he needed to think always before he replied, which made him appear slow and his answers less sure. Weatherhead himself felt that the discussion was very unsatisfactory, and that too much was attempted. It would have been better, he thought, if they had tried to concentrate on one or two questions, 'As it was, we ranged inconclusively over a wide area. One paper wrote that I failed to state the basis of the doctrines which I believed, but since Mrs. Knight mentioned the Incarnation, the Resurrection and the Life after Death in one sentence, it would tax anyone in a few minutes adequately to prove to a sceptic the reasons for our belief in these tremendous fundamentals.' He found himself 'oppressed by the diagnosis I made of her personality', feeling that her hostility was an expression of 'repressed aggression against parental tyranny in her childhood.'

On 15 September 1955, Huw Weldon produced the first of a series of programmes on the theme "Is This Your Problem?" On the panel for the first programme, together with Weatherhead, were J.F. Wolfenden, then Vice Chancellor of Reading University; an unnamed psychiatrist; the barrister and broadcaster, Edgar Lustgarten and the actress Edana Romney. The programme aimed at breaking new ground in dealing with people's personal problems, but the majority of the press attacked it, accusing the B.B.C. of lowering standards. The *Daily Mirror* critic wrote 'I thought the whole programme a cheap, shoddy, shameless business. Little can be gained by presenting this sort of thing before the public gaze of 12,000,000 viewers.' The *News Chronicle* declared 'this kind of curiosity, to put it mildly, can only be called unhealthy.'

The 1955 Methodist Conference met in the Albert Hall Manchester in July. Weatherhead was inducted as President following the usual formal vote, the results of which were presented by the Rev. Frederick A. Steele, who announced 'The Rev. Leslie Dixon Weatherhead 500.' The *British Weekly* wondered 'why Weatherhead should have had to wait so long for the honour now his.' Inducting him, the retiring President, the Rev. W. Russell Shearer, said,

it is a peculiar joy to be able to voice the welcome of Methodism to you as you enter upon this year of special responsibility and honour . . . your name and influence are alike known throughout the whole world. . . . We have all rejoiced in the width and wealth of your powers; and now, at this moment, your own people are inviting you to a year with them at home. I speak for tens of thousands of Methodists whose hearts are going out to you today.

The new President replied, 'I deeply love Methodism, and I owe everything to Methodism, and I shall serve Methodism as well as I can.'

In his Presidential address he decided against ranging across the world and speaking about colour problems, industrial unrest, or the hydrogen bomb, saying,

I want this Conference to keep very close to Jesus Christ. I want us to be aware of His presence in every session. I want us, in that presence to renew our vows and to listen to what He is trying to say to us. Many ministers and laymen have come up to Conference depressed and disheartened. . . . I do not want them to go away from the Conference merely having voted on this resolution and on that. I want them to remember the Manchester Conference of 1955 as an occasion when they were brought face to face with Christ, and went back to their churches with a new sense of power and joy, of faith and love. I am therefore going to call you to: 1. A greater efficiency. 2. A greater tolerance. 3. A greater dedication.

He evidently felt the need to defend himself against those who thought of him as having deserted Methodism, saying that they should not suppose that because Conference had allowed him to serve in 'what is really a supra-denominational church' that he had lost touch with Methodism.

I can tell you I am very unpopular for flying the flag of Methodism on every possible occasion. Once a month a score of Methodist ministers meet for fellowship in my study, and hardly a week passes by but I speak or preach in a Methodist Church.

He claimed to have been able to study Methodism more clearly than if he had been tied to a Methodist Church and circuit. He proceeded to attack the appalling inefficiency which he said he found in Methodism, declaring that he would close four out of five Methodist churches, concentrating instead on 'one thriving vital centre of spiritual life in the town.' He compared the ineffectiveness of the churches unfavourably with the 'efficient aggression' of Communism, which, he said, if given the same opportunities, would make the country Communist within ten years.

He appealed for tolerance, especially toward the Moral Re-Armament movement and Billy Graham, who had been severely criticised by Donald Soper during his Presidential year. He called these 'Gateway Movements' which were not substitutes for the church, but 'bring through the gateway of decision, men and women whom we frequently miss.' He called for tolerance and charity towards other branches of the church, particularly since there were negotiations taking place towards church union, and for a 'wider tolerance' in Christian Missions towards other religions.

> We must not present too rigidly a Western Christ. I believe that Eastern thought has much to teach us and that we have much to teach the East. . . .
> The Christianity we know so far is not the final religion. Christianity may well be – I believe it is – the final religion, but it will be a religion that includes all truth, wherever it is found, in whatever system it is at present enshrined.

The Times (5 July 1955) was so impressed with Weatherhead's address that it devoted part of its leader column to it. The *Methodist Recorder* (7 July 1955) invited W. E. Sangster to write its traditional appreciation of the new President. Sangster described Weatherhead's election as 'an event in world Methodism. It will be noted with delight far beyond the borders of our British jurisdiction.' He scornfully dismissed the criticisms and hostility that Weatherhead had always attracted, quoting one senior Methodist who had informed him that "psychology is shallow thinking about ourselves and theology is deep thinking about God." Sangster referred to Weatherhead's failure to be appointed to Wesley's Chapel as 'the sharpest disappointment of his public life', and regretted the opportunity that Methodism then missed. Discussing 'the secret of the new President's power' he said

> He is a preacher of the first order. There is stuff in his sermons. . . . They have sound homiletical form, logical progression, and illuminating illustrations. . . . He has charm and a most engaging friendliness. I have known people who, though they had never met him, heartily disliked him (largely, I suspect, because they were sick of what seemed to them the fulsome praise of his ardent admirers), but, half-an-hour in his company, and they were entirely changed. Yet, if I were to put the secret of his power into one word, I should use the word "caring". . . . All his high skill in homiletics, and all his honest interest in biblical exegesis, is subordinated to this master-desire to help people. There is nothing mysterious about this man's power. People love him because he loves them. Even those who do not know him personally feel, as he preaches, an almost personal love reaching them. There is nothing deceptive in that. I would say to any of them: "That is how he feels for you." Frankly, I have often wondered how one human heart could feel so much.

The Methodist Conference, which is made up of equal numbers of ministers and lay members, is the supreme authority for the Methodist Church, responsible for all matters of doctrine and discipline, and the assembly in which all Methodism's major decisions are made. Forty years ago, it was still the case that the President, as successor to John Wesley, was regarded during his single year of office, as the embodiment of that authority. Weatherhead, when he took office, was surprised at how much power the President actually possessed.

He handled the business of the Conference with remarkable speed and grace. He was not by nature a 'committee man' and in no sense a church politician. But he was highly organised and efficient, and hated time-wasting and protracted arguments and going over points that had already been made and understood. When he thought something had been made sufficiently clear, and the solution was obvious, he cut short further debate. He was not, however, manipulative, and did not seek to impose his own views and wishes on a meeting which he was presiding over. *The British Weekly* (14 July 1955) reported

> we have finished almost ahead of time. Lively debate has been missing, proposals expected to provoke opposition have been accepted with little question and no conference has ever agreed with quite so much. . . . The wit, wisdom, and winsomeness of Weatherhead have dominated the proceedings as completely as that of some other Presidents who have been sharper figures in argument. It has been leadership by gentleness, but leadership it has been.

In addition to the Conference sessions, Weatherhead was required to speak at lunchtime meetings, and often to preach in the evenings. He also gave time to interviewing patients who had come to Manchester to see him. The weather was hot, and much of the time he was in pain, due to old afflictions which flared up again as he drew on his resources. In what he described as his busiest day, he presided over the Conference in the morning, then went on to address seventy candidates about to be ordained. This was followed by a laymen's lunch at which he gave the address, then it was back to the Conference to give addresses to both the ordinands and the newly-ordained deaconesses, continuing in the chair until 6 p.m. then going on to a church ten miles away to conduct an ordination service lasting two hours.

Weatherhead considered as one of the highlights of the Conference a speech by Harold Roberts on the proposed 'rapprochement' between the Anglicans and Methodists which he found 'brilliant' and 'enthralling.' He felt that any discussion afterwards would have 'lowered the spiritual temperature which the spirit and temper of Dr. Robert's words had engendered', and so asked the Conference to vote immediately without any further debate. This the Conference did, with only two dissentients.

Harold Roberts also presented the report of the Conference Commission on the Missionary Obligation of the Church. In this he took a strongly traditional line which must have sounded like a direct refutation of some of his new President's earlier address:

> Christ gave them a revelation that was final. Tolerance was only safe when there was finality. Tolerance as an end in itself was not a virtue but a vice. . . .
> Christianity was not interested in getting a round-table conference at which the different religions of the world met together to say: "There is no final certainty. We have all got our snippets of truth; let us pool them and make a universal religion." Christ was God's last Word about the redemption of

the world and the universality of Christianity was founded in its exclusiveness. But finality did not mean sterility. . . . The missionary was learning to serve as well as to lead others – but they must not imagine that because of the growth of indigenous Churches the Christian missionary, and financial aid, would no longer be needed.

Weatherhead himself presented the report on the Ministry of Healing. He claimed to be one of the first to have interested the Methodist Church in healing, referring back to a *Methodist Recorder* article of 26 February 1925. It had been at his suggestion that the Spiritual Healing Committee had been set up by the Conference of 1937. He reported that the Spiritual Healing Committee was to arrange at university level a Diploma of Pastoral Psychology. Clinics had been established in various parts of the country, but there were difficulties because of the constant movement of Methodist ministers, so that no sooner had a team of doctors and ministers been formed, than the Methodist left, to be succeeded by one not interested in this particular ministry. Weatherhead admitted he had been fortunate in being for so long in one place, and in London, and therefore able to establish his own clinic at the City Temple with a full team of doctors. He repeated his criticisms of public healing services, warning against the harm done when a patient who did not find healing was led to believe that it was because of their own lack of faith, or came to believe that religion is no good and that God does not answer prayer. He appealed for a recovery of the ministry of intercession for the sick, stating that from his own experience 'the laws of intercession are emerging.' He refused to accept the argument from ministers that they were too busy, saying that they should consider if they were doing what they were ordained and trained to do. Much of what ministers undertake could and should be done by laymen.

At the invitation of the Bishop of Manchester, who had been a guest and spoken at the Conference, Weatherhead preached on Church unity at Manchester Cathedral on 10 July. He said that the need of the Churches was to unite, and that the world was right in refusing to listen to them while they were disunited. Conversations on theological and doctrinal matters might be useful, but 'the way to unity was the way of love.' He also spoke in the Free Trade Hall, about the possession of nuclear weapons. In this he said that the only hope for the world was in the wide dissemination of knowledge of what atomic warfare is likely to do, in the constant expression of the 'passionate desire of the people of all nations to pursue peaceful lives' and 'most of all, in promoting measures aimed at mutual understanding, trust and co-operation, such as the trilateral promise of America, Russia and ourselves not to be first to use the bomb.'

As he had feared, the year of office was very demanding, involving a considerable amount of travel with little time allowed for rest in between. He was expected to visit every Methodist District in the Kingdom. On one weekend, he spoke to 2,000 people on the Saturday night in Birmingham, then to 300 in an overflow hall, and another 1,500 in another part of the city. The next morning he preached at Leamington Spa to 1,300 people and in the evening to another 1,500 in Coventry. A regular sufferer from insomnia, he found staying in so many different houses with complete strangers as hosts a considerable strain.

To co-incide with the Conference, that same month Epworth published *Over His Own Signature*. This book originated in the Perkins Lectures he had given at Wichita Falls during his American visit the previous summer. In his Preface he explains,

When I was asked for a theme it seemed to me that nothing is more important than what I call "looking at Jesus". . . . We can never see Him without being challenged to extend our service to the world and our sense of values, and without being empowered to alter our lives.

He had therefore taken all the 'I am' sayings in which Jesus made statements about himself, and based each of the eleven lectures on one of these.

This book is probably the most deeply felt and personal expression of Weatherhead's own conviction and faith. Even the most critical reviewers were impressed by the devotional power of the book. *Joyful News* declared that this was 'perhaps his greatest' book, and that it contained 'all the qualities and marks of great preaching.' The *Christian World* described the book as 'utterly beautiful', and referred to Weatherhead as 'the greatest Methodist of our time.' Writing in the *London Quarterly and Holborn Review* (October 1955) Dr. Leslie Church said that 'In the expositions there are flashes of genius, but always one is conscious of the steady light of Truth, serene and irrefutable.' He recognised that it was Weatherhead's own very personal statement of faith: 'Perhaps indeed it reveals more of the man who wrote it than he himself realized.' The *Pulpit Digest* (February 1956) chose the book as its selection for the Pulpit Book Club. Patrick H. Carmichael, Dean of the General Assembly's Training School in Richmond, Virginia, writing in *Religious Education* (March 1956) concluded that 'The strikingly varied theological positions reflected in the volume make it very clear that the author cannot be classified as either fundamentalist or modernist.' The *Church of England Newspaper* (30 November 1956) declaring that 'Dr. Weatherhead is nothing if not original', went on to say that he 'gets down to the meaning of life itself: in fairly simple language he brings the wisdom of heaven down to the market-place.'

The book made a deep impression on its readers. A woman from New York wrote to say that reading this book 'was one of the greatest experiences of my life' and sent him a poem she had written in response to it. A man who read it while ill in hospital said that it was for him 'absolutely the start of a new life.' Weatherhead sent a copy to Mr. and Mrs. John D. Rockefeller, who expressed themselves delighted with it, and deeply appreciative of the inscription he had written in it, thanking them for all their kindness and generosity.

Over His Own Signature quickly went into two editions and sold just under 10,000 copies. Weatherhead seems to have been disappointed that it did not sell more, possibly because he had put so much of his own heart and mind into it, and he may have expected it to have the same appeal as his earlier books on Jesus, some twenty five years before. But times had changed and books of sermons were no longer popular. Yet his next book, *Prescription for Anxiety,* produced the following year, showed that he had not lost his ability to speak directly to people's needs in language they understood and to which they responded. Frank Cumbers, from the Epworth Press, wrote to him (12 March 1956)

It is quite true . . . that books of sermons are not likely to sell at quite the same rate as an entirely new book. . . . I have just finished my reading of your new book on anxiety, to be published by Hodders. If you would sometimes give me a book like that, I feel that Epworth would not show to any disadvantage.

On 28 August W. E. Sangster preached at his final service as minister of the Westminster Central Hall. Weatherhead was present on the platform as President and as a close personal friend. The Conference over which Weatherhead had presided had, very much against Sangster's wishes, elected him to succeed Dr. Colin Roberts as General Secretary of the Home Missions Department. Sangster, unlike Weatherhead, accepted the will of Conference as the will of God, and therefore – though reluctantly – obeyed, even when he felt he was being appointed to something he did not want and did not believe himself equipped to do.

At the beginning of the Methodist 'new year' in September, Weatherhead preached at a broadcast service from Wesley's Chapel. According to Edwin Robertson, Weatherhead's broadcast preaching during his Presidential year was disappointing, because apparently he felt he had to mention John Wesley on every occasion, so that the producers became irritated and even talked of refusing to broadcast him unless he omitted such references. Experienced though he was, he seems to have been so awed by the honour and responsibilities of his office, and so anxious to fulfil his duties towards Methodism, that he was in danger when broadcasting of forgetting the wider, non-Methodist public who would also be listening.

In this sermon, Weatherhead appealed to Methodists to be 'bridge builders', not only with members of other denominations but particularly 'to bridge the gulf that separates us from those lovable, attractive, often very fine people who are estranged from the churches.' Since his journey by ship to India in 1916, when for the first time he came into contact with charming atheists and non-churchgoers, he always had a soft spot for those whom he came to regard as 'lovable agnostics'. Saying that intellectual doubt should not be an obstacle since no one would be pressured to believe doctrines they found difficult to accept, he went on to refer to the way he had been charged with heresy before the Methodist Conference. 'Fourteen charges of heresy were preferred against me. Those days are gone. . . . If Methodism could accept me, it could certainly take you.'

A letter to the *Methodist Recorder* accusing Conference of being 'a lumbering leviathan' which 'rubber stamped whatever the Headquarters policy makers required', initiated a debate in the correspondence columns on the way Conference was conducted. Letters in reply argued that 'one of the human sources of the strength of Methodism is that subjugation of extreme individualism to a sense of corporate responsibility of which Conference is . . . both the expression and the guardian.' Some regretted 'the marked decline in debate in Conference' attributing this to an overloaded agenda. Since it was noted that Weatherhead had got through the business very rapidly with very little argument this would appear to be a criticism of the Conference over which he had presided. Conference that year had revised the regulations concerning candidature for the ministry, which provoked another debate on the arguments for women in the ministry. Weatherhead's remarks at the Conference on the Methodist Order of Deaconesses, in which he had praised their training as being 'in many ways as good as the training of ministry' were used as an argument in support.

In a broadcast from Wesley Church, Cambridge, on 16 October, preaching on 'Caring for the Sick', Weatherhead described the work of the City Temple Clinic, and said that at the City Temple there were half-a-dozen prayer groups committed to pray for the sick every day. He spoke of the value of the laying-on of hands and then went on to talk about 'Odic Force', which he said had been discovered by Reichenbach 100 years ago, describing it as 'mechanical rather than sacramental.' Weatherhead had first had his attention drawn to 'Odic Force' by the Bishop of Lichfield, Dr. Woods, after the publication of *Psychology, Religion and Healing* in 1951. Woods, who was a personal friend of the royal family, was concerned about the health of the King. He had learned from the Bishop of Rochester, Dr. Christopher Chavasse, about a doctor in Harley Street, who, although fully qualified in medicine, practised spiritual healing. Woods wondered whether the King might be helped through this treatment, and asked Weatherhead what he thought about this kind of healing. This doctor had heard Weatherhead preach when a student at Cambridge, and had been considerably influenced by him. He demonstrated to Weatherhead that by holding his hand above a person's body, close to it, but without touching it, a point of physical trouble could not only be located but eased. He invited Weatherhead to try it and he discovered that he also possessed this power. Weatherhead became very interested in this, as it seemed to relate to the ancient methods of healing such as anointing with oil and laying on of hands, and he began to use this method of healing himself with successful results.

In October, 1954, he wrote an article for the *London Quarterly and Holborn Review* on 'Odic Force: A re-discovered Healing Power.' In this he explained that the name derived from the Norse God, Odin, and described it as an 'all-pervading energy' which had been re-discovered in the nineteenth century by a Stuttgart chemist, Carl Reichenbach. Weatherhead considered that this psychic energy was the explanation for the healing 'miracles' of Harry Edwards and others. It was not a 'spiritual' property, and did not depend on the faith of either the healer or the patient. Weatherhead was intrigued by Reichenbach's suggestion that there was a 'current of energy which emanates from certain organic and inorganic bodies', and the idea that 'conditions of disease . . . throw out varying wave-lengths according to the nature of the illness' which could be measured from considerable distances. 'I have actually seen a photograph of the tuberculous lungs of a patient, showing clearly the extent of the disease, taken while the patient lay in a London hospital. *The instrument which took the photograph was fifty miles away.*' Believing that this was the 'threshold of thrilling new discoveries in healing,' over the next few years he became increasingly involved and keen to encourage further research. With the Bishop of Rochester he placed an advertisement in *The Times* in June 1956, requesting support for

The Biophysical Research Fund. The Bishop of Rochester and Dr. Leslie Weatherhead ask for contributions for research into the scientific basis of radiesthetic phenomena and hitherto unexplained cases of healing. The fund will be administered on the advice of the medical society for the study of radiesthetics (the perception of radiation)

In spite of the enthusiasm of its promoters, the appeal attracted little response, and nothing came of it.

Preaching at the jubilee celebrations of Princes Avenue Church, Hull, on 8 November, Weatherhead called for the creation of 'one great Free Church of

England'. He said he thought this would be an appropriate time for the Free Churches to approach the Anglicans as well 'to see if we cannot get closer together there.' Although the Methodists and the Anglicans had agreed to enter into bilateral Conversations, he did not regard these as excluding the participation of other denominations, but believed that better progress would be made if more such bodies were involved.

The President of the Methodist Conference, during his term of office, is the official spokesman for Methodism on all matters of public interest. The national and provincial press gave wide coverage to Weatherhead's attack on strikes, his call for a united Free Church, his delight at the vote in Parliament to abolish hanging, his deploring the introduction of Premium Bonds as being 'a bad thing to introduce the element of luck into such a dignified thing as the Budget. It is unsound economy to lead people to think they will receive prizes with no corresponding contribution to the community.' The popular magazine *Picture Post* (17 December 1955) featured him, together with Billy Graham and Group Captain Leonard Cheshire, in an article by Charles Hamblett on 'God's Ambassadors.'

The attitudes of the various Churches to divorce were sought concerning the romantic attachment between Princess Margaret and the previously married Group Captain Peter Townsend. Weatherhead prepared a statement for the press which was published in all the main newspapers on 27 October. In this he said that for a royal princess to marry a divorced person would cause great offence to many Anglicans, since 'If the State Church approved this marriage, it would break its own rules.' If, however, she renounced all claims to the throne for herself and for her issue then they ought to be allowed to marry as private citizens.

An engagement which gave him particular pleasure early in the new year was to meet with all the Methodist commissioned chaplains serving home establishments of the three services at a conference at Westminster. This had become an established tradition, during which they held the annual Covenant Service together. The afternoon conference was presided over by Sangster as Secretary of the Home Mission Department. Weatherhead spoke of contemporary sex problems, and the subsequent discussion ranged around many topics with which chaplains had to deal. Both Weatherhead and Sangster answered questions – though not always agreeing with each other. Weatherhead also visited Cranwell R.A.F. College at the invitation of the Commandant, to preach at a combined Church of England and Presbyterian, Methodist and United Board Parade Service. The *Methodist Recorder* (12 January 1956) reported,

> the occasion was, in fact, a state visit, at which full honours were accorded to the President by the Royal Air Force for the position he holds as one of the leading ecclesiastical dignitaries of the day, as well as his representative capacity on behalf of the Methodist Church.

In February, he produced for the *Methodist Recorder* his reflections on reaching the half-away point of his presidential year, which the paper described as 'one of the most searching analyses of the Church ever published by the *Methodist Recorder*.' He praised the Methodist system and the District Chairmen and ministers with whom he had stayed during his travels, but repeated his call to close down a high percentage of churches and have two or even three ministers work as a team. Ministerial salaries he said should be increased by at least fifty per cent to keep some kind of pace with the cost of living. The size of Committees should be cut down by two-thirds. He would withdraw Methodist ministers from Scotland, with the exception of Edinburgh, Glasgow, Inverness and Aberdeen, or other places where it could be proved that the number of English Methodists made it worthwhile. He called for a new approach to be made to the Congregationalists.

> I feel that if the Congregationalists would unite with us we should both be enriched. . . . If Congregationalism can tolerate one Methodist for twenty years in its most famous pulpit, and another Methodist [A. Victor Murray, President of Cheshunt College] as the head of its Cambridge training college for ministers, what is in the way of union? I hereby invite Congregationalism to examine our Methodist way and see if we cannot unite. It is a sin to remain separate unless some vital principle is involved.

Ignoring the fact that his casual attitude to re-baptism would offend more orthodox Christians and therefore be a further obstacle to a wider union, he called also for 'a new approach made to Baptists,' pointing out that there was nothing in Methodism to prohibit the baptism of an adult person. He could see

> no insuperable reason why an adult person who wished his entry into Church Membership to be marked by a second baptism, doing on his own, voluntarily, what had been done for him in infancy, should not be allowed to do so, if he felt it to be a valuable means of grace. . . . Here again, separateness is sin unless some vital principle is involved. . . . I am quite sure that for most of us denominational differences are emotional, not intellectual. . . . How can we . . . look into the face of Christ and pretend that members of other denominations are in any sense wrong? There is truth in every denomination, and in my view the differences are trifling compared with the great fundamentals about which we are all agreed.

He went on to say that what he considered was most wrong with Methodism (as with every other branch of the Church) was that 'we have not integrated the truths we sincerely believe in with the things we habitually do.' He called for a deepening of the spiritual life of the church, 'which should everywhere be a loving community. . . . The fundamental trouble with Methodism is that . . . her level of spiritual experience is too low to be easily communicable or even desirable. . . . Our main failure is a failure in relationships . . . a failure really to love.'

In March, Hodders produced *Prescription for Anxiety*, which became another immediate best-seller, selling over 30,000 in the first three weeks, and eventually going into six editions and over 100,000 copies. The book's appeal lay in the honesty with which Weatherhead shared his own anxieties, dark periods and fears, and drew on these to offer counsel and advice to others similarly troubled. In this he is not the expert in psychology or the minister untouched by such suffering, dispensing wisdom and comfortable answers, but a fellow sufferer, sharing the hard lessons he has learned through his own experiences in the hope that others might be helped by them. The book therefore conveys an impression of genuine humility, sincerity and a real concern for those he desires to help.

The book received exceptionally wide coverage. *The Publishers' Circular* predicted that it would be 'a very big seller indeed' and reported that 'Sales took a spurt after the first reading on 'Woman's Hour.' Before publication a series of extracts were featured in the *Daily Mail*. In America it was even mentioned in the *Hollywood Features* and the Director of Broadcasting of the Illinois Council of Churches, Raymond B. Knudson, introduced the book on both radio and television, recommending it as 'invaluable' and to be coveted by every religious library. The *Methodist Recorder* (26 April 1956) praised especially the book's lack of psychological jargon, its 'charitable common sense always with a theological foundation,' and its total lack of insipid sentimentality, and concluded that 'Methodism should be proud of its President' for 'He has not done better than this.' J. Baird Ewens in the *Irish Christian Advocate* (27 April 1956) said,

> I feel more than ever that one source of Dr. Weatherhead's power is the peace that follows after us with unhurrying chase and unperturbed pace. . . . And yet peace does not descend at the waving of a wand. . . . It has to be fought for: it comes to us after a battle; shall we call it the Battle of Gethsemane?

This extraordinary sense of peace was remarked on also by Norman Phelps in an article headed, 'The Magnetism of Dr. Weatherhead' for the *Liverpool Daily Post* (21 May 1956), which was also serialising extracts from the book. Phelps said that in his time he had heard many famous preachers, including R.J. Campbell, Studdert-Kennedy, Dick Sheppard, Campbell Morgan and Silvester Horne. Yet,

> Comparing them all, I can truthfully say this, that never, listening to any preacher or meeting him afterwards, have I had a greater sense of peace and serenity than in the presence of Dr. Weatherhead. . . . The curious and unusual thing about Dr. Weatherhead is that, despite this air of dwelling apart in a quiet place . . . there is no mind in modern times more acutely aware of the peculiar human problems and difficulties of the day and of how they can be diagnosed and cured. . . . Of his books, *Prescription for Anxiety* . . . is his latest and among his best. It is not pious or preachy, but at once objective and human, analytical and warmly sympathetic.

The *Church Times* (24 August 1956) thought the book,

> sanctified common sense' but criticised it for its 'major omission of emphasis on sacraments which lessens the value of the book. . . . Dr. Weatherhead is a great believer in confession, but he does not believe in priestly absolution. No reference is made to the solemn words pronounced by the bishop at an ordination.

The American papers tended to describe Weatherhead as being 'to the United Kingdom what Norman Vincent Peale has become to the United States' and to compare his book with Peale's *The Power of Positive Thinking*, even though Peale does not admit to sharing the weaknesses and dark experiences of those for whom he is writing in the way that Weatherhead does.

The book was reviewed for the May 1956 issue of the *City Temple Tidings* by the Rev. J.B. Phillips, who described it as 'vintage Weatherhead' and as

> the antidote to all the smart-alec evangelists of this world who think that all problems are solved if only a man will "surrender all to Jesus." I wish with all my heart that these bouncing evangelical extroverts who have such slick answers for mankind's ills would study this book. . . . It has helped me, and I feel sure it will help many others towards inner serenity.

Phillips's comments were heart-felt and sincere. Like Weatherhead, he also suffered from periods of acute anxiety and dark depression, and sought to help people who wrote to him from out of his own struggles and hard won faith. A few years later Phillips wrote to Weatherhead asking his help and advice, and this led to a correspondence in which they shared their experiences and gained considerable help and sympathy from each other.

There were many others who wrote to Weatherhead, prompted by this book, telling him how much they had been helped by it, and seeking his further advice about their problems. One of these was the writer, Catherine Cookson, who wrote to him when she was herself going through a bad breakdown. She was astonished to receive an immediate reply, in which he thanked her for her letter, saying how much it had helped him. It was only later that she learned that he was also going through another of his 'dark periods' at the time. Dr. William Kyle wrote to him, (14 January 1975) passing on a letter from a doctor friend who had suffered considerably from ill-health:

Lately I have returned to Leslie Weatherhead's *Prescription for Anxiety*. I always seem to read this in times of stress and strain. Dear Dear Leslie Weatherhead – how I've blessed him again and again for helping me through sticky patches. He never allows one to have a sense of guilt about one's fears and failings. I don't think I could have got through these past few years without that book and my own copy is just about falling to pieces and dog-eared.

Weatherhead was present at the City Temple for its Annual General Meeting on 16 April. He was delighted at the way the church was managing to carry on with him away most of the time, and described the meeting as 'one of the happiest that I can remember in twenty years.' He made a point of being at the church for one Sunday each month, and when he did, the church was packed to capacity for him. Visiting other churches made him particularly appreciate 'the spirit of real worship' which marked the services at the Temple, which he said was not common elsewhere. At this meeting Alice Head retired as Church Treasurer after twelve years, and was succeeded by Binstead Griffiths. The rebuilding work was proceeding, but slowly, and the estimated date for completion had again been deferred until early 1958. During May, 1956, the main steel superstructure was put in place, and contracts were agreed for the heating, lighting, ventilating and electrical installations. Weatherhead had written to the Queen at Buckingham Palace to invite her to the opening but received a reply advising him to apply again within a year of the re-opening. This he still continued to hope would be in the autumn of 1957 instead of spring 1958.

In June, he presided over the Welsh Assembly and then flew to Belfast to preside at the Irish Methodist Conference in Cork. He was excited by the crowds which turned out to greet him in both places.

I have rarely seen greater enthusiasm than I came across during my recent visits to Wales and Ireland. . . . In Barmouth, where the Welsh Assembly met, I was on my last evening, sitting peacefully at tea with my host at 5 p.m. when the minister rang up from the church where the final meeting was to be held at 6.30 p.m. He said, 'We have two churches crowded already and three hundred people in the street. What are we to do?' So I hurried off and we began the service an hour earlier than it was announced! In Ireland the enthusiasm was similar and every meeting crowded. . . . Surely such enthusiasm must mean at least the possibility of revival.

In June also the talks between the Anglicans and Methodists were officially begun. Weatherhead, as President, had been given the task of choosing the Methodist team to save delays in waiting for nominations and elections. He had included himself as one of the representatives and was eager to take part, but reluctantly had to withdraw when he entered hospital for an operation. As he came to the end of his year of office he was pleased to be able to tell his City Temple members that although the year had been very demanding, he had felt 'wonderfully sustained' and had only missed one appointment throughout the whole year, due to influenza.

At the end of the month, he summed up his impressions of his Presidential year for the *Methodist Recorder* (28 June 1956). He regretted that

the Presidency comes too late in one's life for one to take full advantage of its tremendous possibilities. . . . During my late forties I think I could have accepted nearly all the invitations that came my way, but . . . it [is] impossible in the early sixties for one to meet all the demands with the resilience and vitality which a President should be able to bring to them.

At sixty-two, he was rather older than was usual. It is more than probable that if Weatherhead had not been serving for so long in a church of another denomination he would have been elected earlier. The Conference even so, felt it was making a great concession in electing him when it did. With these remarks Weatherhead was in danger of seeming ungracious.

He also felt that there were too many special services and that the President should be able to attend an ordinary service without any special arrangements being made. He was even more convinced that they should be closing more buildings and combining congregations with team ministries. He was not alone in urging this. The Methodist Union of 1932 was seen as a chance to rationalise Methodist work by reducing the number of chapels in use, and amalgamating circuits. This had become 'a running sore' by the mid-1950s, when it became urgent to re-deploy resources and ministry to new areas of urban growth, so that Conference adopted special powers to override the local trustees in certain conditions. Weatherhead then repeated his call for greater ministerial efficiency and an increase in ministerial stipends, criticising the giving of the churches. He felt strongly that Methodist ministers were underpaid and badly housed, remembering how difficult it had been for him and his family in the earlier years of his ministry.

Saying that 'The modern age must be offered a much more reasonable presentation of truth than the language of the Churches usually expresses', he admitted, in a revealing piece of self-criticism,

For myself, I feel that my words are too glib. I make the Christian way sound too easy, and talk of Christ's promises as though they had only to be accepted to make life one grand sweet song. Listeners therefore imagine that there is something wrong with *them*: that they have missed something which the preacher always possesses. Their lot is so hard and bewildering, fraught with so much disappointment, frustration and pain. Whereas many of us, who talk a lot, also have hours of problems and days of darkness when we are as much in the dark as they are, and wriggle through, unblest by any light from heaven, or any immediate answer to prayer, offered some-times from the depths of something akin to despair. This we never, or rarely admit, and our people tend to think that we always live on mountain tops and do not know the deep valleys which they so often traverse.

He was relieved to hand over the burdens of office to his successor, Harold Crawford Walters, at the Conference in Leeds in July. He hoped to be back in his own pulpit at the City Temple for the first three Sundays in August, and then to take a holiday before opening his twenty-first year at the church. But before the end of July he was in considerable pain and ordered into hospital for another operation. He wrote in August to his old friend, Raynor Johnson,

> The aftermath of the two operations I have just had has been most unpleasant and painful, but I also had some spiritual experiences which I am glad not to have missed. . . . In quiet hours in the hospital, I became quite convinced of the meaninglessness of a lot of church activity, and I want more time to meditate and prepare for the next phase and to get my perspective corrected as to what is important and what unimportant. Strangely enough, I do not feel a bit attracted now to any form of psychotherapy, though I would still like to help people spiritually.

He returned to the church for his anniversary on 7 October and the Gift Day and Harvest Festival on 14 October (his 63rd. birthday), but the next day was back in hospital for another immediate operation as the one in July had not been a success. He suffered severely from incurable diverticulitis, brought on by the tensions of his way of life, and he had developed an irritating skin condition which plagued him for the rest of his life. The strenuous year of office had left him feeling exhausted and spiritually depleted, and the anxieties and depressions which he had admitted to so publicly in *Prescription for Anxiety* continued to plague him. Much as he felt he ought to be returning fully to his ministry at the City Temple, it became necessary for him to have a complete rest to enable him to convalesce, recoup his nervous energies and restore his spiritual reserves. His recovery was so slow that his doctor advised a further convalescence in the sun, so in February 1957 he went with his friend Ernest Appleyard to the West Indies, where, for the first time since he had taken up the presidency, he was able to sleep without drugs.

22. The City Temple Re-Opens

'to stand by people from the cradle to the grave with that greatest of all dynamic inspirations, that most searching of all challenges, that most heartening of all forms of comfort, the Gospel of Jesus Christ.'

Weatherhead began his twenty-first year at the City Temple on 7 October 1956. In November, England, together with France and Israel, invaded Egypt in order to re-possess the Suez Canal, which had been nationalised by the Egyptian President, Colonel Nasser. This operation caused sharp division in the country, many thinking that it was not only misguided but immoral. Preaching at the City Temple on 11 November, the Sunday after the invasion, John Huxtable, the Principal of New College, London, condemned the government for its actions in collusion with the French. This produced a protest during the service, and a number of members of the congregation walked out. Weatherhead felt bound to comment on this in his December Minister's Letter. In this he said he was sorry to have been away when feelings had run so high, and that the pulpit should never be used to express party political views, though 'if a moral question arises, then I think the pulpit should speak out bravely, as long as the preacher realises . . . that those who differ from him have little chance to express their views and may rightly feel that their point of view is just as Christian as his own.' He went on to give his own opinion, which hardly differed from Huxtable's, that,

> unless there were factors in the situation hidden from the public, the Government did make an error of moral judgment in taking unilateral action and that Britain's moral prestige was seriously weakened in a day . . . we have lost the right to challenge any other power for invading a neighbour country.

Weatherhead was always prepared to identify himself with a cause, even if it meant being accused of taking political sides, if he believed it to be morally justified. In December, 1956, a number of leading South African opponents of Apartheid, including several black leaders, were arrested and charged with treason. In February, 1957, Christian Action launched a fund to pay for their defence and the support of their families. Weatherhead was one of a number of well-known people – which included Trevor Huddleston, Jo Grimond, Donald Soper, Henry Moore, Graham Sutherland, Harold Wilson and the Bishop of Manchester – who signed a letter to *The Times* (8 February 1956) as sponsors of this fund. In March 1958, he was a signatory of another letter to *The Times* supporting the recommendation of the Wolfenden Report that homosexual acts committed in private between consenting adults should no longer be a criminal offence. Among those who signed this second letter, including once again Donald Soper, were Lord Attlee, A.J. Ayer, the Bishop of Birmingham, Canon John Collins, J.B. Priestley, Bertrand Russell, Stephen Spender, Mary Stocks and A.J.P. Taylor.

In January, 1957, Martin Fearn, who had been the City Temple's organist since

1929, decided to retire. The church appointed in his place Dr. Eric Thiman, then organist at Crouch End Congregational Church, where he had been since 1927. Thiman, who was Professor of Harmony at the Royal Academy of Music, and Dean of the Faculty of Music in the University of London, was the most widely known and distinguished musician in the history of Congregationalism. He had been chairman of the music committee and music editor of *Congregational Praise*, the new hymn book published in 1951, which included a number of his hymn tunes. The City Temple had adopted the book in 1956, having received a gift of £500 from the Brixton Independent Church for this purpose.

The church received a severe blow when, in February, Herbert Lewis died very suddenly. Weatherhead received the news while he was away in the West Indies. He was deeply shocked and saddened at the loss of someone he regarded as an 'ideal colleague . . . entirely free from conceit or self-assertion.' They had enjoyed an exceptionally happy relationship, in which Lewis, who was also entirely free from jealousy of Weatherhead's fame or the crowds he attracted, exercised a quiet but greatly appreciated supportive pastoral ministry. The Presbyterians asked Kenneth Slack, then General Secretary of the British Council of Churches, to become their Interim Moderator. Weatherhead found an additional pastoral and preaching colleague in a member of the City Temple, the Rev. T. Charles Brimley, who readily agreed to become Associate Minister. They had known each other from Weatherhead's days in Leeds when Brimley had been minister of Great George Street Congregational Church in Liverpool, and Weatherhead had a high regard for his preaching and pastoral abilities.

Visible progress was being made on the new building. During Weatherhead's absence, and against his wishes, the Church Council had insisted on the enlargement of the planned gallery to accommodate more people. This was also against the preference of the architects, who had designed a smaller gallery that stretched along both side walls of the building. The extended gallery meant that the pulpit had to be placed much higher so that those in the gallery could see the preacher. To solve this, the architects replaced the intended smaller, pedestal pulpit with an extraordinary and huge drum, cantilevered out from the side wall of the outer apse, some twelve feet above the ground.

On 11 July, the *British Weekly* printed an article by Derek Walker on the work of the City Temple. Walker stated that no ministry at the City Temple had had greater significance for the religious life of the country than Weatherhead's, which he referred to as 'the most remarkable pastoral ministry of this century.' He noted that the church was always full when Weatherhead preached, but also Weatherhead's comments that it was no longer as easy to draw a crowd as it had been before the war. According to Adrian Hastings, 'The mid-fifties can be dated pretty precisely as the end of the age of preaching: people suddenly ceased to think it worthwhile listening to a special preacher . . . the sermon as a decisive event was gone.' Hastings attributes this largely to the move towards a more liturgical and sacramental form of worship in the Free Churches; he concedes, however, that while 'Leslie Weatherhead could compete on his own terms well enough with Westminster Abbey, the liturgy of Kingsway Hall [where Donald Soper ministered] could not.'[1]

Weatherhead preached at both services on 6 October, the twenty-first anniversary of his ministry at the City Temple. He was deeply moved when, during the morning, Brimley, who was sharing the services with him, paid tribute to him for his outstanding ministry and then invited the huge congregation to rise and sing the Doxology.

In November, Weatherhead was invited to attend a Luncheon at Buckingham Palace. He was delighted that the Queen spent some ten minutes in private conversation with him and asked about the City Temple, showing 'the greatest interest in our work.' The Queen pointed out to him the ruins of the Palace chapel, which had been destroyed in an air-raid, and asked him what should be done with it. He suggested that it might become a picture gallery – which it now is. He was impressed with her naturalness and lack of stiffness and formality.

At last, in March, 1958, he was able to announce the definite date for the official Re-Dedication of the rebuilt City Temple as 30 October. Moreover, the Queen Mother had consented to be present. Since he had first arrived at the church in 1936, he had received a number of indications that the royal family were aware of his work, and interested in it. The Queen Mother had sent him a personal message after reading *This is the Victory* early in the war, saying that she thought it would help to sustain the morale of the nation during that dark time, and later, the Queen also had sent him a message after reading *Psychology, Religion and Healing*. The Queen Mother indicated that she would prefer to attend a church which was fully functioning before her visit, so it was decided to move to Holborn during the month of August. Weatherhead preached for the last time at Marylebone on 27 July, on 'The Grace of Gratitude.' With the departure of the City Temple congregation, the Presbyterians had decided that the Marylebone church should be closed. Weatherhead expressed the feelings of sadness and gratitude of his church for the exceptional hospitality they had received for over eleven years. He issued an invitation to the now homeless members of Marylebone to stay together with them and join the City Temple at Holborn. During the morning service Kenneth Slack presented the City Temple with the gift of a pulpit edition of the Revised Standard Version of the Bible on behalf of the members of Marylebone. The final services at Marylebone were held on 10 August, and the first at Holborn the following Sunday.

The church held a well-attended press conference on 11 August to view the building, and the subsequent publicity created considerable interest. The *Evening Standard* described the building as 'modern but restrained.' *The Times* which included several photographs, reported that the church had been designed for alternative use as a lecture or conference hall, and that 'This new cathedral of the Free Churches' contained 'several features not generally considered to be part of a church.' The hall beneath the church, which had a seating capacity of 756, including a gallery, was designed for use as either a meeting hall, cinema or theatre. It was equipped with a projection room, stage and orchestra pit, and had separate entrances in Shoe Lane so that it could be used independently of the church. A lift had been installed to reach the floor above the church which contained the church offices, Clinic rooms, flats for the verger and an assistant minister, and a large conference room – which *The Times* described as 'more befitting to an industrial corporation than a church' – with a fully equipped kitchen. Frank Salisbury had painted a triptych which was mounted above the dais in the conference room. The church's links with the City were acknowledged by the Clockmakers' Company who had provided synchronous clocks throughout the building.

The News Chronicle, reporting on the 'vast crowds who turned up for the opening service', referred to the new City Temple 'as one of the finest modern church buildings in Britain'. *THe Daily Telegraph* noted that 'The interior of the church . . . is much brighter with more light from the windows than the old church', and reported Lord Mottistone as explaining, 'We have adopted a restrained modern design and the church is less elaborate than its predecessor. Wedgewood blue is the traditional colour for the City Temple and this is the basis of the colour scheme of the new building.'

On Sunday, 17 August, a day which Weatherhead said was 'one of the great days of my life', the queue began to form before nine for the eleven o'clock service in the morning and before four o'clock for the six-thirty evening service. Weatherhead preached on 'The Gladness of Returning Home', taking as his text the first verse of Psalm 122: 'I was glad when they said unto me, "Let us go into the house of the Lord", which he said, the Bishop of London, Bishop Compton, had preached on at the first service at the re-built St. Paul's Cathedral in 1697, after the great fire of London. In his sermon, Weatherhead recalled some of the 'wilderness experiences' which the church had been through since the destruction of its building in 1941. He appealed to the congregation to make the new building a 'spiritual home', asking them to put themselves out to welcome strangers, and said that it was important that the church should acquire the 'right atmosphere' of love, prayer and worship.

The style of the new building, and the content of the first service, created an extraordinary amount of comment and criticism in the religious press, particularly in the *The Baptist Times* (21 August 1958). A front page article, which headlined the £430,000 cost, described the newly built church as 'very different from the old.' It drew attention to the fact that where the old marble pulpit had formerly stood there was now 'a high apse, the central features of which are the communion table, on which lies an open Bible, and above it a cross 12½ feet high.' It noted that the new pulpit was placed to one side, and that 'for occasions when the church building is used for public meetings, a Japanese silk curtain is lowered to cover the stained-glass window and the cross.' There was also a cinema screen in a box below the apse floor, which could be raised for film services.

Another prominent article in the same issue, by Neville Penry Thomas, attacked the building as

> a contemporary style religious hall which, when I attended the first service in the new building . . . lacked only a Wurlitzer organ rising out of the floor to complete my feeling of being in a gorgeous, up-to-the-minute meeting place of some odd but wealthy American sect.'

He described the building as 'a piece of religious theatricalism, not a church; and for that the architects and those who advised them must share the blame.' He proceeded to criticise the placing of the pulpit, the 'smooth, sophisticated cross . . . so much less disturbing than the rough original.' He disliked the Wedgwood panels placed along the sides of the building, and the design of the lectern and communion table as 'too blatant.' He went on to criticise the service itself.

> There was, of course, a vast crowd at this first service – long queues waiting long before ten o'clock for the doors to open. It was a great occasion.

Yet in addition to my disappointment with the building I felt that Dr. Weatherhead's pre-occupation with the wanderings and experience of the church fellowship . . . and his frequent anecdotes, were a poor substitute for the more fundamental message that such a home-coming should have inspired. . . . I cannot escape the belief that the new building fails to enshrine the unspeakable mystery of the Faith it was raised to glorify.

This article provoked considerable correspondence which continued for several weeks. Most disagreed with Thomas, defending both the building and Weatherhead. Replying to his critics, Thomas revealed that his real objections were to what he regarded as the lavishness of the new building, and its cost. 'I am personally perturbed that £430,000 should have been lavished on the new City Temple . . . luxury, magnificence and, in my opinion, slick, unsubtle modern taste, were the dominating characteristics of the new building. There is no element of humility'.

The British Weekly (14 August 1958), though it described the building as 'having the tone and luxury of a West End cinema,' was, however, more approving: 'it retains the spirit of sacred beauty and retreat.' It found that though 'the Communion Table and open Bible are designed to dominate. . . . They don't. Nor does the cedar of Lebanon Cross, suffused with lilac fluorescent tints. Nor does the organ. No, it is the great ivory-white pulpit and the preacher from it, the Rev. Dr. Leslie D. Weatherhead.'

The criticisms came in the correspondence columns. 'What is the lavish cost and luxuriousness for – the glory of God or the pride of man? It is unnecessary for the former. It is a lot to pay for the latter. This concentration of opulence in one church is wasteful and self-indulgent.' Another letter attacked the replacing of the pulpit with a central cross. 'Preaching the Word and expounding the Scripture is put on one side and bobbing to a piece of wood takes its place. No wonder that lurking in the background is what the late Dr. Grieve called "sanctified psychology." Years ago someone put "Ichabod" [i.e. 'the glory has departed'] in the front of the City Temple; let it now be engraved in stone.' Other writers leapt to Weatherhead's and the City Temple's defence, most notably Dr. William Kyle, who described being present at the service on the first Sunday evening as 'an enriching and never to be forgotten means of grace.'

To coincide with the opening, the City Temple Council published a small book, *The City Temple, Past, Present and Future,* compiled by Bertram Hammond. This contained a short history of the church written by Hammond, an account of the destruction and the re-building by the Church Secretary, John Dewey, and the church's plans and hopes for the future written by Weatherhead. In this he explained that when he became minister in 1936 his main ambition was to make the City Temple a fellowship and not just a preaching centre. He gave an account of the various church organisations, many of which he had started himself. He recalled the chapter he had written on 'The City Temple Tomorrow' for his book *The Significance of Silence,* in 1945, saying that many of the things he had suggested there were now taking shape: the central focus of the new building was the Cross, an open Bible was to be placed at the beginning of each service on the holy table, there was to be a chapel for private prayer and a children's corner, and rooms for the psychological clinic. He declared that the purpose of the new City Temple was 'to offer Christ to men and women,' repeating

The Rededication of the the City Temple attended by the Queen Mother, 30 October 1958

his insistence that the City Temple, though technically Congregational, was 'above all narrow denominationalism', that it did not ask its members to agree to any theological propositions. 'We seek to serve the new age by offering, in the centre of the City of London, all the beauty and joy and meaningfulness of life with Christ at its centre.'

With the church once again back in the City, Weatherhead appealed for teams of visitors who would be willing to make the rounds of the homes in the vicinity of the Viaduct, while the publicity surrounding the re-opening was still fresh in people's minds, and to contact the local offices, distributing leaflets of the churches activities.

The Re-Dedication Service, on 30 October, attended by the Queen Mother was broadcast by the B.B.C. and later transmitted throughout the world on their World Service network. The event received exceptionally wide coverage in the national, and even the international press. Photographs of the new building were published in Swedish, as well as American, Canadian and Australian newspapers. The Temple's close neighbour, the *Evening Standard*, not only produced a special supplement to mark the occasion, but allowed a spotlight to be placed on the roof of their building to illuminate the church's new rose window.

The service was attended by a large procession of representatives of the different denominations, among whom were the Bishop of London, Montgomery Campbell – who was rebuked by some members of his own Communion for giving the blessing at the end of the service – and the Dean of St. Pauls, W.R. Matthews, who had long been a friend of the Temple and of Weatherhead. The

Exterior of the rebuilt City Temple

Dean and Chapter of St. Paul's had donated some marble from their destroyed reredos for the dais of the new Friends' Chapel of the City Temple. The City Temple's host for much of the war, the Rector of St. Sepulchre's, George Salter, was there, and Dr. Lynn Harold Hough, who, though now eighty, had come from America especially for the occasion and to preach at one of the special services which marked the weekend of celebration.

In his address, Weatherhead referred to the day as 'the most important and significant day in the long history of our Church,' and noted that this was the first time in all its history that the City Temple had been attended by a member of the royal family. He outlined the way the church intended to minister to each different age group, 'to stand by people from the cradle to the grave with that greatest of all dynamic inspirations, that most searching of all challenges, that most heartening of all forms of comfort, the gospel of Jesus Christ.' He said that

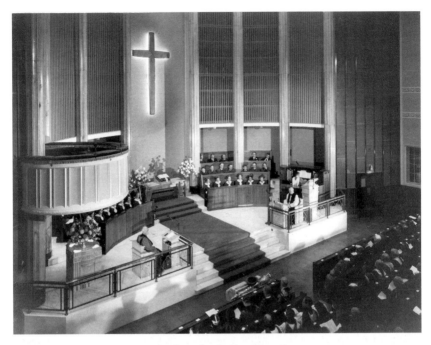

The Re-dedication service in the rebuilt City Temple

though now they had a beautiful building, what it needed was an 'aura, an atmosphere of reverence for God and love for man' such as the old parish churches possessed, where it was easy to pray, because in them people had been praying and worshipping for centuries.

The Christian World produced a lavish four-page supplement in which it described the occasion and the building at considerable length. It noted that although the pulpit was now to one side, it was of so unusual and dominating a design that it still maintained the emphasis on the centrality of preaching in the church's worship.

The Baptist Times (6 November 1958) complained that 'No representative of the Congregational Union or any of the other Free Churches took any part in the service, which while fully representative in its congregation, was entirely domestic in its conduct.' But R.W. Hugh Jones, writing the same day in the *British Weekly*, thought that the service well bore out Weatherhead's claim that the City Temple, though

> technically a Congregational Church . . . is above all narrow denomination-
> alism. . . . You would not often find, met together in one Church for an act of
> worship, such a representative group of people as those who formed the
> procession. . . . We had had evidence before that the City Temple had
> commanded the interest, and caught the imagination, of people across the
> World when it was re-opened last August; and this service but confirmed
> the special place it holds in the life of the Churches in this country. . . . No
> one present is likely to forget the experience . . . we were reminded by the
> Queen Mother that its message has been heard across the World, and one
> could feel that the community of Christ's people here is conscious of its
> immense responsibility.

The following day, Sidney Berry preached at the second of the Re-Dedication services. Berry reminisced about his own early memories of hearing Joseph Parker and R.J. Campbell at the City Temple. He paid tribute to the ministry of Weatherhead, which he said had been largely carried out through years of strain and stress: 'He had the compelling power which brought people to Christ and by his preaching and writing his influence on the religious life of our time had been far-reaching and profound.'

During November, a series of organ recitals by Eric Thiman and other distinguished organists, including John Birch and George Thalben-Ball, were arranged to show off the new instrument, which had attracted a great deal of interest. J.W. Walker and Sons, who built it, set out to 'create the finest instrument to be installed in the City of London since the war.' The original specifications were drawn up in consultation with Martin Fearn and Sir William McKie, the organist of Westminster Abbey, and then with Eric Thiman, after he had been appointed, who suggested his own modifications. The more than 3,500 pipes of the organ were hidden by a louvred screen behind the forty foot cedar of Lebanon pillars which were the main feature of the wide apse.

A new book, *A Private House of Prayer*, had been forming in Weatherhead's mind for some time. He regarded prayer as being of vital importance in any Christian life, and made it a priority in his ministry to maintain the highest possible quality of prayer in worship, and to encourage and help lay people in practical ways in what he himself acknowledged to be 'the difficult art of praying' as well as 'the highest activity of man.' During his time in Leeds, he had produced a prayer card which made suggestions for a brief daily prayer time, giving headings and a sequence of prayers which had proved extremely popular. The framework of the book he had included as an appendix to *Prescription for Anxiety* as 'Everyman's House of Prayer', and he had planned the book in more detail during his time in hospital in 1956. He explained that having had for many years to do a great deal of travelling he had devised a method of praying for his own use. This owed much to a book by H.E. Fosdick, *Successful Christian Living* (1937). Weatherhead's book is made up of prayers, including many of his own, and poems and meditations from various sources which he had collected and used in his own private devotions and found helpful. These are arranged into seven different 'rooms' which represent the different forms of prayer, and grouped for use on each of the different days of the month. The end of the book includes a section of 'Spare Rooms' with additional prayers and prayers for special occasions.

Hodders produced the book in a number of different bindings and prices, anticipating that it would not only be popular, but would also be bought by many as an acceptable gift. In an advance press notice, published in most newspapers, the publishers predicted that over the next two years it would sell more copies than any other book on their lists, including fiction, and that it would even outsell all their other Weatherhead titles, including *Psychology, Religion and Healing,* which had sold over 50,000 copies. The *Irish Christian Advocate* welcomed it as 'a much-needed book on prayer' and compared it favourably with Fosdick's *The Meaning of Prayer*.

Most of the reviewers were impressed with it as a very practical guide and help for those who found it difficult to pray by someone who freely admitted that he also found prayer difficult, and was sharing his own personal method and answers. The *Church Times* (21 November 1958) had its usual reservations about the book's usefulness for Anglicans, since 'The Eucharist is hardly mentioned.' It thought that in some places the book was too sentimental, especially in frequent references to the beauties of nature, but concluded 'This is a minor blemish on a lovely book, and some may think it not to be a blemish at all.' *The Christian World* (4 December 1958) welcomed it as 'the perfect Christmas gift from one Christian friend to another . . . of all the aids to devotion we have perused during the last few years, Dr. Weatherhead's is the most deeply laden with treasure.' Lynn Harold Hough reviewed the book for the American *Pupil Digest* (June 1959). Referring to it as 'a noble book', he declared 'It will take its place among the few really great guides to devotion. It will be read and re-read. . . . It will bring enrichment to the spiritual life of thousands.' Some of the American papers thought the architectural plan was so rigidly adhered to that it tended to be mechanical, but most recommended it for its spiritual depth and practical value.

The publisher's belief in the book was justified. It quickly ran into several impressions, and when, in 1985, Arthur James took it over from Hodders and re-printed it, it again went into several more impressions, and had become an established classic. In 1987, Hodders themselves paid *A Private House of Prayer* a remarkable tribute in commissioning, thirty years after, a companion volume, *A Healing House of Prayer,* from Bishop Morris Maddocks, Adviser to the Archbishops of York and Canterbury for the Ministry of Health and Healing. In his Introduction, Maddocks pays generous tribute to Weatherhead's original work, describing it as

> Leslie Weatherhead's beautiful book . . . [which] has become a classic and will remain so. Born out of the Methodist tradition it has helped Christians of all denominations to draw nearer to their Lord. Here I am able to speak from experience, for its creative spirituality which meets all occasions, has helped Anne [his wife] and me, particularly during the 'wilderness' periods of our lives. . . . I am certain our experience is far from being unique.

On 1 January, 1959, the B.B.C. news broadcasts announced that in the New Year's Honours List, Weatherhead had been appointed a C.B.E. He had always had a high regard for honours and awards, and was more than delighted with his, especially as Free Church ministers were not often recognised in this way. Among Methodist ministers, there were five others who had been made C.B.E., but these were all for military service, particularly as chaplains.

That Weatherhead had been recommended for such an honour was apparently due to Kenneth Slack, who had been consulted by the Archbishop of Canterbury, Geoffrey Fisher, for the name of an appropriate Methodist. Fisher wrote to Slack, saying that he was 'feeling rather at a loss' in being able to think of an outstanding Methodist. In his reply, Slack named Weatherhead, Sangster and Soper, recommending Weatherhead, pointing out that 'his name is almost a house-hold word in the English-speaking Protestant world.' Fisher expressed concern that Weatherhead was 'sometimes tinged with theological or other controversy', Soper was too political and Sangster too ill for consideration[2] Weatherhead's name was submitted on the list of the Prime Minister, Harold Macmillan. This was unique: no Methodist minister had ever before been included in the Downing Street list.

As the year began, Weatherhead was very happy with the strength of the church and its activities. More people were remaining to Holy Communion than at any time in the history of the church, with attendance at the sacrament frequently over 500. The membership of the Friends of the City Temple had reached over 1,100. Teams of young people had visited over 800 flats in the City, and 'the best Carol Service we have ever had, held on a weeknight only a week before Christmas Day', had been attended by over 1000 people. The church was entirely free of debt and new members were constantly being received. The Psychological Clinic was expanding, with ten doctors now giving their services to it. A new organisation was started on the initiative of a church member, Mrs. Joan Seaward, (professionally well-known as 'Nurse Williams' of the magazine *Woman*) who responded to a lecture from Dr. Leslie Cooke on the plight of refugees by setting up the City Temple's own fund for refugee children, which rapidly became an important part of the life of the church.

Winifred Barton was anxious to be allowed to retire, after twenty-three years as Minister's Assistant, but was persuaded to stay until a successor could be appointed. In his January letter, Weatherhead paid tribute to her for her considerable pastoral work, and especially for her highly successful leadership of the Community Evening which she had transformed from the old Friday Fellowship. He was, he said, grateful most of all to her for her complete personal loyalty to him. She was finally able to leave in April, after the church agreed to the appointment as Assistant Minister of Miss Marjorie Inkster, who, some years before, had been a member of the City Temple's Friday Fellowship. Weatherhead was pleased to welcome her as one of their own former young people. After theological training at Cheshunt College, Cambridge, she had spent five years as a Chaplain's Assistant in the R.A.F. before taking a Diploma in Mental Health. She had then joined the staff of the West Middlesex Hospital as a psychiatric social worker. Weatherhead was keen that she should work particularly with young people, where he felt the biggest gap in the church's ministry lay.

Weatherhead's public fame, which was now at its height, increased the demands for his involvement in activities outside the Temple, particularly in broadcasting and television. On 16 April he spoke in the afternoon on the B.B.C.'s 'Woman's Hour' programme, and that same evening he appeared on television in a discussion on Euthanasia. The following week he appeared again in the televised version of the B.B.C.'s 'Brains Trust.' The *Methodist Recorder* (21 May 1959) reported, 'Dr. Weatherhead is rapidly developing as one of the outstanding religious personalities. . . . He is revealing a quickness of intelligent retort and nimble-mindedness which is the life of any controversial discussion.'

Weatherhead was astonished when the B.B.C. suddenly, with no explanation, dropped him from the Brains Trust. It was only much later that he learned that this had happened because a member of the City Temple, unknown to him had sent an appeal, using his name, to the other members of the Brains Trust asking for money for the church. He was very upset, not least because he was given no opportunity to clear his name and put the matter right.

In time for Easter, Hodder's brought out a small book, *The Resurrection of Christ*, which Weatherhead himself described as an 'essay', in which he set out to discuss 'in the light of modern science and psychical research', how the resurrection might have been achieved, taking up a statement made fifty years before by W.H. Myers that 'men would, within a century, cease to believe in the Resurrection unless new evidence in the field of psychic research could be shown to make it reasonable.' Arguing the case for psychical research, Weatherhead prophesied that 'a careful and honest enquiry into psychic phenomena will yield even richer treasures for the well-being of man than physics, chemistry and biology have given us, vast though these treasures are.' As usual, Weatherhead put forward a theory of how the Resurrection happened which he believed was consistent with the ideas of modern science. He had been excited by reading *My Philosophy* (1933) by Sir Oliver Lodge, in which Lodge suggested that Christ's spirit was so 'high' that it possessed the power to change the physical nature of his body – to 'de-materialise' it. Weatherhead, whose early notebooks show how he had long been fascinated with the findings of physics, that matter was 'energy', and the way heat could change the properties of matter so that something solid could be turned into liquid and then into gas, seized on this to suggest that Christ may have disposed of his physical body in the tomb by 'speeding up the molecular movement' and thus transforming it in some similar way.

The Church Times (24 April 1959) found the book 'passionately sincere', but did not think that the 'attempts to rely on inferences from psychic phenomena', would commend themselves to all readers. It criticised Weatherhead for picking and choosing from the biblical accounts, but even so, 'warmly commended' it 'to those who value a "scientific" approach to the mysteries of religion.' The *Christian* (1 May 1959) felt that there was no need to refer to psychical research to explain the Resurrection: 'For our part, we accept the miracle, but we question the value of trying to explain it on psychological grounds such as these.'

The church's activities were continuing to expand. In October, the Thursday lunchtime services, which had been so popular in the days of Parker and Campbell, were re-introduced. Weatherhead himself preached at the first three, attracting sizeable congregations. The Social Hour after the Sunday evening service was also re-started, and a Sunday evening Young People's Fellowship begun. This became known as Young People Unlimited, with its age range restricted to under thirty fives, after the meeting had been crowded out with older members of the congregation who wanted to hear Weatherhead again after an evening service when he had agreed to speak to the Young People's group.

On 29 September, Weatherhead told the Church Council that he wished to retire within a year. A letter was immediately sent to all church members, informing them of his decision, so that they might know before the news broke in the national press, which it did very rapidly. He was astonished to find it reported in over 40 newspapers and on radio and television. In his Minister's Letter for October, he explained more fully why he had come to make what he described as 'the hardest decision I have ever had to make in my life.' He had come to love the new church, which was the fulfilment of his long-held dreams. His health was better than it had been for at least three years, and he had never enjoyed preaching more. The church had never been in such a strong position, both financially and spiritually. New members were joining every month; Marjorie Inkster's youth work was growing; congregations regularly overflowed into the hall below the church. All the organisations were flourishing, and the music, under Eric Thiman, had never been finer. Weatherhead felt that he had completed the job he was meant to do and it was time to hand over to someone younger with fresh energies and ideas.

He believed that as 'a great and successful church' it would have immense opportunities in the heart of the city, but this meant increasing demands on the minister which he no longer felt able to face. He was finding that the demands then being made on him were greater than they had been when he came to the church in 1936, though he was a quarter of a century older. 'I find that after nearly twenty-four years' strain, some of them war years of shattering nervous demand, I now shrink from every new burden laid upon me and from every new demand that is made.' It was not leadership if 'instead of grasping new opportunities eagerly, he has to be prodded from behind. . . . I should be wicked to hang on to a position in which I am very happy, if by so doing, I "let down the side." He did not want the church to suffer, as other churches had done, because the minister had stayed too long, after his powers had declined. He was, he reminded them, sixty-six, and it was time to 'give a younger man a chance.'

Weatherhead had been at the City Temple twenty-four years. Of these, six had been years of war, and seventeen had been spent in churches other than their own. During this time his international reputation, and as a consequence, that of his church, had grown considerably. He had produced more than twenty books, most notably, *Psychology, Religion and Healing*, which had established him as probably the best known and most influential authority in the field of non-physical healing. The establishment of his Psychological Clinic had a pioneering and wide-reaching influence on the development of pastoral psychology as part of the ministry of the church. His tours abroad had enhanced his reputation further, and in particular his fund-raising tour of America had been exceptionally successful, and ensured that the City Temple could build itself a new home entirely free of debt. In spite of the war, and declining congregations elsewhere, he had continued to attract considerable crowds to hear him whenever he preached. As President of the Methodist Conference he had introduced the Anglican/Methodist Conversations to explore the possibility of union between these Churches, and only illness had prevented him taking an active part in these discussions himself. In seeking his successor, the church felt able to consider anyone it wished, from any denomination and from anywhere in the world. And this it proceeded to do.

1. Hastings, *A History of English Christianity 1920-1990* (SCM 1991), p.465.
2. Fisher Correspondence in the Lambeth Palace Archives. I am indebted to Dr. Lynne Price for this information.

23. Into Retirement

'One of the giants of English Nonconformity . . . a dominant figure in the
Christian Churches of the world . . . a pastor perhaps without equal
today. Leslie Weatherhead has had an influence which has transcended
the limits of geography, profession and denomination.'

The news of Weatherhead's resignation came as a considerable shock to most
members of his church. Among the many who pressed him hard to reconsider
was the former Secretary of the Congregational Union, Dr. Sidney Berry.
Weatherhead was taken aback by many of the reactions to his leaving. He wrote
to Raynor Johnson:

> They are reacting quite well, though some to my surprise, are not just
> disappointed but *angry* with me. My voices tell me I am right, although I *am*
> much better than I was in 1955/6 I have a great deal of pain from the
> diverticulitis. For instance I haven't been out of pain for a fortnight. . . . I am
> 66 and I am *sure* it is right to pull out.[1]

Those closer to him were not surprised that now the goal of rebuilding, which
had been such a dominant aim for so many years, had at long last been achieved,
he should feel that his work at the City Temple was done and that this was the
moment to leave. As the delays and frustrations had dragged on and the date of
the return to their own home had repeatedly been put back, Weatherhead had
steadily become convinced that, like Moses, he would never be permitted to see
the promised land. Having held the church together through seventeen years in
several different and borrowed buildings, and having now shared the joy of
seeing the church re-established so speedily and thriving once again on its old
site, he had no doubts that it was time for him to go. He had earned his retirement,
and at sixty-six he wanted the freedom that release from the burdens and responsibilities of ministering to his great church would give him, to explore new
things and seize new opportunities.

Reporting on Weatherhead's retirement in the *News Chronicle* (3 October
1959) Geoffrey Murray referred to him as

> One of the giants of English Nonconformity . . . a dominant figure in the
> Christian Churches of the world . . . the foremost authority on psychosomatic
> illness . . . and a pastor, perhaps, without equal today. Leslie Weatherhead
> has had an influence which has transcended the limits of geography, pro-
> fession and denomination.

Murray went on to say that 'no better person could be chosen for one of the
new life peerages. . . . Leslie Weatherhead is of the calibre of an Archbishop.
Moreover, the honour is one which would thrill the Free Churches.' This
suggestion proved popular with other newspapers also, although nothing came
of it.

At a special Church Meeting on 24 November, Weatherhead was warmly
thanked for his services during the twenty-three years of his ministry. Though
regrets were voiced by several members that the Minister should feel it necessary

to intimate his resignation at this time, but he said that his decision had not been made lightly and he would not reconsider. By a standing vote, he was unanimously invited to become the 'Minister-Emeritus' of the City Temple for life. It was mentioned that Dr. Fosdick had been so designated when he retired from his ministry at Riverside, New York. Weatherhead was more than delighted to accept.

Throughout Weatherhead's ministry, the members of the church had, for the most part, been only too happy to follow where he led. This was so much the case that the Church Council made the mistake of assuming that this ready acquiescence was given to them as well. At the meeting that accepted Weatherhead's resignation, they proceeded to recommend the name of a successor for acceptance by the meeting. This was the Rev. R.W. Hugh Jones, a well-known Congregationalist, then minister of Warwick Road, Coventry. Although Weatherhead was in the chair, he properly refused to take any part in the discussion concerning the proposal. Hugh Jones was well known to the members of the City Temple, and had very successfully led the conference weekends of the Community Evening, but the members objected to his – or anyone's – name being put forward so hastily, and without following the usual Congregational practice of asking the meeting to consider inviting him to preach 'with a view.' The members, led by Dr. Eric Thiman, reasserted themselves, and the Council was forced to give way to the will of the meeting. The Church decided that it did not want to rush to appoint a successor. The Council was asked to draw up a list of those to be invited to preach, and after these had been heard, to submit a list to the members to be voted on later.

Such was the confidence of the church and its sense of the world reputation and importance of its pulpit that the Church Council did not hesitate to range far wider than the available ministers of their own denomination or within the borders of their own country in their search for Weatherhead's successor. Distinguished British Congregationalists, among whom were Dr. Leslie Cooke of the World Council of Churches in Geneva, Dr. Trevor Davies of Richmond Hill, Bournemouth, and the Rev. Hugh Jones of Warwick Road, Coventry, were invited to conduct services during the following weeks after Weatherhead's resignation had been announced. Others invited were Dr. Eric Baker, the Secretary of the Methodist Conference, and a Canadian Baptist of Welsh origins, Dr. Emlyn Davies. The Rev. A. Leonard Griffith from the Chalmers United Church of Canada in Ottawa preached at both services on 8 May.

Several members had contributed to the commissioning of a bust of Weatherhead by a Polish sculptor, Kostek Wojnarowski, to be placed in the church vestibule alongside the bust of Joseph Parker. This was unveiled by a church member, Viscountess Leathers, at a simple ceremony on 1 December. In a short speech, Wojnarowski, who had won the highest award for bravery as a pilot in the Polish Air Force during the war, said that during the sittings with Weatherhead he had been conscious of a great sense of peace which had helped him to recover something he had lost as a result of his wartime experiences.

John D. Rockefeller died on 13 May, 1960. Paying tribute to him in the June , Weatherhead wrote,

The City Temple owes an immense debt to him, and though it is technically a Congregational Church, it must always be remembered that he would never have given to it as he did unless he had believed me when I told him that, like his own beloved "Riverside Church", it aimed at being above all narrow denominationalism. If the City Temple forgot that, it would lay itself open to the charge of having received money under false pretences.

Weatherhead did not reveal in this obituary, and only made public some time after he had retired, that Rockefeller had offered to restrict his gift of a quarter of a million dollars so that it would not be available for rebuilding the City Temple on any site other than one chosen by Weatherhead himself. Weatherhead, who had been keen to rebuild the church in George Street, Marylebone, 'where thousands throng the streets on Sundays, rather than in the deserted City', had turned down the offer of this restriction, saying that he did not feel justified in using Rockefeller's offer 'merely to get my own way.' The decision where to rebuild had in any case finally been resolved two years before Weatherhead met Rockefeller, with the appointment of Lord Mottistone who had advised using what remained of the old church. Work had already started, so that it would not have been either wise or practical for Weatherhead to re-open the question on his return from America in 1954. But it is to his credit that he made no public mention of Rockefeller's offer until so long after he had retired from the church.

In June Weatherhead was interviewed on Independent television for a programme, 'Ministers of Grace', which prompted a letter to the producer from Noel Stevenson, I.T.V.'s Programme Administration Officer.

> I felt I must congratulate you. . . . We thought it was excellent television, and John Thompson's interviewing a model demonstration of how effectively sympathetic courtesy can secure brilliant elucidation. Leslie Weatherhead's personality came out crystal clear.

The Methodist Recorder (23 June 1960) reviewing the programme, asked why it was that Weatherhead 'should face viewers comparatively unknown as a T.V. personality . . . he had not emerged dynamically on television.' The *Recorder* was pleased to report that in a BBC 'Panorama' programme, Richard Dimbleby, interviewing six young women from overseas, asked them which Englishman they most admired and would most like to meet. Along with the expected answers – Prince Phillip, Laurence Olivier and Rex Harrison – one American said, 'Dr. Leslie Weatherhead.'

Weatherhead's interest in the paranormal and non-physical methods of healing involved him in 1956 in a highly publicised and controversial court case which caused him to be seen by many of his critics as credulous and gullible. The case involved a Miss Catherine Philips, who brought a case for damages against Mr. George de la Warr for fraudulent misrepresentation. He had sold her a de la Warr Diagnostic Treatment Instrument, referred to by the press as 'the Black Box' for £110. This box was claimed to be able to heal people at a distance by means of 'radiesthetics'. Weatherhead, who knew de la Warr, had long been interested in this method of treatment, and impressed by demonstrations of its effectiveness which he had witnessed himself. In an article on 'Odic Force' for *The London Qyarterly and Holborn Review* in October, 1954, he stated that some twenty years before

> a specimen of blood from the finger of one of my children, sent on a bit of blotting paper to a 'radiesthetist', led her, by holding a pendulum over it and over certain biochemical salts, to prescribe a remedy which entirely

and over certain biochemical salts, to prescribe a remedy which entirely cured a most obstinate and long standing disability which had made the child's life miserable for years.

Weatherhead was one of twenty-six witnesses for the defence, who included Air Marshal Sir Victor Goddard, a French professor, a barrister and several doctors interested in radionics. In his evidence, Weatherhead said that he had visited de la Warr's laboratory in Oxford three times and was a patron of them, that it was nonsense to suggest that the work was fraudulent, and that the de la Warrs were honest and he was quite certain of their integrity. Mr. David Karmel, Q.C. in his final speech on behalf of the complainant, said that 'All these witnesses had something in common – they lived and thought in a somewhat rare atmosphere. They were all interested in spiritualism and faith healing.' Although the judge found in de la Warr's favour, he stressed that his findings in no way supported the claims that had been made that de la Warr's instruments actually worked. The judge said that he had been impressed by the sincerity of the many defence witnesses even though he regarded many of the claims that had been made for radionics as absurd.

The case was followed avidly by the popular press. The *Daily Express* (19 June 1960) managed to get hold of the Black Box, photographing and describing its components which it said were made up of switches and connections which 'mean nothing to conventional scientists.' Chapman Pincher, the *Express's* most famous columnist, was full of scorn for de la Warr and those who supported him, asking 'how is it that such honest credulity can exist in an age of rank materialism when science is taught in every school?'

The publicity given to this case and Weatherhead's involvement in it was a source of some embarrassment to his friends and followers. (The *City Temple Tidings* ignored it entirely.) More prudent ministers, with stronger instincts for their own self-protection, would surely have avoided being drawn into it. Weatherhead was prepared to become involved, simply because, knowing the defendant, he believed him to be honest and incapable of fraud. At the same time, Weatherhead's own integrity was at stake, since he had for years written and spoken in support of the kind of research de la Warr was engaged in, and he could not, and – being the kind of person he was – would not, refuse to acknowledge his interest and support even though the wide publicity could be damaging to his own reputation and expose him to ridicule.

On 24 May, Wesley day, Weatherhead was told that W.E. Sangster had died that morning. Sangster had been ill for nearly two years with a muscular wasting disease that had progressively paralysed him. Towards the end, Sangster had not wanted any of his close friends to visit him. Weatherhead, who was 'the dearest of his friends', had been particularly hurt and upset by this seeming rejection. In his last letter (15 May 1959) a year before, Sangster had written to him,

> Dear, dear Leslie, don't feel cut off from me. I don't feel cut off from you. No. I can't dictate. If I could, I could talk on the phone. Its your prayers I need – and I know I have them. . . . God is in charge. I am shut up with Him, and that is a wonderful experience. When I come back, I shall have rich things to tell you. As soon as I can, I'll say 'Come!'

Weatherhead provided an obituary appreciation of Sangster for the *Sunday*

Times and was immediately invited to take over his regular monthly religious article for the paper.

That same evening a special Church Meeting had been called to consider his successor. Understandably, Weatherhead, who took the chair, was under considerable strain because of his friend's death, and the importance of the occasion. Several names, including some who had taken up the invitation to preach, were before the meeting for consideration. Speeches for or against any particular one were discouraged, though questions about each were accepted. A question was asked about the theological position of Leonard Griffith, to which Weatherhead replied that he had had a long talk with Griffith, and he 'was convinced that he was more orthodox than the present Minister of the church and that there need be no fear that he held any extreme views which would be out of sympathy with the present outlook of the church.'

The method adopted for choosing the new minister was the transferable vote system used by the Methodist Conference for the election of its President. A first vote was taken on a number of names, then a second vote on the top three. In the final count Griffith received over 70% of the votes cast, and over 160 more than the next nominee. The Secretary then formally moved that a unanimous Call be sent to Leonard Griffith, and this was agreed by a standing vote of all the members. Griffith was notified by telephone immediately after the meeting, and duly accepted, agreeing to take up his ministry in October.

Griffith's name had been made known to the City Temple through a strong recommendation from Dr. John Short, who, after his ministries at Lyndhurst Road Congregational Church, Hampstead, and Richmond Hill, Bournemouth, had gone to St. George's United Church in Toronto. In a letter to Weatherhead the previous November, Short said,

> In my judgment he is the most outstanding of the younger men in the United Church of Canada. He is evangelical in spirit and unique in his approach with a natural sense of drama in his style. He has . . . held great audiences spellbound by his eloquence which is also matched by deep thinking.

Griffith, who was just forty, had been born in Lancashire. His parents, who were professional opera singers, had emigrated to Canada when he was nine. After taking a B.A. degree at McGill University he had studied theology at Queen's University, Kingston, Ontario, gaining his B.D. in 1945, and was then ordained as a minister of the United Church of Canada.

Weatherhead was charmed by Griffith's personality when he entertained him in his home, and impressed by 'his magnificent preaching and devout, sincere spirit in church.' He felt he had made a 'new and lovable life long friend who fully shared one's own aspirations and ideals for the City Temple.' Griffith also felt he had made an 'immediate friend' who 'made no secret in our private conversations that he wanted me to succeed him.' After accepting the Call, Griffith wrote to Weatherhead,

> I do hope that it will be possible for you to come to the Induction on Friday, October 21st. It would give me the keenest pleasure to have you there and I do want the City Temple people to know from the very beginning that by being Minister Emeritus you have a permanent place in their hearts and mine in the life of the Congregation.

Weatherhead was particularly pleased when the Church Council, with the approval of Leonard Griffith, unanimously agreed that one of the Clinic rooms should be re-named 'Dr. Weatherhead's Room' and continue to be available for his use after he had retired. He was unhappy at having to lose the services of Winifred Haddon, his exceptionally efficient and dedicated secretary for over twenty years, and would now become his successor's. After he had retired, he was glad to have the services of another former member of the City Temple, Elsie Thompson, who volunteered to do his typing for him, but she did not know shorthand, and he found it difficult to cope with his large correspondence, and to produce the articles and books he still wanted to write.

The Sunday morning service on June 26, which Weatherhead conducted, was given over to a memorial service for Dr. Ida Scudder, the founder of the Vellore Hospital and Medical School in South India. Among those present were the Indian High Commissioner, Mrs. Pandit, the American Ambassador, and the pianist, Eileen Joyce. Weatherhead had been an enthusiastic supporter of Vellore since his days in India, and each year during his ministry the City Temple had held a special service in support of Ida Scudder and her work. In his Minister's Letter reporting the Memorial Service he expressed the hope that this support would continue after he had left the church.

In September, Hodders produced a new book of sermons, *Key Next Door.* This contained twenty-five sermons selected from those preached during Weatherhead's last months at the City Temple. The book was designed to mark the closing of his ministry, and was presented by the publishers as 'the full flowering of one of the greatest preachers of our time.' The same month, Cassell published in their Red Lion series Christopher Maitland's short biography of Weatherhead which provides a remarkable indication of his public standing at this time. This was intended for young people.

who are of an age to be thinking of their future careers. Each presents a biography of one of the most famous men or women of modern times, all of them at the top of their particular professions, whose achievements the young, depending on their own ambitions, will seek to emulate.

Maitland's book places Weatherhead alongside the others featured in the series: Earl Mountbatten of Burma, Sir Alexander Fleming, Lord Nuffield, Kathleen Ferrier, Sir Malcolm Sargent, Sir Donald Bradman, R.G. Menzies and Harold MacMillan. Weatherhead is described as 'one of those rare people who, like all great men of action, is always guided by that carefully meditated faith which transforms a career into a vocation.'

The church gathered in the hall on 14 October, Weatherhead's sixty-seventh birthday, to wish him well on his retirement and to make a presentation to him and his wife. The Church Secretary, John Dewey, reviewed the twenty-four years of Weatherhead's ministry, saying that he had given the best years of his life to the City Temple. He was then presented with a folio of more than fifty letters from friends all over the world, and a cheque for £1,927 donated by members and friends of the church. The Church Treasurer, Binstead Griffiths, praised Weatherhead as 'a great inspirer and as a tremendous storehouse of power made freely available to the world by his sermons, broadcasts, his writings and his personality.' His retirement was against all the arguments wishes and pleas of his friends. 'He goes while we still want more, with his abilities still strong and matured by experience, and in the knowledge that the future of the Church will be safe in the hands of his successor and colleagues.' He then presented him with a 'substantial cheque' on behalf of the Church and the Church Council.

A tribute and presentation – of a Kenwood electric mixer – was also made to Mrs. Weatherhead, who, although 'she had always felt that her first duty was to her home and her family' had made her own quiet contribution to the life of the church, visiting many who were ill, and giving friendship and support to any in trouble. She had been active in leadership of the women's organisations as President of the Ladies Working Guild and in practical participation in the Women's League of Service Adoption Scheme, as well as in her keen support for the missionary work of the church, having been a missionary herself.

Weatherhead, replying, looked at the cheque and remarked, 'Behold the idle rich!' He added his own tribute to his wife for 'the peace and serenity of their home life together.' He said he had achieved his ambition of leaving no gap between the closing of his own ministry and the opening of another. He was very happy about handing over to Leonard Griffith, of whom he was already very fond.

The Committee set up to sort out matters relating to his retirement had agreed to pay him £4,000 from corporate funds, together with the car. This created some correspondence with Weatherhead who had understood that the car had already been given to him 'many years ago.' The Church had in fact given it to him as a 'thank you' present when he returned from his fund-raising trip to America in 1954. Binstead Griffiths had to explain that as the car had continued to appear as an asset in the church accounts 'it would have to appear as a gift now'.

The Farewell services were held on 16 October. In the morning Weatherhead preached on 'Let's Look Forward'. Refusing to dwell on the past, he described 'Every parting as a kind of death', but said, 'When bereavement happens, those who remain are committed as Christians, not to moan tearfully that life will never be the same again'. Referring to his going to the Brunswick Church in Leeds at the age of thirty-two, he said that his predecessor there, A.E. Whitham, had told his crowded congregation on his last Sunday, 'If you love me, come like this next Sunday and give the young man a chance.' Weatherhead added, 'That is what I now say to you.' Telling them to be ready to accept new ideas he appealed to them to 'offer the new Minister a church on its toes to go forward, a church undivided by quarrels, a church full of people dedicated to the upward climb towards the oneness with God which is the destiny of man.' At his final service in the evening, he preached on 'According to my Gospel', saying that although the Gospel was Christ's and belonged to the whole world, Paul knew that he could only impart that fraction of it which he had made his own. 'So', Weatherhead said, 'I have preached my gospel, the tiny bit that I could see. Now comes the time when you must receive another facet of the truth which my successor will bring to you.'

During the following week he received a letter (17 October 1960) from the Archbishop of Canterbury, saying,

I saw the notice yesterday in which you preached your final sermon as Minister of the City Temple. May I send you a word of deep sympathy. Your conviction that it is right to make way for a younger man will save you from any self-pity but at the same time there cannot but be a wrench in parting. May I also thank you for the grand work for the Christian cause that you have done all through these years. Again, grace will keep you from undue self-congratulation, but we can all openly and thankfully praise God for your work.

1. Raynor Johnson: *The Light and the Gate* (H & S. 1964) p.280.

24. Bexhill

'Weatherhead is to most preachers as a carpet-beater to a feather
duster. When you have heard one of his sermons you have the
marks to show for it.'

The Weatherheads had bought a house at Bexhill-on-Sea, and they moved there
after the final services at the City Temple were over. He still had a number of
engagements to fulfil. One of these was to open the Highgate Centre at Highgate
Methodist Church, where Dr. William Kyle had started a counselling service.

For some time, Weatherhead had been interested in the work of the Churches'
Public Morality Council, and this had become a major concern, which continued
throughout the decade and involved him in a great deal of publicity and
controversy. The Council was receiving reports of increasing sexual activity
among unmarried people, especially teenagers still at school. Weatherhead grew
steadily more alarmed at this, and at what he perceived were the dangers to the
nation of this pattern of behaviour. His public speeches on this theme became
more and more numerous. Soon after his move to Bexhill he was invited to
preach at the Remembrance Day Parade Service at the local war memorial. In his
address he took the opportunity to warn about the dangers to the nation of
sexual immorality among the young.

Preaching at the Manchester and Salford Mission a few days later he attacked
the publication of *Lady Chatterley's Lover* as 'rank poison', declaring that 'Sexual
immorality was one of the mightiest and most terrifying dangers of our time',
and that the effect of the intimate sexual detail in *Lady Chatterley* might have
serious consequences on normal unmarried people with surplus sex energy
which 'cannot be biologically satisfied in our society.'

Another early task after his retirement was to write an obituary of one of the
longest serving of his Clinic doctors, Dr. James Burnet Rae, who died on 31
October. Rae, who had orginally been a Presbyterian minister, had joined the
church and the Clinic when Weatherhead arrived in 1936. He was a Vice-President
of the Guild of Health and had been invited by the Archbishop of Canterbury to
become the Free Church Co-President of the Churches' Council of Healing.
Weatherhead's sadness at losing this old friend and colleague was added to by
his concern for the future of the Clinic which was now so short of medical staff
that its effectiveness was almost halved. Among the other doctors, two had
retired, one was semi-retired and another recovering from a serious illness. He
appealed for new people to offer their help, stipulating three requirements: 'a
real appreciation of the value of religion based on their own experience . . . a
medical qualification . . . a psychological qualification or experience of
psychological treatments.'

Not surprisingly, after the hectic schedule, the publicity and all the excitement
which surrounded his departure from the City Temple and from London, the
considerable contrast of life in retirement in Bexhill affected his spirits. Painful
physical ailments added to his depression. He shared his feelings with Raynor

Johnson, who wrote back in December,

> I was so sorry to read between the lines that you are a bit "down" and feeling a bit like an old crock. Despite the skin and the ulcer, and the deficiencies of the alimentary tract, I insist that you are suffering from an almost inevitable reaction from the fact of retirement. Before you were in the centre and in a pulpit, now you are a private individual (to a considerable extent) and the crowds are elsewhere listening to some other fellow. It is the close of a phase and the psychological passage is likely to hit you a bit hard. I beg you to believe. . .that some of your most important work lies ahead. . . . Don't allow yourself to be tempted to dash all over the country and wear yourself out doing the same kind of things which you have done week in and week out for so long.

At Leonard Griffith's urging, he returned to the church to preach for the first time following his retirement, on the Sunday after Easter, 9 April. He hesitated before accepting, having been firmly told by John Dewey and Marjorie Inkster that he should stay away completely from the church for a year to give Griffith a clear field. He preached at both services and the next day unveiled a plaque during a special evensong service at St. Bride's Fleet Street, to commemorate the close fellowship the two churches shared during the war. St. Bride's had also been destroyed by bombing, but the then Rector, Prebendary Arthur Taylor, had offered the City Temple the use of their schoolroom as a venue for the City Temple's organisations to meet.

Following an article in *The Methodist Recorder* by the Secretary of the Churches' Fellowship for Psychical Study, the Rev. Bertram Woods, Weatherhead was contacted two weeks before his retirement to write an article in support of psychical research for a follow-up Special Supplement to the paper which it was intending to publish in January. Because of other demands on his time Weatherhead was unable to produce his contribution so quickly, and the Supplement eventually appeared on 8 June, 1961. It included a further article by Woods replying to correspondence, and in addition to Weatherhead's, there were two articles by scientists opposed to such research; Professor C.A.Coulson of the Mathematics Institute, Oxford, and Professor D.M. MacKay from the University of Keele. The Symposium was edited by Professor W.D.Wright of Imperial College, London.

Coulson said that the study of psychic phenomena was not popular with professional scientists because it had been 'the happy hunting ground for all sorts of frauds and charlatans,' and because 'Scientists do not like phenomena that are not reproducible.' He was 'prepared to believe that there are experiences of a psychic kind of which we know little or nothing', and that 'God almost certainly wills that we should study them.' He disputed that orthodox science was materialistic and that such research was an antidote to it. He considered that evidence of telepathy provided no proof of the existence of the 'spiritual' world, but was better studied by theoretical physicists 'to devise an account of space-time that fits all the observations.' Nor did Spiritualism prove anything about survival after death. Psychical research ought to be encouraged, but it could not, as Woods had argued, contribute effectively to man's search for God or to Christian evangelism. MacKay supported Coulson, saying that although Christians should not be 'debarred from looking scientifically into this weird

Evelyn and Leslie Weatherhead with Gertie Hutchinson

field, so tangled with the unscientific overgrowth of wishful thinking and wilful deceit,' he was 'dismayed at the *motives* for such inquiry urged by Mr. Woods.' He agreed with Coulson that 'scientific inquiry by its nature can prove nothing about a "spiritual world" because whatever can be scientifically "proved" becomes *ipso facto* a part . . . of the natural world.'

Weatherhead began by agreeing that psychic research was 'under a cloud. . . . No field of human thought and action has been so bedevilled by quacks and charlatans.' He repeated his comment, made 'forty years ago', that 'Spiritualism has not made a single, definite, valuable or original contribution to Christian thought concerning life after death.' But he insisted there was 'a residue of truth' which was 'an authentic part of human experience . . . which Christians, not the bereaved or emotionally unstable, should, as lovers of truth, investigate.' He regarded a refusal to explore truth as 'un-Christian as well as cowardly.' His main argument was that to ignore questions about psychic matters was to leave out significant parts of the Bible. Referring to Christ's resurrection appearances and the account of the Transfiguration in which Jesus was said to have spoken to Moses and Elijah, he said 'He would be a bold man who excluded psychic material from the New Testament.' He went on to justify his own interest from the example of John Wesley, and to give examples from his own experience which he claimed were evidence of psychic phenomena. He appealed for 'the kind of real scientist who, without prejudice, will examine this vast and difficult field of phenomena with the same scrupulous attitude of mind which we so admire, say, in physics.'

Weatherhead was accorded an unusual honour for a Free Church minister when he was invited to be Select Preacher at the University of Cambridge on June 4. In July, he gave a lecture to the annual conference in Wimbledon of the Churches' Fellowship for Psychical Study, on 'Intercession and Healing.' He came back to the City Temple, again at Griffith's personal invitation, to preach at all the services for five weeks from 30 July to the end of August. Griffith returned from holiday to take part in the service on Weatherhead's final Sunday. He had not previously heard him preach and so for the first time experienced for himself the extraordinary impact of his predecessor.

I was magnetised by his pulpit presence, as were all the members of that vast overflow congregation. He preached on the obscure incident of Jesus cursing the fig tree and did so with lucidity, charm, and power that carried the Word of God straight into the hearts of the people. Never have I heard such a superb communicator.[1]

From the start of his ministry, Griffith had felt daunted by the task of following Weatherhead. 'Though Weatherhead gave me his friendship and constant encouragement, I still lived under his shadow and felt like a sparrow sitting on an eagle's nest.' When he met Geoffrey Fisher, the retired Archbishop of Canterbury, Fisher asked him how he was getting on, remarking, 'It must be awesome to succeed Weatherhead.' When Griffith agreed, Fisher said he knew how he felt. 'Don't forget that I twice succeeded William Temple – as Headmaster of Repton School and as Archbishop of Canterbury.' Griffith asked how he had managed it, to which Fisher replied, 'Well, I decided that there must be some things Temple could not do and that I should concentrate on them.'

Although Weatherhead had described his leaving the church as 'a bereavement', neither he nor anyone else had seriously considered or appreciated the effect of his going on those for whom his ministry had been so personal and had meant so much. Weatherhead knew the Methodist system in which a newly appointed minister took up his duties the Sunday immediately after his predecessor had closed his ministry, and this had been the case in each of his former churches. He had therefore been keen that there should be no gap between his ministry and that of Griffith. In this he had been supported by the Church Council, who were no doubt concerned, particularly from a financial and practical point of view, that there should be no falling off of numbers attending the services between one ministry and the next.

But the relationship between Weatherhead and the members of his congregation had been exceptionally close. Not only had they shared together all the dramatic, tragic, frustrating and exhilarating experiences of the past twenty-four years, but the spiritual, emotional and psychological influence of his ministry on so many of them had been so intimate and powerful that even the ones who had not often spoken to him personally felt that he held a place of central importance in their lives. They had come to depend on him, Sunday by Sunday, to an extent which few appreciated until he was no longer with them. As a psychologist, Weatherhead understood the way an individual patient could become dependent on a therapist with whom he spent an hour every week, but neither Weatherhead, nor anyone else, appreciated the degree of dependency which had built up over the years with the regular members of his congregation. For them, as much as for him, it was a 'bereavement', and after such a long and exceptional ministry they needed time to grieve for his going before they could begin to adjust to a new and entirely different ministry and personality. It was unfair and unfortunate for Griffith that they were not allowed to do so, and coming as he did from completely outside the situation, he could have no way of understanding or appreciating the depth of this feeling and this need.

For many of those who had come regularly to hear Weatherhead, Griffith was a shock, and it was not easy for them to adjust. It is not a criticism of Griffith to say that the effect of his preaching was different from that of Weatherhead. He was his own man, with his own considerable gifts, and there was no way he could possibly know, since he had never yet heard Weatherhead preach, how very different his style and personality were. Griffith, who was much more theologically conservative and orthodox than Weatherhead, took his preaching very seriously, as a proclamation of the Word of God. He was dramatic and declamatory, where Weatherhead wooed and persuaded. His voice was resonant and powerful, where Weatherhead's was light and gentle. Those who had for years basked in the warmth of the sheer love of people which emanated from Weatherhead and which had embraced them week by week, found it hard to respond to Griffith's seemingly tougher, more masculine and less outwardly affectionate persona. There was also a misguided attitude among some members of the church, of which again Griffith was probably completely unaware, which implied that any nostalgic mention of Weatherhead was a disloyalty to Griffith. This created an unhappy and totally unnecessary feeling of rivalry and division within the church.[2]

When Weatherhead had come to the City Temple in 1936, he was already well known there and to the country at large. He had no need to prove his powers as a preacher, and the church which had been losing its congregations became packed to the doors from the start. He immediately set out to strengthen the fellowship of the church, starting several new and lastingly successful organisations within the first few weeks. Griffith, whatever his reputation in Canada, was unknown in England and had a daunting task to justify his call as Weatherhead's successor and to establish a reputation for himself in his new sphere. Griffith believed that the greatest need of the Church was 'A resurgence of uninhibited, dynamic preaching', but he was very conscious of the succession of great preachers he had been called to follow, and acutely anxious about his ability to fulfil expectations. In his first pastoral letter he told the church, 'I have come to the City Temple primarily to preach, and to this end study and sermon preparation must always be given priority over all other claims on my time and energy.' He did not, as Weatherhead had been careful to do, take a regular Sunday each month away from the City Temple, but for the first year, preached at almost every service, not only each Sunday, but at the Thursday lunchtime services as well. He reckoned to spend at least thirty hours each week on sermon preparation alone, and each sermon was carefully memorised so that he could preach entirely without notes. This regime inevitably created an enormous strain on him which eventually began to tell.

To begin with, the large congregations were maintained. In his final services Weatherhead had appealed to the congregation to come and support the new minister, and this they did. There was also a considerable curiosity factor, increased by the exceptional publicity Griffith's arrival had received in the national press, to hear what 'this babbler' had to say.[3] As the months passed, however, the numbers attending declined, although in response to his ministry new people were being received into membership, so, in spite of the smaller congregations, at the 1962 Annual Church Meeting the Church Secretary was able to report an increase in membership of nearly four per cent.

There was anxiety about the future of the Psychological Clinic. Griffith felt it necessary to give an assurance in his July Minister's Letter that:

I shall do all within my power to see that this unique and vitally important ministry does have a future in the life of the City Temple. Though not a qualified psychologist, I am a firm believer in the partnership of minister, psychologist and physician. . . . Fortunately, we can count on Dr. Weatherhead's continued association with the Psychological Clinic, and he and I have already made plans for its reorganisation in the autumn.

The meeting of the Clinic took place on 13 September, the 25th anniversary of its inauguration. Weatherhead presided and was delighted that it was attended also by Leonard Griffith and by Noel Shepherd, who had just been inducted as the new Assistant Minister. The Clinic staff consisted of eleven doctors, one of whom, Dr. David Common, a Canadian, held theological as well as medical and psychological degrees. Winifred Haddon and Norman French – a London hotelier and close personal friend of Weatherhead – were appointed as joint secretaries. French had a particular interest in the Church's ministry of healing. Dr. T.P. Rees of Harley Street agreed to act as a consultant. It was arranged that the Clinic staff should continue to meet regularly, 'and where necessary to discuss, under fictitious names, the difficulties which patients bring to them. In this way the maximum help available will be offered.' Weatherhead felt happy that the Clinic's work was continuing and that its future seemed so secure.

Following the successful defence of D.H. Lawrence's book, *Lady Chatterley's Lover*, in a six day trial at the Old Bailey in November, 1960, Penguin had proceeded with the publication of the first complete and unexpurgated edition. The combination of the publicity of the trial and the notorious reputation which the book had gained long before its publication, ensured that within a few months it had sold over a million copies. Weatherhead had, as quoted earlier, refused a request to be a witness for the defence. In a letter to Michael B. Rubinstein, the Solicitor for Penguin Books, (6 October 1960) he deplored the book as capable of doing harm.

On 20 September, 1961, *The Times* published a long letter from Weatherhead under the heading 'A Nation in Danger.' Weatherhead subscribed to the traditional view that sexuality needed to be regulated and controlled if a strong social order were to be maintained. He found his support for this, not only in the traditional teaching of the Church, but in the arguments of Freud and the conclusions of Arnold Toynbee, whose *Study of History* had put forward the view that civilisations collapsed and disappeared when they no longer served the purposes of God. He found further support in the *History of the Decline and Fall of the Roman Empire* in which Gibbon had concluded that 'sexual depravity within, not the hostile enemy without, brought down that great empire.' In his letter to *The Times* Weatherhead gave statistics:

> sinister figures for homosexuality, marital infidelity, and violent sex crimes. . . . One bride in six pregnant on her wedding day . . . one in twenty of all births illegitimate . . . venereal disease in teenagers . . . increased by 66 per cent in the last three years.

He quoted the headmistress of a London girls' school as saying that 'not one girl in her sixth form was a virgin', 'and your paper, Sir, reported the habit of teenage girls of wearing a yellow golliwog, not as a sign of academic or athletic distinction, but as a sign that the wearer had had sexual intercourse with a man.'

This letter attracted a great deal of attention and comment throughout the national press, and the correspondence in *The Times* continued every day for six weeks. Weatherhead was accused of 'attacking modern youth'. A 'clerical correspondent' retorted that 'national decline was no concern of religion.' Weatherhead was pained to find that, having since the beginning of his ministry acquired a reputation for an exceptional ability to speak to and for young people, he was now being labelled as an elderly conservative kill-joy. John Freeman in the *News of the World* said, 'Stop moaning, Britain's kids are fine,' and called him 'a gloomy old bore' and 'the latest of these dismal Jimmies.' He was lampooned in the 'Peter Simple' column of the *Daily Telegraph* for repeating a story, later proved to have little foundation, that a search of handbags belonging to sixth formers at a girls' school had discovered that 80 per cent of them carried contraceptives.

'Demos' in the *Methodist Recorder* rallied to his defence. Quoting further statistics from the Registrar General, he demanded, 'In the face of such figures I do not see how anyone can with honesty lightly gloss over the moral state of the nation.' Canon Wilfred Garlick in the *Stockport Advertiser* declared that Weatherhead had taken on the traditional role of the 'Nonconformist Conscience' in drawing attention to the 'moral turpitude of the nation'. One result of the letter to *The Times* was that Weatherhead was invited to serve on a Committee set up by the British Medical Association to investigate the increase of venereal disease especially among young people.

In addition to his letter to *The Times* Weatherhead had syndicated a similar article to a dozen other newspapers, several of which, such as *The Daily Mail, The Yorkshire Evening Post,* and *The Evening Standard* not only featured it prominently and at length but also made it the subject of their editorial comments. Heading its editorial 'Decadent Britain?' the *Daily Mail* (21 September 1961) said 'Dr. Weatherhead swings statistics like a battle-axe.' It questioned whether the moral climate was in fact worse than in the Victorian period, saying that 'percentages plucked out at random can be as misleading as isolated quotations from Gibbon', adding that Weatherhead's assertion that 'With our present sexual laxity our homes are becoming less and less secure', was not born out by social researchers, who 'investigating home life in Britain have come to exactly opposite conclusions.' It did, however,

> enthusiastically agree with Dr. Weatherhead when he calls for a whole-hearted Christian revival. That is what Britain thirsts for today. Although

the evils and dangers of our society and age are not perhaps as simple or sinful as he paints them.

He continued to write, speak and preach on this theme throughout the decade, and to attract the attention of the press whenever he did so. In March, 1962, after giving a public lecture at the Highgate Counselling Centre on 'A Nation in Danger', he was interviewed for the *Daily Express* (12 March 1962) by Nancy Banks-Smith, who reported that

> This week-end he rocked 'em in the aisles at Highgate, London, with straight-right statistics. That venereal disease has risen by 345 per cent among young girls. That in one class of 14-year-olds 12 per cent of the boys and 25 per cent of the girls had already had multiple sexual relations. . . . Weatherhead is to most preachers as a carpet-beater to a feather duster. When you've heard one of his sermons you have the marks to show for it.

He returned again to the theme of the sexual degeneration of the nation two years later, in October, 1964, when he was invited to address the Annual Public Meeting of the Public Morality Council. Speaking on 'The Moral Climate Today,' he referred back to his original letter *The Times* on 'A Nation in Danger', and said that the question that needed to be answered was 'whether we are witnessing a changed but defensible pattern of sexual behaviour or a dangerous decline in moral standards.' He thought the latter. He said that when he was a teenager, it was the withholding of facts about sex which was so worrying, but nowadays it was the withholding of guidance. The verdict in the *Lady Chatterley* trial had 'opened the gates to a flood of obscene material.' Extra-marital intercourse 'put in jeopardy the homes of the nation.' There was an 'appalling rise in V.D. amongst teenagers.' He repeated statistics of sexual activity among school children, and stated that 'Facts have been collected to show that young girls going up to the university frequently lose their virginity in the first term.' This address again attracted a great deal of notice in the press, and brought him an invitation from the London Committee Against Obscenity to join their campaign.

As the City Temple congregations had steadily fallen, the treasurer, Binstead Griffiths, suggested that the church's new minister should write regular religious articles for the press to make himslef better known, as Weatherhead had done with considerable success throughout his career. Griffiths therefore arranged an appointment for Leonard Griffith with the publisher of the *Daily Mirror,* Cecil King. Griffith was taken aback by King's bluntness and the discourtesy of his reception:

> Mr. King rudely refused my services. 'Why do you want to write for my paper?' he barked. 'Do you think it will fill your church? Nothing will fill yours or any other church ever again! The churches in this country are dead! The Established Church is dead! The Free Churches are deader!'[4]

King's brusque treatment of Griffith indicates how much attitudes had changed since Weatherhead first went to the same church in 1936. It had become much harder to attract the interest and co-operation of the press for the expression of the religious point of view. But it was also the case that Weatherhead, who possessed a natural instinct for journalism, had always caught the attention of the press and public because he dealt with matters which interested them, in a highly controversial, lively, provocative and unconventional way. Griffith's less controversial, more orthodox and conservative opinions, however sound and well-considered they may have been, could not succeed in persuading the editors of the national papers that he had anything new or interesting to say.

Weatherhead returned to the theme of an earlier book, *Why do Men Suffer*, with a new book, *Salute to a Sufferer* published by Epworth in July 1962. This was the subject of the A.S. Peake Memorial Lecture he had been invited to give that same year. He felt greatly honoured and delighted to be asked to deliver this lecture, saying that, unlike all his predecessors in this lectureship, 'I have no claim whatever to be a scholar. I have been a working minister ever since I was ordained.' He had studied under Peake, who had been his Supervisor for his M.A. thesis.

The book reveals Weatherhead's pastoral rather than academic approach to his subject matter, as in almost all his books. Although asked to deliver a formal lecture, he wrote, 'What I have tried to do is imagine that I am writing this book for a Christian friend of ordinary education and outlook who has suddenly fallen seriously ill, perhaps incurably ill, or whose wife or child has done so.' The ten short chapters tackle questions which, Weatherhead says, were in his experience the questions people asked when suffering of body or mind, descended on them. He disclaims having 'any glib or easy answers', but set out to give a Christian response to such questions as 'Does God want me to be ill?' 'Why should this happen to me?' 'Where does God's goodness and omnipotence come in?' 'What sense is there in all this suffering?' The book repeats much of what he had written before about the nature of suffering and the will of God, seeking to give answers that help, but aware that:

> Trying to answer mental problems does little to make pain easier to bear. If all were explained, suffering remains to be faced and borne, and intellectual answers do not supply courage and faith. These are of far greater value than understanding. [p.6f.]

Preaching on Sunday morning, 1 July, 1962, Leonard Griffith was suddenly taken ill. He collapsed and was treated in the vestry by Lord Stamp, who arranged for him to have a complete medical examination. This revealed low blood pressure but nothing organically wrong. This was the second such incident. The first had been during a Thursday service some weeks earlier, but he had managed then to finish preaching. Griffith realised that he was suffering from the considerable emotional strain of the ministry of the City Temple. He dates his illness himself from his return from holiday in time to share the service with Weatherhead at the end of August, 1961. Weatherhead preached to a congregation that overflowed into the hall below the church. The following Sunday 'the congregation fell as predicted, by seventy percent.' Griffith had assumed that his own congregations would begin to grow steadily, but instead they settled to an average of 300 on Sunday mornings with twice that number in the evenings. 'Compared with my first year, the situation resembled a deflated balloon. Obviously the honeymoon was over.' He began to realise then how much the financial solvency of the church depended on him. The members contributed about twenty-five percent of the total budget, and he was required to make regular appeals on the annual Gift Day, and on Missionary Sunday, Home Churches Sunday, and several other occasions for special purposes. The bulk of the church's income came from the weekly offertory, so that it was dependent on large congregations. 'In that respect the Sunday services, and especially the preacher's performance, resembled a West-End show. If the audiences held up, the show stayed open; if they fell down, the show might have to close.'

Another book by Weatherhead, *Wounded Spirits,* was published by Hodder and Stoughton in September 1962. This he explained, was in some sense a footnote to *Psychology, Religion and Healing.* It contained accounts of a dozen unusual cases with which he had been connected. Some of these involved the use of odic force, hypnotism, and healings which had followed confession, laying on of hands and intercessory prayer. Among the stranger cases were some which appeared to involve 'demon possession' and multiple personality. The several different non-medical ways in which healing took place in these cases he argues were evidence that

> around us are vast areas all but unknown. In and through them immense
> energies seem to operate . . . we need to go farther, to understand them, to
> find out the laws which lie behind them, to be able to release them. [p.10]

After preaching at the lunchtime service on 11 October he lectured that evening to the Literary Society on 'Telepathy.' The hall was packed and the lecture was relayed to the conference room for the overflow audience. He defined telepathy as 'the communication of ideas from one mind to another independently of the senses.' He gave instances from his own experience and the work of others in the field such as J.B. Rhine. Weatherhead argued that 'separation of the body does not mean separation of mind, and that at a deep level all minds are connected.' He claimed that a hypnotised patient could sometimes, by means of telepathy, say what was going on in his own home several miles away and even what someone was writing in a letter. Weatherhead thought that telepathy could explain some 'alleged spiritualistic phenomena' and that it played an important part in the effectiveness of intercessory prayer:

> a thousand people praying . . . for a sick person could, because of the
> interpenetration of their minds with his, so alter the patient's mental attitude
> to his illness and change it from despair to hope, as to help importantly in
> his recovery.

In March, 1963, *The Observer* gave considerable prominence to an article by the Bishop of Woolwich, John Robinson, based on his book, *Honest to God.* The publicity given to the book by the article, and the extraordinary controversy it aroused, resulted in the book selling 'more quickly than any new book of serious theology in the history of the world.' Robinson disseminated in an easy, read-able and brief form the radical theological ideas of Tillich, Bultmann and Bonhoeffer. He wanted Christianity to be presented in a new way which would dispense with much of the traditional language and ways of referring to God, to 'de-mythologise' religion to make it more accessible and acceptable to modern minds. Although the book contained little that was new or disturbing to those in the academic circles from which Robinson had come, it was startling and sensational to the theologically uninformed members of the public and the national press. Robinson's readiness to appear as a defence witness in the *Lady Chatterley* trial had previously brought him to the attention of the press and already gained him a reputation as a notoriously unconventional bishop.

The book generated a huge controversy, becoming the subject of radio and television programmes, innumerable sermons and provoking heated debate in churches and newspaper correspondence columns. In a television interview, the Archbishop of Canterbury, Michael Ramsay, declared that the book caricatured the ordinary Christian's view of God, and accused Robinson of 'denying almost every Christian doctrine of the Church in which he holds office.' Leonard Griffith, in a sermon on April 7, described the book as 'a brilliant piece of work', and praised Robinson for his courage in expressing his own doubts and convictions so frankly and fearlessly. Griffith however, felt that the book would 'diminish rather than enlarge the Gospel.' He pointed out that there were other 'theological giants' such as Karl Barth, Reinhold Niebuhr and Emil Brunner, who held 'very firmly to the traditional image of a God separate and distinct from the world which he has made.'

Weatherhead responded warmly to *Honest to God*, finding a kindred spirit in Woolwich's attempt to dispose of unhelpful religious language and concepts in order to reach non-church goers. He was quick to leap to the defence of the Bishop against his critics – as he had previously defended Billy Graham. He particularly protested at the charge of atheism which had been levelled at the Bishop in *The Church Times*. In a letter to that paper (2 April 1963) Weatherhead wrote,

> For myself, I should wish to state my position in different language. . . . No-one can doubt that a sincere Christian is writing. In my opinion no-one in our time has done so much to free essential Christianity from the excess luggage which it has accumulated. . . . I believe that in the dark night which the organised church may be entering, the Bishop's point of view, which he has put forward, with wide knowledge and understanding, and with unusual reverence and humility, may well prove a lamp unto our feet and a light unto our path.

Weatherhead returned to his old pulpit that summer for what was becoming an annual tradition, to preach at each service on July 21 and July 28 and again on August 25. On July 21 he also spoke after the evening service to the young people's group about sexual morality among young people. In spite of his retirement and absence from the church, he had not lost any of his astonishing drawing power. The *British Weekly* (13 August 1963) printed an article by David Storey headed 'Queues at the Church Door', referring to the crowds which had turned up at the City Temple during the last two Sundays in July to hear Weatherhead:

> To anyone who has not seen this phenomenon previously, a queue for church must seem like a fantasy, and yet this amazing, albeit supremely uplifting sight was there for all to see. . . . Passers-by registered blank amazement and, obviously, were finding it difficult to equate the waiting lines of churchgoers with all the stories of 'empty pews' which they had heard.

Storey attempts to explain Weatherhead's extraordinary appeal.

> How is it that a preacher who retired from the pulpit nearly three years ago can bring people to queue for church? There is nothing spectacular: no "added attractions". . . . What then is his secret? Part of it, undoubtedly, is that he has the knack of showing how, in reality, religion is not simply "part" of life, but life itself. . . . His preaching is intellectually honest to the point of ruthlessness. . . . There was no hell-fire preaching, no attempt at sweeping people into an enquiry room on a surge of emotionalism. These were sermons

that brought one quite unmistakeably into touch with the infinite. We were offered the God whose love for His children is boundless in both its compass and duration. To hear such preaching as this people will come to church. . . . Many hundreds of young people are obviously happy to be there. Is there a moral here somewhere?

On 15 October, the day after his seventieth birthday, Weatherhead lectured to the Literary Society on 'The Christian Relevance of Psychic Research', which he defined as 'the study of the supernormal faculties of human personality.' He knew that the subject was under suspicion, but in spite of cranks and frauds, more and more evidence was emerging which could not be dismissed as nonsense. No subject, which was not itself inherently religious, was as relevant to religion as psychic research. He believed that psychic research, using the strict methods of scientific investigation, could enrich Christian faith. Materialism was discredited, the study of apparitions made it easier to believe in Christ's appearances after the Resurrection, and the study of telepathy made it easier to believe in intercessory prayer. The evidence for life after death made survival a more likely explanation of some phenomena than alternative theories. He quoted Professor Alister Hardy of Oxford University as saying,

If only one per cent of the money spent upon the physical and biological sciences could be spent upon investigations of religious experience and psychical research, it might not be long before a new age of faith dawned upon the world.

1. Leonard Griffith: *From Sunday to Sunday: Fifty Years in the Pulpit* (Irwin 1987) p.122.
2. W.E. Sangster, who had the same daunting task of following Weatherhead at Leeds, told his new congregation, 'Never hesitate to praise your former minister to me. Never water your words down, because when you praise Mr. Weatherhead, you will be praising him to a friend.' 7 September 1936.
3. The title of his first sermon was 'What Will This Babbler Say?'
4. Leonard Griffith: *From Sunday to Sunday: Fifty Years in the Pulpit* (Irwin 1987), p.123f.

25. The Christian Agnostic

'Why is so much space being given to yet another extensive publicising of the heretical views of the Rev. Dr. Leslie Weatherhead?'

Having retired, Weatherhead looked forward to being free to travel, to spend a longer time in America with his family and friends there, and to return to Australia, where he and Raynor Johnson planned to write a book together, expressing their dissatisfaction with conventional religion and presenting what they regarded as a more acceptable form of religion for the 'modern man.' They had first considered doing this during Weatherhead's stay with Johnson in Melbourne in 1951. In the years that followed they continued to share their ideas through correspondence. Although an academic scientist by profession, Johnson was becoming increasingly interested in spiritualism and Eastern mysticism, and between 1953 and 1959 produced three books of his own on these subjects. That Johnson, as a distinguished physicist, was able to believe in the existence of spiritual and psychical realities, so often regarded with scepticism by scientists who studied the physical world, was a significant factor in their relationship, and Weatherhead, who had a high regard for scientists, treated Johnson's views with considerable respect. He contributed a laudatory Foreword to Johnson's book, *The Imprisoned Splendour* (1953) which Johnson described as 'An approach to Reality, based upon the significance of data drawn from the fields of Natural Science, Psychical Research and Mystical Experience.'

Johnson urged Weatherhead to read the collected poems of the mystic F.W.H. Myers and the books of the spiritualist Geraldine Cummins, in particular her writing about the concept of 'Group-Souls.' Cummins, whom Johnson had met in 1953, practised 'automatic writing' through which she received messages from the dead. She communicated to Johnson a message from a mystic friend, Ambrose Pratt, who had been dead for several years. This told Johnson that he and Weatherhead belonged to a 'Group-soul' together with 'F.W.H. Myers, Henry Sidgwick, Verrall, Butcher, Gurney etc. those Cambridge scholars who founded the Society for Psychical Research.' Pratt also told Johnson to write another book on the subject of 'Imaginism' based on the works of E. Douglas Fawcett. This book, *Nurslings of Immortality,* was published in 1957. Again Weatherhead contributed a Foreword. Describing it as 'a wonderful book', he said he was not competent to comment on the philosophy of 'Imaginism' but on the sections concerning religion his own beliefs were very much in harmony with the author. Expressing the thinking behind his own subsequent book, *The Christian Agnostic,* he said that Christians should always be open to receive new truths, they must free themselves from the 'superstitions of the fundamentalists' and from the imprisonment of creeds which, 'devised fourteen hundred years ago', could not contain 'the entire nature of the Eternal and Infinite God.' The archaic language of the Church was putting off many thoughtful people who were 'hungry for what religion can offer.'

Johnson passed on to Weatherhead the scripts of the messages from Ambrose Pratt which he had received through Geraldine Cummins. He was fascinated by them, but kept his feet on the ground. He wrote to Johnson (29 August 1956):

I sat down and read the whole thing at a sitting and must tell you that in this field it is the most amazing and convincing document I have seen. There are difficulties, of course, which I cannot possibly understand. For example, if Ambrose could show Miss Cummins a picture of the word 'electron', and then explain that it means 'amber', and then show her a rose, why couldn't he show her the word 'Ambrose'? And if he made a little fish, a sprat, and apparently wrote the word since he talks of crossing out the sign of 'S', why couldn't he write the word 'Pratt' straight away?

Weatherhead was by this time in correspondence with Cummins himself. Some years before, she had been consulted by Frederic Lawrence, the original architect chosen for the new City Temple. In one of her letters to Weatherhead Cummins wrote, 'I know of no-one whose opinion I value more than yours.' He shared this with Johnson saying that he felt flattered, but he could not understand why she should value his opinion. He wanted to know where he fitted into 'this whole set-up .... I cannot understand very much, but if I can understand, I think I have the gift of making other simple people do so also.'

During the following months Johnson sent Weatherhead several suggested titles and outlines for their joint book, sharing with him the development of his own thinking, which was moving steadily away from conventional Christianity. Soon after Weatherhead had retired, Johnson wrote to him saying that while his admiration for Jesus remained as great as ever, he now found Christian doctrine unsatisfying, and even a perversion of what Jesus had intended to convey. At the same time, Weatherhead was having to put off his plan to go to Australia due to his own uncertain health and the reluctance of his wife to be parted from him for the necessary length of time.

Their views were now diverging so markedly that the possibility of them producing a joint work was becoming increasingly remote. Johnson went ahead with a book on his own, *A Religious Outlook for Modern Man* (1963). Weatherhead again provided a Foreword. In this, he explained the circumstances in which the book came to be written. He said that he was 'delighted to find how closely' he agreed with Johnson, though 'I did not feel too happy after reading his chapter on "How am I to regard Jesus Christ?"' He also thought more highly of public prayer and of the Church than Johnson did.

In 1964, Johnson produced *The Light and the Gate.* This was a study of four friends whom he said had most influenced him, and he presented them as 'Lights which may show the traveller through life that Gate which leads to the Path.' The four were the Irish mystic, 'A.E.' George Russell; Ambrose Pratt; an American, Robert Clifton, who had become a Buddhist monk known as Sumangalo; and Weatherhead himself, who was the only one then still living. Johnson tells of his friendship with Weatherhead since they first met in London in 1928, describing his infectious sense of fun and charm of personality, his essential humility, and his dislike of pomposity and self-importance. He refers to his 'great gift of a very flexible and sympathetic speaking voice' and his use of 'simple and appropriate language.' He notes also Weatherhead's 'extreme sensitivity and marked self-criticism.' [p.243f]

Weatherhead's own book, *The Christian Agnostic,* came out in September 1965. The title had been in his mind for some considerable time. In his Preface he explains that he gained the phrase 'Christian Agnostic' from a private conversation with the famous judge, Lord Birkett, just before he died in 1962. The idea, and the attitude to religion of respectful doubt it represented, was very much in the air. Joseph McCulloch, the vicar of St.Mary-le-Bow, Cheapside, had given this designation to a group which included Tony Benn, John Freeman, Malcolm Muggeridge and Sir Richard Acland, and was preparing to produce his own book of essays with this title. Weatherhead, who had headed one of his weekly sermonettes for the *Sunday Times* 'The Creed of a Christian Agnostic', and had been interviewed under a similar heading by David Frost for the *Daily Mail,* corresponded with McCulloch, who immediately agreed to Weatherhead using the title for his book, saying that his own book would not be ready for some time, and in any case there was no copyright on the title.

The publication of *Honest to God* and the controversy it aroused not only initiated a public debate on religious truth but also removed the inhibition that many people in public life felt towards making known their true beliefs, or lack of them. In April 1964, *The Sunday Times* (29 April 1964) printed an article headed, 'Atticus Among the Godless', which stated –

it is now respectable not to believe in God . . . . In the past five years, public opinion in this country has at last grown up enough to acknowledge that a man in public life can be a Humanist, Agnostic, or even an Atheist, and need not hypocritically conceal his views.

A year later (21 March 1965), the paper carried a leader commenting that there had been –

a revival of interest in religious questions within the past five years, with religious books becoming the badge of an enterprising publishing house . . . . . Religion can now stir the feelings of the readers of the *New Statesman* in a way only politics used to do. In *The Sunday Times* we have had our largest quantities of correspondence over religious and moral questions, and it is obvious that these questions are alive in people's minds, more alive now than questions of party politics or theory.

The paper attributed this revival of interest in particular to the pontificate of Pope John and to the Bishop of Woolwich. But Weatherhead's weekly articles had also made their own contribution to the number of letters on religious subjects *The Sunday Times* was receiving. He had a remarkable gift for sensing and responding to the climate of the time, and with *The Christian Agnostic* he succeeded once again in reaching a wide audience who were ready and interested to read what he had to say.

The City Temple's lunchtime service on Thursday, September 16, the fiftieth anniversary of Weatherhead's ordination, was given over to a 'theological teach-in' arranged by Hodder and Stoughton to publicise *The Christian Agnostic.* A panel of speakers were invited to lead the discussion and to represent different theological points of view. These were John Wren-Lewis, a research scientist, writer and Anglican lay theologian (replacing the Bishop of Woolwich who was ill), the Bishop of Llandaff, Dr. Glyn Simon; Father Thomas Corbishley, Superior of the Jesuit House, Farm Street; Weatherhead himself, with Leonard Griffith in the chair.

Well over a thousand people attended the debate which continued for two hours. Weatherhead, who spoke first, explained that his reason for writing the book was to appeal to people who were attracted to Christ but put off by much of the Church's teaching. The Bishop of Llandaff said that people ignored the Church, not because of its teaching but because of the way it was run, and its failure to speak out on such political issues as nuclear war and racialism. He agreed with Weatherhead that people found the recital of creeds confusing, but they were meant for instruction, and he would not himself remain an official teacher in the Church unless he accepted the creeds. Father Corbishley agreed that the Church was finding it difficult to win over thinking people. He argued that God was a God of reason as well as of love. The Church, as an organisation, needed to have a frame of reference, and this was the creeds. He agreed with Weatherhead that the Church had gathered a great deal of unnecessary clutter around the creeds, much of which Weatherhead was right to reject. He pleaded however for 'the word of the expert' to be accepted in matters of belief as it was in matters of science. John Wren-Lewis described himself as a typical representative of the group for which Dr. Weatherhead had written his book. He saw modern science and technology as a product of the Christian spirit. Questions and comments from the audience provoked a debate about the Virgin Birth, which Weatherhead said did not concern him emotionally, and was a matter for historic judgment alone. Corbishley felt very involved emotionally with the doctrine since it was a 'question of humanity's relationship to God.' Wren-Lewis declared his belief in a literal resurrection, which he said showed that Christ's life had some effect on material circumstance. 'If I didn't believe in the resurrection literally, I wouldn't be interested in Christianity.'

The teach-in was recorded by the B.B.C., which broadcast extracts from it and from the book on its daily 'Ten to Eight' programme during the week of 18 to 21 October. It also received wide coverage and comment in the national as well as the religious press, which ensured that, as Hodder's had hoped, it became an instant best-seller, selling out its initial printing of 6,000 copies within the first three weeks.

In the book, Weatherhead describes himself as 'an angry old man, and I feel I must get the fire out of my bones . . . before I die.' All his life he had been outspokenly critical of dull and lifeless worship, unintelligible language and outdated creeds which he believed kept many intelligent people away from accepting the Christian faith. Having, in his retirement, spent more time in the pew than in the pulpit, he had become even more impatient with boring services and tedious and irrelevant sermons:

> Not for much longer will the world put up with the lies, the superstitions and the distortions with which the joyous and essentially simple message of Christ has been overlaid . . . the message of Galilee is overlaid with creeds and ceremonies and doctrines, and what with denominational squabbles, mutual disapprovals and intolerance, one can hardly catch the message of the Son of Man or be lifted up and strengthened by its beauty and power. Every declaration of that message should bring the listener into communion with the living Christ and into touch with the unseen world of the spirit. [p.3.]

Although the book was attacked by his critics, and interpreted even by some of his friends as representing disillusionment and loss of faith, it is in fact a passionate defence of what Weatherhead calls 'our most holy religion.' In it he attempts to separate what he regards as the essentials of the Christian faith from the doctrines and accretions, customs and traditions which he considers inessentials, and which it was therefore possible to either dismiss or to take an agnostic attitude towards:

> I am writing for the "Christian Agnostic", by which I mean a person who is immensely attracted by Christ and who seeks to show His spirit, to meet the challenges, hardships and sorrows of life in the light of that spirit, but who, though he is sure of many Christian truths, feels that he cannot honestly and conscientiously "sign on the dotted line" that he believes certain theological ideas about which some branches of the church dogmatise; churches from which he feels excluded because he cannot "believe". His intellectual integrity makes him say about many things, "It may be so, I do not know." [p.x.]

Weatherhead quotes with approval from *Christianity and History* (1949) by his fellow Methodist, Herbert Butterfield, 'We can do worse than remember a principle which both gives us a firm Rock and leaves us the maximum elasticity for our minds: the principle: "Hold to Christ, and for the rest be totally uncommitted".' It was Weatherhead's 'holding to Christ', his refusal to make any compromise concerning his personal loyalty and faith in Jesus, that prevented him following Raynor Johnson any further along the road towards an individualistic and quietistic Buddhism. But this apart, he was equally committed to allowing the exploration of truth to lead him wherever it would, and a major purpose of his book is to defend and assert the right of every person to do so for themselves, in the belief that since all truth is of God, who is himself the source of all truth, then the most truly religious and Christian attitude is to welcome truth, from wherever it comes, and however revolutionary it may be, since insofar as it is true, it can only be a step closer towards the knowledge of God himself.

In defence of this belief, *The Christian Agnostic* discusses the most fundamental Christian beliefs and doctrines: the nature of God, of 'Christ and His Achievement,' the Holy Spirit, the Church, the inspiration of the Bible, providence, prayer, faith, evil and sin, death and survival, heaven and hell. Weatherhead does not set out to present and defend Christian orthodoxy, but presents his own very personal speculations, questions, doubts and conclusions, not in order to persuade his readers to accept everything he believes, but to persuade them not to let their doubts and difficulties prevent them from discovering a real faith in Jesus Christ:

> This book would say to the modern layman, "Don't exclude yourself from the fellowship of Christ's followers because of mental difficulties. If you love Christ and are seeking to follow Him, take an attitude of Christian agnosticism to intellectual problems at least for the present. Read this book to see if the essentials of the Christian religion are clarified for you and only accept those things which gradually seem to you to be true. Leave the rest in a mental box labelled, "awaiting further light". In the meantime, join in with us in trying to show and to spread Christ's spirit, for this, we feel, is the most important truth in the world. [p.xlv.]

In spite, therefore, of all its apparent challenges to Christian orthodoxy, *The*

Christian Agnostic is at heart as keenly evangelical as any of Weatherhead's previous books, and its aim is no different – though its approach and style are very different – from that of a first book of City Temple sermons by Leonard Griffith, published a year or two earlier, called *Barriers to Christian Belief* (1961), in which Griffith sets out to 'give answers to the basic problems that hinder the acceptance of the Gospel of Christ.'

Even so, some the ideas in *The Christian Agnostic* caused considerable surprise and offence to many religious people, and more than anything else Weatherhead had written, caused him to be branded 'heretic' by more conservative and fundamentalist Christians. Although Weatherhead in this book was exceptionally careful to give copious references and quotations from a host of sources to support each of his propositions, he succeeded in arousing a great deal of abuse for what he had to say about many cherished beliefs. For example, he not only dismisses the doctrine of the Virgin Birth as 'though of great interest, . . . of no *importance* at all', but in discussing how it came about, gives as 'One explanation' a suggestion that Mary's pregnancy was the result of a 'sacred marriage' to a temple priest, possibly Zacharias. Weatherhead carefully examines this theory, and indicates how the details in the biblical account fit in with it as a possibility. He does not commit himself to saying that this is what he believes took place, but the fact that he gave space at all to considering such a theory caused outrage in some quarters. He was amused at finding himself anathematised by the fierce Ian Paisley in *The Revivalist* (November 1965), together with the theologian, Nels Ferre, for holding 'certain unitarian beliefs' and for saying that 'Jesus was the offspring of a Temple prostitute and Zacharias the Priest.'

Much of what he says in this book about miracles, the divinity of Christ, the Atonement, the Trinity, the Bible and other traditional beliefs he had written before in earlier works, so that the book is a summing up of the theological ideas he had developed throughout the length of his ministry. But the tone of *The Christian Agnostic* is more provocatively argumentative, less concerned about upsetting the feelings and sensitivities of those whose cherished beliefs he was challenging.

The book ends with a summary, 'Credo and Commitment'. In this he sets out his personal beliefs, which have been stated throughout the book, gathering them together in order 'to end the book on a positive note'. He believes in God, who is

loving, suprapersonal, everywhere available . . . but concerning His activities in His vast, mind-staggering universe I have no means of knowing more than a minute fraction, and whether He can be described as three in one or three million in one, who can say . . . and what does it matter?

He believes in 'the divinity of Christ, though I do not know what divinity means', and 'No one, short of information not available, can say that Christ is "the *only* begotten Son of God". One can only say "only" if one can exclude all other possibilities.' He remains agnostic about the Holy Spirit. 'Few Christians, whom I know, think of the Holy Spirit as a separate Person . . . for myself I see no need of the concept of the Holy Spirit as a third person in a Trinity.' He says that he 'believes intensely in *the* Church. . . . Its missionary activity is the chapter in its history which enheartens me the most . . . . I regard the Church on earth as a human copy of a divine original, a fellowship stretching across the world' which includes all Christians, whatever their theological beliefs and denominational allegiance 'who love and serve Christ and adore and worship and move forward to the unimaginable unity with God which is His will.' The Bible he regards as 'a marvellous library of writings which depict man's developing and increasingly successful search for God.' The Bible writers were 'often inspired' but much of the Bible is not, and could be omitted without loss. [p.246f.]

He accuses St. Paul of having a guilt complex that caused him to distort the teaching of Jesus, and to put an emphasis on sin which did not derive from Jesus himself. He believes in 'God's providence and care' and that therefore all the pain and suffering of the world does have meaning and is within the 'mighty purposes' of an all-wise and all-loving God. He believes in prayer, 'that it is possible to have communion with God and that He can sometimes use our prayers to help others', and 'in the value of faith in the sense of trustful commitment to God whatever happens.'

Acknowledging that 'sin is a dark fact of human life which cannot be dismissed by euphemistic and psychological labels' he yet 'believes intensely in forgiveness, a restoration of relationship which has immense therapeutic power, both . . . between man and God, or man and man.' He believes 'that every soul survives death . . . though survival does not of necessity involve living for ever.' 'Eternal life' refers to the 'quality, not the quantity of life', and 'both heaven and hell describe a temporary existence.' Some souls may 're-enter an incarnate life', and 'For all we know, life on other planets in other forms than "flesh" may be open to the spirit after death, and this may account for the very few people one knows who have any glimmering of having lived before.' But the soul after death 'goes on spiritually where it left off', maybe as part of a group soul. 'We shall rejoice in our fellowship with others, especially those we love and those with whom we shall co-operate, and I hazard a guess that though we keep our identity we may lose our separateness.' He believes that 'the redemption of the world by our Lord Jesus Christ' means that 'the whole human race' will be 'won back into harmony with God's will' and therefore though 'Much may be suffered . . . bliss at last seems to me certain for all.' In his final paragraphs Weatherhead re-affirms his faith and allegiance to Jesus Christ:

> To that Person, so august, so high above me and yet so human, so lovable, so knowable, so utterly forgiving, understanding and ready to accept me, I desire to commit myself, and, affectionately and humbly, I invite the reader to do the same. [p.257.]

In spite of his unorthodox views, his stated disillusionment, disappointment and agnosticism, this is the same Weatherhead who wrote *The Transforming Friendship* forty years before, with the same evangelical urge to persuade others to share that faith, the same belief in the possibility of every person to enter into a loving relationship with Christ, and to find themselves and their lives transformed by his presence and his power.

The book was serialised before publication in the *Methodist Recorder* and it was then reviewed for the *Recorder* (16 September 1965) by Leonard Griffith, who predicted at least 'one thing about this book – it will be read. It is too important to be ignored, and too fascinating to lay down once you have picked it up.' Griffith is generous in his appreciation of the book, acknowledging that there was much that he could not endorse, but saying,

> I do not have to agree with a book in order to appreciate its positive value. *The Christian Agnostic* has greatly enriched my thought and challenged me, as it will challenge the most orthodox reader to re-sharpen his thinking and to re-define his own theological position.

No other book of Weatherhead's so clearly revealed the differences between his critics and his supporters. In the *Recorder* correspondence columns he was accused of being 'a pre-Barthian liberal whose book makes no distinctive contribution to the contemporary theological debate', of 'not being in line with Methodist doctrine', of being 'indistinguishable' from Unitarianism, of 'studied vagueness in expression.' The Rev. Frank Ockenden (9 September 1965) demanded to know

> Why is so much space being given to yet another extensive publicising of the heretical views of the Rev. Dr. Leslie Weatherhead? As one of the major contributors to the hazy and nebulous theological outlook of the present time, he has long forfeited the right to be regarded as a teacher of the things that become 'sound doctrine.'

An Anglican, Canon N.S. Power (30 September 1965), leapt to Weatherhead's defence, saying that reading the extracts in the *Recorder* had for him been

> a moving and rewarding experience. It is however, disturbing to find so many critics who seem unaware of Dr. Weatherhead's greatness. He has over the years, helped hundreds of thousands of people to find a faith; he has helped thousands of sufferers with personal difficulties and problems. He has helped many to find the Christian way who would be repelled by a more dogmatic approach . . . . Some of the ideas which seem to have given offence have, after all, been advanced (though seldom in such a readable way) by many of the greatest Christian thinkers for the past fifty years. It is a pity that those who are offended by such thinking cannot express themselves with some deference to a man who has done as much as any man living in our time to commend a living Christian faith to thoughtful people.

The Epworth Press made *The Christian Agnostic* its book of the month for its *September News Notes.* In this it was reviewed by the Editor, Gordon Wakefield, who sent a draft of his notice to Weatherhead before publication 'because I have had to be rather severe . . . there are certain parts of your argument with which I am not at all happy. I only hope that I have not been too severe to one who through the years has shown me nothing but kindness.' Wakefield's review was a considerable shock to Weatherhead, not lessened by a letter from the Managing Editor of Epworth, Frank Cumbers, who explained that, he had persuaded Wakefield to moderate and omit some of his harsher comments before publication.

Wakefield began by commenting that 'this volume presumably offers us what the author regards as the quintessence of his teaching and his final reflections on life.' Weatherhead, he said, belonged to 'the generation when historical and dogmatic theology were in abeyance.' His judgments were subjective: He was 'inclined to want the strawberries and cream from all religions'; the book was mistitled, since he was

> agnostic only about the claims of orthodox Christianity . . . . He is willing to

give very free rein to eclectic attempts to penetrate to regions where the Church has deemed it wise to acknowledge ignorance. The book could well be called *The Christian Gnostic* – and I fear that the author's Christology is precisely such.

His creed is 'syncretistic, and probably a collection of items incompatible in logic'. Weatherhead's theology 'is not strong enough to stand the strain of his good intentions.' Wakefield concluded that

> *The Christian Agnostic* may not be taken very seriously by the theologians. It is not likely to be another *Honest to God* – it derives from pre-Barthian liberalism. But some of our more thoughtful people will . . . find that it tries to answer many of the questions which baffle them, and which do not seem to interest the "new theologians". In fact it is a "genuine lay theology", if by "layman" we mean the man at present in the pew, and not the "involved" university-trained Christian by whom the Bishop of Woolwich sets such store.

Woolwich himself wrote to Weatherhead, (14 September 1965) saying how 'desperately disappointed' he was to have to drop out of the City Temple Teach-in.

> I have read your book with much interest and appreciation. Naturally, I fully sympathise with your purpose and approach. I think the differences in our position derive from the fact that the shoe pinches at rather different places. The kind of mill that I have been through is different from yours, but I recognise in many of the letters I receive just the sort of people to whom I am sure your book will speak . . . one thing that struck me about your book was that it seemed to me that you took a number of texts more literalistically, and in a way more conservatively, than I would . . . . I find myself much nearer to the neo-orthodox theologians and biblical theology than to the older liberal modernism. But this I suspect simply reflects the fact that all the old lines are now criss-crossed.

Woolwich understood that Weatherhead was setting out to deal with the questions that throughout the years his many correspondents had raised with him in their letters, rather than the topics which were interesting the new theologians. Weatherhead was a preacher, not an academic. His experience, apart from his war-curtailed period at Richmond, was wholly in the pastoral ministry. His chief aim was to communicate the religious truths that he deemed of practical help to lay people and that related to their daily lives. But it was the religious professionals, rather than the lay people for whom he was writing, who in the main reviewed the book, and this is reflected in their criticisms. One of the most savage came from Canon Gordon Phillips, Chaplain to London University, who was asked by Hodders to review the book for the November edition of their own publication, *Focus*. Phillips's remarks were so uncomplimentary that Hodders refused to publish them, though they sent Weatherhead a copy. Phillips wrote that Weatherhead's 'notions of orthodox, mainstream Christian ideas are so bizarre as to suggest that his theological reading lacks both breadth and depth.' He criticised him for making

> no reference to anything written in France or Germany (except, inevitably, Dr. Schweitzer) in the last century or in this. Can one seriously confront an educated "Christian agnostic" of today and not refer to de Lubac, Teilhard de Chardin, Hans Urs von Balthazar, Karl Rahner, Hans Kung and the rest?

The book will be valuable mostly to those aged 60 and over, whose undergraduate days were disturbed by Julian Huxley's *Religion Without Revelation* and have not looked at many religious books since then.

Eric Routley, who reviewed the book for the *British Weekly* (16 September 1965) began by paying tribute to Weatherhead's ministry.

There must be few Christians among those who can read English who do not owe Dr. Weatherhead a debt of some kind; many owe him an immeasurable debt. Who has not been at some time heartened by some word of his during his fifty year's ministry?

But Routley greatly disliked the book.

I do not believe that this is a good piece of apologetic. It may be an impressive piece of personal testimony, but it is not going to help people to believe . . . . That which he seeks to do is so profoundly right . . . and yet he has not found the secret of proclaiming the Faith without disparaging other people's versions of it.

He accused Weatherhead of lacking sympathy for 'those whose temperaments, education or experience would make them dissent from his liberal and humane vision.'

K.C. Dykes, in the *Baptist Times* (7 October 1965) described the book as 'the mature reflections of an outstanding preacher on what kind of Christian faith can reasonably be held today'. He thought that 'Many readers will be helped: some will be infuriated.' Though he felt 'bound to dissent from many of his conclusions' he was

full of admiration for Dr. Weatherhead's courage . . . . He is putting the deep human questions. Into his answers there comes a fine blend of common sense and penetrating wisdom. In a word, he is preaching to our condition.

Dykes wished that Weatherhead had not been so hard on St. Paul, and considered that the basic weakness of the book was 'the author's failure to realise with Dale that Jesus came not so much to preach the Gospel as that there might be a Gospel to preach. Too readily he makes the exclusive court of appeal what Jesus *taught*. His thinking about the Person of Christ . . . surely leaves us with Adoptionism.

John Wilkinson, in the *London Quarterly and Holborn Review* (September 1965) described the book as Weatherhead's *'confessio fidei* . . . . It is the fearless and candid writing of a man of humble mind in search for Christian truth.' He thought that the more theological chapters of the book were the ones most open to criticism, since Weatherhead presented a 'binitarian' rather than a Trinitarian view of God, and 'his Christology . . . verges upon a vague gnosticism which obscures the real quality of his own experience of the divine grandeur which is Jesus.' While rejecting the 'sacred marriage' explanation of the Virgin Birth, Wilkinson agreed that it was not an essential part of the Christian faith, and praised the work as a 'courageous book . . . the precipitate of the thought of one who is essentially close to Christ as the Lord of all good life.'

The Friend (17 September 1965) which devoted a long editorial to the book, considered that it would not 'prove very acceptable or convincing reading to the agnostic in the true sense – the man who has already decided that Christianity has probably nothing to contribute to him in his search', but that the real aim of the book was to 'stab the people already in the pew into a healthy aliveness that includes vigorous questing and questioning.' It found Weatherhead's style 'garrulous' 'jesting' and 'anecdotal', and considered the book

> far too long, and actually rather frivolous . . . on a subject of the gravest importance . . . . By comparison, *Honest to God* is severe, strenuous, laconic; and so should books on this subject be. *The Christian Agnostic* comes dangerously near to playing with the matter.

The reviewer accused Weatherhead of 'urging Christians to travel light' by getting rid of 'much of the lumber of the Church', and then – through his speculations about the birth of Jesus, the possibility of Christ appearing on other planets, and repeated re-incarnations – of greatly adding to

> Christian impedimenta instead of subtracting from them . . . the impression is left . . . that one has been (not unwillingly) persuaded to keep the wariest eye open to detect absurd accretions upon the Gospel of Jesus, only to find oneself saddled at the end with more accretions than ever one started with.

The writer however, apologised 'for the severity of this judgment' and said that there were many passages 'which taken in isolation, could appeal very feelingly and deeply to many Friends.'

A Baptist minister, Paul Cook, in *The Banner of Truth* (January/February 1966) found Weatherhead highly subjective and blasphemous, and his sympathies 'not as much with the Church as with the world.' Cook accused him of 'profane sophistry and misrepresentation' declared 'His pious profanity knows no bounds', and pronounced that 'From whatever point of view it is considered the book is a failure.' Weatherhead, he said, was guilty of 'mock humility' and he rejected his presentation of Jesus as being not the Jesus of the Bible, but merely a projection of himself. 'He is none other than what Dr. Weatherhead would like to be in his better moments.' *The English Churchman* (8 October 1965) was equally 'appalled and disgusted', and, obviously unaware of how much support and apppreciation Weatherhead was already receiving from Anglicans, urged that 'proposals for union with the Methodists shall include safeguards to prevent a flood of unorthodoxy sweeping in to the Church of England from Methodism.'

A scathing review by Richard Tatlock in *The Church Times* stung Weatherhead into writing to Tatlock, (21 September 1965) whom he knew personally, and had regarded as a friend. He wrote that while he had not expected him to agree with his views, 'the *bitterness* in your language astounded me.' He signed his letter, 'Affectionately, as in the old days.' Tatlock replied (30 September 1965)

> I felt it necessary to write as I did . . . . I should have been extremely dishonest if, for friendship's sake, I had written otherwise. The truth is that I believe that all this "candid scepticism" is doing the Christian faith a disservice . . . .
> Was it necessary to publish your doubts? You clearly think it was. I don't.

Tatlock's article brought Weatherhead several letters from Anglican correspondents deploring the tone of the review and saying how much Weatherhead's book had meant to them. One woman, having read the review, promptly went and bought the book. She wrote to him, 'It has given me a sense of liberation. . . . . Dr. Robinson's *Honest to God* did me good. Your book has made me happy.' Weatherhead received more personal letters about *The Christian Agnostic* than any other book he had written. Most of them were complimentary, finding the book challenging and stimulating, even where there was much that the writers could not agree with and wanted to argue with him about. Several of his ministerial friends and colleagues, and also those from other denominations, thanked him for putting into words much that they had felt themselves, particularly with regard to the sacraments and the theories of the atonement. Several churches, in America, Canada and Australia as well as in Britain, made the book the basis for a series of discussion groups.

The book was seen by many as a major contribution to the debate set off by *Honest to God* and appreciated as being more positive and less vague than Robinson's book. Joseph McCulloch wrote (12 September 1965) 'What an admirable book! I am about to tell the flock at Hampstead that it is far more important and far more intelligible to read this than *Honest to God.*' Another Anglican rector, D. Berners Wilson, wrote (11 October 1965) 'Your new book has moved me profoundly: and the whole church *ought* to be grateful for it. 'Honest to God' rang a bell in the minds of many bewildered by the churches' dogma, but they were left suspended, as it were, in space with their thoughts circling round and round; your 'The Christian Agnostic' will bring them safely to earth – perhaps even into the Kingdom!' Dr. Thomas Jessop, who had been Vice-President of the Methodist Conference during Weatherhead's Presidential year, declared, (11 September 1965)

> It's as bold as, but *far* better than, the Bishop of Woolwich's curiously confused writing. I'm very glad you've published it. My grumble at the theologians is that they haven't given us a *preachable theology* . . . they've lost contact with the ordinary mind . . . so do go on, in your inimitable way, distinguishing between conviction and theorising, life and the ivory towers, religion and ecclesiastical haberdashery.

J. R. Berry, the Master of Divinity at Manchester Grammar School wrote (25 September 1965) to thank Weatherhead, saying, 'I am profoundly grateful to you for a book which I can confidently place in the hands of my Sixth Form students who are, so very often, the very types for which you have so wisely and courageously written.' Other teachers and lecturers in religious studies wrote in similar vein.

There were some, even among his closest friends and admirers, who were distressed by it. One of these was the eminent Scottish preacher and New Testament scholar, Professor James Stewart, who had received an advance copy of the book, and for whose opinion Weatherhead had the highest respect. Stewart, who had a special admiration for St. Paul, was far from happy about the book. He wrote (17 September 1965), 'it has made me feel dreadfully sad . . . you are now bound to write another book with all the anger left out – and perhaps . . . a little more sympathetic appreciation of St. Paul, the most loyal and understanding interpreter Jesus ever had.'

Five days after the publication of Weatherhead's book, SCM brought out *A Religion for Agnostics*, by the former Principal of Mansfield College, Nathaniel Micklem. Micklem's book was much briefer than Weatherhead's but his purpose was the same. He too, was writing 'for people who, without being hostile to Jesus', were 'puzzled or offended by traditional Christianity' and believed that 'the traditional Christian doctrines must be radically revised.' Micklem also stated that 'About many things he remains an agnostic. About the essential things, his life had made him convincingly clear.'

Inevitably, coming out so close together, and with such similar titles, the books were compared. Under the heading, 'Agnostics Again', Father Thomas Corbishley reviewed it for the *Catholic Herald*. Corbishley thought Micklem's book would be at a disadvantage appearing so soon after Weatherhead's, but he regarded it as 'much better as a reasoned argument'. John Willoughby in the *Oxford Mail* (7 October 1965), noting that Weatherhead's book had 'received a rough and rather derisive handling from some critics on the strictly orthodox side', thought that Micklem's approach was 'more scholarly' than Weatherhead's, and that while Weatherhead had 'for many years been . . . something of a deviationist', Micklem's position 'as a theologian who demands respect is surely unassailable.'

Owen Chadwick, in *The Sunday Times* (26 September 1965) described Weatherhead's book as 'gentle, humane and friendly . . . . It is marked by sympathy with everything but orthodoxy and the Book of Common Prayer.' He referred to Weatherhead as 'a Christian agnostic in . . . the sense of all reverent men that the ultimate realities of the world are a mystery and that we live in shafts of light in the darkness.' Chadwick thought the book would have two critics, 'one will say that for an agnostic, or even for a Christian, he believes a great deal too much, especially about the evidence for survival after death; the other will say that, if you are going to have religion at all, it is better to have it tough – blood and nails and vinegar.' Like other critics, Chadwick thought Weatherhead too literalistic in his approach saying that 'To strip religion of old, literally obsolete formulas is not like stripping philosophy of what is disproved. It is more like ridding "Hamlet" of every line of familiar beauty, and leaving a play . . . which sane theatregoers will not pay to see.'

The *Times Literary Supplement* (9 December 1965) declared that *The Christian Agnostic* was not a good book; that the writing was 'distractingly author centred, and any preacher who thoroughly presented Weatherhead's 'somewhat tenuous' version of Christianity 'would undoubtedly lose most of his congregation.' Weatherhead felt it necessary to defend himself and correct 'one irritating inaccuracy'; the claim that he had suggested that Zacharias committed adultery with Mary in a "sacred marriage."' Weatherhead objected to the accusation that he had used the 'label' 'adultery' saying that modern standards of morality did not apply, and a sacred marriage then would have been regarded as 'the highest possible degree of spiritual dedication on the part of a young girl.' He said that he had merely put forward the idea as a possible explanation, and not as a theory of his own to which he was committed. 'I do not expect your prejudiced reviewer to praise my book, but, in a paper like the *Times Literary Supplement*, one does expect accuracy and fair play.' He also pointed out that under his ministry 'the City Temple was full for 24 years!'

A remarkable appreciation of the book came from a most unexpected quarter: an 'independent Christian newsletter', *Search* (October 1965) produced by Michael de la Bedoyere, a former editor of the *Catholic Herald*. Bedoyere wrote that Hodder and Stoughton had sent him a copy of *The Christian Agnostic*, and

> I picked it up without any great excitement and began a rather desultory reading. Very soon, however, my attention was caught and I read during every spare moment in a state I can only call 'thrill'. The book . . . is anything but orthodox and Catholic, but every page in it seemed to me to breathe the love of Christ, the vital importance of religion, a sense of

constructive freedom, and a genuine spiritual enthusiasm with which one rarely meets. . . . For general circulation Dr. Weatherhead's book would loudly call for the sternest blasts of the *Index Expurgatorious*! [Sic.] By Catholic standards, it is chockfull of the grossest heresies! Yet, to me at least, the love of our Lord and the dedication to truth and common sense, as Dr. Weatherhead sees it, make an overwhelming appeal particularly at the present time . . . . Let us put to one side what we really cannot, by our Catholic faith, accept, and concentrate on what it is that makes the Methodist Dr. Weatherhead so much better seeming a Christian than I and perhaps you are.

The American reviewers, though puzzled by the title, were on the whole friendly, if not entirely favourable. Alan G. Gray, in the *Michigan Christian Advocate* (December 1965) who referred to Weatherhead as 'my best beloved author whom I have leaned to these many years', felt the title did not fit the book, since 'he's the same old Weatherhead he has always been.' He considered the book 'well worth examination' and a serious work, but was unhappy about Weatherhead's views on the Virgin Birth and miracles: 'On these two issues alone the book leaves me sad' since 'he feels it so essential to explain everything with a neat formula. Must the awe, mystery and wonder of our faith be lost in this scientific probing and historical documentation.'

Religion and Life (Summer 1966) also thought the title misleading, since the contents of the book were typical Weatherhead, though it suggested that some would find him 'too mystical'. It did not think that the book provided 'the kind of Christian apologetic that will find a ready response on the American campus.' The Philadelphia *Friend's Journal* (15 February 1966) thought that the book was part of a 'recent trend in Protestant theology purging Christianity of the supernatural, the miraculous, and the dogmatic accretions of millennia.' It bracketed Weatherhead with 'Christian existentialists' and 'certain younger theologians' as 'the Protestant counterpart to the Catholic aggiornamento.' It considered that Weatherhead, 'like many theologians before him, has slowly moved towards the Quaker position' since his views on authority were very similar to the Quaker emphasis on the 'inner light.' It regarded the theory of reincarnation as 'the only weakness' in the book, and as 'at least as fantastic as some of the Christian dogma he questions.' Richard R. Baker,III, in *The Virginia Churchman* (March 1966), though he felt that Weatherhead was 'largely right in spirit, and in the concern that motivates the book,' would not recommend it. He criticised Weatherhead for not paying sufficient attention to the theologians, saying that there was 'a strong strain of anti-rationalism' which had 'marred his message', and that 'without the rational structure of theology, Christianity would long ago have sunk into noxious superstition.' He closed its review: 'You will like this old warrior and you will agree with what he wants to say and do. We need this kind of bull in our neat little intellectual china shops. But it is still bull.'

The *International Journal of Parapsychology* (September 1966) was enthusiastic. Their reviewer, the Rev. James Cope Crosson, declared, 'This is an exciting book! It is also one of the most sensible and stimulating books I have read in a long time.' He described Weatherhead as 'not only a scholar but a cleric so far ahead of his contemporaries that he has almost become a legend as a pioneering spirit, a prophet and a seer.' Crosson, more than almost any other reviewer, understood the source of Weatherhead's concern and those whose doubts he was seeking to answer. Crosson said that as an army chaplain in World War II, he had found that

> many of the traditional cliches and platitudes were sorely lacking in the search for answers to head-on questions of men facing the uncertainties of combat experience; they wanted facts, not theories or theoretical possibilities.

He greatly approved of the way Weatherhead sought to deal with such questions and provide answers. The book, he concluded, would help people 'to plant their religious feet firmly on solid earth . . . it is a "must" for every thoughtful person interested in hammering out a faith of his own.'

A Methodist bishop in Iowa recommended the book to a meeting of a hundred ministers in Des Moines, and it was given another strong recommendation on a 'For Your Information' programme broadcast by the largest radio and television station in Washington D.C.

In an article for *The British Weekly* (24 December, 1964) the religious television and radio producer, Edwin Robertson, said:

> Anyone who has broadcast knows that the programmes about which he receives several letters of commendation from faithful Christians are nearly always the programmes in which he has failed to talk to those really outside the church . . . we should have learnt from the scandal of *Honest to God*, that when we do speak to someone other than ourselves *the world listens, it is the church that refuses to hear* . . . . There are other writers – alive and dead – who have been telling us for a long time that we must stop talking to ourselves and start talking to those for whom the old phrases about "atonement," "salvation," "blood," are not meaningful. We have to talk in terms of the future, in terms of man's great becoming, in terms of responsibility . . . we can speak out to others the liberating word of the Gospel in a language that is not fogged with religious terms and about matters that have vital concern to more than theologians.

Though the book may have deserved many of the severe criticisms made of it by its serious critics, the responses it received, from the religious professionals who reviewed it, the orthodox and conservatives inside the churches who generally disliked it, and the lay people all over the world, who read it, who in the main found it spoke to them and were grateful for it, and wrote to Weatherhead about it, bear out Robertson's assertion. One correspondent, Ian Gregory, summed up this response when he wrote to Weatherhead,

> We are astonished at the rot being written about your new book by people who obviously have a vested interest in traditional religion. On behalf of the salesmen, water engineers, accountants, teachers, centre lathe turners, window cleaners, housewives, schoolboys and girls and me, a journalist, thank you, thank you, thank you. . . . '

Thirty years after it was first published, *The Christian Agnostic* continues in print. One American minister was so impressed by the book that he personally paid for sixty copies to give one to every family in his congregation. An African American pastor, brought up in a fundamentalist church, wrote about the book's impact on him.

> It was for me the turning point in my faith journey and remains the one volume that is an indispensable part of my library . . . . If I can point to any

one time of total conversion, it was when I read the preface and first chapter of this book. I have been free ever since.

The Christian Agnostic was re-published in Britain by Arthur James in 1989. In an introductory Preface, the Managing Editor, Denis Duncan, said that this book was the one by Weatherhead most requested in second-hand religious bookshops. Since it was written, the growth of unorthodox religious groups under the general label of the 'New Age' movement has made many of the things Weatherhead wrote about matters of fresh enquiry and speculation outside the traditional Christian churches and denominations. In this setting, the unconventional nature of the book, with its open attitude to truth, combined with its passionate conviction of the need of every soul for the love of God made real in Christ, give it a fresh and increasing relevance.

26. The Last Years

'By any standard of greatness (and one which specially appeals to me is that
of "comprehensive goodness") Dr. Weatherhead was a great man . . .
he commanded "eminence with words" and he splendidly compressed
it in a blend of simple, muscular language, deep-felt religious
conviction, oratorical skill, and that additional quality that
belongs to genius and is indefinable.'

The publication date of *The Christian Agnostic* was chosen to coincide with
the fiftieth anniversary of Weatherhead's ordination. In a tribute to him in the
British Weekly (16 September 1965) under the heading, 'Thanks Leslie
Weatherhead', Principal Charles Duthie recalled 'very vividly' the first time he
had heard him speak, to a group of young ministers, shortly after he had begun
his ministry at the City Temple.

> His message that day has remained with me ever since. . . . He spoke with
> such directness, simplicity, humour and charm that it was not at all difficult
> to understand why thousands came to the Temple every Sunday, nor why
> even larger numbers were avid readers of his books.

Weatherhead was now seventy-two, and although in his public appearances
his vitality and cheerful good humour seemed as great as ever, he was feeling
the strains of age, tiredness and ill-health. In March, he had, like Leonard Griffith,
felt dizzy while preaching at the City Temple, and had only just managed to
continue and complete the service. He wrote to a friend, Frank Eden (23 August
1965):

> I came over giddy in the pulpit and at one point – where I could not remember
> the name of Abraham Lincoln, I had to hold on to the side of the pulpit. I
> thought I was going to faint. That pulpit is too high – as you will remember.
> I hope this is not a sign that I should chuck up preaching. . . . Old age is
> frustrating, but "I'll . . . while I've breath" You know the line.

He was becoming increasingly nervous about his health, and as he preached
less and less, so the strains of doing so became greater. On his doctor's advice
he cancelled several important engagements: at Brunswick in Leeds, at Leicester
Cathedral for the opening of the University, at Richmond College in Bournemouth
and with the B.B.C. The invitations were still arriving in considerable numbers,
but he was feeling less able – and less willing – to accept them.

> I find myself depressed that now I am too old and tired to accept, thrilling
> invitations keep coming. York Minster and Bristol University this week
> alone! Life *is* a puzzle isn't it. I'd have jumped at these opportunities years
> ago.[1]

Donald Soper, who visited him in Bexhill, thought he was becoming unnecessarily
preoccupied with the state of his health.

> He was frightened of his own health, I think. I went to preach at Bexhill and
> I went down in the afternoon to see him before I was preaching in the
> evening. He said (this is not a criticism, it is just a fact) 'I don't think I can

get to the meeting tonight', but he was as fit as a flea as far as I could see. He was frightened of himself. There was a valetudinarian aspect to his later years. He became unduly sensitive, I think, as to how well he was or wasn't.[2]

On 12 March 1966, Weatherhead took part in a Teach-In on Healing at the Westminster Central Hall. This was sponsored by the National Federation of Spiritual Healers with the aim of providing a common platform for representatives of different approaches to the ministry of healing, in order, the programme stated, 'to show that the various avenues of healing are complementary and not competitive, and to seek the common denominators which bind them all together.' Twenty-three different speakers shared the platform throughout the day, among whom were Brian Inglis, Donald Soper, Harry Edwards, Beverley Nichols, Brother Mandus, and various other leading members of healing organisations. Weatherhead considered that the Teach-In was 'a rag-bag of ideas but I thought it right to go.'

That same month, Leonard Griffith announced that he was leaving the City Temple and returning to Canada, where he had accepted a call to become minister of Deer Park United Church, Toronto. Griffith had become increasingly disheartened by the shrinking congregations and the general indifference to his ministry, as he later recalled, with remarkable honesty,

> At this point I began recording my morning devotions in a spiritual diary. . . . Looking back over its pages, I am appalled by the constant confession of such moods as impatience, apathy, anxiety, weakness, despair, exhaustion, egotism, faithlessness, depression, forsakenness, frustration, discourage-ment, futility, bitterness . . . in my diary I described those years as 'the years of the locust' and wrote, 'How long O Lord, how long . . . ?'[3]

He was also up against a number of unforeseen obstacles about which he could do little. Soon after he arrived in London, a sharp cut-back in public transport meant that both the main-line station at Holborn Viaduct and the nearby underground stations were closed on Sundays, and several bus schedules were also reduced, making it not only more difficult but also more costly for people to get to the church. Public attitudes towards the churches were also changing. A sympathetic London minister friend, the Rev. Harry Jacquet, who was having to face similar difficulties at Whitefield's Church, Tottenham Court Road, told him that he had come to London

> at the worst possible time. . . . The whole spiritual climate of this country seems to have become cold and cynical and atheistic. Once people were simply critical of the church. Now they have become hostile or indifferent to it.

Early in 1965, Griffith carried out a preaching tour in Australia. Such was the warmth of his reception and the response to his preaching that he felt it was 'like being raised from the dead. . . . I came to life again and felt a reawakening of the vigour and enthusiasm that had been dormant for so long.' The contrast with his situation in London, and its effects on him, could not have been more marked. 'The message came across loud and clear. Obviously my ministry in London, however challenging and rewarding, placed an intolerable burden on my spirit.' He returned to London resolving to give the City Temple one more try, only to find that all the old stress symptoms, which had disappeared during his time in Australia, re-emerged. Nothing had changed. He therefore began to make enquiries of his friends in Canada, actively seeking a fresh pastorate there.

Leonard Griffith closed his ministry on 26 June. In his farewell sermon he described himself as being 'emptied of easy speech and utterly drained in spirit.' Recalling his six years at the church he praised the loyalty of the members, saying that during his ministry, '246 names had been added to the roll, bringing the present total to 544 of which about 200 worship and contribute regularly.' He expressed concern for the future of the church saying that with the current 'mistrust of pulpit rhetoric' and the widespread hostility and indifference to the church, the City Temple was 'bound to fall on lean years.'

A Vacancy Committee had been appointed to consider his successor. Weatherhead was consulted and gave his opinion on several names which had been suggested. Among these were Howard Williams, then minister of the City Temple's close neighbour, Bloomsbury Baptist Church. Weatherhead commented that he had 'a reputation for being a little pink', with which Griffith agreed. Weatherhead thought that as a 'temporary expedient' either Dr. Leslie Cooke or Professor James Stewart might be considered for a short ministry, 'perhaps five years.' He also suggested considering Dr. John Vincent of the Methodist Central Hall, Rochdale, and Edmund Heddle, the minister of Beulah Baptist Church in Bexhill, with whom Weatherhead had become very friendly.

Weatherhead returned to the church to preach several times during the vacancy, and, with concern over loss of income due to falling congregations in mind, he was asked to take both services on the church's Gift Day, 25 September. Mrs. Weatherhead underwent a serious operation during that month, and though this was pronounced to be entirely successful, her health remained a constant anxiety. His own health continued to trouble him, and he was forced at the last minute to drop out of an engagement to preach at the Ordination and Induction service of a former member of the City Temple at Christ Church and Upton Chapel on October 19.

He received an honour which meant a very great deal to him when on 6 July he was elected the third President of the recently established Institute of Religion and Medicine. This had been formed following a Working Party set up in 1962 by the Archbishop of Canterbury, Dr. Michael Ramsay, to investigate ways of closer co-operation between the medical profession and the churches. Weatherhead's election was a significant recognition by members of the churches and of the medical profession of his life's work to bring them together in co-operation and partnership. Weatherhead's standing in this field is indicated by the fact that the first President was the Archbishop of Canterbury and the second the President of the Royal College of Surgeons, Sir Arthur Porritt, which meant that Weatherhead was the first freely elected religious leader to be so honoured. Introducing him, Porritt said that

Dr. Weatherhead has an excellent link with the Institute through his psychological clinic and his contact with doctors, which have given him considerable knowledge of both vocations represented here today. . . . He has that vision essential for the Institute, and the ability to look at all subjects from a human point of view.

In his response, Weatherhead referred to his meeting with the R.A.M.C. doctor 'in a tent on the Euphrates, 50 years ago, in 1916', when they talked about 'the very thing that we are gathered here to discuss.' He went on to speak about the weekly group called together by the Bishop of Madras, of doctors, clergy and ministers, in which they discussed the new books being published on the new psychology by 'Crichton Miller, Hadfield, William Brown etc.' He described the City Temple Psychological Clinic, which was 'staffed by a group of 10 Christian, medically qualified psychiatrists, four ministers and two lady psychiatric social workers', saying that its aim was also 'the aim of this Institute of which I am so proud to become President.'

Weatherhead's involvement with the IRM was much more than that of a non-active figurehead, since the formation of the Institute meant a great deal to him, as the fulfilment of a dream for which he had worked and campaigned for most of his ministerial life. Being retired, it also gave him, during his official year, a new sphere of activity to engage in, and helped to counter some of the frustrations and sense of uselessness which his retirement made him feel. In spite of his indifferent health, he eagerly undertook his new responsibilities.

At the end of his year of office, the I.R.M. Assembly met at Halifax, on 12 July, 1967. In his opening Report, the Chairman, Dr. Kenneth Soddy, paid particular tribute to Weatherhead

> for the inspiration of his presence amongst us. Because of the nature of the structure and functioning of IRM it is not easy for a President to take an active part in day-to-day affairs, but Dr. Weatherhead has made his influence felt helpfully in many ways, and especially in some of the "back room" work. Our President's reputation too, has given IRM a boost among many people who would not otherwise have been interested in the Institute.

In his Presidential address Weatherhead expressed his sense of having received 'a very great honour', and said that the I.R.M. was the development of a movement to bring together the two professions of the church and medicine which he had longed for for thirty years. He recalled how he had proposed to the Methodist Conference in 1935 that students for the ministry should be given some psychological training, that every Methodist District should have a regularly meeting group of doctors and ministers 'so that the energies released in religion, medicine and psychology could all be focused on human need', and that every church should have 'groups of devoted people making intercession for the sick' and also 'carefully guarded services in which the laying on of hands for healing could be practised in accordance with New Testament teaching.' He stressed the importance of intercession for the sick, describing it as a way of co-operating with God in his will for health for each individual. He spoke about the laying on of hands, which he said should sometimes be 'regarded as a sacramental rite in which grace is symbolically conveyed' but sometimes also as 'a treatment without any necessary link with religion.' He distinguished between the pastoral ministry in which the laying on of hands put the emphasis on forgiveness and the person's unity with God, and the activities of lay healers who possessed the gift of 'odic force' which was 'a *treatment* not a *sacrament*'. He repeated again his warning about the dangers of healing missions which held crowded and emotional healing services. In his final remarks he spoke about anxiety, and referred especially to the unique privilege that clergy and ministers had in being able to visit people in their homes, which gave them an opportunity to recognise stress and unhealthy factors within the home situation and put them in a position to offer guidance and help and to exercise a preventive ministry.

Weatherhead continued to contribute occasional articles and letters to the press. On 18 March, 1967, *The Times* published a contribution by him headed 'A Way Forward for the Church.' In this he repeated the central ideas of *The Christian Agnostic,* not a bit inhibited by the critical reviews of that book. He proposed that the Church should welcome into membership 'those who believe that the spirit of Christ is a clue to the meaning of life' without first requiring them to subscribe to any creeds or articles; it should not go on 'dishonestly clinging for comfort to beliefs we do not believe in' or insist on beliefs about which Christ said nothing. He said that there must be a new concept of unity which did not expect everyone to believe the same things, or worship in the same way, but was based on the recognition of a common heritage, and a determination to work together 'united in action against evil.' There should be a 'new vision of service' in which instead of too many churches being open only on one day a week, most church buildings could be dispensed with, and the remaining ones kept open day and night, as counselling centres to which anyone in need might turn for help.

For some time Weatherhead had been in correspondence with J.B. Phillips, the famous Anglican translator of the New Testament into popular speech. Weatherhead had eagerly seized upon Phillips's *Letters to Young Churches* when it was first published in 1947 and they found that they had much in common. Phillips had contacted Weatherhead in 1961, seeking his help, when he was going through a particularly bad period of deep depression, from which he frequently suffered. Weatherhead replied, (1 June 1961) saying that he too had been through 'this valley.' He had known Phillips was ill, since they had been due to appear on a television programme together which had had to be cancelled. On receiving Phillips's letter he had immediately contacted his friend Dr. Percy Backus, and urged Phillips to contact him and make an appointment. He also suggested he read *Prescription for Anxiety* which Phillips had reviewed and about which he had been 'good enough to say kind words.' He recommended 'Rest without letting people worry you' and suggested a holiday in Scotland, telling him to try the P⁻ɔkfoot Hotel in Moffat, 'mention my name. I have found health and God there.'

Phillips wrote to him again in 1967. Weatherhead, who had sent Phillips a copy of *The Christian Agnostic*, replied (3 February 1967)

I feel concerned about what you describe as depression because I went through that hell thirty years ago. I had over 200 hours of "analysis" with J.A. Hadfield and finally emerged but it took years. If there is any possible way I could help I would do anything I could. I still have charge of the City Temple Psychological Clinic and have 10 Christian, medically qualified psychiatrists working with me as a team. Surely *something* can be done for you, who have done so much for others. I found DRYNAMIL an enormous help to dispel early morning depression.

These tablets are the basis of "purple hearts", but in spite of all the talk about them, and their obvious dangers to foolish young people, under medical advice I think them invaluable. I still take *1* before a Sunday at the City Temple; a challenge which still makes me "anxious". Let me know if there is anything I can do.

Phillips replied, and Weatherhead wrote again at some length in a highly self-critical and revealing letter (17 February 1967) in which he identifies himself with Phillips's experiences :

> I wish we could talk! If ever you come this way come and have an hour or so. For we seem to have had so many similar experiences. Nowadays, I feel fine for weeks together then there will come down a black cloud when I wish, quite sincerely, that I could die. I have thought so much about you but it would be presumptuous to guess at causes in your case. I can only say briefly what happened to me in case anything in my case helps you. You have read the psychology doubtless. I was crushed between the super-ego and the id! I think success wrought my downfall, that is why I wondered if it might apply to you, far more successful and famous than I! Your name and fame are world wide.
>
> I now look back and see this situation. I was a popular preacher, packing the City Temple, people queuing to get in, selling my books etc. etc. when all the time I knew myself inwardly to be a lover of applause. The conflict between what I pretended to be – or at any rate was thought to be – in the pulpit and what I really was, was too much and broke me in two. Could part of your trouble be that you do not deserve the praise of the whole world for your translations. You know they are jolly good. So were my sermons! But human praise blows up the super-ego and makes bigger the contrast with the id, the gap widens when mental health demands they should be drawn together. This may be no use at all, but I have noticed again and again, that in the very hour of triumph, when the whole world applauds, men suffer a "breakdown". The world's estimate and what a man knows is the truth makes his mind split. Does this make sense? We are alike in the parental situation. I had a dominating mother whom I idolised until Hadfield revealed, through my dreams of a powerful witch, that she was completely cramping my free development. I was terrified of her disapproval. . . . I hated her dominance but could not live without her approval and became a wheedling little rabbit as insecure as one could be. A great many things which I have done with the supposed motive of altruism and Christian service, I have *really* done to buy other people's approval because this gave me a sense of security. I now look back and see what a mess my life has been and I only cheer up by trying to move forward in the comfort that God knows all, forgives all, will never cast me away, and even now, in the next dimension, can work out purpose in my life, for, in my best moments, I *do* love Him, and want to be more worthy of the word "Christian". . . . Well, my dear J.B., I don't know why I am tipping all this out on you . . . but my heart goes out to you, because in some ways we seem to have been in the same dark valley. We *shall* triumph, I am sure of that, if we endure to the end and soldier on as you say. Please *don't* resort to L.S.D. . . . The dangers are too great. Whatever happens in your mind you have wrought a mighty work for the Kingdom of God. No one in your generation has done more. God bless you. You will find the way through and so shall I. May it be soon!

No doubt Weatherhead knew himself very well, but in this astonishingly frank and self-disparaging letter, he hardly does himself justice – as Phillips was well aware. Weatherhead's psychology had taught him that even the best of a person's motives were invariably mixed, and in accusing himself of self-serving and unholy motives he was not telling the whole story. He fails to mention here, what was very obvious at the time, that a major reason for his breakdown was his impossibly high work-load, combined with the equally impossibly high stand-ard he set himself. There may have been an element of pride involved; believing that he could help the thousands of people who wrote to him where others without his specialist knowledge and skills could not – as many of those who wrote to him pleaded was the case. But there was also the excessive stress of anxiety and guilt caused by his not being able to do all that he set out to do, which meant that however hard he worked, and however many hours he put in, there were always some left unseen and unhelped. This conflict was as much, probably much more, the cause of his breakdown than the explanations he gives to Phillips in this letter.

Phillips at any rate, was comforted and helped by the letter. As he replied (19 February 1967):

Your letter was an enormous help to me! Not only have you gone up in my estimation by several hundred per cent, but now I feel we are really communicating. Years ago at a Christian Books Exhibition in London you spoke to me most kindly, and I can remember saying to my wife and various friends afterwards, "Here is a man who is just as friendly off the platform as he is on it!" And you know, as well as I do, that that is not always true of the world's greatest preachers. Through the years I have read all your books, and strangely enough the last one which you kindly sent me revealed to me more of you than it did of the Christian faith, if you see what I mean. But now you have trusted me with such complete candour I feel I know you, and I shall certainly try to see you when I can.

There is a great deal of similarity in our experience of life. . . . I was trying to please an exacting and rather tyrannical father. . . . I did not realize how subtle continued success and being in demand everywhere could be . . . your telling me of your own experiences is far more help than any book of conventional pious comfort. . . . You yourself have helped so many people all over the world that I refuse to accept that your motives were quite so selfish as you make out; they were probably mixed like mine and most people's. Don't, I beg you, turn against yourself. "If our heart condemn us, God is greater than our heart and knoweth all things."

Weatherhead replied (12 March 1967)

I certainly feel we are on the same wavelength and I wish we were geographically nearer. I think I too suffered a sad loss of security. Under Hadfield's analysis I felt I wasn't wanted as baby, though through a medium my mother (?) assured me she loved me. I think I have collected University degrees in order to compensate for being a frightened, much caned duffer at school. How I *hated* school!!. . . . Of course, you know, as I do, that most awful loss of ability to *feel*, is a symptom of anxiety-neurosis, but how devastating it can be. Even now I have patches when I have no feeling at all about God, and feel a hypocrite if I am suddenly called on to help another. At other times – for me often when trying to prepare sermons, He is gloriously real. I love walking along the beach here and repeating some of Charles Wesley's hymns which have helped me in time past. (He wrote a lot of tripe too, of course).

No, whatever you do don't let anybody persuade you to have L.S.D. *NOTHING* would persuade me to try it. . . . I felt, when I was in my darkest valley, that one or two facts sustained me. I said to myself:

1.So and so went through this and he is now all right so why not I?

2. I *sometimes* feel radiantly happy, full of life and fun and if I can *sometimes* reach these heights I can do so again and since the *trend* is always towards health (the cut finger tends to heal) then the "vis medicatrix naturae", which is true of mind as well as body, is working towards my full recovery.

3. God can use *everything* that happens to me for His glory and weave it all into a better qualification to understand and to help others. Even forgiven sin can become an asset I feel. I am sure from your letter you will know all this. . . . I thought old age (I am 73) would be calm and serene. I want to be a benevolent, white-haired serene old gent. The white hair is true and that is all!!

Weatherhead's articles for *The Sunday Times* had been appearing regularly for six years, when a new Editor, Denis Hamilton, decided that it was time to end this particular feature of the paper. Weatherhead's style, which had been so effective for so long, was now felt to be no longer in tune with the mood of the late 1960s. This rejection must have been a blow to him, making him feel even more that he was getting old and out of touch. However this blow was softened somewhat by The Lutterworth Press which took the opportunity to publish, in July 1967, a collection of his *Sunday Times* articles under the title, *Time for God*.

This book was divided up into six sections, 'The Inviolate Soul', 'Motives and Ends', 'Sight and Insight', 'The Incentives of Prayer', 'The Christian Year', and 'The Things Which Remain'. Reviewing the book for *Tidings* (August 1967) Kenneth Slack said that the most striking thing about the articles was that

They are richly human. Here, in the unerring power of communication is surely to be found the secret that has perplexed so many of Dr. Weatherhead's fellow preachers. Why, in a day when preaching is at a discount and much of conventional church life has been eroded, has this man gone on being heard gladly by the masses of men? This book shows us why. He loves people, and writes of the Gospel with a simple directness that can only be achieved with immense effort over the years. A younger generation of preachers would have differences of approach and emphasis. We can all learn from his secret.

At a meeting of City Temple members on 31 May, a unanimous call had been sent to Slack, then minister of St. Andrew's Presbyterian Church, Cheam, to become the next minister of the church. In a private memorandum in March, Weatherhead had informed the Vacancy Committee that Slack had 'told him he was unhappy at Cheam and would eagerly welcome a call to the City Temple.' Slack was already very well known there since he had been Interim Moderator of the Marylebone Presbyterian Church after the death of Herbert Lewis, and from that time until the move back to Holborn he had been Weatherhead's close ministerial colleague. He had been General Secretary of the British Council of Churches for ten years, and as the author of a book, *The British Churches Today*, he knew their current situation better than anyone and had no illusions about the realities of the task he was taking on at the City Temple. Slack had an additional considerable advantage over Griffith in that he was well known, at least among church people in England, as a preacher, writer and as a frequent and successful broadcaster, and in ecumenical and international church circles as a British representative at the World Council of Churches and as a member of the Advisory Committee Conference of European Churches. He admitted to being both excited and 'mildly scared' about the prospect: 'all the central churches in our big cities, especially in London, face acute problems and the City Temple's fame alone is daunting.' Slack's Induction took place on Monday, October 2. In his Statement, he expressed his awareness of the situation which faced him. 'It is humanly speaking, appalling in its difficulty, as the whole country seems to have entered a religious ice-age, certainly as far as the habit of worship goes.'

In February, Weatherhead's main publishers, Hodder and Stoughton, celebrated their centenary with a Literary Luncheon, hosted by the *Yorkshire Post* in the Queens Hotel Leeds. The three speakers invited by Hodders from among their most successful authors were the former British Ambassador to Moscow, Sir William Hayter, the novelist Mary Stewart and Weatherhead himself. In his address, Weatherhead recalled how Leonard Cutts, then head of the religious books department of Hodders, had come into his vestry in Leeds in 1932 to ask him if he would write for his firm. Weatherhead had replied that he was too busy, but Cutts had noticed from an order of service on Weatherhead's desk that he was preaching a series of sermons on the life of Christ which he had called *His Life and Ours*. This had become the title of the first book of his which Hodders had published. Since then they had sold more than a half a million of his books, 'Hence my present affluence and part of their prosperity!'

Weatherhead's appearances at the City Temple were becoming less frequent. He preached at the morning service only on April 21. Slack was eager for him to preach again in July while he was away at the World Council of Churches meeting in Uppsala, but before this Weatherhead suffered a slight heart attack. His doctor warned him that he should not take on the responsibility for a full Sunday's services for some time, but he agreed to preach on the morning only of July 14. He became ill again and was admitted to hospital so that this engagement had to be cancelled.

In June, Epworth produced a compilation by Frank Cumbers of *Daily Readings from the works of Leslie D. Weatherhead* as a companion to a previous volume of selections from W.E. Sangster. In his Foreword, Cumbers describes Weatherhead as

> easily one of the best known ministers in the world. Yet humility always clothes him. . . . Leslie Weatherhead always seems to men and women to speak with marvellous understanding of their situation. This arises partly from a generous love and concern for ordinary folk, and also from an amazing ability to enter into their position. . . . The man who speaks to men and women in their difficulties has been there himself . . . he has known the dark places, and his friends have watched with sympathy, and also with gratitude for an example of positive heroism and constructive patience. His books have put the world in his debt.

The *Church of England Newspaper* (23 August 1968) headed its review, 'Weatherhead a genius but, . . .' saying

> As one moves through the pages of the book one is convinced of a great

mind whose genius for insight into the human situation is enhanced by his training as a psychologist. Dr. Weatherhead's devotion to Christ is simple but certain. . . . The orthodox evangelical who may well prefer *Daily Light* or daily readings from Spurgeon or Sangster nevertheless with careful handling of the book will find much for his own benefit.

The Methodist Recorder (5 September 1968) chose it as its 'book of the week', and praised it for revealing Weatherhead's special qualities, not only of 'lucid language', 'simplicity' and discipline', but also 'his courage, the kind of courage which faces awkward and difficult questions without hint of evasion.' The book contained the essential Weatherhead.

Compassion for the sufferer and the anxious; practical guidance in Christian living; replies to honest enquiry; the link between religion and healing; teaching on the festivals of the Christian year . . . his deep conviction that the living Christ is sufficient for all our needs.

Cumbers later followed with *Daily Readings from the works of Martyn Lloyd Jones.* One American critic who reviewed the three together for the *Asbury Seminarian* (Spring 1971) wrote,

What profit! What insight! What reward! This is especially true of . . . the Sangster and Weatherhead anthologies. One will look a long time elsewhere to find something devotionally comparable. . . . This reviewer finds difficulty with Lloyd Jones – he does not communicate with the sharpness of Sangster and Weatherhead. He lacks warmth, human contact. But he does place emphasis on the Word of God, and that has its own rewards.

Weatherhead, who made a habit of noting the sales of his books inside the front cover, recorded that this book had sold 2,276 copies by December 6, and 6,000 in America. By September, over £300 from the royalties had been sent to the Methodist Homes for the Aged. But there was an earlier, sadder note.

I received this early copy on June 14th 1968 in Bexhill Hospital on one of the unhappiest days of my life. Having had on May 3rd a Coronary Thrombosis, I had an attack of diverticulitis and an abscess formed which perforated the colon and landed me with peritonitis. They could not operate because of the heart condition and I nearly died – and wanted to, as it seemed so attractive to GO ON but antibiotics brought me back. It was misery to be brought back after a glimpse of the next phase.

Weatherhead expressed his frustration with age and retirement in a letter to Edmund Heddle (9 November 1968)

Old age, no demanding job, the irritations of being at home so much instead of here there and everywhere, make life dull, gloomy and monotonous, and radiance departs. I feel this ought not to be and that if I really *had* all I long for, and if I *were* the kind of chap people think the author of "The Transforming Friendship" *is* I would always be serene and joyous.

While Slack was on holiday in September it was hoped that Weatherhead would be well enough to preach at services on the eighth and twenty second, but he had to decline the eighth as he was suffering from throat trouble. Against his doctor's advice he preached at the evening service on September 22, on 'Loving Matters Most'. A recording was made of this service for sale on the church bookstall. It is clear from this that Weatherhead had lost none of his persuasive pulpit power, though the content of his sermon had now been refined down to

Leslie Weatherhead with The Archbishop of York, Dr Donald Coggan, 1968

a very basic message of what he regarded as the essential gospel, which he presented without complicated or sophisticated argument. Preaching less, and feeling constantly unwell, he was becoming much more nervous about entering the pulpit, finding it a considerable strain, and he was less sure of his memory. He was using fuller notes, though still far short of a complete manuscript, since merely to stand and read a sermon was something he deplored, and even now, would not do. Yet it was not only because he was finding the effort of preaching more exhausting that he was simplifying his message; it was also that he was less interested in engaging in the old battles and arguments, more concerned to share the things he felt really mattered.

The Archbishop of Canterbury, Michael Ramsey, was the guest preacher at the City Temple on Sunday evening, 19 January 1969, during the Week of Prayer for Christian Unity. Weatherhead was present and led the opening prayer, but he found it a considerable ordeal. He thought he was going to faint during the service and needed to be helped to the robing room afterwards. The nervous strain of the service came on top of his personal troubles, not least the failing health of his wife, which was now causing him considerable anxiety. He was also having further spells in hospital himself. In a letter two months later he wrote,

I am home and making progress but we are rather a sad household. Gertie [Gertie Hutchinson the Weatherhead's housekeeper who had been with them over thirty years] hobbles around with an ulcerated leg and Lyn really had a stroke, though we don't like the word. Her speech and movements are affected. And I have had 2 heart attacks in 8 months on top of that serious abdominal illness in July. However we plod on. I am 75+ and there must be an end to some activities though I hate to say "No" to the many invitations that reach me. One yesterday to Oxford Undergraduates but – there it is. I daren't say "Yes."[4]

Increasingly, Weatherhead was becoming pre-occupied with the nature of life after death. In March 1969, the National Christian Education Council's Denholm House Press brought out *Life Begins at Death*, a small book based on taped conversations in which Weatherhead, returning to the subject of one of his earliest books, *After Death*, replies to questions put to him by his friend, the Secretary of the City Temple Psychology Clinic, Norman French. Among these are, 'why do Christians believe in life after death?'; 'is it unreasonable to believe that death is the end?'; 'Does this life decide our destiny for the next?'; 'What did Jesus mean by eternal life?'; Do sinners get a second chance?'; 'Do the mentally sick go into the next life mentally ill?'; 'can Christians believe in reincarnation?'

Weatherhead's answers are not just intellectual replies, but deeply personal responses, reflecting not only his beliefs, but his own feelings and longings at this late stage in his life. Only a belief in another life

can make sense of this one. . . . The physical body wears out or it suffers from disease, it cannot, after a certain period, be the home of the spirit. . . . I am not afraid to die. . . . I do rather dread the interim period between my present health and my death – the period when one might be ill and useless, a burden to oneself and others. But the idea of dying, taken by itself, is attractive to me. To wake up amongst old friends with a new body that doesn't hurt anywhere and is not worn out is most attractive. . . . I believe that when you die you go on where you left off. I can't believe that the accident of dying . . . determines our eternal destiny. . . . no man at his death has exhausted his possibilities. . . . If there is no further plane on which those possibilities can be expressed . . . then it seems to me that the whole of human life is irrational.

Referring to the evidence of Spiritualism, he quotes F.W.H. Myers, as saying, via the medium Geraldine Cummins, how marvellous and beautiful the next life is. He expresses his universalist belief in the ultimate invincibility of the power of God's love to save:

I don't see how God who is Love can be satisfied if there is one soul in an endless hell, if there is one soul lost. That is a defeat of eternal purpose and that I don't believe is possible. . . . I don't think there will be heaven – not the highest heaven – for anybody, least of all for God, unless we are all in it. . . . My own view is that God wills that every living soul shall at last be brought by free choice into harmony with his will. [p.64]

Life Begins at Death had been featured as a series of articles in the *British Weekly*, which then asked Eric Routley to review it. Routley, who began by declaring himself 'unqualified to do so', did so at some length in two articles printed in succeeding weeks. He acknowledged that the book was intended to offer comfort, but said that he himself was unable to respond to it, since 'for the most part I find that I don't myself want to say these things, or hear these things about death.' He disagreed with Weatherhead's use of scripture, describing his biblical interpretations as 'folklore' rather than the result of critical and precise study. Concerning what happens after death, Routley says, 'I don't disbelieve anything that Dr. Weatherhead says – but neither (I think) do I believe it. I really don't think we know, or are required to know, anything about this.' Any assurance to a bereaved person that they might be reunited with loved ones after death is offering false comfort, because it is saying what cannot be proved. In Routley's view a Christian teacher should be less concerned with the power of death to separate people from one another and more concerned for what in this life separates people from faith and from God:

> It is not what may happen to them in another world that would worry me, but what is going to happen to them in this one. And it is in terms of this one, and in those terms alone, that any Christian friend, teacher or minister, can comfort a bereaved person.

David James, in *The Methodist Recorder* (6 March 1969) found the book much more helpful, though he was not convinced by what Weatherhead had to say about the possibility of reincarnation. Picking up his frustration with his physical frailty and longing for release and the new beginning which he believed death would bring, James criticised Weatherhead for treating this life as 'only a prelude . . . one could follow him more easily here if he did not seem to regard this present life as so preliminary and almost incidental; one does not feel that he attaches to it the decisiveness that we find in the New Testament.' He finds 'the real Weatherhead' in what the book conveys of his 'deep and loving sense of God in Christ. . . . The Christ who takes the terror from dying, and makes it a moment of peace, of happy anticipation and the beginnings of reunion.' He recognised the book as 'a record of a search for truth which must always be too great for us', and thought that as a basis for group discussion, and as a help to any person genuinely seeking guidance 'it cannot fail to do great good.'

The Christian (28 February 1969) quoted passages from the book, saying that Weatherhead was 'always good for making Christians think – if they are not too dogmatic to do so.' Even *The Church Times* (28 March 1969) called it 'a stimulating little book'; Weatherhead's 'profound knowledge of the results of psychical research' was 'invaluable' and his discussion of reincarnation also deserved to be taken seriously. *Psychic News* (1 March 1969) headed its report, 'There's Hope for non-Christians in the next world!' and thought that Weatherhead 'spoke like a veteran Spiritualist' in his replies to Norman French, and that his comments on life after death owed more to Spiritualism than they did to Christianity.

Once again, Weatherhead received a great many letters from people who, in spite of the strictures of critics like Eric Routley, found the book of the greatest comfort and help, especially the elderly and recently bereaved. In less than a month after its publication, stocks had sold out, and a third printing was being arranged. All Weatherhead's royalties were donated directly to the City Temple Psychology Clinic.

In March, Weatherhead was featured on Anglia Television in a programme presented by Kenneth Slack, part of a regular series, 'Men Who Matter.' Slack described Weatherhead as 'a fantastic phenomenon', referring to his ability still to fill a vast building every time he preached, his having thirty books still in print, some of which had been selling steadily for forty years, and his pioneering influence in making 'psychology a handmaid of faith and a means of Christian healing.' Asking what was the secret of Weatherhead's extraordinary success in continuing to attract large crowds 'that has enabled him to run counter to the experience of almost all other preachers since 1918', Slack offers as part of the explanation,

> Here was a man who knew what was going on in men's minds . . . he's unravelled the questions in men's minds and in deceptively simple fashion shown them the Christian answer. I say deceptively simple, for let no-one imagine from the popular style of his writing that it does not conceal a vast amount of difficult reading. Again, his hearers felt "Here is a man who understands". This could be dangerous: it could tread near to sentimentality . . . there was a rich humanity – a gift of humour that broke out continually, and that never-ceasing interest in the movement of the human mind that his psychological study and practice had given him . . . his superb gift was communication; religiously he was always gripped by the power of Jesus of Nazareth. He really believed that to know him *was* "a transforming friendship."

Weatherhead's doctor advised against his accepting Slack's invitation to preach during Slack's absence on holiday during September. He had preached at the City Temple for the last time. Both he and his wife suffered from influenza during the epidemic which hit the country during the winter months. Though he never entirely lost his sense of humour, he was finding little to be cheerful or optimistic about.

> We are in a very dark valley with a day and night nurse in the house. We both had flu all over Xmas. (My Xmas dinner was an antibiotic tablet and a cup of tea!) But Lyn is very ill with this arterio sclerosis which is much worse. I cannot understand what she is trying to say. She has choking fits, distressing to witness, and her walking is very wobbly. . . . I find I can't take in more than the "Adventures of Sherlock Holmes" at the moment. My mind is deteriorating also and quickly. . . . Just now I feel how difficult it is not to fall into anxiety. Every thing is a burden – income tax for instance – but prayer does help.[5]

Two months later he writes again, describing how his wife's condition has worsened, and how difficult he is finding it to cope, even with both day and night nurses.

> Lyn's illness is a fatal one and it is terrible to see her getting weaker every day. . . . My doctor wants her to go into a Nursing Home but she is against it and I don't want to drive her out of her house. . . . I feel the strain is getting *me* down and I think the doctor's advice about a Nursing Home is partly in *my* interests but one hears of such neglect and incompetence in these Homes that I don't want her to be deprived of the comfort of her own home if I can help it. What *shall* I do? I think the only answer is to keep her here as long as I can. I do find great help in prayer and in the prayers of friends. . . . Memory is still a blessed thing but I have never been so un-happy and wish the end could come for both of us. Lyn is nearly 80.

A few weeks later:

> I am a prisoner here although we have a day and a night nurse. Lyn is slowly dying of the kind of sclerosis that killed Dr. Sangster and there is no cure. . . . She can't speak now . . . she can't walk although the nurse gets her up to sit in a chair. . . . It is *very* hard that she can't make us understand what she wants.

He was disappointed not to be able to attend the opening of William Kyle's Westminster Pastoral Foundation at the Westminster Central Hall, where a room had been named in his honour.

I am glad Bill Kyle has got going and wish I could get up to see the room they have kindly called after me but my own health is precarious. You will come up against many snags trying to work with the average G.P. and psychoanalyst. I had a hard battle there until I started the C.T. Clinic which seems to be dead now. . . . Don't let work overwhelm you. A church will cheerfully kill the parson if he lets them. . . . I hope you can make out this scrawl I have rheumatism in my right wrist . . . keep on praying for us.

Evelyn Weatherhead died on 29 July, just a few weeks before their Golden Wedding. A short act of thanksgiving for her life was included in the Communion Service at the City Temple on the Sunday morning after her death. *The City Temple Tidings* contained tributes to her from Winifred Barton and Alice Head. They described her as retiring by nature, preferring to stay quietly in the background, but giving her husband strong and loyal support. She had become actively engaged in the Women's organisations at the church, being President of the Ladies Working Guild and the Women's League of Service. She maintained her strong interest in mission, and organised a Missionary Birthday Scheme. They paid particular tribute to 'the stability of her presence' during the dark and terrible years of the blitz. Alice Head described her as a perfectionist, who had a 'meticulous sense of responsibility in regard to all rules and regulations and took the utmost care to see that they were kept.'

After much debate the church decided to reduce the size of the worship area and to install a smaller pedestal pulpit in place of the existing lectern. The glass screens at the back of the church were brought forward to reduce the seating; at the same time doubling the size of the Friends's Chapel and creating a large room opposite it. The gallery ceased to be used except on special occasions when a larger congregation was anticipated. This decision, coming so close to Weatherhead's last preaching appearance at the church, and coinciding with the Methodists' decision to sell the Kingsway Hall, for so long the place of Donald Soper's outstanding ministry, gave a symbolic physical and architectural expression to the final end of the era of star preachers in central city churches, which, because of Weatherhead's extraordinary appeal, had lasted at the City Temple well after it had ceased almost everywhere else.

On 3 October, the Samaritan League celebrated its Diamond Jubilee, with Weatherhead's protege, William Kyle, as the guest speaker. Among the greetings received was a telegram from the Queen. Weatherhead, now widowed and chronically unwell, did not feel fit enough to attend. His seventy-seventh birthday on 14 October was a lonely affair, in spite of the greetings he received.

I had over 40 cards and letters, 3 lots of flowers and a box of fudge from Dr. Backus! Spoilt! It was a sad and lonely day. I miss her more than I thought I should, and if they play a hymn on the wireless which was a favourite of hers – and many were – I find my eyes pricking with tears and I can't control my voice – so preaching, dear boy, is out of the question until I can learn control. I've got a fit of nervous exhaustion and find it hard to sleep. Only 3 hours last night even with drugs. But the boys both going back to USA made a crisis which I found difficult. I can't get my mind working – except letters. I feel I have said my say and I wish I could quickly slip away and join Lyn![6]

However, he was happily present once more at the City Temple on 25 April 1971, to dedicate and name the extended former 'cough-box' at the rear of the church, which had been turned into a sizeable meeting room, as the Leslie Weatherhead Room. Kenneth Slack, reporting with pleasure on Weatherhead's presence, remarked that

his voice was strong and his bearing erect, and his power coming through with the old force. It was an unforgettable morning. I shall long treasure the time after the service when hundreds were milling around . . . and queuing up to where Dr. Weatherhead most appropriately held court in an armchair within the room that now bears his name.

Writing soon after, Weatherhead expressed his own pleasure at the event, though it had been a strain.

I was glad I was able to get to the C.T. and was delighted to find that it has not spoilt the look of the old place as much as I thought it would. I was very nervous. . . . I simply hate growing old. I have about six things wrong with me which I won't list. It would bore you, but they make you continually conscious of your body and that makes you get hypochondriacal and unhappy. My specialist (heart) says no more preaching and indeed I go through agonies of apprehension that I shall have a heart attack on the pulpit steps somewhere and make a scene. I dodged as many steps as I could at the C.T. but the benediction nearly did me in at the top of those 3 stairs. . . . Perhaps one ought to be told to "trust in the Lord" but I've had 4

With Dr Kenneth Slack at the dedication of the Leslie Weatherhead Room

coronaries and other troubles. I'm really eager now to see what the next life is like. I feel I've done all the good I can do here and would like to pass on to the next phase. I hope that doesn't sound morbid to you.[7]

He returned to the subject of his first published work with his very last book, *The Busy Man's Old Testament,* published simultaneously in July by the Denholm Press in England and Abingdon in America. Weatherhead said that the aim of the book was to persuade people to read their Bibles. He set out 'to provide the busy man with the richness the Old Testament contains, while avoiding matter which is not relevant to his needs.' The book includes a chronological list of all the Old Testament books and the dates of the main events they describe, with a short explanatory paragraph and references on the passages from each book which Weatherhead considers worth reading, as well as reasons for omitting those he dismisses as unhelpful. He had indicated in *The Christian Agnostic* that he had thought of producing such a book, and this had led to several letters urging him to do so.

The Methodist Recorder welcomed the book warmly, saying 'It could only have been written by one who knows and loves the Bible', and that its effect would be to encourage people to read the Old Testament as its author hoped. But Weatherhead himself was not happy with it:

It isn't a good work. I have strayed into country (O.T.) where I am not at home and have no right to speak. But so much of the O.T. is nonsense to the modern busy man that I took pity on him and suggested what bits he could blue-pencil without loss![8]

With the death of Alfred Torrie, on 25 April, 1972, Weatherhead lost a colleague who had been closely associated with his psychological work almost from the beginning. Torrie had been medical officer of health in Barnsley in 1925, when Weatherhead had frequently lectured there. It was at Weatherhead's persuasion that Torrie had taken up psychiatry. He had moved to London in 1936 and immediately joined the staff of the City Temple Psychological Clinic when it was set up. The Clinic was now fading out of the life of the City Temple. Sympathetic though he was, Kenneth Slack was too much involved in the establishment of the United Reformed Church and wider ecumenical activities to be able to devote much time to the Clinic, even if he had been more inclined towards that kind of ministry. Increasingly, therefore, though people were still being helped by it, the Clinic was becoming merely a left-over from Weatherhead's ministry, and remained in existence mainly out of respect for him. The real initiative in the development of psychological counselling as part of the ministry of the church had now passed effectively from the City Temple to William Kyle's Westminster Pastoral Foundation at the Westminster Central Hall.

On 14 October, 1973, Weatherhead celebrated his eightieth birthday. Hodders wanted to give him a birthday party in London, but he did not feel up to making the journey or to facing the fuss. He was surprised and gratified by the amount of greetings and good wishes he received, following the event being mentioned in the national press and on the radio. He wrote to Frank Eden (9 January, 1974)

I had 273 letters and cards 9 telegrams 14 lots of flowers 5 boxes of chocolates, 2 book tokens and umpteen telephone calls including from my two boys in America. My daughter and her husband and 2 sons came for the weekend. . . . It was a thrilling day and I feel most grateful.

He went on to describe his health and situation:

> I am affected with many bodily ailments, diverticulitis – inflammation of the colon due to nervous strain over a long period – rheumatism in my right leg, heart trouble (3 coronaries) and a wretched skin trouble which makes sitting painful. Otherwise I am quite fit! and can still laugh and, sitting on an air cushion, can write. I can't go away or go out for a meal as I get sick. I have all meat minced and all vegetables sieved. Meals are a misery as I feel sick all the time. Luckily I have a devoted housekeeper who has been with us 38 years. You would know that my wife died in 1970 after a very painful illness. The last two years were hell. I have been a member of F.K.[the Fellowship of the Kingdom] for 50 years but cannot now go to the meetings. Sitting on a hard chair in a church vestry is too much for me, most months, though Harry Facer, our excellent minister here, takes me in his car sometimes and also takes me to church on Sunday mornings if he is preaching. I like him very much and admire him. I am nervous of driving my car.

He was not by any means as depressed and depressing as his letters make him appear. Harry Facer, recalling their relationship, gives a happier picture. He remembered his regular Saturday morning visits to the Weatherhead home as 'always a delight. Our conversations covered a very wide field, and so often were illuminated by his irrepressible sense of humour.' Facer was especially appreciative of the unstinting encouragement he received from Weatherhead, so that he never felt daunted by having to preach when he was in the congregation. 'It was', Facer wrote,

> always a spur to do one's best, and a disappointment on the Sundays when he wasn't well enough to be there . . . he was always so loyal to the local church, and so encouraging to the preacher. Never did he let the opportunity go by of expressing thanks and appreciation for anything in the service that had helped him. . . . He retained his love for the well ordered, well prepared and relevant form of worship. . . . Certainly no privilege could have been greater than being "his minister". . . . Not all preachers are good listeners, but all I can say is that as one who ministered regularly to this Prince among Preachers, no listener could have been more attentive and encouraging.[9]

Apart from mention of the room named after him, Weatherhead's name now rarely appeared in *Tidings,* except for his regular tributes to old friends, church members and colleagues as they died. Another of the Psychology Clinic's first doctors, Edith Hudgell, died on 19 May. In his tribute to her, Weatherhead mentioned that he had persuaded her to give up her general practice in Harrow to concentrate on psychotherapy. 'When I started the Psychological Clinic in 1936, she asked if she might join the staff. We were a happy team, with Dr. Burnett Rae, Dr. Torrie, Dr. White, all of Harley Street, and now, with Dr. Hudgell, all dead.'

In May, 1974, the City Temple celebrated its centenary on Holborn Viaduct. A short history, *The City Temple: A Hundred Years,* written by Kenneth Slack, with a Foreword contributed by Weatherhead, was produced to mark the occasion. Weatherhead, commenting on the closure of public transport and the influence of television in tempting people to stay at home, acknowledged

> that immense difficulties now face us. . . . The present may seem the end of a battle, but it is not the end of a war. Young people may desire different

tactics but modern youth has, I am convinced, a real passion to make a new world and to present Christ in a new way – witness 'Godspell' and 'Jesus Christ Superstar.'

Slack, in turn, gave considerable space to recounting Weatherhead's ministry at the church, describing his call as 'something of a special providence.' Referring to Weatherhead's considerable success as an author, Slack wrote,

It would be impossible to exaggerate what this popular literary power did, and still does, for the continuing fame of the City Temple. Had his primary wider fame been as a broadcaster this would have meant little beyond the United Kingdom. The fact that anywhere in the Protestant (and not only the Protestant) English-speaking world if a man ever read a religious book he would at least have read one 'Weatherhead' meant that his name carried the name of the church he served in central London into all the lands where such people lived. It was natural if they came to London to seek his church. [p.32]

Slack, who knew Weatherhead very well, goes on to describe his personality, and notes the jealousy which Weatherhead's extraordinary success and popularity inevitably attracted.

Underlying this galaxy of powers was a sensitive nature, with antennae of feeling that were easily bruised, and a nervous system which however resilient it had already proved to be in demanding and exposed ministries, exacted a toll commensurate with his achievement. Nor does a man possess such amazing popular gifts without attracting the envy of lesser men, or the sour comment that he lacks some other gift. He made no claim to be a dogmatic theologian, but he was more generous in acknowledging his debt to scholars than some of them were in admiring the degree to which he conveyed their thought to the multitude.

As part of the centenary celebrations, the eminent Baptist historian of the Free Churches, Ernest Payne, gave a lecture on 'The City Temple and the Free Churches: Retrospect and Prospect', on 19 June. Reviewing the history of the church on the Viaduct, Payne quoted Albert Clare's remark in his tercentenary volume, that when Weatherhead was called to the City Temple in 1936, he belonged to

"that select and much-sought-after company of preachers of whom it can be said that they do not seek congregations but that congregations seek them". . . . Leslie Weatherhead spoke to a generation that was puzzled and a little frightened by what giants like Freud and Jung were saying, as well as the many amateur psychologists and quacks . . . in the years before, during and after the war . . . the City Temple congregation was unsurpassed as a nucleus of Christian witness and influence.

Weatherhead was unable to take part in the service of Thanksgiving on 30 June, but recorded a message for the occasion which was played during the service. *Tidings* reported,

The familiar and well loved voice was heard once more in the City Temple. Dr. Weatherhead in his message helped the congregation to face up to the difficulties of worshippers today, brought about by poor public transport, petrol shortages, etc. He clearly acknowledged that we live in changing times and that now our focus for ministry in God's name to the world has to change.

Early in 1975, the City Temple was hit by two sudden and unexpected blows. In January, Kenneth Slack announced that he had been invited to become Director of Christian Aid, and would therefore be ending his seven year ministry at the church that Easter. The following month, Eric Thiman died suddenly, after an operation. He had been organist for sixteen years. Both had made their own considerable contribution to the continuing fame and reputation of the church.

It was now fifteen years since Weatherhead had retired: his links with the church were growing more tenuous, and the influence of his ministry on the life of the church was becoming more remote. Many of those who had been most closely associated with him in his ministry had also gone. John Dewey, who had been a major force in the affairs of the Temple since he was first elected to the Church Council in 1926, had died suddenly in Peru, in January, 1973. Following Slack's resignation, Weatherhead's former secretary, Winifred Haddon (now Mrs. Weddell) who had continued as minister's secretary to both Griffith and Slack, was recruited to become secretary to the Rev. Arthur Macarthur, the newly appointed General Secretary of the United Reformed Church. She had served the church for thirty-four years. The District Council of the United Reformed Church, to which the City Temple now belonged, appointed as Interim Moderator a former Presbyterian, the Rev. David Holt Roberts. There was now no-one on the ministerial staff of the church who had had any direct association with Weatherhead's ministry.

In September, Hodders produced a substantial biography, *Leslie Weatherhead: A Personal Portrait*, written by his son, Kingsley. This was a tribute by a son to his father, in the last years of his life, and a tribute too, from Weatherhead's chief publishers, for whom his books had been steadily on the best seller lists for more than forty years. Weatherhead himself was pleased with the book.

> Kingsley and Hodders have done a good job. There are a few passages that I wish he had left out concerning other people but I am glad he has presented "warts and all" in his picture of me.[10]

Kenneth Slack, reviewing the book for *Tidings,* praised the author for succeeding in the difficult task, for a son writing about his father, of being objective, and producing 'an honest portrait of a real man' and not 'an artificial piece of hagiography'. Saying 'It is very hard to see how it could have been done better', Slack still feels that,

> in the end, when the biographer has done his excellent best, a mystery remains. What was it about this man that made his gifts add up to the extraordinary phenomenon that he has been? Some clues are here. His almost terrifying sensitivity, that was so personally costly, enabled something of that strangely intimate relationship between preacher and congregation. He had some skins missing, and was raw to the harsh rubs of life. People in trouble discerned that he knew what they felt like. His antennae were delicate; they transmitted messages that others missed. Even then, the mystery remains.

Weatherhead's eighty-second birthday, in October, 1975, again attracted some attention, especially as he had been on the radio twice during the previous weeks. In spite of his continued ailments, he had regained some of his serenity and cheerfulness.

> Since I was on the wireless I have had over a hundred letters and 68 cards

on my recent 82nd birthday. Brother body gives a lot of trouble but I can hobble about with a stick and have many blessings.[11]

Describing his father in those last years after the death of his wife, his son says,

He was lonely. Even with the extraordinary and selfless devotion of Gertie, the housekeeper, who continued to look after him, life was unavoidably empty. He didn't want to write any more books; he dared not preach; he no longer felt well enough to go to London. He had had his life, he felt, and now was impatient to be translated into the life beyond death in which his belief never faltered. "I long to slip away," he wrote in these months. "There are so many people waiting for me on the other side."[12]

Leslie Weatherhead died in his sleep on Saturday, 3 January, 1976. The City Temple, which at this time was without a senior minister, quickly contacted Kenneth Slack, who immediately agreed to take part in the service there the following morning, though it meant driving through the night from the north of England to be there on time.

The B.B.C. broadcast the news and substantial obituaries appeared in all the national newspapers. *The Daily Telegraph* gave most space to his ministry at the City Temple, saying that 'He more than kept it in its place of pre-eminence among nonconformist churches.' It suggested that part of his success as a preacher 'may have been the fact that he was an expert psychologist.' *The Times* described him as 'one of Britain's outstanding preachers of this generation', saying 'Leslie Weatherhead had the supreme gifts of presence, voice and a sense of the power and place of preaching in the worship of the Free Churches.' When he was called to the City Temple in 1936 he had 'already become a national figure in the world of the churches.' It called him 'a pioneer of psychiatry in the field of Christian counselling using methods widely developed in the United States but giving them a British accent.' (This was inaccurate, since Weatherhead had developed his psychological ministry independently of America, and was in many ways ahead of developments there.) *The Times* quoted his critics as accusing him of

lacking the "metropolitan note" in his preaching and of playing down to his congregations. Weatherhead knew how to "pre-digest" his material and how to present it to a popular audience. There were "tears in his voice", and he was not above using the appropriate doses of emotion. His sermonic recipe was the personal story, the biblical event, a touch of sex, a reference to loneliness and then that peculiar Weatherhead appeal which moved the congregation emotionally. It was a powerful combination which drew regular congregations of great size. . . . Weatherhead had style and panache in preaching without becoming a mere pulpiteer. He cared for people, and his prayers in public worship had a winsome personal touch which made the worshipper feel that it was his prayer too.

The religious press gave considerable space to personal tributes and assessments of his ministry. In *The British Weekly* Roy Trevivian, a former Methodist minister who became a well-known religious broadcasting producer and presenter, said that Weatherhead's 'courage was awe-inspiring', and described the effect that reading *The Transforming Friendship* had on him when he was sixteen.

Until then I hadn't read a religious book. I simply devoured it. . . . I finished reading it late one Sunday night – as I closed the book I decided to go for a walk to look for this Jesus. On a hill a mile away from my home Jesus came to me – I mean that – *came* to me and offered me his love and forgiveness. No one could ever take that experience away from me. What Leslie did for me he must have done for hundreds of thousands of people all over the world where his words were heard and his books read. People found Jesus through the way he talked and wrote about Jesus . . . his courage was awe-inspiring. He served the truth as he saw it – but always from a Jesus centred base.

Colin Evans, in the same paper, described him as 'far ahead of his time. . . . He dealt fearlessly with the worries of modern man actually attempting to answer the questions people were asking, instead of just positing those they weren't.' Dr. Ernest Payne, in the *Baptist Times,* recalling the remarkable ministries of Weatherhead, Soper and Sangster in London during the Second World War, wrote,

Their contribution to the maintenance of the courage and morale of the metropolis was a very great one. . . . Not all his fellow Christians passed under Dr. Weatherhead's spell, accepted all his New Testament interpretations or approved his interest in spiritualism, but that does not lessen our gratitude to God for one of the outstanding preachers of our time.

The Methodist Recorder tributes ran through several weeks. Its leader column described him as 'a preacher of the first rank' and expressed 'our admiration and gratitude for the distinguished ministry of a superb craftsman and good friend. Many of an older generation of Methodists still wistfully speculate on what might have happened if Leslie had been allowed to accept the invitation to Wesley's Chapel.' Donald Soper said:

By any standard of greatness (and one which specially appeals to me is that of "comprehensive goodness") Dr. Weatherhead was a great man . . . he commanded "eminence with words" and he splendidly compressed it in a blend of simple, muscular language, deep-felt religious conviction, oratorical skill, and that additional quality which belongs to genius and is indefinable.

To William Kyle, he was simply 'the greatest human being I have known'. John Crowlesmith, dealing with Weatherhead's influence on the revival of the healing ministry in all the churches, wrote, 'Today the new ecumenical movement towards Christian Healing owes him a great debt. He may rightly be called the Father of its present development.' Harold Roberts, recalling being impressed by him in his Manchester days, described his preaching as 'inimitable', adding, 'The secret of his ministry cannot be understood apart from a recognition of the extent to which he cared about prayer.'

A private family funeral, conducted by his friends Harry Facer and Edmund Heddle, was held in Bexhill, and they also conducted a memorial service there. Weatherhead had left very careful and detailed instructions with Kenneth Slack for a service of Thanksgiving at the City Temple. These included a request that

I should like my ashes to rest under or behind a stone at the foot of the Cross in the chancel of the City Temple with the words: 'Here lie the ashes of Leslie D. Weatherhead. He loved the City Temple and was its minister from 1936-1960.'

This apparently simple request was the cause of a protracted correspondence and argument between the church and Weatherhead's friend and executor, Norman French. The Elders and the new minister, a South African, Brian Johanson, who was inducted on 11 May, were opposed to an easily visible plaque on the grounds that Weatherhead himself had been against memorials in the church, and they did not want the chancel to become a 'shrine to Leslie Weatherhead.' There was also some debate on architectural grounds that the apse was not sufficiently deep to provide enough room for the ashes to be interred there. The dispute became acrimonious and led to French resigning his membership of the church.

At Weatherhead's request, the service on 29 January was conducted by Kenneth Slack, who also gave the address. The prayers were led by Donald Soper. In his address Slack referred to Weatherhead's ministry at the City Temple and his genuine pride at standing in the succession of ministers there. 'In a line of giants like Joseph Parker, R.J. Campbell and F.W. Norwood he stood out as great or greater than any . . . his fame – because of his writing – became more world-wide than any of his predecessors.' This he had achieved 'in an age which was no longer the age of the preacher.' The whole of Weatherhead's ministry had been in times of exceptional stress, from his chaplaincy in the First World War, through the depression years, to the London blitz in the Second, and the post-war period of re-building and reconstruction. Though he

believed in the relevance of the Gospel to society as a whole' his 'all-absorbing, passionate interest was in men and women in their personal lives.' 'He was no theologian . . . and had a real distrust of dogma. . . . But he had a real grip on the heart of our Faith . . . that it is above all else faith in a Person. . . . Many of the loveliest and most deeply felt passages in his books are in fact descriptions of Jesus, what he is and what he did and what he can do . . . he was a man moreover with less than the usual number of skins, unduly raw to the rubs of life, over-sensitive to its harshnesses and cruelties. . . . [In his preaching,] he didn't orate; he had no trumpet tones of rhetoric. . . . But he had a remarkable range of persuasion over a congregation that could sweep in a moment from laughter to tears, from the lightest of touches to the deep swell of emotion, from the most human of anecdotes to the most compelling descriptions of some biblical scene. . . . But . . . he was indescribable. There were far better scholars in the pulpit than he was . . . far more remarkable orators. . . . There were possibly – though this is far more doubtful – men of equal psychological penetration. . . . But what none of them had – and he had with unique power – was the ability to make every man and woman feel that what was being said was being spoken to their individual mind and heart.

Throughout the service, a casket containing Weatherhead's ashes had been standing on the communion table. After the singing of a hymn, Slack spoke the words of committal, and placed the ashes into a niche in the wall of the apse, at the foot of the cross beneath which Weatherhead had so often knelt, and where he had asked for his mortal remains to lie.

1. Letter, to Travell, 1 April 1966.

2. Interview with Lynne Price, 9 April 1992.
3. *From Sunday to Sunday, op. cit.*, p.130.
4. Letter to Travell 20 March 1969.
5. Letter to Travell 8 January 1970.
6. Letter to Travell 19 October 1970.
7. Letter to Travell 7 May 1971.
8. Letter to Travell 7 May 1971.
9. The *Methodist Recorder* 15 January 1976.
10. Letter to Travell 22 October 1975.
11. *ibid.*
12. K. Weatherhead, *Leslie Weatherhead, A Personal Portrait,* (H & S) p.221.

27. ENVOI

On a Sunday in October, 1993, a large congregation gathered at Wesley's Chapel in London for a service to commemorate the centenary of the birth of Leslie Dixon Weatherhead. This was an appropriate place for such a service to be held, since it was where his parents had first met and married, and where, as a tiny child, he had first been taken to worship.

Friends and admirers came from all over the United Kingdom, as well as from Canada, Australia and the United States. Weatherhead's three children were there: his sons came with their families from America, and his daughter Margaret from her home near London.

Professor Dixon Weatherhead, looking and sounding remarkably like his father, read a lesson from St. Paul's letter to the Romans, chapter 8. The address was given by a former President of the Methodist Conference, Dr. Colin Morris, well-known as a distinguished preacher and broadcaster.

Saying, 'I yield to no-one in my admiration for him', Morris spoke about the impact Weatherhead had made on him personally, as theologian, pastor, prophet and preacher. Talking about his remarkable personality, he described him as 'debonair: wit, eloquence, courtesy, handsome, always this serene confidence in the presence of God.' Commenting on the criticisms of Weatherhead as lacking a sound and systematic theology, Morris said,

> I would gauge that Leslie Weatherhead as a theologian did more to shape and help the theology of ordinary Christians throughout many decades of this century than all the great theological names put together.
>
> If there is one lesson that he has taught us, it is that if theology is too complicated or too abstruse to be converted into sermonic form, then it is irrelevant. . . He tackled the big, the difficult theological subjects . . . he wrestled with them and translated them into a language which ordinary Christians could understand.
>
> The kind of pastoral techniques and practices, which theological students of our day take totally for granted, Leslie Weatherhead fought for sixty years ago, when it was believed that psychology was subversive of faith and that it would tend to foster moral anarchy.
>
> He brought to bear on Christian doctrine, sanctified common sense, intellectual honesty, and vast pastoral experience. . . . He had no intellectual pride at stake, his only concern was to make God real, to change people's lives.

The interest in this centenary service and in the writing of this book, brought letters from all over the world, from people whose lives had been significantly influenced by Weatherhead's preaching and books, and who were eager to share their memories of him. A member of the United Church of Canada recalled meeting him in Toronto, and said, 'his books did much to make Jesus come alive in my life and I feel I owe a great debt to him.' A retired Methodist minister, now living in Portugal, wrote to say how he had first come under the spell of Leslie Weatherhead during the latter part of the 1920s, when, a student at Leeds University, he would join the queues at 5.30 for the 6.30 evening service at Brunswick. An American pastor from Alaska spoke of the deep impact that Weatherhead's writings had upon his ministry:

> his small book, *The Will of God* kept me in the ministry in my early years. As I dealt with parish personal tragedies, the reaction of thinking that somehow God was behind the tragedy was really turning me off God. Reading his book helped me to know that it was possible to look at reality in a new and fresh way.

A former President of the Methodist Conference said 'he has had a greater influence on my ministry than any other minister, or indeed, any other person.' A retired Baptist minister recounted the effect that reading Weatherhead's books such as *Discipleship* had on him, and the impact of his personality when they met: 'one recalls his humour, his conversational style of preaching which came over so personally, the clarity of his sermons and books and his deep devotion to Jesus Christ. My wife and I are so thankful to God for him.' Several letters came from people in Australia who vividly remembered the impact of his visit there in 1951.

> Listening to him was sheer magic. For the first time in my life the Christian faith came alive. He had a charming presence, a beautiful face and voice, and a capacity to make Jesus's teaching relevant to us in the here and now. . . . He was indeed God speaking to us at that time and thus was one of the very great influences on my life.'

The Rev. Harry Facer, who had been Weatherhead's own minister during his retirement years in Bexhill, recalled that as a teenager, he had been greatly helped and encouraged by his Christ-centred preaching and writings. 'In his preaching it always seemed to me that he had been talking to Jesus a few minutes earlier.' A woman in Nottingham, who shared cherished memories of his ministry, wrote 'He made Jesus so real to so many of us and memories such as these, and all he gave us through his preaching and living, still have the power to sustain us today.' Another former member of the City Temple also found that through his writing he was still speaking with a relevant voice:

> We were so privileged to have had Leslie's influence - the inspiration that one got week by week. . . . One has had many influences in life since the days when he was around, but whenever I go back to the books I'm surprised by how resonant they still are, how much I still find helpful.

Although it is now thirty years since Weatherhead preached his last sermon, such memories of the inspiration of his preaching and the impact of his personality keep his influence alive in the lives of those who recall with gratitude to God the difference his life and teaching made to them. The fact that several of his books are still in print, in America and in this country, means that he is still a living influence on the lives of those who discover him in the present generation, too young to have heard him for themselves.

In 1989, for example, Weatherhead's *The Transforming Friendship* was picked up and read by Dr. Lynne Price, who was looking for a short devotional book to read. At the time she was engaged on research in interfaith encounter and dialogue from a Methodist perspective. The book so impressed her that she decided to discover more about him. She was further impressed by his undogmatic approach to religion and his remarkable success as an evangelist. This led her to make Weatherhead's approach to mission and evangelism the subject of her doctoral research, subsequently published as *Faithful Uncertainty* (1996). Lynne

Price demonstrates that far from being outdated, Weatherhead's writing and approach to evangelism are now being appreciated afresh, as having a particular relevance and practical value for today. Her research shows that he anticipated much that is now current in evangelical methodology and theological ideas. Price states that 'The common processes of the emerging theologies of the last twenty-five years or so (Liberation, Feminist, Interfaith, Process, Asian, Black)' which she describes as 'identification', 'dialogue', 'the validation of personal experience' and 'the recognition of the need for religion in every day life', were articulated by Weatherhead. She suggests that he remains a model for contemporary mission in Britain.

Leslie Weatherhead believed intensely in the necessity of God, in the reality of the transforming friendship of Jesus Christ, in the pursuit of truth, and in the will of God for the ultimate salvation of every individual. Through his preaching and writing he conveyed these ideas with remarkable power and success for nearly five decades to many thousands of people throughout this country and abroad. Any adequate account of the Free Churches during the first two-thirds of the twentieth century, of the changing appeal of popular preaching, of the development of pastoral psychology and the healing ministry, of the changing social and religious attitudes to sex, of the growth of interest in 'complementary' or 'alternative' medicine, of popular religious and devotional literature, of religious broadcasting, and of attempts to engage in debate with the religiously doubtful and disaffected, must include some reference to Weatherhead.

His friend, Professor James Stewart, called him, 'God's great gift to the Church.' In an interview with Lynne Price, another friend, Dr. Donald Soper said of him,

Weatherhead is an enduring person, that is to say people will be continually coming back to him whereas some are forgotten. I think he has a place
in the history books whereas others only have a fly leaf.

Weatherhead's two most distinctive qualities, his intense love of people and his passion for truth and interest in new ideas, would have made him outstanding at any time. Since human nature remains much the same in every generation, in any age he would always be able to speak to its innermost need and condition, as is evident from the continuing popularity of such books as *The Will of God* and *The Christian Agnostic*. At the end of his very first book, *After Death*, he wrote: 'through every activity of life the only thing that matters is that we should allow the life of the ages [by which he meant the quality and power of the life of Jesus] to express itself, and that we should infect with it the lives which, from day to day, we touch.'

It is because he did this through his preaching and writing so remarkably and with such success during many decades of the twentieth century that there are thousands still, all over the world, who hold his memory in the greatest affection and regard, and why, even in a much changed world, his words are able to excite, challenge and influence those who still read them today.

CONCLUSION

For fifty years, from the mid 1920s to the end of his life in 1976, Leslie Weatherhead attracted publicity and comment. His extraordinary success in drawing large crowds to hear him whenever he preached or spoke aroused a curiosity which led to many published articles describing his personality and style and attempting to analyse his 'secret.' I have made use of these throughout since they show how his contemporaries saw him, and provide the most accurate record of the impression he made on them.

The approach of this study is chronological rather than thematic, since this shows how Weatherhead's ministry developed from his background in a nineteenth-century Wesleyan Methodist family and was influenced by his interest in psychology and healing, and his experiences in India and in two world wars. He had an extraordinary ability to sense and respond to the concerns of ordinary people and to changing social attitudes, especially as these were affected by the 'new psychology' (of which he was an influential populariser) and the widespread doubt and disillusionment with religion which followed the First World War.

Leslie Weatherhead stood in the tradition of the Free Church, and especially Methodist ministry, in which preaching was at the centre of worship. This was a consequence of the Protestant Reformation when the authority of the Holy Catholic Church was replaced by that of Holy Scripture as the revealed Word of God. The development of critical scholarship during the nineteenth century, which cast doubt on the literal interpretation of the Bible as a basis for Christian truth, served to undermine the authority of the pulpit, which was further challenged by the mistrust of the claims of authority following the First World War.

The search for a reliable source of Christian truth led to a new interest in the historical Jesus, with books like Schweitzer's The Quest of the Historical Jesus (1910), Fosdick's The Manhood of the Master (1914) and Glover's The Jesus of History (1917) – books which were cherished by Weatherhead, who turned for authority to the person of Jesus as the one whose life most truly revealed God, and provided a standard and guide for human life. Weatherhead frequently said that the Bible (and by implication, all other claims to religious truth and moral authority) should be judged by Jesus and not Jesus by the Bible. As a result, his use of the Bible was selective. Even words attributed to Jesus in the New Testament could be discounted if they did not accord with the character of Jesus as Weatherhead understood it. He did not, for example, believe that Jesus ever said what St. John's Gospel (chapter 14 verse 6) reports him as saying, 'no one comes to the Father except by me.' In books such as The Transforming Friendship (1928), Jesus and Ourselves (1930) and His Life and Ours (1932) he presented a romanticised, even a Boys Own Paper picture of Jesus as a great captain, hero and leader, who called his followers to adventure, and was available to every individual as guide, companion and friend.

Weatherhead coupled this presentation of Jesus as the source of Christian truth with the assertion that truth had to be perceived, not merely received. All truth that mattered had to be recognised at first-hand. No statement of doctrine by Pope or preacher needed to be believed or accepted as true unless the individual 'felt it in his ductless glands.' Weatherhead therefore set aside the authority of both Church and Bible, freeing himself to preach ideas from any source which were attractive and convincing to him, measured only by his understanding of the truth as he interpreted it in the life and and personality of Jesus. His book, *After Death* (1923) led to his arraignment for heresy before the Methodist Conference. Although he was acquitted, he was frequently accused of not conforming to Methodist doctrine. Unlike W.E. Sangster, he rarely preached doctrinal sermons, and when he became minister of the Congregational City Temple, had no obligation to do so. His oft repeated statement that 'no-one was ever converted by a sermon on the Trinity' indicates his preaching aims as well as his theological limitations.

Weatherhead's insistence on the right of people to think for themselves and only to accept as true those things which they found convincing was liberating to those who flocked to hear him and was a major part of his appeal, since it freed them from the necessity to accept everything the Church taught, regardless of their difficulties and doubts. But Weatherhead's approach could seem dangerously subjective, as became evident in his last major work, *The Christian Agnostic* (1965). This reveals his attitude to truth and authority at its most uninhibited.

The reactions of the orthodox to *After Death* also made Weatherhead less impressed with academic theology. He concluded that the theologians were always fifty years behind the poets, and that they did not deal with the problems which worried ordinary people. (He was delighted when I sent him Stevie Smith's poem, 'How do you see?', published in the *Guardian* (16 May 1964) which he quotes appreciatively in *The Christian Agnostic* [pp.70, 244, 249] as it expressed his own frustration with Christianity's unanswered questions.) Thereafter he was less interested in what contemporary theologians were saying. In *The Christian Agnostic*, while he quotes many authorities in support of his views, he offers few theological guides to his readers other than himself. As a preacher, he was more interested in the lives of Christians than in their theology: it was the German theologian Dietrich Bonhoeffer's courage in opposing Hitler rather than his Christology that appealed to him.

Weatherhead belonged to a liberal tradition which he continued to preach successfully long after it was generally considered outmoded. In his book, *The Living of These Days* (1957), H.E. Fosdick, the foremost exponent of this tradition in America, and an important influence on Weatherhead, accepted the criticisms of this theology that –

There were distortions of perspective, lack of depth, oversimplification, too complaisant optimism, too easy surrender to current categories of modern thought. [p.66]

Weatherhead's preaching was not immune from these defects, but Fosdick's defence of liberalism also applies:

Of course it left out dimensions in Christian faith which would need to be rediscovered! Despite that, however, it offered to a generation of earnest youth the only chance they had to be honest while being Christian . . . the revolt . . . was in the interest of a deeper, more vital, more transforming Christian experience than literalism, legalism and authoritarianism could supply. [*ibid*]

During the first half of this century, serious Bible study lapsed in many churches. Weatherhead most often preached on a biblical theme, but his approach was imaginative and inspirational rather than academic. The questions discussed at the Friday Fellowship and Community Evening groups at the City Temple reflected Weatherhead's own preoccupations, and were mainly to do with intellectual difficulties of belief and problems of Christian living, with almost no Bible study.

Weatherhead's appeal was mainly to intelligent office workers, students, teachers, nurses and professional people, although there were some working-class members in his churches and he was proud of the wide social mix of his congregations. He was not primarily concerned with social justice, the inequalities in society, or with poverty and homelessness, although he did care about these things. He was more concerned with the practical problems of individuals, their psychological adjustments, relationships, ability to cope with suffering and tragedy, their perplexities over the meaning of life, their anxieties and aims, their religious questions and doubts and their relationship with God. He sought to give rational, 'common sense' answers to difficulties of belief, and to remove obstacles and obscurity. He attacked orthodoxy, ancient creeds and biblical fundamentalism which he believed put unnecessary difficulties in the way of belief, and he aroused hostility and criticism from those for whom these things were precious.

His writing about psychology, and particularly *The Mastery of Sex Through Psychology and Religion* (1931), which gained him a world-wide reputation, also offended more conservative Christians. His use of hypnotism, his interest in spiritualism and psychic research, in unorthodox methods of healing and in euthanasia and reincarnation made him appear eccentric, and even gullible, and made his judgment suspect to many. In the 1960s, his 'Nation in Danger' speeches and articles attracted some ridicule, particularly as some of his statistics and stories of teenage sexual behaviour were of doubtful origin.

His most significant work, *Psychology, Religion and Healing* (1951), established his reputation as perhaps the world's foremost authority on all non-physical methods of healing, and played a considerable part in the revival of the healing ministry in churches of all denominations. Although his theology was criticised and his arguments from the evidence of spiritualism and the paranormal were not acceptable to many, the book was acknowledged as a seminal work, the most authoritative and comprehensive yet produced, and became an essential study for those interested in this field for the next thirty years.

His last major work, *The Christian Agnostic,* attracted some of the most serious criticism and sharply divided his critics from his admirers. The book was intended to encourage those with doubts about religion to follow their own insights in arriving at religious truth. In doing so he presented his own ideas and speculations which took little account of current trends in theology or of the leading contemporary theologians. In 1977, Professor William Strawson, in a lecture on 'The Significance of the Rev. Dr. Leslie Dixon Weatherhead as a Preacher', criticised the book as failing to achieve its objects because it was aimed at the wrong questions, and answered the difficulties felt acutely in the pre-war and immediate post-war period, which were no longer real issues. Academic theology had moved on to other matters, as shown by *Honest to God*. But if Weatherhead appeared out of touch with the universities, he still knew his own readers. His book was (as another critic described it) 'a genuine lay theology', and was welcomed as such by those who bought it in considerable numbers and who continue to do so (it remains in print); and it appears to have a fresh relevance in the eyes of the 'new age' seekers after religious truth.

Although he came from a structured and hierarchical church tradition, Weatherhead cannot be fitted easily into the picture of the mainstream churches during the decades in which he was active. When churches in general were losing their congregations, he continued to draw large crowds. He was a superb communicator, with an exceptional personality, and like Spurgeon and Parker, attracted some to hear him who were more interested in the style than the content of his preaching. Apart from his year as President of the Methodist Conference he held no administrative office, and was not involved in church politics. He pursued his interests in psychology and Christian healing in the main independently of official church bodies. He took a keen interest in Church unity, and often spoke in favour of it, but apart from his Presidency, when the Anglican-Methodist Conversations began, played no active part in ecumenical affairs. Theological and denominational differences meant little to him, and he was impatient with debates which attempted to find a consensus on doctrine.

The Methodist historian, Norman Goldhawk, says that traditional Methodist piety was made up of three elements: an urge to holiness, an evangelical missionary impulse, and an adherence to a distinctive church order. For Weatherhead the first of these, influenced by evolutionary theory and the new psychology, became interpreted as 'the soul's urge to completeness.' He was keenly missionary, committed to pressing the claims of Christ at every opportunity. His adherence to Methodism, though strong, was sentimental and fraternal rather than theological and doctrinal. He was less willing than his friend W.E. Sangster to defer to Methodist authorities. Accepting the ministry of the Congregational City Temple led some of his fellow Methodists to accuse him of deserting Methodism, but his church origin was evident in the emotional warmth of his preaching and his emphasis on experience.

Weatherhead's career was that of an exceptional individual who, although clearly belonging to the Methodist tradition, was unrepresentative of his denomination as a whole. If his critics were many, he also attracted many people of all denominations and none, through the extraordinary appeal of his personality and the persuasive power of his preaching. Especially attractive was the devotional context of the worship he led, which combined dignity and reverence with an atmosphere of warm friendliness and humour, and yet conveyed a powerful sense of spiritual reality. He was exceptionally successful in persuading thousands of the reasonableness of the Christian faith and in influencing many to enter the Christian ministry. Paying tribute to him in an article in the *British Weekly* (16 September 1965) to mark the fiftieth anniversary of Weatherhead's ordination, Principal Charles Duthie said:

In the thirties and again after the Second World War I was often struck by the fact that Leslie Weatherhead's books figured more prominently than any other man's in the list given by young men presenting themselves as candidates for the Christian ministry. It was clear that he had helped them decisively on their way.

When Weatherhead is compared with his contemporaries in the areas in which he was most well-known: in pastoral counselling and psychology with Norman Vincent Peale, Harry Guntrip or J.G. McKenzie; in his contribution to the debate on religion, sex and morals with Maude Royden and Herbert Gray; in his published books of sermons with Fosdick or Sangster; in broadcasting with Dick Sheppard and Donald Soper; in his books on the problem of suffering and pain with C.S. Lewis; in his approach to the difficulties of belief with John Robinson, Nathaniel Micklem or H.A. Williams; in the revival of the Church's healing ministry, and in the investigation of all non-physical methods of healing, then he is not only being measured with the leading figures in each of these fields, but even when such comparisons are made to his disadvantage, they demonstrate the extraordinary range of his industry and the remarkable scope of his ministry.

The last three decades of this century have seen a sharp decline in the fortunes of all the English Churches, and the Free Churches most of all. Those who began the century full of confidence, numerically strong, with the power to sway governments, are now largely ignored and disregarded by the mass media and treated as of little or no importance in the life of the nation. Mass immigration from Commonwealth countries has brought to England a wider choice of religion. Hinduism, Buddhism, and above all, Islam, have attracted adherents from those who in earlier times would have found their spiritual homes among the churches. There are now more Muslims in England than Methodists. Congregationalism, so strong at the beginning of the century, experienced its greatest loss after the First World War, with the fall of the Liberal Party, with which it was too closely identified. In 1972, two-thirds of the Congregational churches voted to join with the Presbyterians to form the United Reformed Church, which resulted in a new denomination actually smaller than the previous two bodies had been when they were separate. Membership of the URC has fallen steadily ever since. Congregationalism survives mainly in two small bodies, the Evangelical Fellowship of Congregational Churches, and the Congregational Federation. With the death of Lord Soper, who died while this book was being produced, in an age of 'celebrities' there is now not a single Free Church personality recognisable to the general public.

After his death Weatherhead became a neglected figure. He was the most widely known, popular and successful preacher of his day, yet no ministerial training colleges in England appear to have recommended him to their students as an example to study and copy. Weatherhead stood outside denominational structures. He was an exceptional individual, whose most distinguished ministry was in an independent, self-governing church which, although it belonged to the Congregational Union (and, after 1972, the URC), he proudly declared to be 'supra-denominational'. Although, especially during the 1930s and 1940s, he attracted many imitators, the old criticisms of him and his preaching style continued to be made, and even his great popularity was held against him. His use of psychology, his personal anecdotes, his irrepressible sense of humour, his references to sex, the accusation that he over-simplified and sentimentalised the gospel, his dismissal of parts of the Bible as incompatible with the teaching of Jesus, his undogmatic, open-ended attitude to religious truth, did not endear him to those who taught homiletics in theological colleges, in spite of his brilliance as a communicator. The academic revival of evangelical theology and biblical conservatism also meant that there was no place for Weatherhead in such circles. His liberal theology was considered out-moded and out of touch.

This neglect of Weatherhead must also be seen as part of the general loss of faith in preaching which had been taking place over many years, even in the Free Churches. Weatherhead was the supremely successful practitioner of an art form which, by the time he died, had generally lost its appeal. Busy ministers no longer considered several hours each day spent in sermon preparation as the best use of their time. Preaching, no longer regarded as a central act of worship, was discussed only as an out-dated and not very effective method of teaching Christian doctrine. Many within the churches were arguing the case for more modern methods of communication. It was said that the attention span of modern audiences was only a few minutes, and, through the influence of television, was visual rather than verbal. In 1967, a Canadian sociologist, Marshall McLuhan, proclaimed, 'The medium is the message'. Churches strove to be up-to-date in their attempts to hold and build their congregations. Film and overhead projectors, cassette recordings, flannel graphs, drama, dialogue and discussion were all held to be superior to a man speaking from a pulpit, 'six feet above contradiction.' The Free Churches, as they sought the goal of Christian unity, became more sacramental. Holy Communion began to take a more integrated and regular place in worship, and preaching tended to be reduced to a short homily preparing worshippers for the sacrament. In this climate, it is not surprising that Weatherhead's name was rarely mentioned in theological colleges.

The fortunes of the City Temple have declined. The kind of media interest that reported the appointment of Leonard Griffith or Kenneth Slack to its pulpit has long gone. Even among the Free Churches it is no longer regarded as the most internationally famous and prominent Free Church in the land. From the time of the ministry of Brian Johanson, inducted just four months after Weatherhead's death, the leadership of the church was steadily taken over by those of a different (and more conservative) theological persuasion, and most of those who had been drawn to the City Temple by Weatherhead's ministry gradually fell away.

Although Weatherhead's bust still stands beside that of Joseph Parker in the entrance to the church, ten years after his death, the City Temple was being run by a group of young, earnest evangelicals, with no interest in the history of the church, who actively disapproved of Weatherhead, not only regarding him as a heretic, but even as not a Christian, because of his views on the Virgin Birth, his rejection of substitutionary theories of the Atonement, and his interest in spiritualism. In 1986 they planned a service to mark the first anniversary of the death of the charismatic Anglican, David Watson. When they were approached that same year to hold a similar service of commemoration to mark the tenth anniversary of Weatherhead's death they refused, saying that the church should be looking to the future and not back at the past. The minister of the Westminster Central Hall, Dr. John Tudor, was more welcoming, and a memorable service and seminar commemorating Weatherhead's ministry was held there instead.

Happily the situation is changing. The present incumbent of the City Temple, Dr. David Hilborn, a conservative evangelical but also an historian, is more sympathetic and ready to acknowledge Weatherhead's achievements and the debt that the church owes to him. In September 1997, on the initiative of a former consultant of the Psychological Clinic, Dr. David Common, the City Temple hosted a well attended and very successful conference with the theme: 'Leslie Weatherhead: A Voice for Today?'

In the United States of America Weatherhead has continued to be appreciated, even in academic circles (perhaps because success is more admired there), and been the subject of some post-graduate research. As early as 1959, Harry Alonzo Shuster presented a dissertation to the Temple University, Philadelphia with the title: 'Preaching to meet human needs: a study of the sermons of Dr. Leslie D. Weatherhead.' This, with Stephen Odum's 1985 Ph.D. dissertation for the Southern Baptist Theological Seminary: 'Identification as a Key to Effectiveness in the Preaching of Leslie Weatherhead' indicates a desire to understand the reason for his remarkable popularity and to learn from it. A black American theologian, Henry H. Mitchell, in a book calling for *The Recovery of Preaching* published in America in 1977, argues the case for the effective use of imagination in the interpretation of Bible stories, and gives particular praise to Weatherhead's *Personalities of the Passion* saying that more such books are needed.

Popular culture has now come to accept to a remarkable extent many of the things which interested Weatherhead but which in his day were regarded as peculiar and strange. This is particularly so with what is now known as 'alternative' or 'complimentary' medicine. Unorthodox practitioners have established clinics for an extraordinary range of therapies and treatments in every town. In 1993, Exeter University appointed the first Professor of Complimentary Medicine, and the *Guardian* reported (21 July 1998) that according to surveys, up to 40% of G.P.s are happy to refer patients to complimentary therapists. The concept of 'holistic' medicine – treating the patient as a whole personality – which Weatherhead argued for and sought to establish in his City Temple Psychological Clinic, is now generally accepted. Healing services with intercessory prayers for individuals and the laying on of hands are now part of the regular pastoral ministry of many churches in all denominations.

It is tempting to speculate how Weatherhead might have related to the religious scene as it is in the closing years of the twentieth century. He would welcome the new interest in preaching demonstrated by the 'Preacher of the Year' competition. He would have rejoiced at the modern charismatic movement's ability to attract young people, and that it shares his belief that at the heart of Christianity is a personal relationship with Jesus Christ – although neither its music nor its conservative theology would have been to his taste. There can be little doubt that he would have been much more in tune with the current religious trends in society outside the mainstream churches than most of the clergy are today. He was always eager to enter into discussion with members of other faiths and would have responded to the challenge of their presence in such numbers in this country, and welcomed the religious insights they have brought with them, while welcoming every opportunity to press the claims of Christ to them. All his life he attacked religious fundamentalism, and would have been greatly concerned about its current revival in all religions, regarding it as the greatest obstacle to progress in the exploration of religious truth. He would have recognised the growth of interest in the supernatural, as indicated by the popularity and number of television programmes devoted to the subject, and continued to press for psychic phenomena to be taken seriously, and for rigorous scientific testing of the evidence. As a psychologist as well as a minister he would have been fascinated by the search for spiritual enlightenment of those involved in all the different manifestations of the 'new age' movement. He always encouraged individuals to explore religious ideas for themselves, and only to accept as true what they found personally convincing. *The Christian Agnostic* is evidence that he would have been well equipped and ready to engage with tolerance, understanding and sympathy in dialogue with these 'new age' seekers after religious truth.

In an article for the *Expository Times* (April 1995) Martin Camroux says,
Growing up in a liberal Congregational Church in the late 1950s Leslie Weatherhead seemed an awesome figure. People bought his books, talked of the occasions when they had heard him preach, and frequently re-used his sermons and illustrations. What Fosdick was to America, Weatherhead was to England'.

In her researches into Weatherhead's ministry and influence, Lynne Price found that,
mention of Weatherhead's name to a variety of Christians of all ages and denominations, and also non-church attenders, met with recognition, affirmation and, often, enthusiasm. They knew people who had been helped by his psychological counselling, had read *The Christian Agnostic* and continued on their Christian journeys, or had been helped to make important life decisions through hearing his broadcast talks.

This has been my experience also. I began my own research out of a deep sense of gratitude and obligation to Leslie Weatherhead for his personal kindness to me, and for his ministry, which has been one of the major influences on my life. It has been a considerable joy to recall those crowded, deeply moving and inspiring services at Marylebone and Holborn Viaduct, to be in touch again with old City Temple friends and acquaintances, and to relive with them the precious memories we share. My appreciation of his remarkable ministry and admiration for his achievements has been greatly increased through the letters I have received from all over the world from so many people eager to seize the opportunity to tell how much this man meant to them. Through him, countless numbers have been encouraged and liberated to explore the ultimate truths of religion, to discover the practical realism of the Christian faith in their daily lives and, most precious of all, to know the 'transforming friendship' of Jesus Christ for themselves.

BIBLIOGRAPHY

Archive and Library Sources

The Weatherhead Archive at the University of Birmingham
The City Temple
The Methodist Missionary Society
The Wesley Historical Society
The British Council of Churches
The Leeds Record Office
The Leeds Local History Library
Dr. Williams Library
The British Newspaper Library
Dr. Weatherhead's personal files, papers and documents in my possession. These include Weatherhead's correspondence with Raynor Johnson and private letters relating to his books, in particular, *The Christian Agnostic*, as well as my own correspondence with him.

Unpublished university research documents

J.J.W. Edmondson: 'The Doctrines of Hell and Judgment and the need for personal conversion as an index to the development of liberal theology within the theological colleges of the Methodist Church in England from 1907 to 1932.' M.A. thesis, Durham, 1990.
Eric Lord: 'English Protestant Religion in the 1940s' M.Phil. dissertation, Sheffield 1993.
Stephen Odum: 'Identification as a Key to Effectiveness in the Preaching of Leslie Dixon Weatherhead'. Ph.D. dissertation, Southern Baptist Theological Seminary, 1985.
John Handby Thompson: 'The Free Church Army Chaplain 1830-1930' Ph.D. dissertation, Sheffield, 1990.

Books by Leslie Weatherhead

After Death (James Clarke 1923)
The Old Testament and Today [with J. A. Chapman] (Epworth 1923)
Coming to Christ in Modern Days [FK Pamphlet] (Epworth 1927)
The Transforming Friendship (Epworth 1928)
The Afterworld of the Poets (Epworth 1929)
Psychology in Service of the Soul (Epworth 1929)
Can We Really Find Jesus Today? [Broadcast Talk] (Epworth 1930)
The Presence of Jesus [FK Pamphlet] (Epworth 1930)
Jesus and Ourselves (Epworth 1930)
Every Man's Hour of Destiny [Broadcast Talk] (Epworth 1931)
The Church and the New Order [Broadcast Talk] (Epworth 1931)
The Mastery of Sex Through Psychology and Religion (S.C.M. 1931)
Every Man's Hour of Destiny [Broadcast Talk] (Epworth 1931)
The Guarded Universe (H. & S. 1932)
His Life and Ours (H. & S. 1932)
Jesus of Nazareth, King! [Broadcast Talk] (Epworth 1932)
Pain and Providence [Broadcast Talk] (Epworth 1932)
The Strength of Christian Confidence [Broadcast Talk] (Epworth 1932)

Pain and Providence [FK Pamphlet] (Epworth 1932)
Individual Happiness (Epworth 1933)
Discipleship (S.C.M. 1934)
Psychology and Life (H. & S. 1934)
Why Do Men Suffer? (S.C.M. 1935)
Fellowship in God's Family [Broadcast Talk] (Epworth 1935)
In the Place Where He Was Crucified [Broadcast Talk] (Epworth 1935)
The Power of God [Broadcast Talk] (Epworth 1935)
It Happened in Palestine (H. & S. 1936)
Ten Minutes a Day for Health's Sake [Broadcast Talk] (Epworth 1936)
The Inescapable God [Broadcast Talk] (Epworth 1936)
A Shepherd Remembers (Epworth 1937)
Sacrament of Nature's Beauty [Broadcast Talk] (Epworth 1937)
Think Before You Fight [Broadcast Talk] (Epworth 1938)
The Eternal Voice (S.C.M. 1939)
Prayer in Wartime [Broadcast Talk] (Epworth 1939)
Things Which Cannot Be Shaken (with others) (1939)
Thinking Aloud in Wartime (H. & S. 1939)
This is the Victory (H. & S. 1940)
The World's A Stage [Broadcast Talk] (Epworth 1940)
Is It Courage We Need? [pamphlet] (H. & S. 1940)
Guarding Our Sunday [pamphlet] (H. & S. 1941)
The Significance of Advent [Broadcast Talk] (Epworth 1941)
Rebuilding the Temple (City Temple 1941)
International Christianity [Broadcast Talk] (Epworth 1942)
Personalities of the Passion (H. & S. 1942)
In Quest of a Kingdom (H. & S. 1943)
How Can I Find God? (H. & S. 1943)
The Will of God (Epworth 1944)
A Plain Man Looks at the Cross (Independent Press 1945)
The Significance of Silence (Epworth 1945)
Healing Through Prayer [pamphlet] (Epworth 1947)
When the Lamp Flickers (H. & S. 1948)
The Holy Land (St. Hugh's Press 1948)
The Resurrection and the Life (Epworth 1948)
Psychology, Religion and Healing (H. & S. 1951)
'Really Mr. Hoyle' [pamphlet] (City Temple 1951)
That Immortal Sea (Epworth 1953)
Over His Own Signature (Epworth 1955)
Prescription for Anxiety (H. & S. 1956)
A Private House of Prayer (H. & S. 1958)
The Case for Reincarnation (Peto 1958)
The Resurrection of Christ (H. & S. 1959)
Key Next Door (H. & S. 1960)
Salute to a Sufferer (Epworth 1962)
Wounded Spirits (H. & S. 1962)
The Christian Agnostic (H. & S. 1965)
On Being a Minister (Lecture) (Selly Oak 1966)
Time for God (Lutterworth 1967)
Daily Readings from the works of Leslie D. Weatherhead (Ed. Frank Cumbers)
    (Epworth 1968)
Life Begins at Death (with Norman French) (Denholm 1969)
The Busy Man's Old Testament (Abingdon 1971)

Books, articles and papers about Leslie Weatherhead

M.F. Camroux: 'Liberalism Preached' articles on H.E Fosdick and Leslie Weatherhead for the *Expository Times* April 1995.
Christopher Maitland: *Dr. Leslie Weatherhead* (Cassell 1960)
Lynne Price: *Faithful Uncertainty* (Peter Lang 1996)
William Strawson: 'The Significance of the Rev. Leslie Dixon Weatherhead as a Preacher.' Unpublished lecture to the Lincolnshire Branch of the Wesley Historical Society, 17 May 1977.
Kingsley Weatherhead: *Leslie Weatherhead, A Personal Portrait* (H & S. 1975)

Also chapters in

Albert Clare: *The City Temple 1640-1940* (Independent Press 1940)
  The City Temple, Past, Present and Future (City Temple 1958)
Horton Davies: *Varieties of English Preaching 1900-1960.* (S.C.M. 1963)
Leonard Griffith: *From Sunday to Sunday – Fifty Years in the Pulpit* (Irwin 1987)
Raynor Johnson: *The Light and the Gate* (H. & S. 1964)
Kenneth Slack: *The City Temple 100 Years 1874-1974* (City Temple 1974)
W.J. Smart: *Miracles of Achievement* (Peter Davies 1961)
Sydney Walton (Ed.): *The League of Good Samaritans* (Leeds 1944)

Methodist and Church Histories

D. W. Bebbington: *The Nonconformist Conscience, Chapel and Politics 1870-1914* (Allen and Unwin 1982)
Clyde Binfield: *So Down to Prayers: Studies in English Nonconformity 1780-1920* (Dent 1977)
Kenneth Brown: *A Social History of the Nonconformist Ministry in England and Wales 1800-1930* (Oxford 1988)
Brunswick Chapel: Minutes of Leader's Meetings 1911-1945
  A Brief Statement of the Circumstances connected with the . . . dissension (1828)
  A Brief Account of the Church's History 1918-1952 Compiled by Three of its Members (1952)
  Centenary Booklet, compiled by A.E. Whitham (1925)
Ed. Board of the Fellowship of the Kingdom: *Quest and Crusade, The Story of a Spiritual Adventure* (Epworth 1939)
J. Wesley Bready: *England Before and After Wesley* (H. & S. 1938)
Barbara Bunce: *So Many Witnesses, The Story of the CFPSS.* (The Churches Fellowship for Psychical and Spiritual Studies 1993)
Herbert Butterfield: *Christianity and History* (Bell 1949)
Jeffrey Cox: *English Churches in a Secular Society, Lambeth 1870-1930* (OUP. 1982)
Frank H. Cumbers (ed.): *Richmond College 1843-1943.* (Epworth 1944)
Horton Davies: *The English Free Churches* (Oxford 1963)
Rupert E. Davies: *Methodism* (Penguin 1963)
  (ed) *A History of the Methodist Church in Great Britain Vols* 2-4 (Epworth 1978-88)
Christopher Driver: *A Future for the Free Churches?* (S.C.M. 1961)
Norman Dunning: *Samuel Chadwick* (H. & S. 1935)
David Edwards: *The Honest to God Debate* (S.C.M. 1963)
Sheila Fletcher: *Maude Royden: A Life* (Blackwell 1989)
George Fowler (Pub.): *London's Great White Pulpit* (1924)
Brian Frost: *Goodwill on Fire: Donald Soper's Life and Mission* (H. & S. 1996)

Alan D. Gilbert: *Religion and Society in Industrial England: Church, Chapel and Social Change 1740-1914* (Longman 1976)
  The Making of Post-Christian Britain (Longman 1980)
John W. Grant: *Free Churchmanship in England, 1870-1940* (Independent Press 1968)
James Hanby: *Old Times and New at Brunswick* (Leeds 1909)
Adrian Hastings: *A History of English Christianity 1920-1990* (S.C.M. 1991)
Silvester Horne: *A Popular History of the Free Churches* (Clarke 1903)
Dorothea Price Hughes: *The Life of Hugh Price Hughes, By His Daughter* (H. & S. 1905)
John Huxtable: *As It Seemed to Me* (URC 1990)
Daniel Jenkins: *The British, Their Identity and Their Religion* (S.C.M. 1975)
R. Tudur Jones: *Congregationalism in England 1662-1962* (Independent Press 1962)
E.K.H. Jordan: *Free Church Unity: History of the Free Church Council Movement 1896-1941* (Lutterworth 1956)
Stephen Koss: *Nonconformity in Modern British Politics* (Batsford 1975)
James Laver: *John Wesley* (Nelson 1932)
William H. Lax: *Lax of Poplar* (Epworth 1927)
Viscount Mackintosh: *By Faith and Work* (Hutchinson 1966)
Hugh McLeod: *Class and Religion in Late Victorian England* (Croom Helm 1974)
James Munson: *The Nonconformists* (SPCK 1991)
Iain H. Murray: *The Fight of Faith 1939-1981: David Martyn Lloyd Jones* (Banner of Truth Trust 1990)
E.R. Norman: *Church and Society in England 1770-1970* (Oxford 1976)
E.A. Payne: *The Free Church Tradition in the Life of England* (S.C.M. 1944)
Vera Phillips and Edwin Robertson: *J.B. Phillips, The Wounded Healer* (SPCK. 1984)
William Purcell: *Portrait of Soper* (Mowbrays 1972)
Ian M. Randall: *Quest, Crusade and Fellowship: The Spiritual Formation of the Fellowship of the Kingdom* (Bell 1995)
  'Southport and Swanwick: Contrasting Movements of Methodist Spirituality in Inter-War England.' Proceedings of the Wesley Historical Society, Vol. 50. Pt 1 February1995.
David Raw: *'Its Only Me' A Life of Theodore Bayley Hardy, V.C.* (Frank Peters 1988)
John Read: *Christ Church Jubilee Year Book* (Christ Church 1926)
Edith Riley Richards: *Private View of a Public Man, The Life of Layton Richards* (Allen and Unwin 1950)
Paul Sangster: *Doctor Sangster* (Epworth 1962)
  A History of the Free Churches (Heineman 1983)
Kenneth Slack: *The British Churches Today* (S.C.M. 1961)
Gerald Studdert-Kennedy: *Dog Collar Democracy: The Industrial Christian Fellowship 1919-1929* (Macmillan 1982)
John H. Taylor: *LCU Story 1873-1972.* (London Congregational Union 1972)
David M. Thompson: *Nonconformity in the 19th Century* (Kegan and Paul 1972)
Leslie Tizard (ed. H. Guntrip): *Facing Life and Death* (Allen and Unwin 1959)
Alec Vidler: *The Church in an Age of Revolution 1789 to the Present Day.* (Penguin 1961)
Gordon Wakefield: *Robert Newton Flew 1886-1962* (Epworth 1971)
Alan Wilkinson: *Dissent or Conform? War, Peace and the English Churches 1900-1945* (S.C.M. 1986)
Daniel Day Williams: *Interpreting Theology 1918-1952* (S.C.M.1953)
Janet Williams: *First Lady of the Pulpit, A Biography of Elsie Chamberlain* (The Book Guild 1993)
K.M.Wolfe: *Churches and the British Broadcasting Corporation 1922-1956* (S.C.M. 1984)

Other Histories

C.T. Atkinson: *The Devonshire Regiment 1914-1918* (Simpkin, Marshall, Hamilton and Kent 1926)

John Black: 'Can't Pay, Won't Pay' article on the Passive Resistance Movement, *History Today* Vol.40. June 1990.

Asa Briggs: *A Social History of England* (Weidenfeld and Nicolson1983)

Martin Ceadel: *Pacifism in Britain 1914-1945* (OUP 1980)

Winston Churchill: *The World Crisis 1911-1918* (Butterworth 1931)

R.C.K. Ensor: *England 1870-1914* (Oxford 1936)

Derek Fraser (ed.): *A History of Modern Leeds* (Manchester 1980)

Peter Jupp: 'From Dust to Ashes: The Replacement of Burial by Cremation in England 1840-1967.' The Congregational Memorial Hall Lecture, 1990.

Alan MacFarlane: *The Origins of English Individualism* (Blackwell 1978)

David C. Marsh: *The Changing Social Structure of England and Wales 1871-1961* (R.K.P. 1965)

L.A. Monk: *Britain 1945-1970* (Bell 1976)

Percival Spear: *A History of India Vol.2.* (Penguin 1965)

A.J.P. Taylor: *English History 1914-1945* (Penguin 1970)
The First World War (Penguin 1966)

John Terraine: *The First World War 1914-1918* (Secker and Warburg 1965)
To Win a War: 1918, The Year of Victory (Papermac 1978)

David Thomson: *England in the Twentieth Century* (Pelican 1965)

Trevor Wilson: *The Myriad Faces of War* (Polity Press 1986)

Psychology and Counselling

David Black: *A Place for Exploration: The Story of the Westminster Pastoral Foundation 1969-1990* (WPF 1991)

John Carl Fluegel: *A Hundred Years of Psychology 1833-1933* (Duckworth 1951)

Erich Fromm: *Psychoanalysis and Religion* (Yale 1950)

J.A. Hadfield: *Psychology and Morals* (Methuen 1923)

L.S. Hearnshaw: *The Shaping of Modern Psychology* (Kegan & Paul 1987)

Roger Hurding: *Roots and Shoots, A Guide to Counselling and Psychotherapy* (H. & S. 1985)

William Kyle: *Healing Through Counselling* (Epworth 1964)

J.G. McKenzie: *Souls in the Making* (Allen and Unwin 1928)
Psychology, Psychotherapy and Evangelicalism (Allen and Unwin 1940)

Surjit Singh: *Christology and Personality* (Westminster Press 1961)

Ian Suttie: *The Origins of Love and Hate* (Kegan Paul 1935)

Healing

John Crowlesmith (ed.): *Religion and Medicine* (Epworth 1962)

David Dale: *In His Hands: Towards a Theology of Healing* (Daybreak 1989)

R.A. Lambourne: *Community, Church and Healing* (Arthur James 1987)

Morris Maddocks: *The Christian Healing Ministry* (SPCK. 1981)
A Healing House of Prayer (H. & S. 1987)

William Sharpe: *Medicine and the Ministry* (Meredith 1966)

Godfrey Winn: *The Quest for Healing* (Muller 1956)

Sexology

Mike Brake (ed.): *Human Sexual Relations - A Reader* (Penguin 1982)

Edward Bristow: *Vice and Vigilance: Purity Movements in Britain Since 1700* (Gill and Macmillan 1977)

Paul Ferris: *Sex and the British. A Twentieth Century History* (Michael Joseph 1993)

A. Herbert Gray: *Men, Women and God* (S.C.M. 1923)

Jeffrey Weeks: *Sexuality and its Discontents* (Kegan and Paul 1985)
  Sex, Politics and Society: The Regulations of Sexuality Since 1800 (Longman 1989)

General

Margery Allingham: *The Oaken Heart* (Hutchinson 1941)

John Attenborough: *A Living Memory, Hodder and Stoughton Publishers 1868-1975* (H. & S. 1975)

H.W. Austin: *Frank Buchman as I Knew Him* (Grosvenor 1975)

W. Beresford and G.R. Jones; *Leeds and its Region*

H.E. Fosdick: *The Living of These Days* (S.C.M. 1957)
  The Meaning of Prayer (Fontana 1960)

Leonard Griffith: *Barriers to Christian Belief* (Harper N.Y. 1961)

Norman Hillson: *Inquiring Christian in England* (Religious Book Club 1940)

Raynor Johnson: *The Imprisoned Splendour* (H. & S. 1953)
  Nurslings of Immortality (H. & S. 1957)
  A Religious Outlook for Modern Man (H. & S. 1963)

D.M. Lloyd Jones: *Preaching and Preachers* (H. & S. 1971)

C.S. Lewis: *The Problem of Pain* (Centenary Press 1940)

Derek Linstrum: *Historic Architecture of Leeds* (Oriel Press 1969)

Alice Linton: *Not Expecting Miracles* (Centreprise Trust 1982)

John B. Magee: *Reality and Prayer* (Harper N.Y. 1957)

Nathaniel Micklem: *A Religion for Agnostics* (S.C.M. 1965)

Henry H. Mitchell: *The Recovery of Preaching* (H. & S. 1979)

Alan Richardson (ed.): *A Dictionary of Christian Theology* (S.C.M. 1969)

Eric Routley: *Companion to Congregational Praise* (I.P. 1953)

Charles Smyth: *The Friendship of Christ* (Longman Green & Co. 1945)

Laurence Temple (Fdk. Lawrence): *The Shining Brother* (Pelegrin Trust 1990)

B. Randall Vickers: *This Family Business* (Vickers & Son 1954)

Virginia Vickers: *Spin a Good Yarn, The Story of W. Farrar Vickers* (Leeds 1978)

A.R. Vidler: *Twentieth Century Defenders of the Faith* (S.C.M. 1965)

John Waddington-Feather: *Leeds the Heart of Yorkshire* (Basil Jackson 1967)

Index

Aberdeen, 76
Abingdon Press, 110, 155, 289
Abyssinia, 93, 105-7,
Acland, Sir Richard, 138, 139, 259
Adam, A. C., 168
Adelaide, 111
Adler, Alfred, 82, 187, 188
Advertiser (Melbourne) 182
Advisory Committee Conference of European Churches, 281
Africa, 18, 37, 106, 138, 149
After Death, 32, 47, 48, 187, 284, 299, 301
Afterworld of the Poets, The, 48-50
Age, The, 182
Agnew, Nettie, 105
Alaska, 298
Albania, 121
Alderman Newton School, Leicester, 17
Aldershot, 21, 23, 25
All Hallows by the Tower, 197
Allbutt, Dr. H. A., 64
Allen, Clifford, 193
Allen, Mr. and Mrs. Robert, 119
Amara, 28
American Church Month, 69
American Section of the World Council of Churches, 129
Amritsar, 38
Amsterdam Youth Conference, 200
Andrews, Charles, 24
Anglia Television, 285
Apartheid, 224
Appleyard, Ernest, 89, 223
Aquinas, Thomas, 103
Arabs, 27, 28, 31, 89
Arizona, 207
Armagh, Cardinal Macrory of, 157
Armistice, 30, 157
Armstrong, Walter, 94
Arnold, Matthew, 49
Arthur James, Publishers, 233, 272
Arvidson, Bishop, 178, 179
Asbury Seminarian, 282
Attlee, Clement, 170, 171, 224
Auckland, 183
Australia, 47, 68, 69, 70, 109, 169, 180-4, 191, 229, 257, 258, 268, 274, 297, 298
Australian Communist Party, 180
Australian Forces, 21, 27, 98, 102
Austria, 129
Ayer, A. J., 224

Backus, Dr. Percy, 186, 277, 287
Badoglio, 107
Baghdad, 28, 31
Baker, Eric, 238
Baker, Richard R., 270
Bakubah, 28, 31
Ballantyne, R. M., 50

Baldwin, Stanley, 117
Balfour, Arthur James, 98
Balthazar, Hans Urs Von, 265
Baluchistan, 91
Bangor Youth Conference, 200
Banks-Smith, Nancy, 252
Banner of Truth, 267
Baptists, 133, 166, 172, 219
Baptist Temple, Philadelphia, 148
Baptist Times, 156, 227, 231, 266, 294
Baptist World Alliance, 131
Bardsley, Cuthbert, 88
Baring, Maurice, 89
Barmouth, 221
Barnsley, 117, 289
Barratt, Rev. T. H., 20
Barrett, Arthur, 80
Barriers to Christian Belief, 262
Barth, Karl, 255
Barton, Winifred, 105, 127, 143, 197, 234, 287
Basra, 27, 28, 30, 157
Bates, H. E., 89
Bath, 106
Battle of the Atlantic, 149
Battle of Britain, 127
Beales, W. Harold, 83
Beckenham, 198
Bedoyere, Michael de la, 269
Beecher, Henry Ward, 98
Beecher Lectures on Preaching, 203
Beethoven, 146
Belgium, 125, 129, 163
Belgrave Central Church, Leads, 53
Bell, George, Bishop of Chichester, 151, 152, 164
Benn, Tony, 259
Benson, Dr. Irving, 68, 181, 182
Beresford Street Congregational Church, N. Z., 183
Berlin, 117, 120, 169, 170
Berry, J. R., 268
Berry, Dr. Sidney, 96, 122, 131, 135, 157, 232, 237
Beulah Baptist Church, Bexhill, 275
Beveridge, Sir William, 139
Beveridge Report, 128, 139, 143, 163, 165
Bexhill-on-Sea, Foreword, 245-95, 298
Beyond Personality, 154
Biophysical Research Fund, 217
Birch, John, 232
Birkett, Lord, 259
Birmingham, 166, 214
Birmingham, Bishop of, 224
Birmingham Post, 151
Birth Control News, 67
Bisseker, Rev. Harry, 20, 21
Black, Rev. Dr. James, 126
Blakeney, Rev. Dr., 148
Bloch, Iwan, 64

Bloomsbury Baptist Church, 275
Bodelschwingh, Pastor, 160
Bohemia, 120
Bombay, 31
Bond, Robert, 94
Bonhoeffer, Dietrich, 254, 301
Bonnell, John Sutherland, 151, 203
Bookseller, 89
Bournemouth, 79, 153, 273
Bowater, Sir Noel, 201
Boy Scouts, 64, 143
Boyd, Rev. T. Hunter, 115
Boys' Brigade, 54, 64
Brackenbury, Sir Henry B., 81, 84
Bradman, Sir Donald, 242
Brahman, 35
Brahmin, 39
'Brains Trust', 234
Brash, W. Bardsley, 174
Bridges, Robert, 50
Briggs, Asa, 85
Brimley, T. Charles, 225, 226
Brisbane, 182
Bristol, 93, 111, 273
Britain, 106, 115, 117, 120, 122, 123, 128, 131, 148, 153, 158, 163, 170, 224, 268, 293, 299
British; Army, 125, 126; Empire, 13, 26, 37, 39, 115, 126; Government, 37, 38, 107, 125, 126, 133, 139, 152, 170, 224
British and Foreign Bible Society, 97, 209
British Broadcasting Corporation, 86-8, 111, 115, 121, 125, 180, 196, 210, 211, 229, 233, 234, 239, 260, 273, 293
The British Churches Today, 280
British Council of Churches, 139, 225, 280
British Legion, 174
British Medical Association, 81, 251
British Medical Association Central Ethical Committee, 192
British Medical Journal, 192
British Museum, 132
British Society for the Study of Sexual Psychology, 64
British Somaliland, 106
British Weekly, 46, 57, 66, 75, 76, 77, 83, 98, 102, 125, 129, 134, 135, 151, 167, 173, 201, 211, 213, 225, 228, 231, 255, 266, 271, 273, 284, 293, 303
Brittain, Vera, 166
Brixton Independent Church, 225
Broadway Tabernacle, New York, 204
Bromley, 176
Bronxville Reformed Church, 202-4
Brooks, Edgar H., 75
Brooks, Phillips, Foreword
Brotherhood Movement, 97
Brown, Ernest, 122
Browne, Dr. William, 60, 76, 81, 84, 276
Browning, Robert, 48-50
Bruce, A. B., 151
Brunner, Emil, 255

Brunswick Church, Leeds, 45, 48, 52-62, 75, 78-96, 108, 135, 243, 273, 298
Buchman, Frank, 74, 75, 77
Buddhism, 34, 138, 261, 304
Buckingham Palace, 109, 221, 226
Buckley, Herbert, 42
Buenos Aires, 119
Bulletin, (Hartford Seminary) 69
Bultmann, Rudolf, 254
Burma, 45
Busy Man's Old Testament, The, 46, 289
Butler Education Act, 163, 170
Butterfield, Herbert, 261

Cadbury, confectioners, 14
Cadoux, Dr. C. J., 72, 174
California, 207
Cambridge, 75, 153, 171, 172, 217, 257
Cambridge University, 17, 248
Campbell, Montgomery, 229
Campbell, Dr. R. J., 94, 98, 100, 101, 220, 232, 235, 295
Camroux, Rev. Martin, 307
Canada, 47, 75, 93, 109, 110, 129, 131, 168, 174, 183, 202, 229, 238, 241, 249, 268, 273, 297
Canberra, 182
Canterbury, Archbishop of, 115, 136
Canterbury Cathedral, 202
Canterbury, Convocation of, 195
Canterbury, Dean of, 157
Carmichael, Patrick H., 215
Carrs Lane Church, Birmingham, 113
Cassell & Co., 242
Caste system, 35, 39
Catholic Herald, 269
Caunt, Mrs. Margaret (nee Weatherhead) 15, 45, 81, 153, 181, 289, 297
Central Association for Mental Welfare, 81
Central Religious Advisory Committee, 87
Ceylon, 24, 34, 45, 181
Chadwick, Owen, 269
Chadwick, Samuel, 19, 24
Chalmers United Church of Canada, 238
Chamberlain, Neville, 115, 119, 122, 125, 126
Chamberlain, Rev. Elsie, 70, 172
Chandler, Rev. Edgar H. S., 129
Channel Islands, 178
Chaplains, 31, 32, 43, 98, 139, 140, 143, 147, 148, 171, 172, 218, 234
Chapman, J. Arundel, 46, 66, 72
Charterhouse, London, 197
Cherry, W. M., 54
Cheshire, Group Captain Leonard, 218
Cheshunt College, Cambridge, 94, 219, 234
Chesterton, G. K., 98
Chevasse, Dr. Christopher, 217
Chicago, 206
Chicago University, 92, 194
Child Psychology and Religious Education, 113
China, 37, 109, 138, 163

Chirgwin, Dr. A. M., 157
Christ Church, Oxford, 76
Christ Church, Westminster Bridge Road, Lambeth, 93, 94, 95, 275
Christchurch, N. Z., 183
Christ of the India Road, The, 119
Christian, The, 235, 285
Christian Action, 139, 224
Christian Advocate, 178
Christian Agnostic, The, 49, 50, 257-72, 273, 277, 289, 299, 301, 302, 307
Christian Aid, 292
Christian Century, 158, 167
Christian Herald, 60
Christian Legion, 138
Christian Literature Society for India, 46
Christian Science, 186-7, 191, 194
Christian Science Monitor, 140
Christian Socialism, 44
Christian World, 66, 76, 151, 156, 158, 159, 177, 192, 194, 200, 215, 231, 233
Christianity and History, 261
Christianity and Social Order, 98
Christianity and the Rise of Capitalism, 42
Christus Veritas, 45
Church, Dr. Leslie, 75, 200, 215
Church of England, (Anglican) 41, 94, 101, 102, 134, 138, 143, 150, 157, 166, 167, 170, 171, 172, 174, 195, 196, 199, 200, 218, 233, 252, 264, 267
Church of England Newspaper, 83, 174, 194, 215, 281
C. of E. Social and Industrial Council, 77
Church of Ireland Gazette, 69
Church of Scotland, 84, 126
Church Times, 154, 156, 193, 200, 201, 220, 233, 235, 255, 267, 285
Church Unity, 101-2, 137, 166, 171-3, 199-200, 209, 214, 219, 277, 283, 303, 305
Churches' Council of Healing, 192, 200, 245
Churches' Fellowship for Psychical and Spiritual Studies, 187, 246, 248
Churches' Public Morality Council, 245
Churches Survey Their Task, The, 136
Churchill, Winston, 125, 133
Churchman, 69, 156
Cinema, 41, 68, 85, 92
Cinema, 68
City of London, 97, 102, 175, 177, 197, 201, 226, 229, 232, 234, 239
City Temple, Preface, 13, 14, 26, 31, 35, 43, 45, 54, 59-60, 65, 86, 87, 94, 95-6, 97-245, 246, 248, 249, 250, 252, 253, 254, 255, 256, 259, 260, 273, 274, 275, 277, 280, 281, 282, 283, 286, 287, 288, 289, 290, 291, 292, 293, 294, 295, 301, 302, 303, 305, 306, 307; Advisory Committee, 174, 176, 177; Choir, 197-8; Community Evening, 197, 234, 238; Constitution, 120-1; Council, 99, 100, 107, 108, 111, 120, 121, 128, 131, 132, 133, 149, 174, 175, 176,

177, 198, 202, 209, 225, 228, 235, 238, 242, 243, 248, 292; Friends Organisation, 170, 183, 234; Home of Service, 121; Ladies Working Guild, 287; Literary Society, 59, 94, 121, 150, 180, 198, 200, 254, 256; Prayer Groups, 198, 217; Psychological Clinic, 104, 105, 109, 111, 134, 150, 151, 190, 191, 195, 198, 214, 215, 226, 228, 234, 236, 242, 245, 250, 275, 276, 277, 284, 285, 287, 289, 290, 306; Rebuilding Committee, 135, 153, 175, 177, 196; Rebuilding Fund, 130, 135, 141, 183-4, 196, 201, 202, 204; Re-Dedication, 229-32; Tercentenary, 125-6; *Tidings*, 50, 101, 102, 110, 111, 121, 122, 126, 142, 145, 146, 148, 151, 153, 162, 174, 176, 205, 220, 240, 280, 287, 290, 291, 292; Young People Unlimited, 235; Womens' League of Service, 287
City Temple: A Hundred Years, The, 290
City Temple, Past, Present and Future, The, 125, 228
Clare, Albert, 126, 128, 130, 135, 139, 141, 142, 143, 153, 291
Clark, Stephen, 204
Clarke, James & Co., 47
Clayton, John, 133, 139
Cleveland, 206
Cliff College, 19-20, 24
Clifton, Robert (Sumangalo), 258
Clockmakers' Company, 226
Clough, Arthur Hugh, 49
Cockin, F. A., 87
Coggan, Archbishop Donald, 283
Coke, Thomas, 24
Cole, Stewart G., 68
Collins, Canon John, 139, 224
Collins Street Congregational Church, Melbourne, 181, 183
Colombo, 181
Colonial Missionary Society, 108
Commission of the Churches for International Friendship and Social Responsibility, 138
Common, Dr. David, 250, 306
Common Wealth Party, 139
Communism, 180, 212
Complimentary (Alternative) Medicine, 306
Compton, Bishop, 227
Compulsory Military Service Bill, 121
Conference of Life and Work, 136
Conference on Christian Politics, Economics and Citizenship (Copec) 65
Congregationalism, 26, 43, 46, 61, 93, 94, 96, 97, 99, 107, 108, 113, 120, 122, 135, 166, 172, 173, 177, 181, 204, 209, 219, 225, 229, 238, 301, 303, 304, 307
Congregationalist, 101
Congregational Federation, 304
Congregational Praise, 225
Congregational Quarterly, 89
Congregational Union, 96, 111, 120, 131, 134, 135, 157, 173, 231, 237, 304

Congregational Union Reconstruction Fund, 196
Convocation of Canterbury, 195
Cook, Paul, 267
Cook, Rev. Thomas, 19
Cooke, Rev. James, 18
Cooke, Dr. Leslie, 234, 238, 275
Cookson, Catherine, 221
Corbishley, Father Thomas, 90, 259, 260, 269
Cork, 221
Corpus Christi College, Cambridge, 56
Costain, A. J., 66
Coulson, Prof. C. A., 246, 247
Coventry, 214
Cripps, Sir Stafford, 170
Cromwell, Oliver, 97
Crosfield, Colonel George, 174
Crosson, Rev. James Cope, 270-1
Crouch End Congregational Church, 225
Crowlesmith, Rev. John, 294
Crozen Quarterly, 68
Crozen Theological Seminary, 69
Cumbers, Rev. Frank, 63, 200, 215, 264, 281, 282
Cummins, Geraldine, 153, 257, 258, 284
Cutts, Leonard, 281
Czechoslovakia, 115, 116, 123, 129, 163

Daily Express, 240, 252
Daily Light, 282
Daily Mail, 85, 201, 220, 251, 259
Daily Mirror, 13, 201, 211, 252
Daily News, 98
Daily Readings From the Works of Leslie D. Weatherhead, 281-2
Daily Readings From the Works of Martin LLoyd Jones, 282
Daily Sketch, 151, 198, 200
Daily Telegraph, 227, 251, 293
Dale, Dr. R. W., 14, 266
Danzig, 120
Darjeeling, 34
Davies, Emlyn, 238
Davies, Trevor, 238
Davison, Principal W. T., 20
de Chardin, Teilhard, 265
de la Warr, George, 239, 240
de Lubac, 265
Deer Park Church, Toronto, 183, 274
Demant, V. A., 157
Denholm House Press, 284, 289
Denmark, 125, 129, 163, 179
Des Moines, Iowa, 271
Detroit, 206, 207
Devonshire Regiment, 28, 30
Dewey, Cyril, 108
Dewey, J. H. J., 125, 153, 167, 175, 177, 197, 201, 228, 242, 246, 292
Didsbury College, 44, 46, 47
Didsbury Literary Society, 38
Dimbleby, Richard, 239
Disarmament Conference, 78

Discipleship, 35, 75-6, 298
Ditzen, Dr. Russell Lowell, 202, 204
Dixon, Rev. W. G., 14
Doe, Jane, 78
Douglas, Lord Alfred, 153
Doyle, Conan, 50
Downing Street, 122, 142, 170, 233
Drew Theological Seminary, 110, 140, 167
Drummond, Henry, 55
Du Maurier, Gerald, 79
Duncan, Denis, 272
Dunedin, N. Z. 183
Dunkirk, 125, 126, 161
Dusseldorf, 120
Duthie, Principal Charles, 273, 303
Dyer, General, 38
Dykes, K. C., 266

Eastern Daily Press, 194
Eddy, Mary Baker, 187
Eden, Anthony, 148
Eden, Rev. Frank, 273, 289
Edinburgh, 134
Edinburgh Evening News, 154
Edinburgh University, 61, 108, 156, 173
Education Act 1902, 98
Edward, Prince of Wales, 38, 39
Edwards, Dr. Maldwyn, 194
Edwards, Harry, 217, 274
88th. Carnatic Infantry Regiment, 27
83rd. Wallajabad Light Infantry, 27
Egmore Church, Madras, 34
Ego and the Id, The, 21
Egypt, 27, 106, 186, 224
El Alamein, 149
Elizabeth the Queen Mother, 157, 226, 229, 231
Elliott, Canon G. H., 166
Elliott, W. H., 86
Ellis, Havelock, 64, 65
Ellis, Thomas, 18
Eltham College, 61
Elton, Lord, 173
English Churchman, 267
Epworth Press, 47, 63, 87, 166, 200, 214, 215, 253, 264, 281
Epworth Review, 70
Epworth *September News Notes*, 264
Eternal Voice, The, 124
Ethiopia, 106
Eton College, 197
Eugenics Review, 67
Europe, 25, 27, 80, 93, 106, 108, 109,116, 117, 123, 128, 136, 148, 157, 163, 171
Euthanasia, 90, 185, 234, 302
Euthanasia Society, 90
Evangelical Fellowship of Congregational Churches, 304
Evans, Rev. Colin, 214
Evans, Dr. Geoffrey, 168
Evans, Sir Robert, 174
Evening News, 191

Evening Standard, 226, 229, 251
Evolution, 29
Ewens, J. Baird, 220
Exeter University, 306
Expository Times, 46, 151, 307

Facer, Rev. Harry, 290, 294, 298
Faithful Uncertainty, 299
Farnham Methodist Church, Surrey, 21, 23, 81
Fawcett, E. Douglas, 257
Fearn, Martin, 224, 232
Federal Council of Churches of Christ in America, 110
Federal Council of the Churches (USA) 129, 133, 140
Fellowship Groups, 34, 42, 53, 74, 104, 105, 109, 111, 121, 128, 129, 134, 137, 147, 190, 197, 234, 302
Fellowship of the Kingdom, 40, 43-5, 46, 58, 70, 151, 290
Fellowship of Reconciliation, 117, 118, 148
Ferre, Nels, 262
Ferrier, Kathleen, 242
Ferris, Paul, 71
Fifth Avenue Presbyterian Church, New York, 110, 151, 179, 203
Fiji, 183
Finchley, 134
Findlay, J. A., 44, 45
Finland, 179
First World War, 19, 21, 25-33, 37, 41, 53, 61, 64, 65, 70, 85, 98, 100, 117, 118, 136, 151, 157, 159, 161, 164, 187, 295, 300, 304
Fish, Harry, 204
Fisher, Dr. Geoffrey, Archbishop of Canterbury, 171-2, 196, 233, 243-4, 248
'Five Peace Points', 136
Fleming, Sir Alexander, 242
Flew, Newton, 38, 39, 43, 44
Flying Ace Service, 141
Flying bombs, 152, 162
Focus, 265
Foreign Office, 120
Forsyth, P. T., 98
Fosdick, Harry Emerson, 45-6, 55, 131, 179, 202, 207, 232, 238, 300, 301, 304, 307
Foundry Methodist Church, Washington, 205
Foyle's, 89
France, 25, 31, 115, 120, 123, 125, 126, 129, 161, 224, 265
Free Churches, 14, 41, 78, 95, 97, 99, 100, 101, 103, 120, 123, 125, 134, 135, 144, 145, 148, 157, 171, 172, 175, 199, 217, 218, 225, 226, 231, 237, 248, 252, 291, 293, 299, 300, 304, 305
Free Church Council, 64, 97, 125, 136, 157
Free Thinker, 67
Free Trade Hall, Manchester, 214
Freeman, John, 251, 259
French, Norman, 250, 284, 285, 295
Freud, Dr. Sigmund, 21, 62, 64, 82, 140, 187,

188, 189, 250, 291
Friend, 69, 266
Friends' Journal, 270
Friends' Meeting House, Euston Road, 167
Friendship of Christ, The, 56
Frost, David, 259
Fry, Christopher, 50
Fry, confectioners, 14
Fulham Palace, 197

Gable, Clarke, 79
Gandhi, 37-9
Garbett, Cyril, Archbishop of York, 164, 195
Garlick, Canon Wilfred, 251
Garrington, Rev. J. L. St. C., 70
Garvie, Principal A. E., 58
General Council of Congregational Churches in the United States, 129
Geneva, 78,106,238
Georgetown Church, Madras, 24
Germany, 92, 109, 116, 118, 119, 120, 122, 125, 126, 127, 133, 137, 148, 149, 151, 156, 157, 159, 160, 161, 163, 164, 170, 171, 197, 209, 265, 301
Gibbon, Edward, 251
Gibbs, Phillip, 89
Girl Guides, 143
Glasgow Evening Citizen, 84
Glover, T. R., 300
Goddard, Sir Victor, 240
'Godspell', 291
Goldhawk, Norman, 303
Gollancz, Victor, 166, 171
Gone With the Wind, 89
Good Housekeeping, 153
Goodall, Tom, 180
'Goodwill invasion', 120
Goodwin, Thomas, 97
Goudie, Rev. William, 18
Gower, Wilfred, 54
Graham, Rev. Billy, 205-6, 212, 218, 255
Gray, Dr. Herbert, 65, 69, 304
Great George Street Congregational Church, Liverpool, 225
Greaves, Dr. Marion, 65
Gregory, Ian, 271
Gregory, T. S., 44
Grensted, Canon L. W., 75, 83
Griffith, A. Leonard, Preface, 99, 238, 241-2, 243, 246, 248-250, 252, 253, 255, 259, 262, 263, 273, 274, 275, 281, 292, 305
Griffiths, Binstead, 145, 221, 242, 243, 252
Grimond, Jo., 224
Guarded Universe, 91
Guardian, 301, 306
Guardian, (C. of E.) 86
Guild of Health, 186, 195, 245
Guild of Health Review, 67
Guild of Pastoral Psychology, 186
Gundry, Ivor, 132
Guntrip, Dr. Harry, 185, 304

Guy's Hospital, 192

Haddon, Winifred (Mrs. Weddell) 143, 242, 250, 292
Hadfield, Dr. J. A., 21n., 60, 61, 139, 188, 276, 277, 278, 279
Hadfield, Rev. James, 61
Hageman, Wanda, 50
Haggard, Rider, 50
Haile Selassie, 106
Halifax, 276
Halifax, Lord, 148
Hamblett, Charles, 218
Hamburg, 116, 152
Hamilton, Denis, 280
Hammond, Bertram, 228
Hampstead, 268
Hampstead Garden Suburb Free Church, 93
Hankey, Maurice, 120
Hardy, Prof. Alister, 256
Harlesden, 13
Harley Street, 8, 61, 87, 105, 134, 217, 250, 290
Harmon, Dr. Nolan B., 203
Harringay, 205
Harris, Dr. Frederick Brown, 205
Harrison, Dr. A. W., 178
Harrison, Rex, 239
Harrogate, 166
Hartley, Marshall, 24, 25, 26
Hastings, Adrian, 225
Hawkridge, Dr. P. B., 168
Hayter, Sir William, 281
Head, Alice, 153, 164, 204, 221, 287
Headingly Methodist College, Leeds, 72, 94, 101, 155
Healing, 14, 30, 31, 58, 73, 82, 83, 93, 105, 110, 146, 178, 179, 185-95, 198, 201, 209, 214, 217, 233, 239, 240, 248, 250, 254, 274, 276, 282, 294, 300, 302, 303, 304, 306
A Healing House of Prayer, 233
Hearst, William Randolph, 153
Heddle, Rev. Edmund, 275, 282, 294
Helsingfors, 63
Henty, George, 50
Herbert, A. M., 127
Hest Bank Congregational Church, Lancaster, 113
Highgate Counselling Centre, 245, 252
Highgate Methodist Church, 245
Hilborn, Dr. David, 305
Hill, Dr. Charles, 180
Hill, Erskine, 76
Hill, Rowland, 94
Hillson, Norman, 85
Hiltner, Professor Seward, 194
Himalayas, 19, 26, 34
Hindle, Major, 31
Hinduism, 29, 35-6, 39, 138, 144, 304
Hiroshima, 152, 166
Hirschfeld, Magnus, 64
His Life and Ours, 57, 72-4, 281, 300

History of the BBC., 85
History of the Decline and Fall of the Roman Empire, 251
Hitler, Adolf, 80, 92, 115, 116, 118, 120, 122, 123, 125, 127, 134, 146, 148, 152, 159, 160, 164, 170, 301
Hoare, Sir Samuel, 106
Hobart, Tasmania, 182
Hodder and Stoughton, 90, 215, 219, 232, 233, 234, 242, 254, 259, 260, 265, 269, 281, 289, 292
Holborn, 13, 100, 121, 126, 131, 148, 167, 175, 176, 177, 196, 226, 274, 280, 290, 307
Holland, 125, 129, 163
Holland, Canon Scott, 138
Hollywood Features, 220
Holy Trinity, Kingsway, 134
Honest to God, 145, 254-5, 259, 265, 267, 268, 271, 303
Horder, Lord, 112, 119, 133
Hornabrook, J. Oliver, 41
Horne, Silvester, 220
Hough, Dr. Lynn Harold, 110, 131, 140, 141, 203, 207, 230, 233
Houghton-on-the-Hill, 18, 19
House of Commons, 117, 119, 131, 148
House of Lords, 38, 151, 180
Howard, Willert F., 46
Huddlestone, Trevor, 224
Hudgell, Dr. Edith, 134, 290
Hutchinson, Gertrude, 283, 290, 293
Hutton, John A., 102
Huxley, Julian, 266
Huxtable, John, 224
Hypnotism, 30, 59-60, 93, 185, 186, 188, 254, 302

Illinois Council of Churches, 220
'Imaginism', 257
Immortality, 33, 74, 163, 263, 234
Imperial College, London, 284
Imprisoned Splendour, The, 257
In Memoriam, 49
In Quest of A Kingdom, 44, 151
In the Steps of the Master, 89
India, 18, 23-40, 42, 43, 45, 47, 106, 103, 111, 138, 144, 172, 174, 216, 242, 300; Army, 26, 28, 31, Religion, 14, 25, 35-8; India Act, 37
Inge, Dean, 69
Inglis, Brian, 274
Inkster, Marjorie, 234, 235, 246
Institute of Medical Psychology, 31
Institute of Religion and Medicine, 275-6
Institute of Sexual Science, Berlin, 64
International Christian Movement, 117, 137-9
International Journal of Parapsychology, 270
International Psycho-Analytical Society, 21
Interpretation of Dreams, The, 21
Ireland, 178, 221
Iremonger, F. A., 86, 87

Irish Christian Advocate, 47, 220, 232
Irish Times, 69
Is It Courage We Need?, 159
Isis, 90
Islam, 35-6, 38, 39, 138, 304
Islington, 105
Israel, 224
It Happened in Palestine, 89-90
Italian Air Force, 107
Italy, 106, 109, 126, 149

Jackson, Rev. Dr. George, 21, 47
Jacquet, Rev. Harry, 274
James, David, 285
Japan, 133, 166
Jeffrey, E. Foster, 135
Jeffs, E. H., 177, 192, 194
Jenkinson, Rev. Charles, 53
Jerusalem, 174
Jessop, Dr. Thomas, 268
Jesus Christ, 17, 18, 19, 21, 29, 30, 33, 35,
   36, 44, 45, 46, 49, 54, 55, 56, 57, 58, 59,
   60, 72-4, 83, 89, 93, 98, 103, 104, 107,
   110, 137, 138, 140, 151, 154, 155, 156,
   158, 161, 173, 174, 186, 200, 201, 211,
   215, 224, 230, 235, 247, 248, 258, 260,
   261, 262, 263, 266, 267, 263, 269, 282,
   285, 286, 294, 295, 297, 298, 299, 300,
   301, 305, 306, 307
Jesus and Ourselves, 45, 55, 57-8, 72, 140, 300
Jesus of History, The, 300
Jews, 115, 117, 118, 119, 148, 155
Joad, C. E. M., 166
Johannesburg, 131
Johanson, Rev. Dr. Brian, 295, 305
John, Augustus, 157
John Milton Society for the Blind, 204
John O'London's Weekly, 193, 201
Johnson, Raynor, 153, 181, 223, 237,
   245-6, 257-8, 261
Jones, R. W. Hugh, 231, 238
Jones, Rev. Dr. Stanley, 119
Journal of the Wesley Bible Union, 56
Jowett, Dr. J. H., 46, 102
Joyce, Eileen, 242
Joyful News, 215
Judaism, 138
Judas, 140
Jung, Carl Gustav, 62, 82, 187, 188, 291

Karmel, David, 240
Kashmir, 105
Keats, John, 145
Keeble, S. E., 44
Keele, University of, 246
Keller, Helen, 204
Kensal Rise, 39, 41
Kenya, 209
Keswick Convention, 74
Key Next Door, 242
King, Cecil, 252
King Edward VIII, 107

King George V, 87
King George VI, 109, 125, 157, 217
Kings College, London, 61
King's Weigh House Church, 176
Kingsway Central Hall, 96, 225, 287
Kingswood School, Bath, 81
Kinsey, Alfred, 65
Kirk Memorial Church, Edinburgh, 61
Kirkham, W. A., 24, 25, 26
Knight, Margaret, 210
Knudson, Raymond B., 220
Kraft-Ebing, 64
Kristallnacht, 118
Krupp, Alfred, 197
Kung, Hans, 265
Kyle, Rev. Dr. William, 142, 221, 228, 245,
   287, 289, 294

Labour Government, 170, 175
Labour Party, 170, 173
Lady Chatterley's Lover, 69, 245, 250, 252, 254
Lamberene, 93
Lambeth Conference, 173
Lambeth Palace, 132, 197
Lamont, Thomas W., 202
Lancet, 67, 83, 192
Lancashire, 241
Lancaster Advertiser, 154
Lang, Archbishop Cosmo Gordon, 66
Larwood, Harold, 79
Laski, Harold, 157
Laval, Pierre, 106
Lawrence, D. H., 250
Lawrence, Frederic, 153, 175, 196, 258
Lawrence, T. E., 28
Lax, William H., 58
League for the Prohibition of Cruel Sports, 90
League of Good Samaritans, 42-3, 53, 104,
   109, 287
League of Nations, 53, 74, 93, 106, 117
Leamington Spa, 214
Leathers, Lord, 149, 164, 174
Leathers, Viscountess, 238
Leeds, 42, 52-62, 72-96, 104, 118, 121, 135,
   223, 225, 231, 281, 297
Leeds City Council, 53
Leeds City Council Improvements Commit-
   tee, 53
Leeds Free Church Council, 53
Leeds Mercury, 62, 66, 80, 81, 84, 87, 89,
   90, 92, 93, 106, 116, 117, 144
Leeds Protestant Methodists, 52
Leeds University, 59
Leeds Vigilance Association, 64
Leicester, 14, 17, 18, 209, 273
Leicester Mercury, 83
Leicester Wesleyan Methodist Messenger, 19
Lennard, Lady, 174
Leslie Weatherhead: A Personal Portrait,
   Preface, 292
Letters to Young Churches, 277

Lever, W. H., 14
Lewis, C. Day, 50
Lewis, C. S., 154, 304
Lewis, Rev. Herbert T., 174, 225, 280
Liberal Christian Church, Cedar Rapids, Iowa, 98
Liberal Party, 41, 99
Lichfield, Bishop of, 217
Lidgett, Dr. J. Scott, 67, 93, 94, 106
Life Begins at Death, 284-5
Life of Faith, 166, 173, 191
Light and the Gate, The, 258
Lightly, J. W., 94
Lincoln, Abraham, 160
Lincoln and Stamford Mercury, 140
Listener, 109
Liverpool, 76, 166, 179
Liverpool Daily Post, 220
Living of These Days, The, 301
Lloyd George, David, 31, 78, 100, 124
Lloyd, Canon Roger, 89
LLoyd-Jones, Dr. Martyn, 134, 159
Lloyds of London, 201
Lodge, Sir Oliver, 235
Lofthouse, Principal W. F., 65
London, 13, 31, 42, 94, 96, 97, 98, 105, 107, 117, 125, 127, 128, 129, 131, 133, 134, 147, 152, 158, 162, 175, 205, 206, 209, 227, 274, 281, 289, 291, 294, 295; Bishop of, 131; Committee Against Obscenity, 252; Congregational Union, 133; Free Church Federation, 106; Missionary Society, 108, 134; University, 17, 30, 185, 225, 265
London Quarterly and Holborn Review, 201, 215, 217, 239, 266
Los Angeles, 207
Lourdes, 179-80, 186, 191, 193
L.S.D., 278, 280
Luccock, Dr. Halford E., 203
Lunk, Leonhard, 197
Lustgarten, Edgar, 211
Lutterworth Press, 280
Lyman Beecher Lectures, 179
Lynch, James, 24
Lyndhurst Road Congregational Church, Hampstead, 241

Macarthur, Rev. Arthur, 292
MacCormick, Pat, 86
McCulloch, Joseph, 259, 268
MacDonald, Ramsay, 117
McDougall, Dr. William, 61, 187
McGill University, Montreal, 93, 109, 110, 241
Mackay, Prof. D. M., 246
McKenzie, Dr. J. G., 61, 185, 304
MacKenzie, Dr. Marion E., 66
McKie, Sir William, 232
Mackintosh, H. V., 14
MacLennan, Rev. David A., 131
MacLeod, Dr. George, 86, 87
McLuhan, Marshall, 305

Macmillian, Harold, 233, 242
Macmillian, Lord, 136
Maddocks, Morris, 233
Madras, 23-7, 31, 34-40, 42, 55, 275
Maitland, Christopher, 242
Maltby, William Russell, 44, 45, 54, 55, 73, 74, 94, 155
Malvern, 138
Man and Woman, 64
Manchester, 21, 41-50, 54, 55, 59, 63, 81, 86, 211, 213, 294
Manchester and Salford Mission, 48, 245
Manchester, Bishop of, 214, 224
Manchester Cathedral, 214
Manchester Grammar School, 268
Manchester Guardian, 47, 60, 66, 89
Manchester University, 42, 46, 48
Mandus, Br., 274
Manhood of the Master, The, 45, 300
Mansfield College, Oxford, 61, 113, 268
Mansion House, London, 66, 139, 201
Married Love, 64
Marshall, Howard, 109
Martin, Hugh, 87
Marx, Karl, 44, 143
Marylebone Presbyterian Church, 167-84, 197-226, 239, 280, 307
Masefield, John, 50
Mastery of Sex Through Psychology and Religion, The, 63-71, 72, 93, 302
Mathematics Institute, Oxford, 246
Matthews, W. R., 86, 87, 229
Mau Mau, 209
Mayo, Rev. J. A., 86
Meaning of Faith, The, 45
Meaning of Prayer, The, 45, 55, 232
Meaning of the Resurrection, The, 55
Medical Press, 192
Medway Street Board School, 16
Melbourne, 181-3, 257
Melbourne University, 181
Melbourne Herald, 68
Memel, 129
Memorial Hall, Farringdon Street, 131, 177
Memphis, 207
Men, Women and God, 65
Menzies, Sir Robert, 180, 242
Mesopotamia, 19, 27-31, 34, 39, 40, 45, 49, 116
Methodism, 19, 21, 29, 43, 44, 47, 52, 67, 70, 73, 78, 79, 86, 93, 94, 95, 96, 97, 100, 102, 107, 108, 133, 135, 166, 172, 173, 180, 181, 183, 195, 204, 209, 211, 212, 213, 216, 218, 219, 222, 233, 248, 267, 287, 294, 298, 300, 301, 303, 304
Methodist: Centenary Fund, 20; Church Bill, 79; Class meeting, 29; Committee on Spiritual Healing, 93, 105, 110, 185, 195, 214; Conference, 24, 26, 41, 47, 77, 93, 94, 95, 101, 105, 109, 118, 144, 178, 179, 185, 195, 202, 209, 211-14, 216, 218, 222, 223, 238, 241, 268, 276, 297, 298, 301; Deed of

Union, 79; Home Missions Department, 216, 218; Homes for the Aged, 282; ministry, 24; Order of Deaconesses, 210; Reunion, 79, 101, 222; Sacramental Fellowship, 52; Social Welfare Department, 157; Society for Medical and Pastoral Psychology, 185, 186; Uniting Conference, 79

Methodist/Anglican Conversations, 101-102, 144, 213, 218, 222, 236, 267, 303

Methodist Church in America, 203

Methodist Magazine, 52, 61

Methodist Recorder, 46, 55, 56, 57, 61, 66, 78, 79, 80, 86, 89, 108, 122, 142, 143, 174, 178, 194, 195, 201, 212, 214, 216, 218, 220, 222, 234, 239, 246, 251, 263, 264, 282, 285, 289, 294

Methodist Times and Leader, 41, 46, 56, 66, 80, 83, 90, 102, 103, 106, 111, 112

Metropolitan Church, Toronto, 93

Metropolitan Tabernacle, Elephant and Castle, 133

Meyer, Dr. F. B., 64, 65, 94

Michigan Christian Advocate, 270

Micklem, Dr. Nathaniel, 76, 268, 269, 304

Midgley, Wilson, 97

Midnight in the Place Pigalle, 69

Millar, Dr. Crichton, 60, 276

Miller, Alexander, 99, 108, 125

Milne, A. A., 118

Mines, Mrs., 199

Miracles of Achievement, 62

Mitchell, Henry H., 306

Modern Discoveries in Medical Psychology, 193

Moffat, 14, 17, 277

Monahan, C. H., 25

Moor Allerton Parish Church, 80

Moore, Henry, 224

Moral Re-Armament, 77, 212

Moravia, 120

Morgan, Dr. Campbell, 134, 220

Morgan, J. P. Company, 202

Morley, Samuel, 14

Morning Post, 38

Morris, Dr. Colin, Foreword, 297

Morton, H. C., 56

Morton, H. V., 89

Moscow, 281

Mottistone, Lord, 196-7, 227, 239

Mountbatten, Lady Louis, 134

Mountbatten, Lord Louis, 242

Mozart, 146

Muggeridge, Malcolm, 259

Muhammad, 36

Munich, 115, 120, 122

Murray, A. Victor, 219

Murray, Geoffrey, 237

Murray, Iain H., 134

Mussolini, 105, 106, 107, 121

My Philosophy, 235

Myers, Rev. Sydney, 194

Myers, W. H., 235, 257, 284

Myriad Faces of War, The, 27

Nagasaki, 152, 166

Nasiria, 28

Nasser, Gamal Abdel, 224

National Children's Home, Preface

National Christian Education Council, 284

National Federation of Spirtual Healers, 274

National Peace Council, 156

National Service of Thanksgiving, 157

Nazis, 118, 120, 122, 129, 148, 160, 161, 164

Neill, Bishop Stephen, 172

Nervous Disorders and Religion, 185

'New Age', (New Order') 129, 135, 137, 139, 151

'New age' movement, 272, 303, 307

New College, London, 143, 224

New Orleans, 207

New Outlook, 76

New Statesman, 259

New Theology, The, 98, 156

New York, 110, 183, 201, 202, 204, 207, 215

New York Herald Tribune, 192

New York Sun, 167

New Zealand, 27, 109, 180, 183

News Chronicle, 66, 211, 227, 237

News of the World, 251

Newton, Dr. Joseph Fort, 98

Nichols, Beverly, 118, 274

Niebuhr, Reinhold and Richard, 179, 255

Niemoller, Pastor, 164

Nixon, Richard, 205

Nonconformity, 14, 41, 78, 86, 97, 98, 100, 146, 148, 150, 237, 293

North West University, Chicago, 206

Norway, 125, 129, 160, 163, 178, 179

Norwich, 194, 195

Norwood, Dr. F. W., 94, 97, 98, 99, 100, 102, 104, 108, 135, 176, 199, 202, 295

Nottingham, 298

Nuffield, Lord, 242

Nursing Mirror, 67

Nursing Times, 192

Nurslings of Immortality, 257

Oberammergau, 84

Observer, 89, 254

Occupying Powers in Europe, 171

Ockenden, Rev. Frank, 264

Odic Force, 217, 239, 254, 276

Odum, Steve, 50, 306

Old Bailey, 250

Old Testament Today, The, 46

Olivier, Lawrence, 239

Olympic Games, 173

Oman, John, 49

On Being a Minister, 142-7

Onebarrow Lodge, 17

Onions, Rev. W. G., 168, 174

Opie, Gladys, 183

Orchard, Dr. W. E., 45, 176

Order of Christian Witness, 169

Orpington, Kent, 152
Oslo Youth Conference, 200
Over His Own Signature, 57, 214-5
Oxford, 74, 136, 139, 240, 284
Oxford Group Movement, 74-7, 84
Oxford Mail, 269
Oxford Road Church, Manchester, 41-50
Oxford Union, 90, 129
Oxford University, 75, 90, 113, 256

Pacific School of Religion, Berkeley, 207
Pacifism, 118, 123
Paget, Paul, 196
Paisley, Rev. Ian, 262
Palestine, 89, 140
Palmer, Dr. William N., 131
Pandit, Vijaya Lakshmi, 242
Paranormal, 14, 91, 93, 185, 239
Paris, 117, 118
Park Avenue Church, New York, 204
Parker, Dr. Joseph, 14, 97, 107, 125, 130,
    147, 167, 232, 235, 238, 295, 303, 305
Parliament, 87, 106, 117, 121, 138, 148,
    157, 218
Pastoral Psychology, 194
Passive Resistance Movement, 14, 98
Paton College, Nottingham, 61
Patten, John A., 97
Payne, Dr. Ernest, 291, 294
Peace Pledge Union, 118, 120
Peake, A. S., 48, 253
Peale, Dr. Norman Vincent, 192, 220, 304
Pearl Harbour, 133
Peel, Rev. Dr. Albert, 131
Penguin, Publishers, 250
Perkins Lectures, 206, 214
Persia, 27, 31
Personalities of the Passion, 140, 306
Perth, Australia, 181
Peru, 292
Phelps, Norman, 220
Philadelphia, 204, 205
Philips, Catherine, 239
Phillips, Canon Cordon, 265
Phillips, Dr. J. B., Foreword, 220-1, 277-280
Picture Post, 218
Pigeon, George C., 75
Pincher, Chapman, 240
Pitt Street Methodist Church, N. Z., 183
A Plain Man Looks at the Cross, 20, 155
*Plan of the Society for the Establishment of
    Missions Among the Heathens*, 24
Poland, 120, 122, 123, 129, 163
Poling, Dr. Daniel, 148
Polish Air Force, 238
Pope, 121
Pope John, 259
Pope, Pius XII, 136
Porritt, Sir Arthur, 275
Portsmouth Cathedral, 197
Portugal, 297

Powell, Rev. Dr. Gordon, 22n., 181, 183
Power, Canon N. S., 264
Power of Positive Thinking, The, 220
Prague, 115, 120
Pratt, Ambrose, 257, 258
Premium Bonds, 218
Presbyterians, 14, 16, 113, 166, 167, 168,
    172, 173, 174, 177, 218, 225, 292, 304
Presbyterian Messenger, 66
Prescription for Anxiety, 113, 215, 219-21,
    223, 232, 277
Pretoria University, 75
Price, Dr. Lynne, 236n., 298-9, 307
Priestley, J. B., 224
Primitive Methodists, 79
Prince Phillip, Duke of Edinburgh, 180, 239
Princes Avenue Church, Hull, 217
Princes Street Congregational Church, Nor-
    wich, 194
Princess Elizabeth, 176, 180
Princess Margaret, 218
Private House of Prayer, A, 232-3
Profumo, John, 140
Psychic News, 194, 285
Psychic research, 14, 153, 173, 185, 186,
    187, 193, 234, 235, 246-8, 256, 257, 285,
    302, 307
Psychologist, 83
Psychology, 21, 30, 31, 34, 57, 58, 61, 63, 64,
    68, 69, 73, 76, 80-4, 93, 105, 110, 112, 113,
    122, 129, 144, 156, 173, 181, 185-95, 198,
    212, 219, 220, 228, 236, 276, 291, 297, 300,
    304
Psychology and Life, 15, 31-84
*Psychology For Ministers and Social Work-
    ers*, 185
Psychology in Service of The Soul, 57, 58,
    59-62, 63, 69, 84
Psychology, Religion and Healing, 30, 81,
    185-95, 198, 217, 226, 232, 236, 254,
    302
Public Morality Council, 252
Public Opinion, 166
Publishers' Circular, 219
Puget Sound College, Washington, 183, 207
Pulpit Digest, 192, 215, 233
Punshon Memorial Church, Bournemouth, 153

Quakers, 14, 30, 40, 106, 146, 166, 172, 270
Queen Elizabeth II, 221, 226, 287
Queen Mary, The, 110
Queen Victoria, 13
Queen's College, Belfast, 46
Queen's College, Oxford, 61
Queen's Hall, 108
Queen's University, Kingston, Ontario, 241
Quest of the Historical Jesus, The, 300
Quetta, 91
Quiver, 146

Radio, (Broadcasting) 41, 85-8, 93, 100, 122, 137, 220, 235, 254, 260, 271, 281, 289, 293

Rae, Dr. J. Burnett, 174, 245, 290

Ratiner, Karl, 265

Ramsay, Michael, Archbishop of Canterbury, 255, 275, 283

Rand Daily Mail, 129

Rankine, Mrs. Keith, 140

Rath, Ernst Von, 118

Raven, Canon C. E., 193

Rayne Memorial Church, 207

Reading University, 211

Rebuilding the City Temple, 13

Recovery of Preaching, The, 306

Rees, Dr. T. P., 250

Reformation, 300

Regent Street Polytechnic Hall, 152

Reichenbach, Carl, 217

Reincarnation, 263, 267, 270, 285, 302

Reith, John, 86

Religion and Education, 215

Religion in Life, 151, 270

'Religion and Life Weeks' 138

Religion for Agnostics, A, 268-9

Religion Without Revelation, 266

Religious Book Club, 89, 167

Religious Outlook for Modern Man, A, 258

Repton School, 248

Resurrection and The Life, The, 173

Resurrection of Christ, The, 234-5

Revivalist, 262

Rhine, J. B., 187, 254

Richards, Rev. Leyton, 118

Richmond College, 20, 21, 23, 43, 45, 61, 273

Richmond Hill Congregational Church, Bournemouth, 238, 241

Richmond Times, 129

Richmond, Virginia, 215

Ridge, Rev. Charles, 13

Ripon, Bishop of, 92, 117

Ritson, Dr. J. H., 209

Riverside Church, New York, 131, 204, 207, 238, 239

Roberts, Dr. Colin, 216

Roberts, Rev. David Holt, 292

Roberts, Rev. Dr. Harold, 101, 209, 213, 294

Robertson, Dr. Edwin, 210, 216, 271

Robins, H. C., Dean of Salisbury, 195

Robinson, John, Bishop of Woolwich, 145, 254-5, 259, 265, 267, 268, 304

Rockefeller Foundation, 204

Rockefeller Jr., John D., 131, 196, 204, 207, 215, 238-9

Roman Catholic, 44, 150, 179, 269, 270

Romney, Edana, 211

Roosevelt, President Franklin D., 133, 135, 148

Roscoe Place Chapel, Leeds, 75

Rotary Annual Conference, 79

Round, Dorothy, 79

Routley, Dr. Eric, 266, 284, 285

Rowanwood, 81

Rowntree, confectioners, 14

Royal Academy of Music, 225

Royal Air Force, 123, 139, 158, 218, 234

Royal Albert Hall, 78, 79, 90, 101, 108, 118, 137

Royal Army Medical Corps, 30, 275

Royal College of Surgeons, 275

Royal Navy, 61, 153

R.S.P.C.A., 90

Royapettah Girls' High School, 34

Royden, Dr. Maude, 65, 69, 98 157, 304

Rubenstein, Michael B., 250

Russell, Bertrand, 224

Russell, George, (A. E.), 258

Russell, Gilbert, 192,113

Russia, 27, 133, 163, 130, 214

Sabbathu, 26

St. Andrews Church, Holborn Viaduct, 13, 112

St. Andrews Presbyterian Church, Cheam, 280

St. Andrew's Church, Vancouver, 183

St. Bartholomew's Church, New York, 179

St. Bartholomew's Hospital, 153

St. Bartholomew's Hospital Journal, 67

St. Bride's, Fleet Street, 134, 246

St. Francis of Assisi, 153

St. George's Chapel, Windsor, 197

St. George's United Church, Toronto, 241

St. Giles Cathedral, Edinburgh, 108

St. Louis, 206, 207

St. Martin's-in-the-fields, 86, 100

St. Mary-le-Bow, Cheapside, 259

St. Mary Woolnoth's, 138

St. Mary's, Islington, 197

St. Michaells, Chester Square, 86

St. Paul, 50, 155, 173, 263, 266, 268

St. Paul's Cathedral, 128, 131, 157, 196, 197, 199-200, 227, 229-30

St. Sepulchres, Holborn Viaduct, 94, 131-47, 196, 230

St. Thomas Mount, 24

Salisbury, Frank, 202, 226

Salt, Sir Titus, 14

Salter, Dr. Alfred, 106

Salter, Rev. G. H., 131, 132, 148, 151, 230

Salute to a Sufferer, 253

Salvation Army, 166, 172

San Francisco, 157

Sandys, Duncan, 152

Sangster, Dr. W. E., Foreword, 26, 43, 54, 134, 157, 212, 216, 218, 233, 240, 256n, 281, 282, 286, 294, 301, 303, 304

Sargant, Dr. William, 192

Sargent, Sir Malcolm, 242

Sassoon, Siegfried, 50

'Save Europe Now' campaign, 171

Save Our Sunday Campaign, 92

Saxe Coburg (Saxby) Street Church, 14, 18, 19, 209

Schweitzer, Albert, 92, 93, 155, 300

Science, 14, 17, 30, 49, 91, 158, 173, 200, 234, 235, 246-8, 256, 257, 260, 307

Science and Health, 187

Scotland, 87, 277

Scots Presbyterian Church, Melbourne, 183

Scouter, 67

Scudder, Dr. Ida, 35, 242

Seagar, Sir Leighton, 202

Search, 269

Seaward, Joan, 234

Second World War, 44, 45, 50, 70, 74, 87, 122-66, 170, 202, 226, 271, 294, 295, 303

Selby-Wright, Ronald, 88

Selly Oak Colleges, Birmingham, 144

Service of Anglo-American Friendship, 148

Sex and Common Sense, 65

Sexual Behaviour in the Human Male, 65

Sexual Behaviour in the Human Female, 65

Sexual Life of Our Times, 64

Shafto, G. R. H., 72

Shapland, Rev. R. B., 86

Shea, General Sir John, 174

Shearer, Rev. W. Russell, 211

Shelley, 49

Shepherd, Rev. Noel, 250

Shepherd Remembers, *A*, 89

Sheppard, Rev. Dick, 86, 102, 118, 220, 304

Shining Brother, *The*, 153

Short, Dr. John, 241

Shuster, Harry Alonzo, 306

Sidgwick, Henry, 257

Significance of Silence, *The*, 158, 166, 228

Silcoates School, 93

Silvey, Robert, 87

Simon, Dr. Glyn, Bishop of Llandaff, 259, 260

Simon, Sir John, (later Lord) 120, 122, 125, 126

Sims, Ronald, 196

Sinfield, Joshua R., 67

Singer Sewing Machine Company, 204

Slack, Dr. Kenneth, 100, 225, 226, 233, 280, 281, 282, 285, 286, 288, 289, 290, 291, 292, 293, 294, 295, 305

Smart, W. J., 62, 84, 178, 179

Smith, Prof. David, 46

Smith, C. Ryder, 43, 201

Smith, Rev. John, 175

Smith, Roy L. 178

Smith, Stevie, 50, 301

Smithers, Waldron, 87

Smyth, Canon Charles, 56

Social Service Review, 67

Society for Psychical Research, 74, 187, 200, 257

Sockman, Dr. Ralph, 204

Soddy, Dr. Kenneth, 276

Somalia, 106

Soper, Dr. Donald, Foreword, 15, 43, 55, 86, 87, 88, 96, 101, 118, 134, 137, 157, 159, 169, 171, 194, 212, 224, 225, 233, 273, 274, 287, 294, 295, 299, 304

Soudan, 106

Souls in the Making, 61

South Africa, 47, 75, 116, 129, 131, 169, 224, 295

South America, 119

South Australian Methodist, 192

Southampton, 119, 166

Southern Baptist Theological Seminary, 306

Spender, Stephen, 224

Spiritualism, 33, 185, 187, 191, 194, 240, 246, 247, 257, 284, 285, 302, 305

Spurgeon, Dr. C. H., 13, 133, 282, 303

Stafford-Clark, David, 192

Stamp, Lord, 164, 174, 253

Stansgate, Lord, 172

Star, 97, 111, 113, 133, 143

Steele, Rev. Frederick A., 211

Stevenson, Dr. G.H., 76

Stevenson, Noel, 239

Stewart, Prof. James, 268, 275, 299

Stewart, Mary, 281

Stock Exchange, 201

Stocks, Mary, 224

Stockholm, 178

Stockport Advertiser 251

Stockwood, Bishop Mervyn, 174

Stoke Newington, 99

Stopes, Marie, 64

Storey, David, 255

Stories of the Kingdom, *The*, 72

Strawson, Prof. William, 44, 45, 302-3

Streatham Congregational Church, 175

Street, O. Dickenson, 202, 204

Studdert-Kennedy, G. A.. 220

Student Christian Movement, 45, 157

Student Christian Movement Press, 63, 124, 268

Studies in the Psychology of Sex, 64, 65

Study of History, *A*, 250

Successful Christian Living, 232

Suez Canal, 224

Sunday Graphic, 157, 166, 195

Sunday School Chronicle, 166-7

Sunday Times, 195, 240, 241, 259, 269, 280

Sutherland, Graham, 224

Sutherland, Rev. James, 53

Swanwick, 43-4, 45, 46, 58, 70, 75

Sweden, 178, 179, 229

Swedish Methodist Conference. 178, 179

Swinburne, Algernon Charles, 49

Switzerland, 178

Sydney, 183

Tacoma, Washington, 183, 207

Tanooma, 27

Tasmania, 182

Tate, Henry, 14

Tatlock, Richard, 267

Tavistock Clinic, 61

Tawney, R. H., 42

Taylor, A. J. P., 224

Taylor, Prebendary Arthur, 246

Taylor, Myrom, 204

Taylor, Vincent, 155

Telepathy, 187, 246, 254, 256

Television, 210, 211, 220, 234, 235, 239, 254, 271, 277, 290, 305
Telling, Maxwell, 59, 62, 63
Temple, Archbishop William, 45, 78, 86, 138, 148, 164, 248
Temple, The, 45
Temple University, Philadelphia, 306
Tennyson, 49
Texas, 207
Thalben-Ball, George, 232
That Immortal Sea, 16, 200-1
Theology, 192, 193
Thiman, Eric, 225, 232, 236, 238, 292
Thinking Aloud in Wartime, 31, 124, 128
Thirty Nine Articles, 199
This is the Victory, 128-9, 131, 226
Thomas, Neville Penry, 227-8
Thompson, Elsie, 242
Thompson, John, 239
Thorndike, Dame Sybil, 157
Thorner Methodist Church, 55
Three Essays on the Theory of Sexuality, 64
Tibet, 34
Tillich, Paul, 254
Time For God, 280
Times, The, 66, 120, 123, 124, 126, 136, 148, 157, 195, 209, 212, 217, 224, 226, 250, 251, 252, 277, 293
Times Literary Supplement, 46, 156, 269
Times Review of the Year 1936, 105
Timothy Eaton Memorial Church, Toronto, 131, 183
Titus, Joseph H., 156
Tombleson, Captain, 30, 40, 42, 275
Tomlinson, George, 175
Tone, Franchot, 79
Toronto, 76, 131, 183, 241, 297
Torrie, Dr. Alfred, 105, 290
Totem and Taboo, 21
Townsend, Group Captain Peter, 218
Toynbee, Arnold, 250
Toynbee Hall Settlement, 140
Trade Unions, 170
Transforming Friendship, The, 55-7, 119, 263, 282, 293, 298, 300
Trevivian, Rev. Roy, 293-4
Triggs, Rev. Arthur, 34
Trumbull Avenue Presbyterian Church, Detroit, 206
Tudor, Rev. Dr. John, 305
Tunbridge, Rev. William J., 39
Tunnicliffe, H. G., 44
Turks, Turkey, 27, 28, 31, 38

Union Theological Seminary, New York, 179
United Church of Canada, 75, 131, 241, 297
United Church of South India, 172, 200
United Churchman, 193
United Free Church of Scotland, 14
United Methodist Free Churches, 52, 79
United Nations, 148

United Reformed Church, 289, 292, 304
United States of America, 47, 65, 68, 69, 75, 98, 109, 110, 116, 129, 131, 133, 140, 141, 146, 148, 151, 154, 155, 156, 163, 166, 167, 170, 178, 179, 180, 183, 191, 197, 201, 202-8, 209, 214, 220, 229, 230, 233, 236, 239, 243, 257, 268, 270, 271, 282, 287, 289, 293, 297, 298, 306
U.S. Senate, 205
U.S. State Department, 141
Universe, 193
Uppsala, 281

V2 rockets, 152, 162
Vancouver, 183
Vanderbilt lectures, *The Fact of Conversion*, 21
Vansittart, Lorl, 164, 180
Varley, Henry, 64, 65
Vatican, 204
Vauxhall station, 19
Vellore Hospital, 35, 242
Venkatachari, 25
Vienna, 21, 115
Vienna, University of, 64
Vickers, John, 75
Vickers, Anne Elizabeth, 75
Vickers, W. Farrar, 75
Victoria, Australia, 181
Victorian Independent, 68
Vincent, Dr. John, 275
Vipond, Rev. J., 194
Virgin Birth, 72, 96, 260, 262, 266, 270, 305
Virgin Mary, 94, 262, 269
Virginian Churchman, 270

Wagner, Dr. James A., 154
Wakefield, Dr. Gordon, 264
Wales, 75, 221
Walker, Derek, 225
Walker, J. W. & Sons, 232
Walters, C. Ensor, 94
Walters, Harold Crawford, 223
War Damages Commission, 176, 196, 197
Ward, Ronald, 108, 109, 143
Warwick Road Congregational Church, Coventry, 238
Washington, D.C., 141, 148, 201, 205, 206, 271
Waterhouse, Dr. Eric, 61, 66, 67, 93
Watson, Rev. David, 305
Wavell, Field Marshall Lord, 50
Weatherhead, Alice, 14
Weatherhead, Andrew, 14-6, 18, 297
Weatherhead, Dr. Arthur Dixon, 35, 81, 119, 153, 179, 183, 207, 287, 289, 297
Weatherhead, David, 80
Weatherhead, Mrs. Elizabeth (nee Dixon), 14-6, 18, 33, 90, 297
Weatherhead, Mrs. Evelyn, 34, 112, 133, 199, 242, 243, 258, 275, 283, 286, 287, 290
Weatherhead, James, 14
Weatherhead, Professor Kingsley, Preface,

15, 17, 41, 81, 145, 153, 183, 207, 287, 289, 292, 293, 297
Weatherhead, Dr. Leslie Dixon: Arab Liaison Officer, 28; Broadcasting, 72, 74, 85-8, 100, 109, 111, 115, 116, 118, 119, 121, 125, 135, 137, 154, 163, 164, 170, 180, 183, 206, 210, 216, 234, 291, 292, 304; CBE, 233; Chaplaincy, 23, 25, 28-33, 34, 38, 55, 123, 158, 295; Christology, 72-4; Education, 16-21; Home and family, 14-8; Ministry, 29, 96, 98, 108, 110, 142-7, 158-65, 179, 295, 304; Mystical experiences, 18-9; 'Nation in Danger' campaign, 251-2, 302; Nature mysticism, 17; Ordination, 23, 24; Pacifism, 31; Politics, 44, 170, 224; Prayer, 45, 110, 143, 146, 187, 232, 254, 263, 293, 294; Preaching, 102-4, 107, 144, 158-65, 167, 201, 206, 212, 215, 225, 246, 248, 249, 252, 255, 269, 278, 280, 282, 283, 285, 287, 291, 292, 293, 294, 295, 298, 301, 303, 304, 305, 307; Presidency, 101, 144, 172, 209-23, 236, 268, 303; Problem of pain, 80, 90, 121, 253, 304; Psychology, 15, 16, 20, 29, 42, 50, 57, 59-62, 63, 81-4, 111, 139-40, 143, 151, 155, 161-162, 185-95, 201, 249, 278, 286, 293, 302, 303; Universalism, 33, 50, 284; Worship, approach to, 103, 145-7, 150, 169, 189, 190, 303
Weatherhead, Muriel, 14, 90
Weigle, Dean L. A., 179
Weldon, Hugh, 211
Wellington, N. Z., 183
Werner, Prof. Hazen G., 167
Wesley, Charles, 279
Wesley Church, Cambridge, 216
Wesley, John, 19, 20, 47, 49, 79, 94, 213, 216, 248
Wesley Methodist Church, Melbourne, 181, 183
Wesley, Samuel, 52
Wesley Deaconess Order, 44, 45
Wesley's Chapel, 14, 93, 94, 96, 167, 212, 216, 294, 297
Wesleyan Methodists, 14, 29, 79, 106, 300
Wesleyan Conference, 209
Wesleyan Methodist Missionary Society, 18, 24
West Indies, 223, 225
West Middlesex Hospital, 234
Westhill College, Selly Oak, 113
Westminster, 218
Westminster Abbey, 78, 132, 197, 202, 225, 232
Westminster Assembly of Divines, 97
Westminster, Cardinal Archbishop of, 136
Westminster Central Hall, 54, 96, 166, 216, 274, 287, 289, 305
Westminster Chapel, 134, 159
Westminster Hall, 132
Westminster Pastoral Foundation, 142, 287, 289
Westminster Training College, 21
Westminster Theological Journal, 193
Whale, Dr. John S., 86, 94, 125
When the Lamp Flickers, 173-4, 180

White, Dr. Ernest, 290
Whitham, A. E., 45, 48, 52-3, 243
Whitefield's Church, Tottenham Court Road, 274
Whitehead, William, 29, 30
Why Do Men Suffer? 90, 193, 253
Wichita Falls, Texas, 206
Wife's Handbook, 64, 215
Wilde, Oscar, 147, 153
Wilkinson, Alan, 50, 163, 164
Wilkinson, John, 266
Will of God, The, 153-5, 204, 298, 299
Williams, Darkin, 146, 147
Williams, H. A., 304
Williams, Dr. Howard, 275
Willingdon, Viceroy Lord, 34, 38
Willoughby, John, 269
Wills, W. H. & H. O., 14
Wilson, D. Berners, 268
Wilson, Rev. Dorothy, 113, 121
Wilsort, Harold, 224
Wilson, Rev. J. M., 64
Wilson, Trevor, 27
Wimbledon, 248
Winchester, Bishop of, 78
Winnipeg, 183
Winnington-Ingram, A. F., Bishop of London, 86
Wise Parenthood, 64
Wojnarowski, Kostek, 238
Wolfenden, J. F., 211
Wolfenden Report, 224
Women ministers, 113, 121, 216
Woods, Rev. Bertram, 246, 247
Wordsworth, 49
World Alliance for the Promotion of International Friendship Through the Churches, 92, 117, 133
World Council of Churches, 202, 238, 281
World (Sydney) 68
Wounded Spirits, 254
Wren-Lewis, John, 259, 260
Wright, J. Stafford, 191
Wright, Prof. W. D., 246

Yale Divinity School, 203
Yale University, 179, 203
Yeats, W. B., 50
York, Archbishop of, 173
York, Duke and Duchess of, 79
York Minster, 273
Yorkshire Evening News, 66, 78, 79, 80, 156
Yorkshire Evening Post, 60
Yorkshire Observer, 173
Yorkshire Post, 281
Y.M.C.A., 19, 30, 32, 49, 63, 80, 90
Young, Dinsdale, 96
Youth Council on Jewish and Christian Relationships, 148

Zaccharius, 262, 269
Zaccheaus, 140